Toward a More
Organizationally Effective
Training Strategy & Practice _____

Toward a More Organizationally Effective Training Strategy & Practice

Richaurd R. Camp
P. Nick Blanchard
Gregory E. Huszczo
Eastern Michigan University

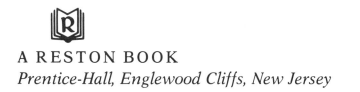

A RESTON BOOK
Prentice-Hall, Englewood Cliffs, New Jersey

TO
Peggy and Lauren in gratitude for their support and tolerance.
                                                              R.R.C.
Lisa for believing and to Mike, Amy, and Brandon for inspiration.
                                                              P.N.B.
Sue and Sam for their stimulation and support.
                                                              G.E.H.

Library of Congress Cataloging-in-Publication Data

Camp, Richaurd R.
    Toward a more organizationally effective training
    strategy and practice.

    "A Reston book."
    Bibliography:
    Includes index.
    1. Employees, Training of.   I. Blanchard, P. Nick.
    II. Huszczo, Gregory E.   III. Title.
HF5549.5.T7C25 1986   658.3'12404   85-14319
ISBN 0-8359-7771-4

A Reston Book published by Prentice-Hall
A Division of Simon & Schuster, Inc.
Englewood Cliffs, N.J. 07632

©1986 by Prentice-Hall, Englewood Cliffs, N.J. 07632

        1   3   5   7   9   10   8   6   4   2

Printed in the United States of America

CONTENTS _____

Preface   ix

1 Improving Training Effectiveness Using an Organizational Perspective   1

THE FIELD OF HUMAN RESOURCE DEVELOPMENT/TRAINING   2
DEFINING TRAINING/HRD   3
OUR MODEL OF THE TRAINING PROCESS   4
WHAT DO TRAINERS/HRD PROFESSIONALS DO?   6
WHERE DO HRD RESPONSIBILITIES FIT IN ORGANIZATIONS?   9
AN OPEN SYSTEMS THEORY PERSPECTIVE FOR TRAINING   10
CHANGE   16
THE EMERGING DISCIPLINE OF ORGANIZATIONAL DEVELOPMENT (OD)   17
SUMMARY   18   DISCUSSION QUESTIONS   20
INTERVIEW on "Organizational Perspective" with the President of Arnoudse and Ouellette
    Associates, Inc.   22

2 Training Needs Assessment   25

WHAT IS A TNA?   25
TYPES OF TRAINING   28
REACTIVE AND PROACTIVE TNAs   29
HOW SHOULD A TNA BE CONDUCTED?   31
OVERVIEW OF TNA   53
WHAT IMPLICATIONS DOES RESEARCH HAVE FOR IMPROVING THE TNA
    PROCESS?   53
SUMMARY   57   DISCUSSION QUESTIONS   58
INTERVIEW on "TNAs" with a Ford Motor Company Specialist   59

3   Learning and Behavior   62

HISTORICAL ROOTS OF CONTEMPORARY APPROACHES TO LEARNING   63
OPERANT CONDITIONING: A BEHAVIORAL APPROACH   67
EXPECTANCY MODEL: A COGNITIVE APPROACH   72
LEARNING VS. PERFORMANCE   74
SOCIAL LEARNING THEORY   75
A LEARNING HIERARCHY   78
ADULT LEARNERS   88
SUMMARY   91   DISCUSSION QUESTIONS   91
INTERVIEW on "Learning Theory and Adult Trainees"   93

4   Designing Training for Effective Learning   97

THE ROLE OF THE TRAINER   99
LEARNING OBJECTIVES   100
FACILITATING THE LEARNING PROCESS   109
ARRANGEMENT OF TRAINING ACTIVITIES   116
SUMMARY   125   DISCUSSION QUESTIONS   126
INTERVIEW on Designing Training for Learning   127

5   Evaluation   130

ARGUMENTS FOR AND AGAINST EVALUATION   131
TYPES OF EVALUATION   135
CRITERION DEVELOPMENT   139
INTERNAL VALIDITY   143
WHAT'S A CRITERION DEVELOPER TO DO?   147
CRITERION EVALUATION   151
DESIGNING THE EVALUATION   156
PRAGMATIC RESTRICTIONS ON EVALUATION   166
RETURN ON THE TRAINING DOLLAR INVESTMENT   167
SUMMARY   172   DISCUSSION QUESTIONS   172
INTERVIEW on Evaluation of Training Efforts   174

6   Nonexperiential Training Techniques   178

LECTURE: DEFINITION AND FEASIBILITY   179
AUDIO-VISUALS: DEFINITION AND FEASIBILITY   188
PI AND CAI: DEFINITION AND FEASIBILITY   198
SUMMARY   206   DISCUSSION QUESTIONS   207
INTERVIEW on Training Styles and Techniques   208

7   Experiential Training Techniques   211

EXPERIENTIAL LEARNING PHILOSOPHY   211
SIMULATION   215
IN-BASKET TECHNIQUE   221

CASE-STUDY METHOD   221
THE INCIDENT METHOD   224
ROLE PLAYING   224
BEHAVIOR MODELING TRAINING   230
T-GROUPS, SENSITIVITY TRAINING, AND LABORATORY EDUCATION   235
SUMMARY   236   DISCUSSION QUESTIONS   236
INTERVIEW on Training Styles and Techniques   238

8   Technical Training   242

TYPICAL APPROACHES TO ON-THE-JOB TRAINING   243
OFF-THE-JOB TECHNICAL TRAINING   249
INNOVATIVE APPROACHES: SOCIALIZATION   250
THE TECHNICAL TRAINING SYSTEM   256
SUMMARY   265   DISCUSSION QUESTIONS   266
INTERVIEW on Technical Training   268

9   Training and Developing Managers   271

WHY MANAGEMENT DEVELOPMENT?   271
THE NATURE OF THE MANAGERIAL JOB   272
KNOWLEDGE AND SKILL REQUIREMENTS OF MANAGERS   276
SOURCES OF KNOWLEDGE/SKILL ACQUISITION   282
MANAGEMENT DEVELOPMENT PROGRAMS AND TECHNIQUES   286
SUMMARY   289   DISCUSSION QUESTIONS   290
INTERVIEW on Management Development   291

10   The Role of Training in OD   295

SIMILARITIES BETWEEN ORGANIZATION DEVELOPMENT AND TRAINING   296
WHY TRAINERS SHOULD BE TRAINED IN OD   300
WHY OD PRACTITIONERS NEED TRAINING KNOWLEDGE, SKILLS, AND
     PROGRAMS   302
TECHNIQUES OF OD   305
FIELD EXAMPLES   311
SUMMARY   319   DISCUSSION QUESTIONS   319
INTERVIEW on The Role of Training in OD   321

11   A Strategic Planning Approach to Training   324

STRATEGIC PLANNING FOR TRAINING   325
CORRESPONDENCE BETWEEN STRATEGY, ENVIRONMENT, AND
     TECHNOLOGY   327
STRATEGIC APPROACHES   333
SKILL AND KNOWLEDGE NEEDS OF TRAINING   337
DISCUSSION QUESTIONS   339
INTERVIEW on Strategy Planning Approach to Training   340

Appendix A: An In-depth Review of T-Groups as a Training and an OD Strategy   345

Appendix B: A Guide for Trainers to the Techniques of Organization Development (OD)   357

References   371
Index   399

PREFACE

For more than ten years, we three authors have had many satisfying experiences as trainers and consultants to a variety of organizations. Moreover, as teachers and colleagues we have enjoyed working with many students of Human Resource Development. We also have been and are pleased that both the business and academic communities show an increasing interest in HRD. This interest is stimulating, but we remain concerned about two things: 1) the scarcity of solid academic research and theory development in this area; and 2) the disproportionate amount of attention practitioners and students give to the training event without commensurate attention to the process and environment integral to the use of that training.

This text attempts to address the two problems comprehensively. First, we reviewed the training literature in academic and practitioner journals. Then we supplemented our reviews by examining the research and theories of related disciplines. We also interviewed practitioners who, typically, are too busy to publish their insights. Our combined efforts produced a comprehensive set of frameworks. These are designed to assist the planning of the strategies and practices that make training and development activities an effective force for constructive change in organizational settings.

We also found the literature and practices of the emerging field of Organization Development to be particularly useful. Indeed, many teachers and expert practitioners recommend the integration of the "OD" and "HRD" fields. We intend our book to provide some specific how-to procedures for such integration.

We focus on both the strategy and practice of training. We review the pre-training situation because the events before as well as those after an actual training event are crucial to success. This is true from both the organization's and the individual person's perspective. However, we do not ignore the event itself. In fact, we give considerable attention to the styles and the content of training relevant to most organizational settings. It is our hope that this book will provide both students and practitioners with insights needed for both the planning and the implementation of HRD activities.

We mean the book to be useful in undergraduate courses in Human Resource Development in colleges of business or education or in departments of psychology. It may also be used as a text in graduate level courses in Human Resource Management, Industrial Organizational Psychology, Organizational Development and Instructional Technology.

*   *   *

There are many people to thank for their help and support throughout the writing of this book: We are truly grateful to our wives and children for their patience and interest. The joys and fulfillment of family life considerably eased the rigors of writing this book.

We also greatly appreciate the help of the many practitioners and academicians who shared their insights with us and were at the same time splendid models of professionals devoted to human resource development. In particular, we wish to thank Alan R. Bass and Lynn Anderson of Wayne State University; Carl Frost of Frost, Greenwood and Associates; and the thirteen professionals whose interview comments are published at the end of each chapter.

We also thank the experts who reviewed our text and the many students in the Masters Program in Organizational Development who provided us with helpful comments on an early draft of the text. Ann Williams provided help on content and style that deserves special mention. We want to express the same thanks and appreciation to the publisher's staff. We must also express our special thanks and appreciation to the cadre of typists who worked on the many drafts of this book. Linda Grady, Lisa Woodbury, Diane Dufek, Vicki Hoevemeyer, Tammy Lay, and Rei Etheridge evidenced only patience and professionalism in performing this task.

Finally, we invite you our readers to provide us with feedback so we can learn how this book has contributed to your effectiveness as a trainer or as a student of training. We expect to continue in our careers as HRD/OD professionals and would appreciate comments that will enhance our own development.

Richaurd Camp
Nick Blanchard
Greg Huszczo

Chapter 1

IMPROVING TRAINING EFFECTIVENESS USING AN ORGANIZATIONAL PERSPECTIVE _____

The following questions will be answered in this chapter:

1. What constitutes the field of human resource development/training?
2. What do HRD professionals do?
3. How can knowledge from the behavioral sciences be utilized to develop a more effective training strategy and practice?
4. How can this book help someone who is already an HRD professional?

This book is designed to help organizations make effective use of one of their most important resources—people. The book is also designed to help workers. It is our view that, through training employees, both objectives not only can but must be obtained. In the following pages, we demonstrate how the planning and implementation of training can be improved.

Some people no longer use the word *training* but advocate the idea of *human resource development (HRD)*. However, as Nadler (1984) noted, some would argue that there is no definition for this term. Others disagree with definitions that have been provided. In our view, HRD involves training workers (in some way) to increase their skill and knowledge. Therefore, we will use the terms *HRD* and *training* interchangeably throughout this book.

THE FIELD OF HUMAN RESOURCE DEVELOPMENT/TRAINING

Training magazine recently (*Training*, 1984) surveyed the chief executive officers and chief personnel officers of 10,500 American organizations about training activities in their organizations. The results of the survey and its projections provide a most comprehensive view of the HRD field. Today, an estimated quarter of a million professional trainers are currently employed in United States' organizations on a full-time basis. There are perhaps three times that number of employees for whom training is a formal but not a full-time responsibility. Fifty-eight percent of all organizations of 50 employees or more have at least one full-time formal training position. The survey found that more than a billion dollars was budgeted in 1984 for seminars and conferences. This figure doesn't include the additional billions of dollars budgeted for salaries of trainers inside these organizations or of trainees while attending training sessions. The survey projected a total training budget for 1984 of slightly over 4 billion dollars. However, Davis (1984) reported estimates as high as $40 billion a year being spent on HRD in the private sector of the U.S. alone when one considers all the costs involved in training.

What has organizational America received in return for this huge financial and human resources investment? Nearly all (99.79 percent) of the respondents to the above survey conducted by *Training* magazine agreed that training was a good investment, something important to provide. Yet, when executives of Fortune 1000 companies were surveyed by Booze-Allen and Hamilton, they rarely chose training as an effective means of accommodating rapid technological change in their organizations (Zemke, 1982). It is the contention of the authors of this book that a key to the future of the field of training is its ability to effectively resolve problems faced by organizations while enhancing the knowledge, skills, and abilities of individual employees. Perhaps the following examples will illustrate our point.

> Supervisors in a large high-tech company recently attended an off-site workshop on performance appraisal interviewing skills. The supervisors became quite adept at using the "problem-solving" approach to the appraisal interview (see Maier, 1970). The evaluations taken immediately after the workshop clearly showed that they understood the steps and processes involved and that they liked the style of such an approach very much. The workshop cost the company nearly $7,000. Follow-up evaluations taken two months after the workshop showed that none of the supervisors used the problem-solving approach in their performance appraisal interviews. The trainers discovered that the corporate personnel department had issued a policy statement related

to performance appraisal procedure about two weeks after the original workshop. The new policy stated that formal evaluation documents with the supervisors appraisal of each subordinate's performance must be signed and forwarded to the Personnel Department before face to face feedback sessions with subordinates are undertaken. Supervisors thus needed to resort to a "tell and sell" approach (Maier, 1970) to the appraisal interviews, defending their opinions to their subordinates.

A manufacturing facility recently trained its engineering and accounting staffs in tools used by the Japanese in their now famous "QC Circles." (c.f., Dewar, 1980) Each trainee was then assigned to a group of employees to solve quality control problems throughout the plant. The engineers and accountants used the tools they had learned to solve a variety of problems. However, they failed to notice the processes and reactions emerging from their small groups. The employees resented the invasion of these "outsiders" into their work groups. The communications skills of many of the engineers and accountants were so poor that further resentment was created. As a result, even solutions that logically should have resolved many of the company's production quality problems were not implemented correctly and some attempts were actually sabotaged.

The above examples illustrate situations where trainers failed to take into account features of the organization other than acquiring the knowledge, skills, and abilities (KSA) specified in the training objectives. This resulted in training programs initially perceived as successful by the trainees but lacking in elements necessary for successful use within their respective organizations. Other observers have undoubtedly seen similar examples of training efforts that might be labeled good ideas that have gone bad. Advancements in organizational theories over the past two decades provide useful constructs and frameworks from which trainers can improve the effectiveness of their efforts.

Jamieson (1981, p. 13) suggested, "Whether our specialty be training, organization development, industrial engineering, organization design or data processing, in many ways we have all failed to recognize the complexity of organizational systems." By integrating the theories, research, and practices of the behavioral sciences and organizational development into our discussions of the various elements of the training/human resource development process, we hope to provide the reader with the concepts and practices needed to plan and execute effective training programs in organizational settings.

DEFINING TRAINING/HRD

Most HRD authors feel obligated to define the term *training*. After all, how can books be written on the topic if we don't know what it is. One of the most commonly quoted definitions was provided by House (1967): *"Employee training and development* is any attempt to improve current or future employee performance by increasing through learning an employee's ability to perform, usually by changing the employee's attitudes or increasing his or her skills and knowledge." Some feel that it is important to distinguish activities aimed at generating learning to enhance one's current job performance from those aimed at preparing an employee for some future job assignment and from those activities aimed at generating learning for the growth of the trainee without any direct ties to job performance, current or future. Nadler (1984) labeled the first as *training*, the second as *education*, and the third as *development*. Others have also distinguished *training* from *education*. For example, Jucius (1971) suggested that *education* increases "the knowledge, understanding, or attitude of employees so that they are better adjusted to their working environment" (p. 243). Although training and education obviously share many similarities (Goldstein, 1974), we see little value here in focusing on any distinction between the two. We wish to emphasize the broader impact of HRD activities on the effectiveness of the organization which provides the training and on the enhancement of the trainee's quality of work life experience. Thus, we advocate developing training programs that benefit the *organization* and the *individual* involved.

Upon reviewing the variety of definitions of training available in the literature, we offer the following list of characteristics as key elements for effective training;

1. Effective training is a learning experience/activity.
2. Effective training is a planned organizational activity.
3. Effective training is a response to identified needs.
4. Effective training is an attempt to further the goals of an organization while simultaneously providing an opportunity for individual employees to learn, grow, and/or cope.

OUR MODEL OF THE TRAINING PROCESS _____

To clarify our definition of the training process, we offer a skeletal model in Figure 1.1. Many other models of the training process exist (see, for example, Goldstein, 1974; Nadler, 1982) and we have attempted to integrate some of the best features of several.

Our model reveals some of our biases, beliefs, and philosophies concerning how training should be conducted in organizations. In particular, we believe in the need for data gathering, for systematic planning, for viewing training as a process not a program, and for a genuine concern for the utility of training efforts. Notice that conducting the actual training sessions doesn't appear until Step 6 of our model. Our experiences as trainers and our review of the HRD literature has demonstrated to us that the preparation steps are just as important for the success of training as the conduct of training sessions.

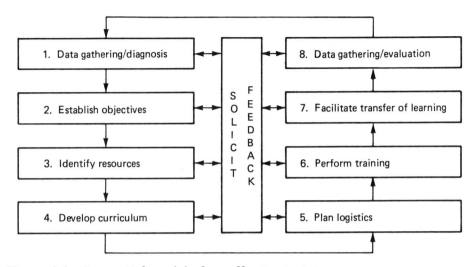

Figure 1.1   Sequential model of an effective training process.

Training must be needed and desired or the likelihood of reaping its benefits will be quite low. Thus, a considerable amount of data must be gathered and analyzed as indicated in Step 1. Chapter 2 is designed to assist the reader in deciding how to go about this task. Once it is clear what the needs of the organization and the characteristics of the potential trainees are, specific objectives of the type described in Chapter 4 should be written as guidelines for the development of every subsequent step in the training process.

We believe that the development of training programs must deal with organizational and human realities. A given set of training objectives could conceivably be addressed in many ways. However, no organization has unlimited resources and therefore must make training decisions based on the identified resources (time, money, people, materials) available. Once identified, the planning of the agenda (the curriculum, if you prefer) and the logistics should occur. These steps will also be discussed in Chapter 4.

Today, there are many styles and techniques being successfully utilized by HRD professionals. The objectives of a training session might best be accomplished by using experientially oriented techniques to increase the likelihood that the trainees will discover the learnings connected to the objectives. However, some types of objectives might better be accomplished in a more didactic fashion. Chapters 6 and 7 will discuss these two basic approaches to training and will also present the research evidence regarding their effectiveness.

As the examples at the beginning of the chapter indicate, training programs can be needed and desired; have clear objectives; and use appropriate resources, curricula, and techniques; yet fail to impact on the subsequent performance and work lives of the trainees back on their jobs. Throughout this book you will hear us emphasizing the need for HRD professionals to take the extra steps necessary to facilitate the actual use of the outcomes of training. In many ways, Step 7 of our model is improperly placed. If you wait until after the performance of a training program before planning and facilitating the transfer of the learning, the battle will be lost. The ideas we present under the topics of conducting training needs assessments and planning and designing the training programs will all be offered with the thought of facilitating transfer of learning.

The reader might also note that our Step 8, "Data Gathering/Evaluation," does not signify the end of a training effort. We emphasize the utility of viewing training as a *continuous process* rather than *discrete programs*. Thus, evaluation is merely another data collection activity, the outcomes of which get translated into subsequent needs analysis efforts. In Chapter 5, we present an overview of the many approaches to designing and conducting evaluations of training efforts. As the box in the middle of our model infers ("Solicit Feedback"), we do not believe that data gathering/evaluation is an activity that only occurs at the end of a training cycle. Descriptive and evaluative feedback should be solicited throughout the steps of needs assessment, program development, and delivery.

More details regarding the steps of the training process will be shared throughout the remaining chapters. Our point in presenting an overview at this point is to forewarn the reader of our biases and philosophies. We urge you to form your own model of the training process as you absorb the material of the subsequent chapters. In fact, you may want to review the models presented by other authors (e.g., Goldstein, 1974; Nadler, 1982) and incorporate the verbal labels of their steps when forming your own model. You will find more similarities than differences when reviewing various models of the training process.

WHAT DO TRAINERS/HRD PROFESSIONALS DO? _____

The American Society for Training and Development (ASTD, 1983), the major association for professional trainers, suggests that there are 15 key roles performed by people in this field. Following is a listing of these roles:

- Evaluator
- Group Facilitator
- Individual Development Counselor
- Instructional Writer
- Instructor
- Manager of Training and Development

- Marketer
- Media Specialist
- Needs Analyst
- Program Administrator
- Program Designer
- Strategist
- Task Analyst
- Theoretician
- Transfer Agent

As the titles indicate, trainers/HRD professionals perform a great variety of services in performing their jobs. Not all trainers fulfill all 15 roles, of course; to do so would require competency in a wide range of knowledge and skill bases. Knowledge bases include understanding how organizations work (both theoretical and practical), understanding human behavior in work settings (e.g., motivation, personalities, leadership), understanding how humans learn and knowledge of the topic areas designed to be subjects of given training programs. We believe that a sound knowledge foundation in the behavioral sciences and the emerging field of *organizational development* will prove to be particularly useful to those entering the HRD profession. We will have more to say on this matter later in this chapter.

Competency in such skill areas as quantitative methodologies (e.g., development of measurement instruments, analysis of data), interpersonal communications (especially listening skills), presentation skills, planning, writing, consulting, facilitating, managing, and marketing is also needed to fully serve an organization's training needs. Some organizations acquire these knowledge and skill bases by recruiting and selecting a staff of HRD professionals; others supplement their ability to deliver the full range of services by contracting with external HRD specialists to fulfill specified segments of their training needs; still others rely on line management to partially or completely fulfill these roles.

How do HRD professionals acquire the knowledge and skill bases desired by organizations? Some have received formal college training in the HRD field. In the last decade, bachelors, masters, and doctoral programs have been developed at many colleges and universities. In addition, professional associations and private consultation firms offer workshops and seminars to prepare people to be successful HRD professionals. Still, many others learn on the job as training assignments are handed to line managers or group leaders or as managers are rotated through human resource staff positions to prepare them for later career moves. We have also recently noticed an influx of teachers, social workers, and communication skills specialists into the HRD profession. Some of these moves seem to be due to reductions in governmental funding of human services and to the closing of schools necessitated by shifts in the school age population as the "baby boom" generation gets older. The overlap of skills needed to act as a change agent in a counseling or a classroom situation and those needed to succeed as a trainer in industrial settings led many to make what they see as a natural career shift.

Thus, HRD professionals in the 1980s bring a variety of educational and vocational backgrounds to their work. There appears to be no universally superior approach to developing individuals for HRD assignments. While, the human resource development field is not a science there are scientific elements to the profession. Thus, HRD professionals require *performance art skills* in addition to *understanding and applying the scientific* principles of learning design and delivery. Table 1.1 provides some examples of what we view to be the science and art features of the training profession.

Table 1.1 Some examples of the science and art of HRD work.

Science	Art
Measuring organizational variables.	Developing an overall strategy to guide a training function.
Measuring people variables.	
Quantifying training needs.	"Knowing" through some intuitive sense what is needed in a given situation.
Applying relevant theories in a matter that will guide diagnostic activities.	
Using precise language in establishing specific learning objectives.	Integrating all the data gathered and deciding what the learning needs are.
Developing and using a systematic inventory of available training resources.	Selling or communicating the meaning and importance of a set of learning objectives.
Applying project management skills, such as systematic planning methods, to establish time lines and budgets necessary to fulfill training objectives.	Negotiating fees and time commitments of providers of training services.
Estimating the financial aspects.	Knowing how much time to allocate to activities out of the direct control of the trainer (e.g., group discussions, discovery-oriented exercises, etc.).
Developing simulation equipment.	
Developing computer and other self-paced learning programs.	Knowing how much material will be covered by a group of trainees who have never been exposed to the material before.
Applying research on learning theory / principles to aid decision-making during the design of training programs.	
Applying or acquiring the subject matter expertise.	Performing a demonstration in a manner that captures the interest of the trainees but doesn't detract from the learning objective.
Planning the logistics associated with a particular training program.	

Table 1.1 Some examples of the science and art of HRD work. (*Continued*)

Science	Art
Performing precisely a technical skill during a training session.	Sensing the comfort level of an audience for a given topic matter.
Performing time management skills to keep a training program on schedule.	Sensing the impact "office politics" are having on a discussion during a training session.
Testing the amount of change in knowledge or skills acquired as a result of a given training program.	Drawing participation out of an audience.
Estimating the cost/benefit ratio for a given training effort.	Persuading an audience to rethink their assumptions and consider something new.
	Providing a sense of humor that helps deliver a point or relieve tension without detracting from the learning objectives.
	Knowing when it is time to move on to the next topic.
	Presenting material to a diverse group of trainees in a manner that doesn't bore the brightest nor lose the totally unitiated.
	Processing group reactions and statements in a manner that reflects the insights gained.
	Qualitatively judging the effectiveness of a given training program.
	Persuading individuals in the "back-at-work" situation to support a trainee's efforts to apply what he or she learned.

WHERE DO HRD RESPONSIBILITIES FIT IN ORGANIZATIONS?

Nadler (1984) pointed to the growing trend of viewing HRD as a responsibility of the entire organization. At the very least, organizations today insist that each and every manager and supervisor has the responsibility to identify (or participate in the identification of) the training and development needs of each of their subordinates. The extent to which HRD is truly a "line" responsibility varies from firm to firm. However, in all but the smallest organizations, some responsibility for the design, delivery, and evaluation of the actual training is vested in some internal staff function or external HRD vendor. Sometimes, training and development activities are provided through the personnel department. In other companies, it is in the domain of the industrial relations function (which may or may not be a department separate from personnel).

A third and increasingly popular option is to staff an HRD department separate from personnel and reporting directly to a member of top management. An HRD department may also be responsible for manpower planning, recruitment, selection, orientation, quality of work life concerns, and even policy development.

AN OPEN SYSTEMS THEORY PERSPECTIVE FOR TRAINING _____

We believe that an "open systems theory" perspective will help the reader sort out the various factors and responsibilities involved in the training function in organizations. A *system* is simply a series of parts that are interrelated. An *open system* can be thought of as a system that interacts with its environment. Experts in the field of training have been calling for a "systems approach" to training for over 20 years (see, for example, Gagne, 1962; Eckstrand, 1964; Goldstein, 1974; Hinrichs, 1976; Goldstein, 1980; Wexley & Latham, 1981).

> While there are many different systems approaches to training, they share several features: the assessment of training needs and objectives; the development of particular training experiences to fulfill these objectives; the evaluation of the effectiveness of the training program; and a consideration of the complex interactions of the program with the organizational context including personnel selection, managerial style, and work procedures. (Mankin, et al., 1980, p. 172)

The fields of biology and physics grew by leaps and bounds when scientists applied the notion of an open systems perspective to the knowledge already established. Environmental causes of plant and animal diseases became apparent. Newtonian physics gave way to the Einsteinian notions. Behavioral scientists applying and studying theories and techniques affecting human behavior in work settings also moved toward a systems theory perspective (see, for example, Leavitt & Bass, 1964; Quinn & Kahn, 1967; Strauss, 1970; Schein, 1980). In fact, the term *organization development* (OD) was coined in the 1960s to describe a subdiscipline of behavioral science that emerged when organization scientists embraced the open systems theory perspective and integrated portions of the subdisciplines of *organizational behavior* and *organizational theory*.

> The field of organizational studies is commonly segmented into "micro" and "macro" branches, the former typically, but not universally, being labeled

"organizational behavior" (OB), and the latter "organization theory" (OT) although it is by no means limited to theory. By whatever labels, the micro branch is ordinarily thought to comprise the study of individual, interpersonal, and intergroup behavior, as in the study of leadership, motivation, and job design, whereas the macro branch concerns organization-wide aspects such as structure, relations with the environment, effects of technology, and so forth. This distinction is by no means clear-cut, as is obvious from the uncertain placement of studies of organization climate. (Pondy & Mitroff, 1979, p. 4)

A book by Katz and Kahn (*Social Psychology of Organizations*, 1966, 1978) represents a milestone in the establishment of the field of OD and provides us with many insights as to how organizations function. We will be applying these insights to our discussions of the training function. After all, work organizations in general as well as the training function in particular can be viewed as social systems.

The boundaries and state of a *social system* are difficult to define. The "common sense" notion that the boundaries can be determined by examining the organization's title and stated objectives is misleading and naive. Katz and Kahn suggest that social systems are best defined by tracing the pattern of energy exchange or activity of people as it results in some output. Then one should ascertain the manner in which the output is translated into reactivating input energy. The authors also suggest that every system is merely a *subsystem* within a *larger system*. Thus, the training function can be seen as a social system and open systems theory can be applied to it.

Figure 1.2 traces the pattern of energy exchange or activity of people by means of an input, throughput, output model. As indicated in the diagram, the training function reacts to, involves, and affects a variety of elements within the organization as well as elements outside the confines of the company walls. Certainly, changes in the state of art of the technology utilized by the organization, governmental regulations, societal mores, economic conditions, and marketing conditions can all provide the stimulus to an organization that may result in a need for training programs. Similarly, the personnel areas of human resources planning, selection decisions, budgets, and job (task) requirements all influence training activities.

Frequently, the planning of training programs and other elements listed as "inputs" in Figure 1.2 are not accomplished in a coordinated fashion. Certainly, the results of the selection procedures used by an organization affect the activities that should be conducted by trainers in that organization. The degree to which the selectors systematically screen out candidates who lack the necessary skills to accomplish the organizational tasks influences the need to develop basic skill development sessions for new employees. On the other hand, if recruitment and selection procedures result in the acquisition of employees who already know how to perform the required duties of a given position, then the need for such basic training programs is reduced. In fact, it is for such cases that Tauber (1981) suggested using a systems theory approach to develop an effective orienta-

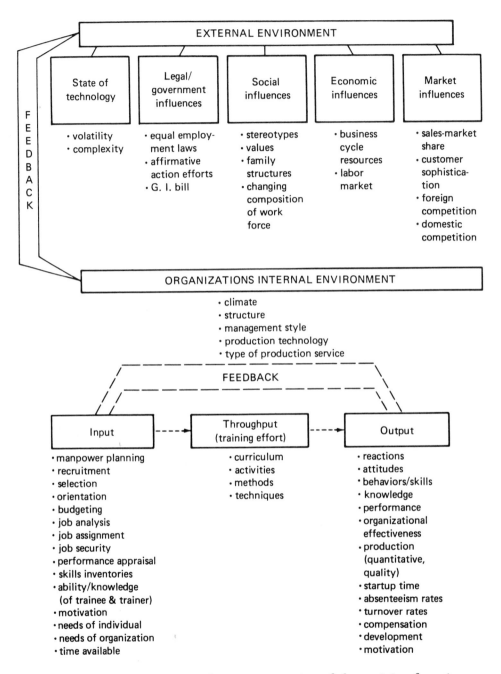

Figure 1.2 An open systems theory perspective of the training function.

tion process. Olivas (1980) also applied a systems theory perspective when he suggested that assessment center results can be used as a guide for designing OD efforts. Thus, it is apparent that an open systems view of organizations improves our use of the "input" subsystems when planning training and/or OD activities.

The arrows surrounding the word "Feedback" in Figure 1.2 imply that the outcomes of training (e.g., improved performance, changes in compensation, advances in career development ladders) are translated into new inputs (i.e., identification of new training needs) for the system. Open systems theory suggests that this is necessary or the entire training system will die. Conversely, some items listed as input in the model (e.g., performance appraisal systems, skills inventories, etc.) may also be viewed as outputs since these products may have been generated as a result of training and as a stimulus for further training. The model suggests that planning training programs should be done in a more *strategy-oriented, coordinated manner* in order to maximize the impact of training activity and other human resources activities on the organization's effectiveness. The relationship between subsystems should be viewed in a symbiotic manner. For example, the criteria and methodology of the organization's approach to selection should influence the training programs that will be offered. The types (and costs) of training programs available within the organization should also influence the procedures utilized by the people involved in selection for the firm. The company could decide to spend its money by hiring a skilled tradesman that is a journeyman or master or hire less expensive apprentices but spend the money training them.

Other principles of open systems theory discussed by Katz and Kahn are also applicable to our efforts to improve training. One principle that is particularly relevant to this book is referred to as the *equifinality* principle. In more common language, this principle states that "There is more than one way to skin a cat." Given a certain training objective, there are several approaches that can be used to accomplish that objective. Taylor's (1911) notion that there is always one best way to perform any job is simply wrong. Individuals are different and where one trainee may acquire a skill best through role playing another may benefit more from a lecture/discussion format. Unfortunately, if a training program succeeds in one organization, it is often offered as a training package to many other organizations. By failing to tailor (not Taylor) the approach to the unique features of the organizations, the equifinality principle is ignored. As trainers, we often have found the energy to plan/develop a program to accomplish an objective once but when facing another situation that seems to have the same objective, the temptation is to pull out the same old game plan. If the success of the first project was really due to the *process* of carefully planning activities to match the needs of a given situation rather than to the *content* of the set of activities, then the application of that content to another situation without replanning may fail. The equifinality principle offers OD practitioners and trainers alike a useful rule to keep in mind. Throughout this book, we stress a contingency notion regarding training. In Chapter 11, we summarize our thoughts on this matter.

Other principles of open systems theory have been alluded to in our previous discussion of the basic input-throughput-output model. Figure 1.1 may seem to be a static picture of training but a system is truly a dynamic process. The principle of negative entropy states that the system's outputs must be translated into the revitalizing energy of input or the system will decay (entropy). The evaluations of the results of training serve as partial needs assessment for the next round of training.

Systems theory suggests that all parts of a system are interrelated and that the system as a whole is greater than the sum of its parts (*synergy*). An organization's recruitment, selection, and training functions may each have been well-developed but, unless care is taken to coordinate these activities, they all may fail. Thus, the overall effectiveness of a human resources department is more than the sum of the effectiveness of the recruitment subsystem plus the selection subsystem plus the training subsystem, etc. The added ingredient to our formula for overall effectiveness is how successfully the outputs of one subsystem can become the inputs of the next subsystem. This illustrates the systems theory principle known as *synergy*.

While an open systems theory perspective is a key characteristic of the OD discipline, many OD practitioners commit *"systems errors"* in their applications. Four such common errors were pointed out by Royland (1980) and provide useful lessons for trainers to consider as well.

First, Royland suggested that OD practitioners all too frequently *define the boundaries* of their client's system on the basis of *accessibility* and *availability*. If a plant manager calls the change agent in, the system is defined as the plant site and corporate and community influences are downplayed or ignored. If the head of a large department brings a consultant in, he or she often treats that department as a whole system. Most consultants or internal staffers would be reluctant to gather data and involve managers outside the entry point department for fear of offending the originator of the change effort. This is done despite the fact it may be very clear that the parts of the larger system are definitely interrelated.

If you are called in to develop a training program in one large department, you are likely to feel inhibited about including managers in the next department or to work with the compensation people to change the reward structure. If you are being paid to do training out of the budget of department X, you will feel compelled to concentrate your efforts there even if you know that support and/or changes from other subsystems are necessary for your training program to really work in the long run. Trainers are often in the bind of having to please the original point of entry rather than concentrate on resolving the problems at hand. Trainers and OD practitioners alike need to better prepare management for spinoff problems likely to result from change efforts. This issue will be further addressed in Chapter 11.

A second system error pointed out by Royland is the change agent's *insufficient specification* of the variables involved. Management often tells OD practitioners (and trainers too) what the diagnosis should be. The consultant is hired to fix that problem not to spend his or her time (and the organization's money) gathering data on possible interrelated factors and attempting to determine the real cause of the problem. Without a thorough needs assessment (as you will learn about in Chapter 2), you may end up treating symptoms, not problems. But, if a company is hurting and seeking help from a trainer or an OD practitioner, they want action, not some outsider poking his or her nose around doing a thorough diagnosis. The repercussions of this problem include an overconcentration on individual deficiencies and failure to notice the relevant problems of organizational climate, leadership style, or environmental influences. We overrely on our entry point person's perception of the situation or quickly attempt to verify it through subjective, intuitive judgments based on observations and/or conversational interviews. By insufficiently defining the variables involved in a given problem, seemingly well-designed training programs may be doomed to failure.

A third common systems error is closely related. The interventions used by OD practitioners may often be *too narrowly focused* on a specific set of behaviors. When exploring whether to launch an organizational change effort, management naturally wants to know what they are getting themselves into. Organizational change may be a process but the client wants to know about its content. It is easier to sell a prepackaged program of known duration than it is to suggest a process of diagnosis and experimentation. However, such a process may be necessary to capitalize on the variety of dynamics that would be uniquely applicable to the organization. Management may feel more secure in contracting for a workshop on problem solving that is scheduled to last X hours, involve Y employees, and deal with Z skills. But a trainer or OD consultant, hoping to help an organization improve its effectiveness by promoting a problem-solving process, may find him- or herself dealing with a wider variety of issues, skills, and employees for an indeterminate length of time. Management may view this lack of certainty as a source of threat rather than the flexibility needed for successful change. Thus, HRD and OD professionals are pressured to limit thinking to simple cause and effect chains in limited areas within a given organization. Chapters 2 and 11 suggest procedures trainers may use to broaden their planning procedures to achieve a more organizational perspective.

Since adult human behavior has multiple causes, training and other interventions must be broad enough to address previous behavior yet specific enough to build new usable skills. OD practitioners and trainers alike have been guilty of overusing their favorite techniques. The comfort that the use of these techniques brings to both the trainer and the client often blinds us to the need for broader, more flexible change efforts. As the saying goes, "When the only tool you have is a hammer, all your problems start looking like nails." Chapters 6 through 10 provide a variety of tools that may help avoid this problem.

The final systems error Royland brings to our attention is the *weak or nonexistent evaluation* component within typical OD interventions. Without a link between the output of a system and revitalizing input energy, a system dies. Trainers and OD practitioners who fail to incorporate evaluation procedure into the design of their change efforts, fail to learn from their mistakes, overrely on short-term reactions of the parties most closely involved, and fail to prove the cost-effectiveness of their actions. Thus, they lose another chance to gain respect and credibility with top management. There are a variety of reasons why trainers (and other change agents) fail to evaluate their interventions properly:

1. A fear of what they may find out.
2. A lack of the skills (especially quantitative skills) necessary to develop a good evaluation component.
3. A fear that management will see the trainer's suggestion for an evaluation as merely a cost-adding element to the service requested.
4. A realization that the management involved prefers a few positive testimonials that the training worked rather than proof that it truly had an impact.

For these and other reasons, trainers and OD practitioners may talk about the importance of evaluation but usually are still guilty of failing to institute this component into their actions (see also Putnam, 1980; Brown, 1980).

It is hoped that the reader now sees the value of open systems theory as a framework for understanding and developing training. Just as it has advanced the study of organizations as a whole, it should also aid our understanding of the training function.

CHANGE _____

As we move toward the 21st century, great changes and transitions are taking place in our society and its business institutions. The rapid advances in technology, increasing foreign competition, and dwindling resources have changed the way Americans conduct their business activities. At the same time, the nature of the American workforce is changing. Today's workers are more educated and are making more demands about the quality of their work lives. As a result of the changes that have taken place in our social systems (e.g., society and in our work places), today's business organizations need mechanisms for planning, managing, and implementing internal change programs.

Training or, as it is more fashionably called, human resource development (HRD) will play a critical role in the ability of American businesses to meet the demands of the complex and volatile environment they are experiencing and can expect to experience into the next century. However, for the HRD function of an organization to meet its responsibilities, it must recognize that business as usual will no longer suffice. The HRD function must become familiar with and integrate into its operations the growing body of knowledge related to organizational, group, and individual change processes. Others have also recognized the need to integrate these change processes into the framework of HRD (e.g., Jamieson, 1981; Lippitt, 1982). This text makes such an integration with a focus on developing a more effective training strategy and practice for the organization.

Trainers can benefit from the perspective of *organizational change* in addition to the traditional focus on *individual change*. The following list displays a sequential model of how organizations change.

1. Stimulus for change is felt within the organization.
2. The organization attempts to cope with the stimulus.
3. A compelling need for change is established.
4. The cause of the change need is diagnosed.
5. Goals are developed and agreed upon.
6. Alternative approaches are identified and evaluated.
7. An approach is selected.
8. The change idea is implemented.
9. The change effort is evaluated.
10. The evaluation is fed back to the organization.
11. The change effort becomes internalized.

Organizations do not necessarily progress from step to step through this model. In fact, resistance to change (a problem no trainer is a stranger to) is typically so strong that companies frequently fail to systematically address the need for change posed by their environment. This model will be more fully addressed in Chapter 10.

THE EMERGING DISCIPLINE OF ORGANIZATIONAL DEVELOPMENT (OD) _____

OD involves a systems perspective but includes much more. One of the earliest definitions of *organizational development* was provided by Bennis (1969): "OD is a response to change, a complex educational strategy intended to change the beliefs, attitudes, values and structure of organizations so that they can better adapt to new technologies, markets, and challenges, and the dizzying rate of change itself." Dozens of definitions of OD have since emerged in the literature. Upon reviewing these definitions, we see four key characteristics:

1. OD utilizes open-systems theory perspectives.
2. OD involves long-term planned change efforts.
3. OD is firmly rooted in behavioral science theory and technology.
4. OD emphasizes that change is a process not a program.

We thus view the field of OD as broader than a systems viewpoint. We will discuss the other characteristics of OD in Chapter 10. One of the goals of this book is to identify, for organizations and trainers, ways to improve training effectiveness by using the discipline known as OD. We feel that it provides a useful perspective, a body of research, and a set of tools for enhancing overall organizational effectiveness and human growth and development. Specific OD implications for the various components of training occur throughout the chapters of this book.

SUMMARY ───

The human, financial, and time resources allocated by organizations to training and development activities is enormous. It has enticed us, the authors of this text, to devote our time and energy to a systematic review of the HRD literature. It is our hope that such a review, combined with our efforts to apply the theories and technologies of the behavioral sciences (including those of organizational development), will provide the reader with a comprehensive view of the field of training and specific ideas on how to practice more effectively within that field.

In this introductory chapter, we provided you with information concerning the size of the field of human resources development; defined what we consider to be the key elements for effective training; outlined the steps of a sequential model of the training process; and discussed the roles fulfilled by HRD professionals and the role HRD plays within organizations. We introduced the fields of organizational behavior and organizational development and focused on how a systems theory perspective serves trainers.

PREVIEW OF THE REST OF THIS BOOK ─────────────

Figure 1.3 illustrates a simplified systems view of training that describes the format of the remainder of this book. The input into the "training system" is the determination of who needs what kind of training. Chapter 2 focuses on this topic. This chapter will answer questions such as "How do you know if training is needed?" and "Who should determine if a training need exists?"

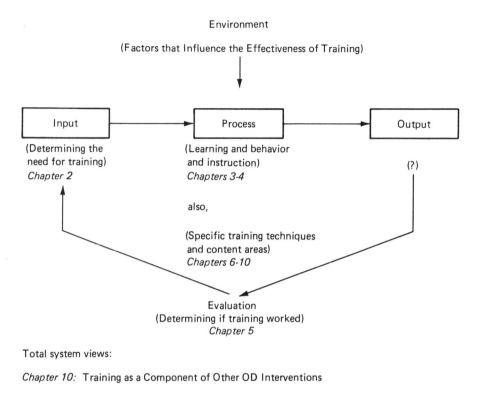

Figure 1.3   Simplified system view of training and overview of this book.

As noted in Figure 1.3, the "process" of training is the particular approach used to change knowledge and/or skills. Chapters 3 and 4 of this book present an overview of the learning process. These chapters focus on how people learn, the difference between learning and behavior, and the factors that influence whether learning gets translated into behavior on the job. The theories and research of behavioral scientists have advanced our understanding of the learning process and provide a useful framework for trainers.

Given this background, the entire second part of this book (Chapters 6–10) focuses in detail on particular training techniques and content areas. A variety of techniques and strategies are presented that focus on non-experiential (Chapter 6) and experiential (Chapter 7) training. Content areas covered in the second part include individualized approaches to training, including manual and technical training (Chapter 8) and management development and human relations training (Chapter 9).

The third part of the book returns the reader to a broader perspective. Chapter 10 discusses the key role that training plays in OD activities. In this chapter, we stress the idea of viewing the trainer as an organizational change agent. In Chapter 11, a discussion of strategy issues to be considered while planning a training system is presented. The effects of the environment on the training system will also be examined.

Although we have previously stated that the objective or desired result of training is a change in behavior, Figure 1.3 lists a question mark as the output of the training system. This is because training doesn't always achieve its objective. Chapter 5 focuses on how to evaluate the effectiveness of a training program. In addition to focusing on evaluation techniques, this chapter also examines how evaluation is beneficial, both to the trainer and the organization. This chapter is purposely placed in the first part of the book because, unless evaluation plans are developed before the implementation of the training techniques, it is virtually impossible to truly evaluate the impact of training.

To summarize, this book is divided into three sections. The first section contains chapters that examine key concepts of a training system (i.e., a systems theory framework for understanding training, training needs assessments, learning theories, program development, and evaluation processes). The second section provides an in-depth analysis of particular training techniques and content areas. The final section of this book takes a total view of the training system by examining the role that training plays in any attempt to change an organization and discussing strategic concerns for trainers.

We will attempt in our discussions of the topics of each chapter not only to reflect the HRD literature on that topic, but also to include the perspectives of practitioners who are wrestling with the issues on a day-to-day basis. To that end, we have included examples from our own experiences as trainers and interviews with HRD professionals. These interviews can be found at the end of each chapter throughout the book.

It is our hope that this book's use of an organizational development perspective will help readers understand why past training activities succeeded or failed. It is also our hope that such information will promote more effective planning on the part of trainers in their efforts to promote change within organizations.

DISCUSSION QUESTIONS _____

1. Are there other business functions that could benefit from an organizational perspective? What are these areas and how would they benefit?
2. What are some of the factors that have led to the importance of HRD/training within organizations? Will HRD/training become more or less important to organizations in the future? Why?

3. What experiences have you had receiving training within organizations? Have they been positive or negative? What do you think caused the training to turn out the way it did?
4. Why do you think system errors occur within organizations? How can they be controlled/eliminated?
5. What skills and knowledge do you think are most important for an effective trainer? Please rank these in priority order.

AN ORGANIZATIONAL DEVELOPMENT (OD) PERSPECTIVE FOR TRAINERS: AN INTERVIEW WITH DON ARNOUDSE ⸻

Don Arnoudse is a management consultant and trainer in productivity and human interaction in the workplace. He is president of the consulting firm, Arnoudse and Ouelette Associates, Inc., headquartered in Dover, New Hampshire. He specializes in designing and implementing development programs that stress shared responsibility by all employees and managers for top quality products and customer service. He works with his clients in efforts to improve communications, participative leadership skills, team development, and problem solving. His firm also specializes in consulting with companies regarding the selection and implementation of computers and other office automation equipment. Their approach to implementation emphasizes training in human interaction skills to assist data processing professionals to communicate with users. Don has over 12 years of experience as a consultant and a trainer to large and small companies. We chose Don to interview for this chapter because he uses a "systems" perspective in the way he integrates his training and consultation services.

Question: Don, you have been very active in the field, providing training to a wide variety of clients. Just how important is having an organizational perspective?

Arnoudse: I have been thinking a lot about that ever since you contacted me to arrange for this interview. I am convinced that having an organizational perspective, as you call it, is crucial for the delivery of successful training. In fact, without that perspective you will find, more often than not, that training occurs without commitment. The training sessions will be viewed as time out from one's job not as part of one's job. The transfer of learning problem you talk about in your book really shows up. As a trainer, I would try to get trainees to develop personal action plans for "on-the-job" application of what they felt they gained from my training sessions. But, unless the organizational environment they came from also changed, I found transfer from the sessions to their jobs unlikely.

It's a seductive situation for a trainer. You want to please your audience. You want to please the personnel director who hired you to deliver the training. But, I learned quite a while ago that if you only respond to these constituencies and fail to spend more time with line management within the organization, working with them on ways to capitalize on the training being delivered to their people, you will often end up with only a stimulating session that produces no real changes. As a result, training becomes viewed in a more jaded fashion within that firm, making it even more difficult to succeed with subsequent training efforts.

Question: What's causing this problem?

Arnoudse: To some extent, trainers and the training industry itself are at fault. We often market training as a product rather than a process. We describe concrete programs in order to get companies to buy into using our services. It's very difficult to succinctly describe the process needed to promote change through training. Management isn't going to sign a blank check for an ill-defined service. So, we describe our efforts as programs that will last X amount of hours, will involve Y number of their people, and will cost them Z amount of dollars.

Another major cause of the problem is that the goals of a personnel or human resources department may be different from the goals of the overall organization. Many of the directors of personnel that I am contacted by will be rewarded within their respective organizations for delivering as many enjoyable training programs as their budget allows. They will receive positive recognition if organizational members return happy and give the programs a "10." When I suggest to them the need to spend more time preparing the organization for the training, I see some of them fearing the trouble this may stir up and/or the costs this may entail. If they already have a notion of what type of training is needed, they wonder "Why should we pay you for the time it takes to clarify needs and generate commitment?" They may see such suggestions as an undesirable delay. They want a program or some quick fix now. And again, their rewards within many organizations may be tied to generating training activities and programs rather than actually solving organizational problems.

Question: What do you do to counter these problems?

Arnoudse: When I first started as an independent trainer, I found myself eager to respond to requests for my services. I found myself generating enthusiastic trainees but questioning whether they or their departments actually experienced productive change. I would frequently get invited back to deliver the same training package to another set of trainees so I began asking questions about what changes actually did occur. This raised the issue of preparing the organization for change with my contact people and we would then schedule more time to plan strategies to capitalize on the outcomes of the training programs.

Now, as a consultant, I see that my greatest leverage point is right up front during the first contact with a client organization. I find it better to raise organizational issues then rather than later. It became apparent to me that doing otherwise was like getting married first and hoping we could work out things later. It's not like that could never work. It's just better to address those issues beforehand.

I have found that asking questions like "What are your desired outcomes? What organizational problems are you hoping to solve with such-and-such training programs? Who do we need to get together to address these problems? What obstacles will these trainees face when they try to apply what they learned in training?" really helps open some doors to promote a more successful training effort. Most of my contact people readily identify the need to solicit the involvement and support of the supervisors or managers of the trainees in order to increase the likelihood that the training will be used. This helps me generate a tie to the line management of that company and I always plan involvement of that contact from personnel/human resources in subsequent meetings with those line managers. Assuming that we can convince the line managers of the benefits and utility of the training proposed for their people, all parties are likely to benefit. These line managers are generally very valuable in identifying ways the training should be designed/modified to meet the unique needs of their group of subordinates. This insures me of a greater likelihood that my training efforts will be perceived as more relevant and valuable. My contact in human resources now has a closer tie with line managers in his or her firm. And, the trainees are less likely to be frustrated by having expectations raised during training but having to return to a climate that doesn't support change. Of course, these sessions do not always go smoothly and this attention to contracting issues does not guarantee success but clarifying expectations in the manner I described up front has certainly helped me promote a more effective organizational perspective in my work.

Chapter 2

TRAINING NEEDS ASSESSMENT _____

Chapter 1 presented an overview of the field of human resource training and development within organizations. A model of change was also presented. This chapter provides an in-depth analysis of how the first four components of this model apply to the training process (see Figure 2.1). This will be accomplished by providing answers to the following questions:

1. What is a training needs assessment (TNA) and why is it important?
2. How should a training needs assessment be conducted?
3. What are the implications of behavioral science research for improving the TNA process?

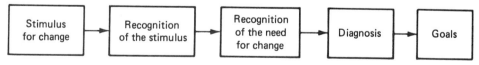

Figure 2.1   The change model.

WHAT IS A TNA? _____

As noted in Chapter 1, there are a variety of internal and external forces on an organization to change. Table 2.1 lists some of these forces and their implications for training within organizations. Often, organizations attempt

Table 2.1 Forces for change and corresponding potential training implications.

Forces	Training implications
1. Increased computerization.	Training in the use and management of computers.
2. Increased demand for employees with high technological skills (e.g., engineering and computers).	Develop these skills in current employees.
3. Changing composition of the work force (e.g., greater education, more minorities and females).	Need for managers who know how to relate to employee problems and can work in a cooperative manner with employees.
4. More demand on management time.	Need for managers who can make quick and accurate decisions.
5. Greater foreign competition.	Need for employees who are skilled in the technical aspects of their jobs.
	Need for managers who are skilled in management techniques (e.g., goal setting) that maximize employee productivity.

to cope with these forces by maintaining the status quo; yet some will respond to these forces and recognize the need to change. The major force for change is often a particular individual, perhaps someone in training or a supervisor in some other function, who recognizes the symptoms that indicate an organization must adapt.

At this point, it is important to differentiate between *symptoms* of the need for change and the *cause(s)* of those symptoms. A symptom of the need for change is a problem and may arise from one of many sources. The cause of the symptom is the factor that must be changed in order to eliminate the symptom/problem. Figure 2.2 lists some typical symptoms of the need to change. As shown in the figure, failure to provide effective training may lead to any or all of the symptoms. Unfortunately, these symptoms may also arise from a variety of other sources. The third stage of the change model (the diagnosis/TNA) is designed to determine the cause that creates the symptom(s).

Training needs assessment (TNA) is the examination or diagnostic portion of the training system. The symptoms that TNA examines are often referred to as perceived performance deficiencies. *A perceived performance deficiency* exists when there is a difference between expected and *perceived* job performance. Since a performance deficiency is based on perception, it

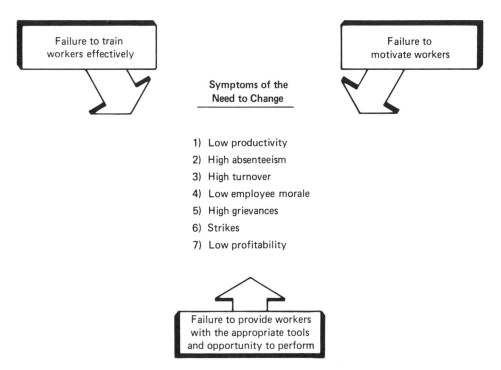

Figure 2.2 Factors that create symptoms of the need to change.

may not reflect objective reality. For example, let's assume a supervisor believes a subordinate's work is of inferior quality. This is a perceived performance deficiency since (from the supervisor's perspective) there is a difference between what is expected (the quality standard) and what is occurring (job performance). Perhaps the subordinate's work is of poor quality. It is equally possible (given what is known about this situation) that the supervisor has inaccurately measured or otherwise underestimated the quality of the employee's work. To complicate matters further, even if the work is, in fact, below the quality standard, there are numerous factors beyond the employee's or training department's control that may be causing the deficiency. These might include:

1. A quality standard set at an unrealistic level.
2. A workload that makes it impossible to focus on quality.
3. Inferior raw materials that cause poor quality.
4. Sabotage by other employees.

This list could be almost endless. These problems should not dishearten one from conducting TNAs. It is realistic to think of the search for the solution to some performance deficiencies as looking for a needle in a haystack.

Nevertheless, if one were to lose a valuable needle, he or she would attempt a search. The search may never uncover the needle. Yet, if it is done in a rational, logical manner, it may eliminate several potential "problem areas" or even uncover the problem.

TYPES OF TRAINING

Before examining the various forms of TNA, it is important to focus on the kinds of training we believe organizations should provide.

Although the discussion above and that which follows implies that training should be provided based on current and/or future job requirements, it should be noted that many times organizations provide training without regard to any job-related deficiency but rather to allow the trainee to grow and develop. While this seems to be a humanistic approach and *may* provide benefits to the organization (e.g., the ability to attract and retain high quality employees), we feel this approach will typically prove frustrating to employees and wasteful to the organization.

As stated in Chapter 1, our view is that training should have a dual goal of organizational effectiveness and an improved work experience for the job incumbent. We feel this dual goal is an appropriate standard for determining the types of training programs that should be provided within organizations. If both parties do not benefit, training should not be provided. Organizations can benefit from training if it increases employee performance by raising skill or motivation levels and/or increases the organization's ability to attract and retain high quality employees. Individuals can benefit from training by obtaining valued rewards as a result of improved performance, through increased job satisfaction and/or through the satisfaction of personal needs (e.g., the need for growth). Training programs that satisfy the latter individual criteria (personal needs) can easily be developed by surveying job incumbents regarding the types of training opportunities they desire. Since this type of training is, only by accident, related to skills needed to perform a current or future job, it can only be organizationally beneficial to the extent that it motivates and/or helps attract and retain qualified employees. In order to be motivational, such training must be offered contingent on effective job performance by the trainee. Care must be taken, however, to assure that training is a highly valued reward compared to the other types of potential benefits that can be offered for high performance (e.g., time off, compensation, etc.). Failure to consider this issue may result in less than optimal employee motivation. The motivational process is described in detail in the next chapter.

We know of no evidence indicating that the use of personal growth programs has resulted in recruitment and/or retention gains. However, if such programs are offered, some type of organizational benefit as well as satisfaction of trainee personal needs should be used in evaluating its effectiveness. Since both individuals and organizations should benefit from training aimed at improving current or future job-related knowledge and skills, the remainder of this chapter will focus on developing a TNA for these purposes.

REACTIVE AND PROACTIVE TNAs

A TNA can be categorized based upon whether it is reactive or proactive. A *reactive* (i.e., *remedial*) *TNA* occurs when the perceived performance deficiency is a discrepancy between perceived and expected performance for the employee's *current job*. Whether the unmet expectations are from a supervisory's or incumbent's perspective, the problem has already occurred and can only be dealt with post hoc. There are, however, different degrees of reactivity. Some organizations may respond to the first example of a deficiency, while others may wait until it occurs numerous times. An investigation of why a particular salesperson failed to meet last quarter's sales quota exemplifies a reactive TNA.

A *proactive TNA* is conducted to respond to the perception that current job behavior reflects an inability to meet *future* standards or expectations. There are two variants of this assessment. The *preventative approach* is designed to assure that an employee will be able to meet future expectations for his or her *current* job. Since the employee is fulfilling current job expectations, the need to take this type of action will be a function of the rate of change of the job and industry in question. These latter factors are influenced by the volatility of the organizations' technology and environment (Perrow, 1970), as was suggested in Figure 1.2. Thus, a computer firm may need to investigate whether its programmers, who are meeting current job standards, have the skill, knowledge and/or ability to adapt to technological advances. Similarly, top management in organizations trying to move from adversarial to cooperative labor/management relations may need to scrutinize whether managers who have been performing effectively in the former case necessarily have the skill or ability to respond to the latter environment.

The second type of proactive TNA is for *developmental purposes*. This type of TNA is conducted when current job behavior leads to the perception that the individual has the potential but is not yet ready to perform at a *higher level position*. Often, such an assessment reveals an individual who is technically proficient in a present position but lacks the managerial skills needed for a higher level job.

Example 2.1 illustrates reactive and proactive perceived performance deficiencies. The reactive and proactive TNAs that would be undertaken to correct these deficiencies would be conducted in basically the same manner. However, they stem from a different base in that they pose different task requirements on the individual(s) who defines the performance deficiency. A proactive TNA rests on the ability of someone to predict or anticipate a future problem. In the preventative version, the individual must know how *or if* the job will change. Similarly, a developmental TNA must compare the individual to a job the employee has (most often) never performed. As illustrated in Example 2.1, top management has to predict what knowledge or skill deficiencies Sandy would have as a manager without the benefit of observing her in this position. Just as with any prediction, these problems may never actually occur. Compare this to the reactive TNA, where the problem is not based on a prediction, but an assessment of past behavior. In the reactive case in Example 2.1, we know Scott is not meeting his quota. True, this "deficiency" may not be due to a lack of training and may actually be due to unrealistic standards on the part of the evaluator. Nevertheless, a reactive TNA is conducted to identify a tangible deficiency.

The point of the above discussion is not that one form of TNA is more desirable than another, but that the proactive version is based on a more uncertain foundation (than the reactive form) and thus may have a lower probability of accurately identifying needed knowledge or skills.

Example 2.1   Examples of reactive and proactive perceived performance deficiencies.

Reactive   Scott is an employee for a large retail organization. He started with the organization as a stockperson and worked his way up to his current position as a salesperson in men's clothes. He has held this position for three years. For the last three business quarters, Scott's sales have not met his quota. Scott's supervisor is extremely concerned about this problem and wants to take some corrective action.

Proactive   Sandy is a computer programmer for a small insurance firm. The manager of the data processing area (Sandy's boss) will be retiring in six months. Sandy is viewed by the organization's top management as the logical successor to the manager's job. Since Sandy has never held a management position, the top management of the organization feels Sandy needs some training, but they're not sure what kind of training she will need.

Value of TNA   Given the discussion to this point, the reader may question the value in conducting a TNA. Combined with the fact that any well done TNA is time-consuming and costly, it may seem logical that many organizations do not conduct a TNA prior to training (Wexley & Latham, 1981). However, the following issues should also be considered:

1. Training is a costly process. When training doesn't achieve its objective(s) (i.e., eliminate the performance deficiencies), an organization spends considerable resources in return for few, if any, benefits. There are several studies (c.f., Miller & Zeller, 1967) that illustrate this point. TNA increases the probability of a successful training effort by determining if and how training can help to solve a particular problem. Training without

conducting a TNA is analagous to a medical doctor performing surgery based (only) on the knowledge that the patient doesn't feel well. The surgery may correct the problem but the odds are considerably against it.

2. During difficult economic times, organizations typically place themselves under self-scrutiny. This self-examination is undertaken to determine the contribution of subunits to the attainment of organizational goals. As will be pointed out in Chapter 5, it is impossible for trainers to *prove* that their training activity caused an improvement in job performance without conducting a TNA. Many training departments do not conduct TNAs; therefore, they cannot prove their effectiveness and it is not surprising that during budget reductions their training department is often the first to go (Laird, 1978).

3. Points 1 and 2 indicate the need for trainers to conduct TNAs but provide little impetus for the line managers to be concerned with this process. Yet, the skill needed to implement a TNA may be a key determinant of managerial effectiveness. The manager's lament that "there aren't enough hours in the day to do my job" is well supported by research (Mintzberg, 1973). Given this hectic existence, the effective manager must maximize his or her resources. Training is one way to accomplish this. However, training or any other type of corrective action probably will not be effective unless there is an accurate diagnosis of the source of an employee's performance deficiency. Unfortunately, evidence exists that managers often err in this type of assessment (Mitchell, Green, & Wood, 1981). This issue will be discussed in detail in the third portion of this chapter. For now, the point is that the skills involved in conducting a TNA are an important aspect of any manager's job and one that typically needs development.

Points 1–3 provide the rationale for why some version of TNA should always be conducted prior to training. Failure to do so is taking a "shot in the dark."

HOW SHOULD A TNA BE CONDUCTED?

Figure 2.3 presents a model depicting the key steps involved in conducting a TNA. Briefly, these are:

1. Defining the perceived performance deficiency.
2. Prioritizing the problem.
3. Identifying job requirements, trainee's skill and ability level, and environmental constraints on correcting the deficiency.
4. Developing a behavioral description of the need.

The remainder of this section is devoted to discussing each of these steps in detail. However, before examining these points, it is important to discuss who should conduct a TNA. As mentioned earlier, TNA is a necessity

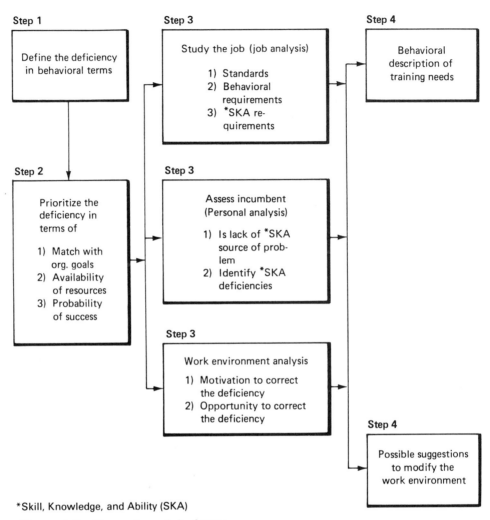

*Skill, Knowledge, and Ability (SKA)

Figure 2.3 General model of TNA.

for effective training as well as a key element of managerial effectiveness. Thus, ideally, both the trainer and the immediate supervisor should jointly implement this process. Later in this section, the importance of the job incumbent's input will be highlighted, both in terms of the quality of information it provides as well as its impact on creating commitment to rectifying the perceived performance deficiency. Peer input will also be noted as a valuable source of information. Realistically, few if any TNAs will use all of these sources. As mentioned earlier, many organizations do not even conduct TNAs. The decision of how many sources the TNA implementor (i.e., manager or trainer) will actually use will be influenced by time pressures, cost, and other situational constraints. Nevertheless, assuming valid information, the more and varied sources of input into a TNA, the greater the probability of an accurate assessment. Thus, the following discussion should be considered a general idealized guideline that the implementor may choose to modify as needed.

Step 1: Define the Deficiency in Behavioral Terms

The first step in the diagnostic process is to clearly define the deficiency that needs to be corrected. In a reactive TNA, the problem is typically identified as a result of a performance appraisal. Problem identification for proactive TNA stems from performance appraisals in conjunction with a planning process. For example, human resource plans may indicate the projected retirement of certain managers with no (currently capable) successors. Whatever the source or type, there is often a tendency to state the problem in terms of a perceived solution (Mager & Pipe, 1984). For example, the manager who states "My supervisors need training in communication" has not indicated what the performance deficiency is (e.g., Are employees not following supervisory orders correctly? Are supervisors giving the wrong orders? Are employees and supervisors arguing over priorities?), but rather what he or she perceives the solution to be. Similarly, an individual who states "Dan needs to develop leadership before he's ready for position X" hasn't specified what Dan isn't doing that he should be. As Mager and Pipe (1984) noted, one way to reduce this tendency of focusing on solutions is to ask the individual defining the problem "What specific behaviors aren't taking place that should be?" Without a specific behavioral description of the problem, an accurate TNA is highly improbable.

Step 2: Prioritize—Organization Analysis

Once the deficiency has been defined in behavioral terms, the next step is to undertake what has been described as an organization analysis (McGehee & Thayer, 1961). Since organizations have limited resources, all problems cannot be handled simultaneously. An *organizational analysis* asks "Which problem should be solved to provide the greatest organizational benefit?"

The answer to this question will be contingent upon the following three criteria:

1. *Organizational Goals.* The issue here is the extent to which the performance deficiency hinders the attainment of organizational goals. One useful technique for specifying this relationship is to ask "What will happen to the organization if the performance deficiency is not corrected?" (Mager & Pipe, 1984). For example, an organization that depends

on the performance of the data processing department to increase its revenues may need to focus on performance deficiencies in this area, even though these deficiencies may not be as large as those in other departments.

2. *Resources.* The capacity to take corrective action must also be considered. Just as any individual has strengths and weaknesses, so too do training departments (and immediate supervisors) differ in their abilities to rectify performance problems. These, along with other resource limitations (such as budget and time constraints), must be considered.

3. *Probability of Success.* The objective of training is to improve performance by changing behavior. This is a difficult and extremely complicated endeavor. As stated earlier, in a developmental TNA you may be attempting to correct a deficiency that will never actually occur. Even if a training need is accurately identified and the correct training is effectively administered, there are still a variety of factors that may inhibit behavioral change. One such factor is the particular climate/culture of the organization. Although there is no one universally accepted definition of this construct (Payne & Pugh, 1976), Payne (1971) defined it as "the prevalent values, norms, attitudes, behaviors, and feelings of the members of a social system" (p. 156). Research by Arval and Stumpf (1981) supported the notion that organization and work group climate are different constructs.

Orientation toward development is a dimension of climate that has been identified by several researchers (c.f., Pace, 1968; Stern, 1970; Gorman & Malloy, 1972). Organizations or work groups high on this dimension are concerned with fostering individual development and encourage the growth and development of new ideas. Evidence exists that a training effort will have a much greater probability of success in this type of organization or work group climate (Allen & Silverzwerg, 1976; Baumgartel & Jeanpierre, 1972).

Table 2.2 lists the variety of resources that can be used in an organization analysis. The diversity of this information illustrates that this phase of TNA is currently more of art than a science. The previous discussion on organizational climate reinforces this point. Although evidence exists that organizational and/or work group climate influences receptivity to training, valid and easy to implement measures of these constructs are not readily available to the TNA implementor. The cost/benefit of such activity (in traditional survey form) every time a TNA is conducted, or for every organizational subunit, is also questionable. Thus, realistically, the best the TNA implementor can do is make a subjective estimate of these climate factors based on observation and any other type of data that can be gathered. Regarding work and organizational climate, the implementor can:

1. *Monitor the attitudes and behavior of key individuals.* One such group are managerial/supervisory personnel since they are responsible for allo-

Table 2.2 Data sources for an organizational analysis.

Data source recommended	Training need implications
1. Organizational Goals and Objectives	Where training emphasis can and should be placed. These provide normative standards of both direction and expected impact which can highlight deviations from objectives and performance problems.
2. Manpower Inventory	Where training is needed to fill gaps caused by retirement, turnover, age, etc. This provides an important demographic data base regarding possible scope of training needs.
3. Skills Inventory	Number of employees in each skill group, knowledge and skill levels, training time per job; etc. This provides an estimate of the magnitude of specific training needs. Useful in cost benefit analysis of training projects.
4. Organizational Climate Indices	These "quality of working life" indicators at the organization level may help focus on problems that have training components.
a. Labor-Management data—strikes, lockouts, etc.	All of these items related to either work participation or productivity are useful both in discrepancy analysis and in helping management set a value on the behaviors it wishes improved through training once training has been established as a relevant solution.
b. Grievances	
c. Turnover	
d. Absenteeism	
e. Suggestions	
f. Productivity	
g. Accidents	
h. Short-term sickness	
i. Observation of employee behavior	
j. Attitude surveys	Good for locating discrepancies between organizational expectations and perceived results.
k. Customer complaints	Valuable feedback; look especially for patterns and repeat complaints.
5. Analysis of Efficiency Indices	Cost accounting concepts may represent ratio between actual performance and desired or standard performance.
a. Costs of labor	
b. Costs of materials	
c. Quality of product	

Table 2.2   Data sources for an organizational analysis. (*Continued*)

Data source recommended	Training need implications

d. Equipment utilization
   e. Costs of distribution
   f. Waste
   g. Down time
   h. Late deliveries
   i. Repairs	

6. Changes in System or Sub-system	New or changed equipment may present training problem.
7. Management Requests or Management Interrogation	One of most common techniques of training needs determination.
8. Exit Interviews	Often information not otherwise available can be obtained in these. Problem areas and supervisory training needs especially.
9. MBO or Work Planning and Review Systems	Provides performance review, potential review, and long-term business objectives. Provides actual performance data on a recurring basis so that base-line measurements may be known and subsequent improvement or deterioration of performance can be identified and analyzed.

From Moore, M.L., & Dutton P. Training needs analysis: Review and critique. *Academy of Management Review*, 1978, *3*, 532–545. Reprinted with permission.

cating rewards. This might be accomplished in a straightforward method by asking about a manager's attitude toward current or past training practices. A more unobtrusive measure would be to examine completed performance appraisals to see when and if training was suggested as corrective action. This might indicate some commitment to the training process. It is also important not to overlook the attitudes and behaviors of top management, since these will influence lower level managerial behavior. An organization that evaluates its top managers (in the formal performance appraisal) on skills in developing subordinates will have a climate more conducive to development.

2. *Pay careful attention to the performance reputation of work groups.* This is related to point 1 in that another group of key players are peers. A reputation of high performance might reflect a norm that would foster commitment to development. Caution is advised, since too high a performance norm may lead to a fear of trying new behaviors that would be acquired in training. This type of data may be gathered through

careful attention to incidental comments about reputation or by examining performance records *across* individuals.

3. *Examine the positive or negative organizational consequences to the job incumbent of correcting the perceived deficiency.* Some organizations have pay systems that increase an individual's salary when organizationally relevant (but not necessarily current job) skills are obtained (Lawler, 1982). Other organizations provide raises and promotions more as a function of seniority. Some organizations never fire anyone, while others are constantly terminating personnel. Attention to these issues will provide some indication of the climate for development.

4. *Pay careful attention to the rumor mill and major organizational events.* An organization that is undergoing restructuring or financial problems might have a climate that hinders a commitment to development since employees may be afraid of attempting new behaviors that may not necessarily succeed on the first try. Even if these events aren't actually occurring, the perception that they are might have the same impact. Thus, rumors should not be dismissed but analyzed in terms of their impact on the developmental climate.

Since there are a variety of other organizational factors that influence the probability of a successful training effort, this topic is covered in more detail later in this book (see Chapter 11). In this chapter, subjective methods of estimating these factors will be noted along with ways in which they can be modified to improve the probability of a successful training effort. The focus will not be on the most scientific (or perhaps accurate) method of measurement but on a practical and realistic approach (given typical time constraints) and one clearly superior to ignoring the influence of these factors on training.

Of all of the sources listed in Table 2.2, the most useful for an organizational analysis are the organization's goals and objectives. These are also usually readily available in one form or another. In larger organizations, a formal strategic planning document typically exists which the trainer should not only read but analyze to get a true feeling for the direction in which the organization is headed. However, the first level supervisor might not be privy to this information. The information may also be too broad for the deficiency at hand. A supervisor can deal with these problems by specifying some time to discuss with his or her immediate supervisor the goals of the subunit and keep these goals in mind in prioritizing perceived performance deficiencies. In smaller organizations, where a formal planning document might not exist, it is important to obtain this type of input from top management. As mentioned in Chapter 1, ideally, the training function should move toward not merely reacting to, but becoming part of the strategic planning process.

Based on the issues described above and using the data sources outlined in Table 2.2, at some point the TNA implementor is forced to come to a judgment as to whether the perceived performance deficiency should be addressed at this time. This will obviously be a subjective judgment, but should be based on the criteria of organizational goals, resource availability, and probability of success.

Step 3: Job, Task, and Work Environment Analysis

If the decision is that the perceived deficiency should be addressed at this time, three further types of analyses are warranted. These are a job analysis, person analysis (McGehee & Thayer, 1961), and what we have called a work environment analysis. Although they will be described separately, these three analyses should be conducted simultaneously.

Job Analysis   As part of a TNA, a job analysis should focus on what the trainee needs to be able to do to perform the job satisfactorily. It should provide information regarding standards of performance, how the tasks are to be performed to meet the standards and the skills, knowledge and abilities needed for performance. In TNA, a job analysis should take both a worker- and task-oriented approach. A *worker-oriented approach* focuses on the skills, knowledge, and ability required to perform the job. These might include elementary motions, job demands (e.g., energy expended), and the specific human behaviors involved such as decision making, communicating, etc. A *task-oriented approach* focuses on a description of the work activities performed. These are typically expressed in terminology used by job incumbents and would involve a description of how, why, and/or when a worker performs an activity. The written description of both of the above is referred to as a *job description*. The differences in these approaches are illustrated in Example 2.2, which depicts a small portion of the job description of a trainer. As the example illustrates, the distinction between task- and worker-oriented statements becomes somewhat blurred in practice. However, each provides enough unique information as to warrant the need for this categorization. Thus, the example of a task-oriented approach focuses more on what the worker would do (i.e., conduct an organizational, job, person, and work environment analysis), while the worker-oriented example focuses more on the knowledge, skill, and ability (KSA) requirements of the incumbent. The KSAs are italicized in the second example and are often listed in a special section of the job description called the *job specifications*.

Example 2.2   Task- and worker-oriented descriptions of the job of trainer.
Task-Oriented   Prior to training, the trainer will assist and/or develop a behavioral description of the perceived performance deficiency by conducting a TNA using an organization, job, person, and work environment analysis. As part of the organization analysis, the trainer will gather data regarding whether organizational goals, availability of resources, and the

probability of a successful training effort warrants dealing with the perceived performance deficiency.

Worker-Oriented Prior to training, the trainer would *question* the
individual who perceives a performance deficiency *to generate a behavioral
description* of the problem. If the trainer is the individual who perceives the
deficiency, he or she would *describe in specific terms* what isn't taking place
that should be. Once the perceived deficiency has been behaviorally defined,
the trainer would infer whether the climate of the organization and work
group is conducive to developmental action. The trainer would also *interpret*
whether the perceived deficiency warrants corrective action based on an
analysis of the organization's goals and objectives.

The job analysis literature (c.f., McCormick, 1979) typically suggests
that a task-oriented approach is beneficial for specifying the training
objectives and is, therefore, extremely valuable for training evaluation. A
worker-oriented approach specifies the skills and abilities that should be
developed and leads to the particular method and content of training. Since
all of the issues addressed above are important for an effective training
system, it is crucial that both types of data be gathered as part of the job
analysis.

Sparks (1982) noted that several questions should be addressed prior to
data collection for a job analysis. These include: (1) What method of data
collection should be used? (2) What should be the data source? and (3) How
should the data be categorized or scaled? Table 2.3 lists some of the methods
that can be used to gather job analysis data. All of the methods are not
equally advantageous for every type of job. As noted in the table (see Table
2.3, technique 3), having the job analyst perform the job may not provide
meaningful information if there is a long time period between performance
and outcomes such as in the job of research scientist. Similarly, observing
the work may be of little value if the job requires considerable cognitive or
artistic skill as in the job of creative writer (Sparks, 1982). Asking questions
about the job (technique 6) requires a determination of format. Interviews
provide the most in-depth information and the opportunity to probe, yet are
extremely time-consuming. The quality of questionnaire data will be influenced by the literacy of the job incumbents. In questionnaires, a decision
must also be made on whether to use an unstructured or structured format.
The former might lead to scaling problems which will be discussed shortly.
While standard job analysis questionnaires are available commercially, the
size of the organization and its training budget may reduce the cost/benefit
of this approach.

Table 2.3 also illustrates that job analysis data can be gathered from job
incumbents, supervisory personnel, or by a job analyst using any or all of the
methods previously noted. Although job incumbents should be the best
source of information about their job, there is no guarantee that the
incumbent(s) will be motivated to represent accurately what their jobs

Table 2.3 Data sources for a job analysis.

Technique for obtaining job data	Training need implications
1. Job Descriptions	Outlines the job in terms of typical duties and responsibilities but is not meant to be all-inclusive. Helps define performance discrepancies.
2. Job Specifications or Task Analysis	List specified tasks required for each job. More specific than job descriptions. Specifications may extend to judgments of knowledge and skills required of job incumbents.
3. Performance Standards	Objectives of the tasks of job and standards by which they are judged. This may include base-line data as well.
4. Perform the Job	Most effective way of determining specific tasks but has serious limitations the higher the level of the job in that performance requirements typically have longer gaps between performance and resulting outcomes.
5. Observe Job—Work Sampling	

6. Review Literature Concerning the Job
  a. Research in other industries
  b. Professional journals
  c. Documents
  d. Government sources
  e. Ph.D. theses
	Possibly useful in comparison analyses of job structures but far removed from either unique aspects of the job structure within any *specific* organization or specific performance requirements.

7. Ask Questions about the Job
  a. Of the job holder
  b. Of the supervisor
  c. Of higher management	

8. Training Committees or Conferences	Inputs from several viewpoints can often reveal training needs or training desires.

9. Analysis of Operating Problems
  a. Down time reports
  b. Waste
  c. Repairs
  d. Late deliveries
  e. Quality control
	Indications of task interference, environmental factors, etc.

| 10. Card Sort | Utilized in training conferences. "How to" statements sorted by training importance. |

From Moore, M.L., & Dutton P. Training needs analysis: Review and critique. *Academy of Management Review*, 1978, 3, 532–545. Reprinted with permission.

entail. Organizational/work group climate, power of the individual gathering the data, and the incumbent's *perception* of the reason for the job analysis are but a few of the factors that might influence how an incumbent describes his or her job. For example, Zeira (1974) showed that organizational climate can make employees reluctant to participate in a TNA. Even if the incumbent does desire to provide accurate data, the individual's verbal and cognitive skills may inhibit his or her ability to do so. Data from supervisory personnel may suffer from all of the problems previously noted. Supervisors may also have little opportunity to observe or truly understand the (subordinate's) job being analyzed. Research has shown that the job analyst also may be somewhat biased (Avery, Passinor, & Lounsbury, 1977) although a more recent study failed to replicate this effect (Arvey, Davis, McGowen, & Dipboye, 1982).

The problems in job analysis regarding method and source of data collection can best be handled by using as many methods and sources of information as practically feasible. An ideal job analysis might include observation, interviews, and questionnaire responses from a sample of the job incumbents and supervisory personnel. The greater the agreement among methods and sources, the greater the probability of an accurate assessment. Unfortunately, the current state of the art does not specify how many sources or methods are needed to obtain a reasonable level of accuracy (Sparks, 1982). These are judgments that must be made based on the perceived necessity for accuracy as well as practical constraints.

For the purpose of TNA, a lack of agreement among sources is only informative if the disagreement is between a job incumbent and his or her supervisor. When an employee describes his or her job duties to be considerably different from others with the same job title, this does not necessarily indicate any problem, except perhaps in how the job(s) is titled. A problem occurs when an incumbent and supervisor perceive a job differently. This is especially true if the difference in perceptions regards task requirements, since the failure to achieve these standards will create a perceived performance deficiency. Therefore, it is crucial that these requirements be agreed upon. The *job expectation technique* (JET) is an OD intervention that may be useful for this purpose. Briefly, this process involves a clarification of the incumbents' job obligations and performance expectations through a series of meetings(s) between the incumbent and other relevant (typically managerial) personnel. All participants (including supervisors) must state their expectations, and this is done for each participants' job. Although some evidence exists that suggests that JET reduces ambiguity and stress for the incumbent whose job is clarified (Dayal & Thomas, 1968), there does not appear to be much hard data documenting its effectiveness.

The third question (How should the data be scaled?) is important for at least two reasons. First, for any particular job, the use of multiple methods requires some format to organize and compare this information. Second, several different jobs may have similar task and/or worker requirements and, in turn, similar training needs. The typical terminology is to describe every individual as having a *position* within an organization. Similar positions comprise a *job*, while similar jobs comprise what is often referred to as an *occupation* or *job family*. *Scaling* is the mechanism by which "similarity" is determined. Unfortunately, the majority of job analysis research has centered around the second goal (developing job families) to the exclusion of the first (i.e., the best format for organizing data). Nevertheless, the scaling methods to be described can serve as a theoretical basis for organizing multiple measures for one position.

A distinction is typically made between quantitative and qualitative approaches to scaling. A *qualitative approach* is based on judgment, while a *quantitative approach* is mathematical. In a pure sense, many quantitative approaches are qualitative judgments that are constructed to lend them-selves to mathematical manipulation. When a job analyst records the frequency of a particular task, that is a judgment that can be quantitatively analyzed by comparing it to the frequency of other tasks involved in the job. Table 2.4 lists a variety of approaches for scaling job analysis data. These are just a sampling of the available alternatives. This table reveals that, currently, there is no universally accepted methodology for scaling job analysis data that fulfills all of the needs of TNAs. The TNA implementor needs to match the scaling approach to the specific needs of his or her organization. In this regard, it seems that the more quantitative and statistically oriented approaches may be best suited for large organizations that can more easily bear the cost of the standarized instrument (e.g., PAQ) or provide a large enough pool of assessees (e.g., as required in factor analysis) for an advanced statistical technique. Organizations that conduct fewer TNAs might find the qualitative approaches, such as functional job analysis, more beneficial for direct use or as a guideline for developing an organizational scaling format.

Person Analysis   The job analysis indicates key elements of the job and how these elements should be performed. A person analysis compares the individual to these task requirements. The first step in this process is to ascertain the source(s) of the performance deficiency. In order for perfor-mance to occur, the individual must have the necessary KSA as well as the motivation and the opportunity to perform the task. Training the incumbent can typically only rectify deficiencies that are due to a lack of skill or knowledge. There are two exceptions to this statement. The first is the situation where an employee's poor performance is due to a lack of motivation caused by the employee perceiving he or she lacks the necessary KSA to be a good performer. Even if the employee is qualified such a perception should result in poor performance. One way of rectifying this misperception would be to provide the employee with the type of training that

Table 2.4 Approaches/techniques for categorizing job analysis data.

Name	Orientation	Description	Reference
Position Analysis (PAQ)	Quantitative Approach	This is a structured job analysis questionnaire that contains 187 job elements. The elements are divided into six divisions. 1 Information Input 2 Mental Processes 3 Work Output 4 Relationship with other Persons 5 Job Content 6 Other Job Characteristics Each job element is rated on one of six different rating scales. The PAQ is scored on several job dimensions derived through factor analysis which provides a profile of the job analyzed.	(McCormick, 1979)
Functional Job Analysis	Qualitative Approach	This approach is based on the notion that all jobs can be classified based on their relationship with people, data, and things. Each of these categories has a hierarchy of performance levels. For example, the lowest level of dealing with data is comparing; middle level behaviors are computing and compiling; while the highest level involves synthesizing. This approach was used as a basis for preparing the 1965 edition of the *Dictionary of Occupational Titles*.	(Fine, 1973)

Table 2.4 Approaches/techniques for categorizing job analysis data. (*Continued*)

Name	Orientation	Description	Reference
Physical Abilities Analysis (PAA)	Quantitative	This approach focuses on the particular physical abilities required for job performance. Nine basic abilities are analyzed such as dynamic strength, gross body coordination, and stamina. An analyst rates the job on each of these dimensions using a seven point rating scale with behavior anchors.	(Fleishman, 1979)
Statistical Procedures	Quantitative	There now exists a relatively large number of purely statistical approaches to organizing job analysis data. These include (a) the Air Force Comprehensive Occupational Data Analysis Program (CODAP); (b) Ward and Hook Hierarchial Grouping Procedure; (c) Analysis of Variance; (d) Factor Analysis.	(Trattner, 1979; Field & Schoenfeldt, 1975; Arvey & Mossholder, 1977)

would lead the employee to believe he or she had the capacity to be an effective performer. However, if the employee does in fact have the ability, this would not be a very economical approach. Perhaps in such a situation some individualized counseling might be a more appropriate strategy. The second exception is the situation where an individual lacks the motivation to perform due to the perception that there are not enough valued rewards associated with effective job performance. If the individual values training and it is provided as a reward for effective job performance, this may raise motivation and, consequently, performance. Yet, as mentioned earlier, caution must be taken to assure that the training is a highly valued benefit relative to others that may be awarded for good performance.

Excluding the two exceptions just noted, performance deficiencies that arise due to the individuals' lack of motivation or opportunity to perform require other types of interventions besides training. More precisely, if a supervisor is not performing effectively due to low motivation as a result of a perceived pay inequity, sending that individual to a training seminar on effective supervision should not raise performance. However, this problem, which is not due to a lack of KSA, may be a symptom of another problem that is. Perhaps the supervisor's low motivation due to perceived pay inequity is due to the fact that the supervisor's *boss* lacks skills in allocating raises. Nevertheless, the previous statement holds true in that there is no training that the *supervisor* could receive that would resolve this problem.

Mager and Pipe (1984) provided a set of questions in a decision tree format (Figure 2.4) that is a useful tool in determining if an individual's performance deficiency is due to a lack of KSA. As noted in the figure, the key issue in addressing this question is whether the employee has previously (*and recently*) performed the desired behavior. If the employee has indicated that he or she has the KSA, then the source of the deficiency must be one of the other two factors. For situations where the desired behavior has not been exhibited, each of the factors is a plausible source of the problem. This situation requires a careful analysis of whether appropriate rewards (i.e., motivation) and opportunity exist *before* the problem can be attributed to a lack of knowledge, skills, or abilities.

Perhaps the easiest way to ascertain if a lack of KSA is the cause of the performance deficiency is to ask the job incumbent to perform the desired behavior. Practically, this is only feasible in a smaller organization where there is a short time span between performance of the behavior and its outcome, and when the performance environment can be effectively simulated. Regarding the latter issue, even if the physical environment can be simulated, it is often difficult to simulate the psychological environment for such a job sample test. For example, asking a salesperson to demonstrate his or her sales technique is not actually a psychologically similar process to the desired behavior since the individual's performance cannot possibly result in a sale.

Assuming that it is not technically feasible to have the incumbent attempt to perform the desired behavior, there are two other issues (besides those listed in Figure 2.4) that should be considered in attempting to determine the reason for the deficiency. These are the *consensus* and *distinctiveness* of the deficiency. *Consensus* refers to whether others (i.e., similar job incumbents) display the same type of behavior as the individual with the deficiency. *Distinctiveness* refers to whether the individual displays the deficiency across situations. These issues should be considered jointly.

High distinctiveness and *high consensus* indicate that a performance deficiency has a low probability of being caused by a lack of KSA. If John is effective at selling all computer lines except for the new personal computer, and all other salespeople are ineffective in selling this model, it is doubtful that John lacks the KSA to sell the product. It is probably more reasonable to attribute John's low sales to a poor market or product (no opportunity) or a low rate of commission (no motivation to perform). Alternatively, it is conceivable, but less likely, that all the salespeople including John, lack the KSA in this particular area.

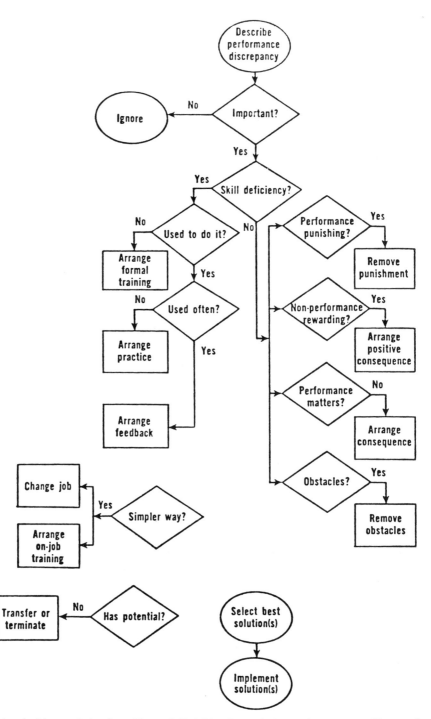

(Reprinted with permission from Mager, R.F., & Pipe, P. *Analyzing Performance Problems or "You Really Oughta Wanna."* 2nd Edition, Belmont CA: David Lake Publishers, 1984.)

Figure 2.4 Decision tree format for determining the source of a performance problem.

Low distinctiveness and low consensus suggests that the deficiency may be attributable to a lack of KSA. Sue is ineffective at selling all products, while others are breaking previous sales records selling the same items. Combined with the fact that Sue has never displayed sales skills (see Question 1, Figure 2.4), the evidence tends to mount that Sue lacks sales ability. Yet, this may not be the case. Perhaps Sue has the most difficult sales territory, or is asked to do a considerable amount of paperwork which takes away from her time to sell. These types of issues would create a performance deficiency in an extremely capable and skillful salesperson.

Distinctiveness and consensus are less valuable indices when they are at opposite levels. When an employee exhibits inappropriate behavior across situations (low distinctiveness) but others also exhibit the same deficiency (high consensus), it tells us little about the source of the deficiency. Similarly, when an employee is deficient only in certain situations (high distinctiveness), yet others do not exhibit the same deficiency (low consensus), a lack of KSA, motivation, or opportunity are equally plausible explanations for this behavior.

Distinctiveness, consensus, and the issues noted in Figure 2.4 refer to the type of information that can be gathered in a person analysis. Typically, this information can be obtained by the TNA implementor through observing the incumbent or questioning the employee's supervisor. Since it is the incumbent's skill, knowledge, and ability that is in question, he or she may well be the most knowledgeable source about the deficiency. Employee input is also useful in comparing differences in supervisor/subordinate job expectations. Finally, since the goal of this entire process is to change the employees' behavior, it seems logical that the employee should participate in this process. Although the importance of employee participation is a controversial topic in the scholarly literature (Locke & Schweiger, 1979), it is important to note that, for the most part, the controversy has centered on whether employee participation in goal setting results in greater commitment and goal attainment (Locke, Shaw, Saari, & Latham, 1981). Research indicates that the latter is obtained, although the former is not. The typical explanation for this occurrence is that more difficult goals are set when employees are allowed to participate in setting their goals. For the purpose of this discussion, it is the outcome, not the psychological processes behind it, that are important. Evidence also exists that when employees feel they have an influence in planning their self-development activities there exists a greater desire to want to improve performance (Burke, Weitzel, & Weir, 1978). This receptivity to modify one's behavior is an important part of the change process (Lewin, 1951). Taking into consideration all of the issues noted above, employee participation seems an essential element of a person analysis.

At some point, the TNA implementor is forced to make a judgment as to whether a lack of KSA is the source of the deficiency. As we suggested in regard to job analysis, it is best to gather as many sources and types of information as possible and look for agreement across measures and sources. The greater the agreement, the higher the probability that training can rectify the deficiency.

Given a judgment that the problem can be corrected by training, the second step in person analysis is to determine the specific skill, knowledge, or ability required and whether the assessee is capable of developing this KSA. Table 2.5 lists the variety of techniques that can be used in this effort. The ideal technique for measuring the employee's current knowledge, skill and ability level (which would then be compared to information obtained in

Table 2.5 Sources of data for a person analysis.

Technique or data obtained	Training need implications

1. Performance Data or Appraisals as Indicators of "Sickness"
   a. Productivity
   b. Absenteeism or Tardiness
   c. Accidents
   d. Short-term sickness
   e. Grievances
   f. Waste
   g. Late deliveries
   h. Product Quality
   i. Down time
   j. Repairs
   k. Equipment utilization
   l. Customer complaints
	Include weaknesses and area of improvement as well as strong points. Easy to analyze and quantify for purposes of determining subjects and kinds of training needed. These data can be used to *identify* performance discrepancies.

2. Observation—Work Sampling	More subjective technique but provides both employee behavior and results of the behavior.
3. Interviews	Individual is only one who knows what he (she) believes he (she) needs to learn. Involvement in need analysis can also motivate employees to make an effort to learn.
4. Questionnaires	Same approach as the interview. Easily tailored to specific characteristics of the organization. May produce bias through the necessity of pre-structure categories.

5. Tests
   a. Job knowledge
   b. Skills
   c. Achievement
	Can be tailor-made or standardized. Care must be taken so that they measure job-related qualities.

Table 2.5   Sources of data for a person analysis. (*Continued*)

Technique or data obtained	Training need implications
6. Attitude Surveys	On the individual basis, useful in determining morale, motivation or satisfaction of each employee.
7. Checklists or Training Progress Charts	Up-to-date listing of each employee's skills. Indicates future training requirements for each job.
8. Rating Scales	Care must be taken to insure relevant, reliable, and objective employee ratings.
9. Critical Incidents	Observed actions which are critical to the successful or unsuccessful performance of the job.
10. Diaries	Individual employee records details of his (her) job.
11. Devised Situations a. Role play b. Case study c. Conference leadership training sessions d. Business games e. In-baskets	Certain knowledge, skills and attitudes are demonstrated in these techniques.
12. Diagnostic Rating	Checklists are factor analyzed to yield diagnostic ratings.
13. Assessment Centers	Combination of several of the above techniques into an intensive assessment program.
14. Coaching	Similar to interview—one-to-one.
15. MBO or Work Planning and Review Systems	Provides actual performance data on a recurring basis related to organizational (and individually or group-negotiated standards) so that base-line measurements may be known and subsequent improvement or deterioration of performance may be identified and analyzed. This performance review and potential review is keyed to larger organization goals and objectives.

From Moore, M.L., & Dutton P. Training needs analysis: Review and critique. *Academy of Management Review*, 1978, *3*, 532–545. Reprinted with permission.

the job analysis) is some form of objective measure (see Table 2.5, items 2, 5, 11 or 13). However, these are costly and many times not readily available. Also, the quality of the information provided in these types of measures depends on the purpose for which they were designed. For example, Boehm and Hoyle (1977) noted the strategic differences in designing an assessment center for a reactive or proactive TNA. Objective measures are also more cost-beneficial in larger organizations that have a greater number of trainees. Smaller organizations may have to rely on a judgment by the TNA implementor based on the use of one or more of the other measures noted in Table 2.5.

Once the employee's KSA deficiency has been identified, an assessment must also be made as to whether the employee is capable of developing the KSA in question. Toward this end, several studies have focused on developing measures of trainability. A variety of measures including life history (Helmreich, Bakeman, & Radloff, 1973), attitudes (Ryman & Biersner, 1975) and early training (Gordon & Cohen, 1973) have been shown to predict training success accurately. Robertson and Downs (1979) developed a trainability test that predicted success in training on a variety of semiskilled manual tasks.

The development and use of the types of tests noted above is an extremely complicated and sophisticated process. The utility of such an approach will be a function of the number of potential trainees, the validity of the measure, and numerous other situational factors (Cronbach & Gleser, 1965). While it is clearly not cost-effective for all organizations, evidence does exist that this type of approach can (in certain situations) significantly reduce the cost of instruction (Reilly & Manese, 1979).

Whatever the source of data, the output of a person analysis should be a specific (behavioral) description of why the employee isn't performing. More precisely, stating that "Sandy needs to improve her decision making," doesn't address why she is making poor decisions (i.e., Are the decisions too slow? Are they of poor quality? Is she basing them on the wrong data?). These are the types of issues that must be addressed in an effective person analysis.

To this point, we have been referring to KSAs as if they are synonymous terms. They are not. We define *knowledge* as information, *skill* as the appropriate application of information, and *ability* as the capability to acquire knowledge or skill. Using this framework, ability is what is assessed in the trainability studies cited earlier. A trainee will not perform, nor is trainable if he or she lacks ability. However, given ability, a performance deficiency may result from a lack of knowledge, skill, or both. A deficiency due to a lack of knowledge is exemplified by a skilled computer programmer who must learn a new language in order to use a new computer. Given the information (knowledge), this individual can apply it (i.e., has programming "skills"). A deficiency due to a lack of skill is illustrated by a manager who takes a course on the problem-solving approach to performance appraisal. The manager may know what is supposed to be done but may use this information poorly. Alternatively, an individual may lack both knowledge and skill. The type of differentiation just noted is very important since, as will be pointed out in the second section of this book, some training techniques are best fitted for knowledge acquisition and others for skill development, while some serve both purposes. Therefore, the more specifically the person analysis states the source of the deficiency, the higher the probability of selecting an appropriate training technique for resolving it.

Work environment analysis An accurate job and person analysis indicates what type of skill or knowledge should be acquired to rectify the performance deficiency. Yet, even if the KS is acquired, there is no guarantee that the deficiency will be eliminated. As we have mentioned several times, performance is a function of KSA, motivation, and opportunity. If any one of these three factors is not present, effective performance will not occur. We have noted that training can only rectify a deficiency which is due to a lack of KS. However, the capacity to perform (i.e., the KS) will not result in performance if the other two variables are not present. The assessment of whether these variables are present is what we refer to as a *work environment analysis*. This data can be gathered as part of the job and person analysis. The issues here are the same ones stated earlier in Table 2.5.

1. What, if any, rewards are available for performing the behavior as well as what, if any, punishments are given for nonperformance? Also, what, if any rewards are given for nonperformance? The latter case might occur when a poor performer is given an easier job assignment.
2. What are the opportunity barriers to effective performance?

These issues were raised earlier in diagnosing the source of the deficiency. For simplicity, we described deficiencies as if they result from only one causal factor. Unfortunately, life is not that simple. An employee may lack all three of the variables (KSA, motivation, and opportunity) needed for performance. Supplying only one (e.g., KSA) is unlikely to result in behavior change. The most difficult aspect of a work environment analysis is to determine whether there is any motivation to perform the behavior. This is difficult because what is rewarding or punishing differs across individuals. Thus, input must be obtained from the job incumbent, either through a questionnaire or interview, as to how that individual perceives the consequences of improved performance. The quality of this data will depend to a considerable degree on the trust between the TNA implementor and the incumbent. If a lack of motivation is a cause of the deficiency, a corrective strategy must be developed. This strategy must be formulated based on the reason for the lack of motivation and the incumbent's perception of a rewarding or punishing experience.

Barriers to performance are somewhat easier to measure. As part of the job analysis, we suggested observing the incumbent and/or actually performing the job. Such actions should provide the TNA implementor with a basis for determining whether the opportunity exists to perform the desired behavior. If not, such opportunity must be provided. This may involve restructuring the workflow or providing additional tools and equipment. Industrial engineering is the discipline that focuses on these types of issues. Martinko and Gardner (1982) noted that, even when environmental changes make successful performance possible, performance may not occur due to the fact that employees have (previously) learned or developed a feeling of helplessness. They suggest several methods of training employees to learn that they now have the capacity to modify their situation. This is an important point, since it is perceived, not objective reality, that will influence behavior.

The discussion above has assumed the problem already exists (i.e., a reactive deficiency). However, as mentioned earlier, a work environment analysis is an important part of a proactive TNA. The redesigning of jobs and/or the implementation of a new technology may generate many training needs.

Trainers should, whenever possible, try to be privy to work environment changes to give them lead time to prepare appropriate training. One way to do this is to be aware of the organization's strategic plan. As previously noted, if a formal plan does not exist, interviews with key corporate personnel are one way to gather this data.

If the types of analyses listed above sound lengthy and complicated, that is because they are. However, it should be remembered that we have progressed to this point because much earlier in the TNA it was determined (in the organizational analysis) that it is important to the organization to correct the deficiency. As we stated at the beginning of this book, training needs to take a broad focus, even if it is lengthy and costly, in order to be an effective force for change within an organization.

Step 4: Develop Objectives

The information obtained in the job, person, and work environment analyses are used to develop the training objectives.

Much has been written in the training literature regarding the value of behavioral objectives. Many advocate this approach (Gallegas & Phelen, 1974), while others have questioned its value (Kneller, 1972; Witrock & Lumsdaine, 1977). Critics have typically stated that behavioral objectives are rigid and fail to consider individual learning styles (Knowles, 1978; Kolb, 1976). Obtaining input from the assessee in the person analysis, as advocated earlier, may be an effective method of dealing with these concerns. Chapter 4 provides a more detailed description of how training objectives should be developed.

OVERVIEW OF TNA _____

Although the process described represents an idealized model of how TNA should be conducted, time constraints may inhibit individuals from implementing all of the component analyses. Given such limitations, the organization analysis is often the first aspect to be excluded. While successful TNAs have been conducted without an organization analysis, this omission increases the risk of focusing on less organizationally beneficial training needs. Similarly, due to time constraints, some individuals may eliminate a job analysis and just focus on the person. Here the risk is the possibility of providing skills that aren't necessarily needed for effective job performance. One training manager was known to brag that he conducted 200 TNAs in one year by simply asking the employee's supervisor to check from a list which courses the incumbent should attend. While this activity was expedient, the majority of training by his department did not seem to meet the organizations' needs. The parent organization subsequently recognized this and removed the manager from the training function.

WHAT IMPLICATIONS DOES RESEARCH HAVE FOR IMPROVING THE TNA PROCESS? _____

The previous section was designed to present a "how to" approach to training needs assessment. Although a four-step approach was outlined, along with a variety of data sources for each step, these sources were often presented without a clear description of how to extrapolate to the desired outcome. This is, unfortunately, due to the fact that such knowledge has not been developed. More precisely, although the desired end product can be specifically defined, the methodology for reaching that state is currently more art than science. One of the reasons for this lack of sophistication is, as Moore and Dutton (1978) noted, due to the fact that TNA suffers from a lack of theoretical development. This section is designed to aid the theoretical development of this area by discussing the implications of behavioral science for improving the TNA process.

One concept described in the OD literature, which seems especially applicable to TNA, is Lewin's (1951) notion of force field analysis. This analysis has most often been applied to group dynamics and begins with the following four steps:

1. Describe the present state of the system.
2. Describe the desired changes.
3. Identify forces pushing toward the desired change.
4. Identify forces resisting the change effort.

The "force field" notion is that any open system is never perfectly static but has forces pushing for and against change. Lewin indicated that tension and conflict are likely to occur when a change effort focuses on developing forces for change without efforts to reduce the forces against it.

Few TNAs correspond to Lewin's advice. Most such efforts try to provide a force for change without corresponding efforts to decrease the forces against change. For example, an individual may be performing a particular task inappropriately because he or she is not aware of the correct method or because of peer pressure to "do it the way everyone else does." Peer pressure would be a force resisting change. A TNA recognizing the skill deficiency would be a force for change. If the former is greater than the latter, given the appropriate training, the individual would still not modify his or her behavior. An effective TNA for this problem would recognize the incumbent's skill deficiency along with the fact that peer pressure is a force for the status quo. Such an assessment might suggest training all incumbents at the same time as a technique for reducing the peer pressure force. A discussion of other typical forces against change will be undertaken in Chapter 11. For now, the point is that an effective TNA should recognize these forces and develop methods to reduce them.

Problem identification stems (at least partially) from performance appraisals for both reactive and proactive TNAs. Although it has been stated by behavioral science researchers (c.f., Schwab, Heneman, & Decotiis, 1971) that the more sophisticated versions of performance appraisal (e.g., behaviorally anchored rating scales) will positively influence training, there currently exists no empirical evidence to support this claim. Yet, this logic is in line with the notion that the TNA problem should be defined behaviorally, as specifically as possible. It also illustrates the concept noted in Chapter 1 regarding the interrelationship of systems within an organization. In this case, the training subsystem interacts with the performance appraisal system. To the extent that the latter is "state of the art," the former should correspondingly be improved.

The source of the information is another factor that should influence the accuracy of problem identification. An assessee's immediate supervisor is the most common source (Moore & Dutton, 1978) and the previous section has noted the importance of gathering self-assessment data from the incumbent. Another potentially useful (but underutilized) source of information is peer assessments (Kane & Lawler, 1978; Love, 1981). Borman (1975) and Zedeck, Imparenta, Kraney, and Oleno (1974) provided evidence that supervisory and peer assessments provide two distinctive (but equally valid) views of an individual's job performance. Similarly, Klimonski and London (1974) showed that self-, supervisory, and peer assessments each present distinctive information. Thus, the use of this additional data source should aid in problem identification by adding a unique perspective. Surprisingly, only one study has attempted to evaluate this use of peer assessments.

Roadman (1964) reported that 98 percent of participants evaluated peer ratings as a valuable educational experience. Perhaps researchers have overlooked this issue due to the high resistance against peer assessments for other purposes, such as promotions (Cederblom & Lounsbury, 1980; Love, 1981).

Equally important for both reactive and proactive TNAs is an accurate determination of the source or causality of the performance problem. A considerable amount of social psychological literature exists regarding the information that individuals use in attributing the cause of someone's poor performance (c.f., Kelley, 1967, 1972a, 1972b, 1973; Weiner, Frieze, Kukla, Reed, Rest, & Rosenbaum, 1972). Mitchell and his colleagues (c.f., Mitchell, Green, & Wood, 1981) have begun to apply these attribution theory concepts to organizational behavior. In summarizing this research, they noted that:

1. There is some evidence that people tend to use "self-based consensus" (Hansen & Lowe, 1976; Hansen & Donoghue, 1977) rather than "sample-based consensus" in evaluating other's performance. "People who use self-based consensus compare the assessee to how they, themselves, would perform in the particular situation, while sample-based consensus judges people in comparison to how a sample of the population has performed in that situation." (Mitchell, Green, & Wood, 1981, page 201).
2. There is a tendency for raters to over attribute the cause of another's poor performance to some internal characteristic (e.g., lack of ability or motivation). Individuals are more likely to over attribute their own poor performance to external or situational factors (Miller & Ross, 1975; Bradley, 1978).
3. There are a variety of factors that moderate to what an individual attributes the cause of another's performance. These include:
   a. The relationship between the rater and the assessee (Regan, Straus, & Fazin, 1974).
   b. Assessee characteristics (Garland & Price, 1977; Deaux & Emswiller, 1974).
   c. Rater expectations (Feather, 1969; Feather & Simon, 1971).

The propositions listed above present a partial summary and do not totally reflect the complexity of the attribution process. Yet, they illustrate that the process contains considerable error. Mitchell, Green, and Wood (1981) stated, "the best way to reduce these errors is to train supervisors to recognize their biases" (p. 229). Perhaps training all individuals involved in a TNA on these common errors will improve the TNA process.

A crucial factor to the success of TNA is getting assessees to accept the need to change based on the feedback that they require skill development in a particular area. As Lewin's model of change suggests, behavior must be unfrozen before it can be modified. (Ilgen, Fisher, and Taylor (1979) developed a model of feedback. They noted that:

1. Task feedback is more likely to be accepted if it is received from someone who is perceived as knowledgeable about his or her job.
2. Trust in the feedback source is a key determinant of feedback acceptance.
3. The consistency of feedback influences its acceptance.
4. The power of the feedback source will influence the desire to respond to the feedback.

The points noted above provide only a partial summary of the Ilgen et al.'s (1979) findings. Nevertheless, they provide several implications for conducting a TNA. One implication is that the individual conducting the TNA must not only be knowledgeable about the assessee's job but be perceived as knowledgeable by the assessee. Recent research (Cederblom & Lounsbury, 1980) on performance appraisal has shown that "perceived accuracy" is a major influence on how an individual will respond to an assessment.

A second implication of the research on feedback is that trainers (or whoever is implementing the TNA) should consider their perceived power within an organization or subunit in assessing the probability of initiating a successful TNA effort. Divisions that do not trust the training department or see it as lacking power will probably not respond to the TNA feedback. This may be especially important in conducting a proactive TNA. Unless some powerful person within the organization also recognizes the need to respond to this anticipated problem, the training department may need to consider carefully the probability of success when initiating such action.

A third implication of the research on feedback is that assessors will need to investigate the amount and type of feedback that the assessee has received prior to the TNA. As previously noted, there are both forces for and against change (Lewin, 1951). If an individual has been performing a task in a particular way for a year and has not received any negative feedback that his or her behavior is inappropriate, the absence of negative feedback becomes a force for continuing in the same manner. If, on one particular occasion (e.g., during a performance appraisal), the individual receives negative feedback about this behavior, this latter force for change may be perceived as inconsistent with the lack of negative feedback during the year and may be negated. Thus, an individual conducting a TNA may need to investigate the frequency with which the assessee has been informed of the inappropriateness of his or her behavior in considering the probable success of a change effort.

To summarize, behavioral science suggests the following for implementing a TNA:

1. Examine the forces for and against change and take action to reduce the latter.

2. Attempt to use some behaviorally based form of performance appraisal to improve problem identification.
3. Use multiple measurement sources. Peer, self-, and supervisory inputs seem to provide complementary sources of data.
4. Train all individuals involved in TNA in typical attribution errors.
5. Take action to assure that assessees perceive the individual conducting the TNA as knowledgeable about the job in question.
6. The perceived trust and power of the individual conducting the TNA, along with the previous feedback given the trainee, are factors that should be examined in considering the probability of a successful TNA.

Further research is needed to verify the impact of these propositions on TNA.

SUMMARY

In this chapter, we have suggested that ineffective performance (i.e., performance deficiency) is a symptom that may arise from a variety of causes. A training needs assessment (TNA) is the process used to diagnose whether training can reduce the deficiency. Some form of TNA should always be conducted as a means of increasing the probability of successfully eliminating the deficiency.

In conducting a TNA:

1. The perceived deficiency should be defined in behavioral terms.
2. An organizational analysis should be conducted to prioritize, from an organizational perspective, the need to modify the deficiency. Organizational goals, resources, and the probability of success should be considered in making this judgment.
3. If a decision is reached to address the deficiency, job, person, and work environment analyses should be conducted.
4. A job analysis should specify the standards of the job, the specific duties, and the skill knowledge and ability requirements.
5. A person analysis should specify whether the deficiency is due to a lack of KSA, the specific KSAs that are lacking, and whether they can be developed.
6. A work environment analysis should specify whether obtaining the necessary KSA will reduce the deficiency. Employee motivation and the opportunity to perform are barriers to performance that must be examined.
7. The output of points 4 through 6 above should be a specific (behavioral) description of the objectives to be achieved in training.

8. TNA can be improved through the application of OD and behavioral science principals and concepts such as force field analysis, feedback, attribution theory, and behavioral methods of performance appraisal.

DISCUSSION QUESTIONS

1. Assume that, as a cost cutting move in conducting a TNA, you were required to eliminate either the organizational, job, person, or work environment analysis. Which would you eliminate and why?
2. Describe a job in one or two sentences. Indicate how you would do a job and person analysis for that job.
3. Many people resist providing accurate information in a TNA. Why do you think that is so? What could be done to reduce resistance to TNAs?
4. Are there some organizations that have a greater need to conduct a TNA prior to training than others. What would these organizations be like?
5. The TNA model presented in this chapter is an idealized model of how to conduct a TNA. In organizations, there is often the need to cut corners (i.e., save time). One way to implement a TNA is for the training department to train managers to accurately assess their subordinates' needs. Can you think of others?

TRAINING NEEDS ASSESSMENTS:
AN INTERVIEW WITH MIKE PROCIDA

Mike Procida is a training specialist for engineers employed by Ford Motor Company. He is energetic, organized, and quite analytical in his approach to his work. His interest and commitment to the topics of training and organizational improvement go beyond his present job. Mike himself has been afforded training opportunities—in his case, as a consultant, through Ford's Corporate Development department. He is also adding a Master's degree in Organizational Development to supplement his MBA and his Bachelor's degree in Education. An important responsibility fulfilled by Mike during his five years at Ford has been to identify and evaluate training opportunities available to engineers. We thus felt he was an excellent candidate to interview for this chapter.

Question: You read our chapter on ways of conducting training needs assessments (TNA). How are TNAs typically accomplished in your area of Ford Motor Company?

Procida: In the past, we just heard from managers what type of training should be delivered because they thought it would be good for their people. In fact, as late as 1974 training was lumped together with recreation programs in our budgetary process. No real TNAs were conducted. Management just declared, "We need XYZ training." We would, occasionally, try to be more systematic by surveying these managers. We would ask them, "What don't we offer that you want your people to have?" "What skills do your people need?" But we didn't look at issues like the motivation for training these managers or the engineers that reported to them. We didn't look at the obstacles that might be present and interfering with identifying training needs. We really didn't attempt to get the key parties to buy into the process of training. We just determined which programs we expected them to show up at.

Question: Has the approach to assessing training needs changed over the years?

Procida: It sure has, especially over the last three to five years. The problems that have rocked the auto industry pushed us to examine many of our practices. We studied our organization, our products, and our resources and attempted to determine what we needed to do across both short-term and long-term time frames. Our cars were becoming increasingly electronically controlled, yet 70 percent of our staff were mechanical engineers, not electrical engineers—a definite skill/mix problem. We surveyed our staff and found we had top-notch people who were sometimes working in the wrong area. We've developed a skills inventory to address this problem.

At the same time, our company invested heavily in training managers to be more participative, to involve their people more heavily in the decision-making process. This led us to seek peer and self-assessments of training needs. We concluded that our people are very trainable and the solutions to several key problems we were facing involved using internal resources rather than recruiting new talent from outside.

Question: Would you consider your approach to be "reactive or proactive" as discussed in our TNA chapter?

Procida: Both really. We reacted to the pressures in the industry and developed a short-term strategy but this in turn pushed us toward developing a longer term perspective. We knew we had bright internal talent we didn't want to lose but their basic skill base didn't match the direction in which our product was moving. We surveyed local universities to discover what programs were already available that might address our problems. We found some were willing to develop specialized programs for us too. We determined what it would cost to recruit and hire new engineers to acquire the talent we needed. Our short-term plan ended up being a contract with a local university to put on an intensive 16 week, 640 hour training program that involved only our people. The cost of the program was still less than the cost of recruiting and hiring one new electrical engineer for one year. Our long-term plan was to develop an on-site Master's degree program in Computers and Electronic Control Systems in conjunction with a local university to update the skills of the entire population. We presently have 150 engineers enrolled at the same cost of hiring four additional engineers. When we presented our more systematic assessment of our needs and the cost analyses of our options, upper management was very pleased with our activity. Partly as a result of all this, our training budget was dramatically increased (this despite the fact that we are downsizing as an organization) and our stature as a function certainly improved. We have now added trainers and even whole new training departments in other divisions of Ford Motor Company. We are now training staff and line managers in how to conduct more systematic TNAs. We are especially using more proactive procedures for our critical technical skills. We have become aware of where our highest attrition and turnover rates are and projecting where they will be. Our key strategy has been to get commitments from line managers to do more thorough TNAs and have our training staff to act as consultants to them.

Question: What would you like to see happening in your area of training at Ford?

Procida: Our training programs have indicated that beyond technical skills training, changing management styles is not an easy task. I think we need to do a better job of assessing styles and assessing situations under which more participative styles are likely to succeed.

We also need more case studies that show the training process from start to finish. This would greatly help our trainers' efforts. It would produce more practical training skills especially in how to conduct TNAs and the connection between TNA and bottom line return for training dollars invested. I know we will become more and more proactively oriented in the next few years, so I hope we make equal strides in developing our trainers in ways that will equip them to assist Ford's challenges. It should be an exciting time.

Chapter 3

LEARNING AND BEHAVIOR

Previously it was suggested that a systems view of training can facilitate the overall effectiveness of not only the training function but the organization as a whole. We have also argued that the focus and content of training activities should be derived from a thorough training needs analysis. Although an accurate needs analysis and a systems perspective are important, the training function is only as good as its ability to transfer new knowledge and skill to trainees. The stimulation of learning, then, can be said to be the hub around which the rest of the training activities revolve. It is, therefore, of considerable importance to understand the learning process and especially the process of learning in adults.

The behavioral sciences (especially the field of psychology) have been examining human learning since the late 1800s. The range of theoretical perspectives has varied widely over the last hundred years and, from a purely intellectual viewpoint, the journey through the rise and fall of the various schools of thought related to this topic is both fascinating and stimulating. However, it is beyond the scope of both this chapter and this book to embark on such a tour. At best, some of the highlights can be viewed and these must serve as background to an understanding of more contemporary thought. While it is the purpose of this chapter to provide the reader with some useful and practical insights, one can become too concerned with tools and techniques. If one doesn't understand the theoretical underpinnings of the techniques, there is a great potential for misuse. Students in business and applied behavioral sciences are commonly stereotyped as being pragmatic and practical in their orientation (and our experience tends to substantiate this). This does not imply, however, that they are or should be atheoretical or antitheoretical. To paraphrase a most productive and respected applier of social science, Kurt Lewin, the most practical tool one can have is a good theory. For example, theories in the fields of physics and mathematics have practical applications in space communications, commercial energy production, and medicine. Theories in the field of human learning have also led to practical application in both educational and industrial settings. This chapter and particularly the following chapter on instruction will show what the theories of learning have to say to the training practitioner.

This chapter is designed to provide answers to the following questions:

1. What are the historical roots from which contemporary perspectives on learning emerged?
2. What are the differences and relationships between learning and behavior?
3. What are the contemporary approaches to understanding learning and behavior?
4. How can cognitive and behavioral explanations of learning be integrated?
5. How does one differentiate between different types of learning and how do the different types relate to each other?
6. What do we know about the characteristics of adult learners?
7. What are the implications of the theoretical and empirical research in human learning for training in organizations?

HISTORICAL ROOTS OF CONTEMPORARY APPROACHES TO LEARNING

Before one can adequately evaluate the usefulness of existing theoretical positions and principles, it must be understood that there are difficulties associated with defining and measuring an event (e.g., learning) that is not directly observable. The choice of a definition has had a considerable impact on the types of learning theory that have developed. For example, *behaviorists* define learning in terms of changes in behavior. *Cognitive theorists* define learning in terms of changes in cognitive (i.e., internal brain activity) processes that may or may not be reflected in behavior. It is hoped that the brief historical perspective presented in the following pages will provide the reader with an appreciation of the advances that have been achieved and the difficulties faced in the more contemporary schools of thought.

Ebbinghaus

One of the earliest scientists to subject both learning and forgetting to quantitative analysis was Hermann Ebbinghaus (1885, 1902, 1911). He introduced scientific safeguards and precautions for the first time to this field of inquiry. Several of Ebbinghaus' concepts remain valid today (although many others have failed the test of time and new data). For example, he discovered that practice of material beyond the point at which it can be perfectly recalled reduces the amount that is forgotten over periods of disuse. This *overlearning* process also reduces the time and effort required for relearning any forgotten material.

Ebbinghaus was also responsible for documenting other principles, such as the fact that we are less likely to forget relevant compared to nonrelevant material. If you were asked to memorize a seven digit number you would have less difficulty if you were told that this was the phone number of a person with a good job opportunity for you rather than just a string of numbers.

Another of Ebbinghaus' discoveries was that *spaced practice*, in which learning is broken up into shorter time periods with breaks between, resulted in better learning (i.e., more resistance to forgetting) than con-tinuous practice over the same length of time. Thus, if you were to attempt to learn how to assemble a bicycle, you would remember the process better if you practiced for three 15 minute periods with a 5 minute break between each, than if you practiced for 45 minutes straight.

Let's take a look at a recent training program in a natural gas utility. The training program was developed for middle managers to give them a better understanding of the whole system and how their respective activities fit in. The program covered the entire operation of the company from exploration to distribution and billing. From Ebbinghaus' principle of relevancy, we can conclude that the distribution and billing managers will remember less than say the personnel and public relations managers since the activities of the former are typically less concerned with the total system. From the principle of *distributed practice*, we can infer that everyone will learn better if we break up the learning segments, and the principle of overlearning indicates that learning will be better if we can get the trainees to practice the material beyond the point at which they can recall it perfectly.

Pavlov

The behaviorist theories of today have their empirical roots in the works of I. Pavlov (1897, 1912), the Russian physiologist. Pavlov, as a result of his now classic studies on the physiology of digestion, accidentally stumbled upon the principle of the conditioned reflex. As nearly all introductory psychology students are aware, Pavlov found that the pairing

Table 3.1 Representation of the classical conditioning process.

STEP 1 UNCONDITIONED STIMULUS ⟶ UNCONDITIONED RESPONSE
(Meat Powder) (Salivation)

STEP 2 CONDITIONED STIMULUS ⟶ UNCONDITIONED RESPONSE
(Buzzer, followed closely in time, (Salivation)
over many trials, by the *unconditioned stimulus*)

STEP 3 CONDITIONED STIMULUS ⟶ CONDITIONED RESPONSE
(Buzzer alone) (Salivation)

over time of an auditory stimulus (e.g., a buzzer) with the placement of meat powder on the tongue of a dog resulted in the dog salivating to the buzzer alone. It could then be said that the dog was conditioned to salivate when presented with the auditory stimulus. This process is called *classical conditioning*.

Table 3.1 presents a graphical representation of the process involved in this type of conditioning. It can be observed from this table that an unconditioned response becomes a conditioned response when it is elicited by a stimulus which, prior to conditioning, was unable to elicit that response. The conditioning process simply involves the pairing of the stimulus one wishes to become capable of eliciting the response with a stimulus that already is consistently able to elicit the response. As we shall soon see, this process matches very closely what would have been predicted from Guthrie's contiguity theory.

Pavlov and his associates also found that a conditioned response could be deconditioned by continuously presenting the conditioned stimulus by itself (i.e., without the unconditioned stimulus) until it no longer produced the conditioned response. This process is called *extinction*. Both the conditioning and extinguishing processes can be said to be learned responses, though Pavlov and his colleagues never referred to them as such.*

Thorndike and Guthrie

The general physiological conceptions of learning at the beginning of the 20th century, as well as Pavlov's work on conditioning, were incorporated by E. L. Thorndike (1905, 1913, 1932) in the development of a set of psychological "laws" of learning. Probably the most famous of Thorndike's laws is the *law of effect*. According to this law, a behavior that is followed by a satisfying experience is likely to be repeated. An action followed by annoyance or dissatisfaction is not likely to be repeated. Thus, Thorndike

---

*These responses were typically refered to as *acquired psychic reflexes* or *extinguished conditioned reflexes*. The process was nearly always simply called *conditioning*.

provided the first documentation of the concept that present behavior is dependent upon the past consequences of that behavior.

As with Ebbinghaus, many of Thorndike's laws have failed to stand in the face of the emergence of new data which have contradicted his "laws." They did, however, conform to the evidence that existed at the time they were generated. In the early years, there were few facts around which to build a theory. The early researchers provided the facts around which later theories were developed. In the process of testing new theories, many of the laws and principles of the earlier period were found to contradict new facts. It is the process of theory building and testing that advances our knowledge in all areas, and even the disconfirmed principles have played a useful role. E. R. Guthrie provides historians with a clear example of how this process works.

Guthrie (1952) developed a theory of contiguity from one of Thorndike's relatively minor laws. Guthrie was a firm behaviorist who rejected concepts that alluded to mental processes, a consciousness or other subjective phenomena. Thorndike had developed a *law of associative shifting* which postulated that all stimuli that are present at the time a response is emitted will become capable of eliciting that response in the future. What he was saying was that if a bear, some trees, and a stream are all present at the same time, and the bear elicits a fright response from the person, then the trees and the stream will also become capable of eliciting fright from the person in the future. This law of association of stimulus and response through contiguity in time was used by Guthrie to build a theory of learning devoid of concepts such as motivation, reward, punishment, and even practice. For Guthrie, the association of stimulus and response was at full strength on its initial occurrence. Reward or punishment served only to mark the end of a particular "stimulus elicits response" sequence. Practice served only to increase the number of associations between stimuli and a particular response. Thus, the more practice, the more stimuli that would elicit that particular response.

Contiguity theory has, of course, proven to be too simplistic to account for human learning. However, Guthrie expanded the behavioristic position by pointing out the associations that are learned between the various stimuli in the learning environment. His empirical work serves as the foundation for discrimination and generalization learning (concepts that are covered later in this chapter).

Tolman

A major break from the behaviorist tradition is evidenced in the work of E. C. Tolman (1932). Educated in the behaviorist school of Thorndike and influenced by Guthrie, Tolman developed a model of learning that incorporated cognitive activities for the first time. He accepted the principle that objects in the environment are perceived as means toward desired goals. He proposed that, between the perception of a stimulus and the acting out of a response, a series of cognitive activities will take place. The response to stimuli in the environment depends upon the interpretation of the stimuli in terms of whether they will lead to goal achievement.

From Tolman's perspective, an individual's goals serve to give meaning to the objects and events in the environment. The response to those objects or events is determined by the relationship between the person's goals and those stimuli. These relationships are contained in what Tolman called a *cognitive map*, which represents past relationships between stimuli, behavior, and goal accomplishment. Ebbinghaus' concept of relevancy can certainly be seen in Tolman's theoretical position. However, Ebbinghaus was more concerned with the development of laws and principles of behavior and never did develop a true theory of learning. Thus, it is Tolman's work that can be said to represent the birth of cognitive psychology. He went far beyond the simple mechanistic-deterministic behaviorism of Guthrie and Thorndike. It is from Tolman's work that we now understand how behavior patterns are formed and supported by feedback from goal accomplishment. It is also in Tolman's work that the origins of the split between the cognitive and behaviorist learning theories of today can be found.

We hope that you now have some flavor for the way in which the different approaches to learning have developed and that you understand the differences inherent in them (i.e., behavioristic and cognitive). The following section describes two of today's most widely accepted models of performance. The behavioristic model (operant conditioning) describes the events surrounding performance and the cognitive model (expectancy theory) describes the mental processes that lead up to performance. As you will see, neither deals directly with learning, but rather with behavior. The vast majority of organizational training techniques derive from one of these two orientations. Thus, it is important that you not only understand their differences but also their respective strengths and weaknesses.

OPERANT CONDITIONING: A BEHAVIORAL APPROACH

Skinner (1938, 1953) defined *learning* as a relatively permanent change in behavior in response to a particular stimulus or set of stimuli. For example, he suggested that, "We learn to perceive in the sense that we learn to respond to things in particular ways because of the contingencies of which they are a part" (1971, p. 179). To paraphrase Skinner, it is not perception that is learned, but rather the relative likelihood of reinforcement for responses relating to the perception. Learning, then, is not some mental event, but a pattern of responses that reflect the contingencies associated with behavior in a given stimulus situation. For Skinner, the brain is an organ that behaves in much the same fashion as the whole organism. Certain neural activities are conditioned to occur or not occur in a given situation depending on the past consequences of those activities. Behavior that has a history of positive consequences for the individual in a given stimulus situation will be reflected by neuronal activity facilitating that behavior. On the other hand, behavior with a history of negative consequences in that stimulus situation will be inhibited by neuronal activity. As the reader may have noticed, Thorndike's law of effect takes center stage in Skinner's model. Thus, Skinner explained thinking, feeling, believing, and all other subjective activities in terms of reinforcement or punishment contingencies. They are experienced as being, for the most part, under the person's control but, according to Skinner (1971, 1975), they are really under the control of the stimuli present in the environment and the past consequences of behavior.

Reinforcement and Punishment

Skinner identified three types of contingencies that may be attached to behavior: (1) *positive reinforcement,* (2) *negative reinforcement,* and (3) *punishment.* Both positive and negative reinforcement increase the likelihood that the behavior they follow will be repeated. Punishment reduces the likelihood of behavior on which it is contingent. *Positive reinforcement* is the administration of a positively valued outcome following some act. *Negative reinforcement* is the removal of a negatively valued outcome following the occurrence of some act. *Punishment* is the administration of a negatively valued outcome following some act. Skinner's behavioristic model is shown in Figure 3.1. The concepts of reinforcement and punishment are illustrated in Figure 3.2.

One of Skinner's primary contributions was to conceptually separate Thorndikian from Pavlovian conditioning. In Pavlovian conditioning, behavior is *elicited* or pulled out of the organism. Skinnerian conditioning (often called *operant* or *instrumental conditioning*) requires the target organism to *emit* the desired behavior which is then either reinforced or punished. We must wait for the behavior to emerge in a particular stimulus

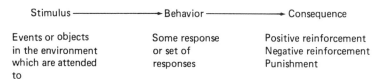

Stimulus ⟶	Behavior ⟶	Consequence
Events or objects in the environment which are attended to	Some response or set of responses	Positive reinforcement Negative reinforcement Punishment

Figure 3.1 Graphic representation of the reinforcement model.

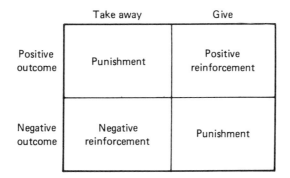

Figure 3.2   Differences in administration of punishment and positive and negative reinforcement.

situation and then administer some carefully predetermined reinforcing or punishing agent.

As the reader may have inferred, the use of punishment is a very risky business in terms of conditioning behavior. Take the example of a child who is punished for sneaking cookies with a spanking when his or her father gets home. The father administers the spanking, the child starts crying, and the father stops spanking. Has the child learned that sneaking cookies leads to a spanking, that crying stops the spanking, or something else? Let's look at a more relevant example.

Suppose, in the training environment, the trainer demonstrates the appropriate set of behaviors for opening and shutting a high pressure pipe valve. He then asks a trainee to do the same thing. Analyzing the situation from a Skinnerian perspective, how would the trainee respond? That would depend upon the trainee's past history of reinforcement and punishment in similar situations. Most of us would probably attempt to replicate the valve operations as demonstrated by the trainer. Perhaps we have been reinforced for obeying those who are in a position of authority or punished for disobeying. Perhaps, when we have attempted new tasks in the past, we have succeeded and the success itself or the consequences of that success have been reinforcing to us in a positive manner. Others may refuse to comply with the trainer because their past experience has reinforced that type of behavior or has punished compliance.

Let us assume that the trainee complied with the trainer's request and, for the most part, was successful in demonstrating the correct responses but shut off the valve too quickly. If the trainer only criticizes the trainee for the error, this may be punishing the trainee for attempting to master the desired behavior. On the other hand, if the trainer only praises the employee for the effort, it may only increase the probability that the error will be repeated. The trainer would have to administer reinforcements after those behaviors he wished to strengthen and punish those he wished to eliminate. As the reader can readily observe, careful attention must be paid to which specific acts are being punished and reinforced.

Let's assume that praise from the trainer is positively valued and criticism is negatively valued by the trainee. If the trainer followed each correct step in the valve opening and closing process with praise, the trainer would be using positive reinforcement. If each incorrect step were followed with criticism, this would be an example of punishing those behaviors. The problem is that even if the trainer succeeds in *extinguishing* the incorrect steps (when a response is totally eliminated to specific stimuli, it is said to be extinguished) the correct steps have not been "learned" yet. In this case, the valve is being closed at a speed that is deemed to be too fast by the trainer. By saying, "No, that's wrong" (i.e., criticizing), the trainee doesn't know whether to slow down, speed up, or quit turning altogether. Even if the trainer says, "No, that's too fast," the trainee doesn't know how much to slow down. If the trainer keeps criticizing until the correct speed is reached and then stops criticizing, what was punishment has now become negative reinforcement. This is because the negatively valued outcome, criticism, was removed immediately following the desired behavior. The best learning (least likely forgotten) seems to occur when mild forms of negative reinforcement are used to shape the behavior into its desired form and positive reinforcement is used to reward correct performance.

Punishment is not usually a very effective behavior modification technique. This is not only true because it is unlikely to produce the desired behavior but also because it requires constant vigilance by the punisher. Reinforcement and punishment have their effects on behavior in a particular stimulus environment. Thus, the punisher or reinforcer becomes a part of that stimulus environment. It doesn't take the recipent of the consequences very long to figure out that when the environment changes (i.e., the punisher is not present) the contingencies attached to his or her behavior are also changed. We've all heard the phrase, "While the cat's away, the mice will play," and it pretty well captures one particular problem with punishment as a behavior modifier. Of course, the same is true of negative reinforcement when some person is responsible for administering the negative outcomes until the desired behavior is achieved. That is because the behavior must be punished until the desired behavior occurs and the negative outcomes are removed. However, with negative reinforcement, the desired behavior is self-reinforcing because it avoids the negative consequences. If the desired behavior is then positively reinforced, the actor will engage in that behavior even in the absence of the reinforcing agent, provided he or she can make the agent aware of the behavior and it continues to be reinforced. In this case, the employee attempts to make the reinforcing agent (the supervisor) aware of the behavior. When punishment is used as the primary behavioral control mechanism, the actor attempts to hide his or her behavior from the punishing agent. One need not examine the implications of this too long to realize that a supervisor's (or trainer's) job is much easier when the workers are attempting to make the supervisor aware of what they are doing rather than keeping their activities hidden. Thus, either positive or negative reinforcement is preferable to punishment as a strategy for changing behavior. The majority of evidence does not indicate that positive reinforcement is more effective than negative or vice versa. Rather, it seems that each, used in conjunction with the other, is more effective than either used alone (Skinner, 1953, 1968).

Shaping and Chaining

From the training function standpoint, two additional concepts associated with operant conditioning should be discussed. The first of these, *shaping*, is crucial for the development of complex behavior. Any complex behavior or set of behaviors can be broken down into a set of simpler behaviors. When arranged in a chronological sequence, these simple behaviors make up the complex behavior. For example, if we were training someone to assemble a chair, the following steps might be involved:

1. Attach padding to top of seat.
2. Cover padding with upholstery and attach upholstery to bottom of seat.
3. Attach seat to top of leg frame.
4. Attach backrest to top of leg frame.
5. Attach legs to bottom of leg frame.

Shaping refers to the reinforcement of each step in the progression until it is mastered, and then withdrawal of reinforcement for that step, making further reinforcement contingent upon that step and the next step in the progression. In our chair assembly example, reinforcement would be administered after the first attempt to attach the padding to the top of the seat. Reinforcement might then be withheld until the next attempt that was superior to the first (i.e., a better job of attaching the padding in terms of placement, amount, etc.). This pattern would be continued until Step 1 was mastered. The next reinforcement would be administered after a successful completion of Step 1 and an attempt at Step 2. This pattern is repeated until the trainee is able to complete all five steps satisfactorily.

The second operant conditioning concept important to training is that of *chaining*. Chaining is related to how outcomes obtain their reinforcing properties. The assumption underlying chaining is that all outcomes acquire their positive or negative value through association with physiological effects experienced subjectively. Food is positively valued because it reduces the pain of hunger. Some food is valued more (or less) because it is pleasing (or displeasing) to our taste. Money is typically a positively valued outcome, yet, it has no direct linkage to a physiological experience. It acquires its positive value because it is linked to things that do create a direct physiological experience. Money, then, can be said to acquire some of the reinforcing properties of those things with which it has been linked or chained. While food is a *primary reinforcer* because it is directly linked to physiological experience, money is considered to be a *secondary reinforcer* because it is linked to primary reinforcers.

In the training environment, we must make extensive use of secondary reinforcers. However, the task of determining whether a particular outcome is chained to positively or negatively valued primary reinforcers is very difficult. For example, some people view close supervision of their work efforts positively while others view it negatively. Even being sent to training itself can be viewed as a positive or a negative outcome. When training is presented as development, it is usually viewed positively because development is typically associated with other positively valued outcomes like promotion, merit increases in pay, etc. On the other hand, being sent for remedial training is usually associated with negative outcomes like low performance appraisals, reduced pay, criticism, etc. Thus, the training experience and what is being taught may become either positively or negatively valued, depending upon the chaining links that have been attached for the trainee.

EXPECTANCY MODEL: A COGNITIVE APPROACH

In 1964, Victor Vroom published a theory of work motivation called *expectancy theory*. While his intent was to explain the cognitive process of motivation, we believe that this theory can provide some explanation of the questions about learning left unanswered by the reinforcement model. In its most basic form, the theory proposes that the force (or energy) that a person directs toward a particular activity can be predicted by three conceptually distinct cognitive processes. These processes are: (1) the individual's *expectancy* (subjective probability) that the effort will lead to the achievement of the activity (or goal), (2) the *instrumentality*, (i.e., subjective likelihood) of the activity for various consequences, and (3) the subjective values of the consequences to the individual along a positive to negative continuum (typically termed *valence*). The variables and their mathematical relationships are symbolized in the formula below.

$$\text{EFFORT} = \text{Expectancy}_i \, \Sigma_{ij} \, (\text{Instrumentality}_{ij} \times \text{Valence}_{ij})$$

Figure 3.3 illustrates the expectancy theory in another manner. Assume Mary is a middle level manager who is deciding whether she should go to training or not. She knows that she can do whatever she chooses in this situation, thus her expectancy (probability) that effort will lead to performance is at its maximum (1.0) in each case. She believes that if she doesn't

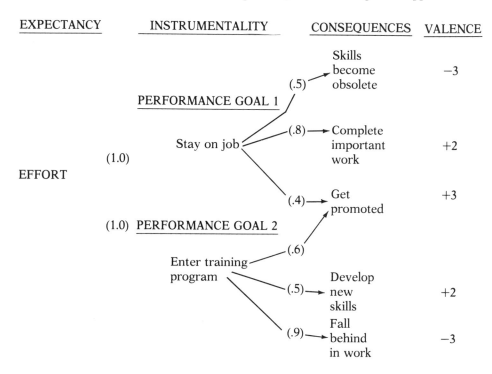

Figure 3.3   Expectancy theory approach to two incompatible performance goals.

go to training there is a 50 percent chance (i.e., instrumentality) that her skills will become obsolete, and an 80 percent chance exists that she will complete some important assignments. On a valence scale of +3 to −3, she positively values completing her assignments (+2) and negatively values (−3) having her skills become obsolete. Calculating the relative force pushing her to stay on the job, we come up with a force of 1.3. Doing the same thing for completing the training program, we arrive at a force of 0.1. Thus, we would predict that Mary would decide to stay on the job and not go to training. This is true because the likely outcomes of going to training are of less value overall than those associated with staying on the job.

The point of the above example is not to illustrate the mathematics involved (although that shouldn't hurt), but to demonstrate that the relationship between a stimulus situation and the ensuing behavioral response requires the concepts of expectancy, instrumentality, and valence.

Presumably, we can all behave in countless ways in a given situation. We choose a particular behavior or behavioral sequence because we expect it to maximize the benefits to us and minimize the cost. In the above example, Mary's two choices are just two among many other potential alternatives. Each of the alternatives is evaluated in the same way and the "best" one is chosen.

Vroom proposed that we all go through these mental gymnastics in arriving at decisions about whether or not to engage in a particular behavior or set of behaviors. His theory states that, after doing the mental arithmetic, we choose the one that provides us with the highest relative force (i.e., the best overall outcomes). Those expectations and instrumentalities must somehow be coded in our memory. His theory implies that we are able to store the relationships between our past behavior and its consequences in combination with current information to make inferences about the consequences of our future behavior. This is very similar to what Tolman once called a *cognitive map*.

LEARNING VS. PERFORMANCE ————————————————

While there is considerable evidence indicating that the operant process describes the physical events surrounding behavior and its modification, it doesn't provide a theoretical model for this process. Skinner (1971, 1950), in fact, rejected theory as at best misleading and at worst damaging. Yet, no explanation exists in the operant literature for the retention of the relationships between stimulus, response, and consequence so that future behavior can be influenced by the past history. Why is it that a given reinforcer is more effective with some people than others? More specifically, why do the relationships between stimulus, response, and consequence hold true? These questions cannot be answered without reference to a dynamically active brain/mind in which the learning and retention of some response capability is separated from its manifestation (i.e., performance). Expectancy theory attempts to describe the mechanisms through which learning and behavior are connected. That is, it describes how and why something becomes performed once it is learned.

Expectancy theory, then, can represent the subjective linkages between responses and their consequences by the concept of instrumentality. The linkage between stimulus and response can be said to be represented by the complete expectancy model. Through the description of the dynamics between expectancies, instrumentalities, and the valences of consequences, a cognitive explanation is provided for the occurrence of a behavior or behavioral pattern.

The major prediction from the reinforcement model is that changing the outcomes contingent upon behavior will produce predictable changes in the behavior. This is nothing more than saying that, by changing the instrumentalities of consequences, one can modify the occurrence of behavior in a predictable manner. The ability of expectancy theory to deal with a complex system of reinforcers and specify relative effects on behavior exemplifies the generality of this theory relative to the reinforcement model which typically deals with a single reinforcer or punisher.

Unfortunately, both the reinforcement model and expectancy theory describe the process of behaving or performing, not learning. While one can include feedback loops from experience into the expectancy model to show how experience modifies the expectations, instrumentalities, and valences, it is still a theory of performance and motivation. A person may act out a set of behaviors and, thus, demonstrate that learning has occurred, but the absence of performance does not necessarily indicate the absence of learning. It may simply indicate a lack of motivation to perform. The reinforcement model and expectancy theory may then provide some explanation as to why people perform, *but not really how they learn.* It is important for trainers to understand both because, unless trainees perform in some fashion, the trainer will never know whether or not they have learned anything. However, that fact does little to explain the learning itself or, for that matter, the reasons for the behavior occurring. Thus, while behavior of some sort is necessary to determine whether learning has occurred, its absence doesn't imply that learning has not occurred or that it has been forgotten. A great deal of evidence has accumulated now to show that learning can take place without the existence of external (i.e., observable) behavior (Bandura, 1977a; Kraut, 1976; Latham & Saari, 1979). Even when trainees have demonstrated learning by some performance in the training environment, this may not indicate that the learning will transfer to the work environment. Thus, learning may occur but not be complete enough to meet the goals of the training function. An effective trainer must understand the dynamics of learning as well as the dynamics of performance.

SOCIAL LEARNING THEORY

As previously stated, the debates between the congnitivists and behaviorists have been going on for a long time and continue even today. However, the gap between the two positions is continually narrowing. As two training researchers, Latham and Saari (1979), pointed out:

> To show that behavior is determined only by cognitions one would have to find a control group consisting of individuals who cannot think. Similarly, to provide empirical support for the argument that behavior is due to environmental consequences alone, one would have the impossible task of forming a control group for which there was no environment. (p. 240)

Thus, it is much more likely that both sides have discovered something important about the nature of human behavior and we should be looking for ways in which the facts supporting the positions are compatible.

Albert Bandura and his associates (Bandura, 1977a, 1977b; Kraut, 1976) have developed a theory of learning that goes by a number of different names. It is sometimes called *observational learning* or *vicarious learning* and most often it is called *social learning theory*. This theoretical perspective incorporates both cognitive and behaviorist ideas in the description of the learning process. Basically, this theory proposes that events and consequences in the external environment must be processed cognitively before they will have an impact on an individual's behavior. The cognitive processes of attention, retention, motivation, and motor reproduction are seen as necessary linkages between an environmental stimulus situation and some subsequent response. These processes will be discussed at length shortly. Figure 3.4 graphically illustrates the proposed relationships between the components of the theory.

Social learning theory shares with operant conditioning models the notion that behavior is affected by its consequences. They differ in terms of the effects that consequences are supposed to have. Whereas the operant approach insists that a reinforcer can *only* act to strengthen the preceding response, social learning theory suggests that it can also facilitate anticipatory learning. For example, the behaviors you need to engage in to reach a desired goal can be more easily learned by watching someone else engage in those behaviors and achieve the goal. By simply observing the other person (usually called a *model*), you can learn the correct behaviors and never once have been reinforced yourself or even behaved in any observable manner. This is called *anticipatory learning* because you have learned in anticipation of the reinforcement. It is also called *vicarious learning* or *observational*

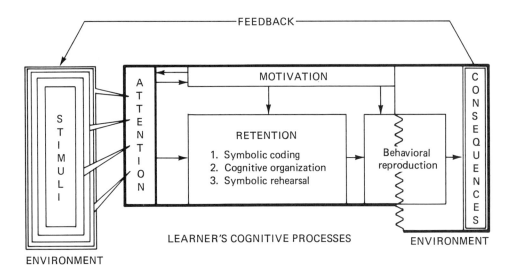

Figure 3.4   Graphic representation of the social learning processes.

learning because it occurs without the learner engaging in any overt behavior other than observing. Clearly understanding these processes should be important to our understanding of how to improve training demonstrations.

Attention

As Figure 3.4 illustrates, the learning process begins with the learner's attention being directed to certain stimuli (e.g., events) in the environment. Thus, things that attract attention are more likely to be observed and learned than others. Models who are more likely to get the learner's attention will be imitated more frequently and more precisely than other models. By developing and calling *attention* to key points, trainers will facilitate learning. The information being observed is then processed for *retention*. The initial phase of retention is the coding of information into symbols (*symbolic coding*). This typically takes the form of internally reducing the perceptual image of the event into cognitively organized verbal symbols that can be easily stored, retained, and retrieved. Thus, events in our environment become encoded internally (probably as electrochemical reactions) and can be manifested in terms of a behavioral code we know as language. We now have a model that specifies how relationships between behavior and its consequences can be retained and recalled to influence future behavior even when the learner has never performed the behavior or been directly reinforced for it.

Symbolic Rehearsal

Symbolic rehearsal is the visualizing or imagining of the behavior by the learner. After the model has been observed and the behavior sequence symbolically coded, the learner can imagine himself actually engaging in the behavior. Although this process may not always occur, the research indicates that learning is facilitated when it does. This can be thought of as practicing in your mind. Research has shown that modeling alone will increase the generalization of observationally learned responses to novel situations. Instructing trainees to symbolically rehearse and assisting them in developing their own symbolic codes will improve the transfer of the learning to different situations.

Behavioral Reproduction

Behavioral reproduction is shown in Figure 3.4 as being both a part of the retention process and a part of the environment. This is because the actual reproduction of the learned behavior sequence improves its retention (known as *practice effects*) but also occurs in some external environment.

While part of the behavioral reproduction is indeed internal to the learner, its final manifestation becomes a part of the environment in which it occurs. Whether the environment delivers positive, negative, or no consequences in response to the behavior, that feedback will influence that behavior in the future.

A great deal of research (see Manz & Sims, 1981) has gone into exploring the ways in which the various characteristics of the model, the learner, and the situation interact to influence the effectiveness of the observationally acquired learning. In general, this research has shown that the application of social learning theory to training within organizations produces positive outcomes. A more detailed description of the theory and how it can be utilized is covered in the next chapter and in Chapter 7.

A LEARNING HIERARCHY

While social learning theory helps us understand more about the learning process, we need to explore more carefully different types of learning. According to Robert Gagné (1962, 1965, 1974), we can distinguish among various types of learning on the basis of the types of activities the trainer and the trainee must engage in for the learning to occur. It is important to differentiate among these various learning types since each builds from the others at lower levels of learning. Failure to understand the more elementary forms of learning will result in an inability to correctly apply higher forms.

Gagné identified the eight types of learning in humans that are presented in Table 3.2. He proposes that Type 1 (signal learning) and Type 2 (stimulus-response) learning are basically unrelated to each other. However, each type of learning (from 2 through 8) requires competence at levels of learning that precede them. For example, Type 4 (verbal association) learning requires competence at Type 3 (shaping) which itself requires competence at Type 2 (stimulus-response learning). The principles discussed earlier in this chapter explain Gagné's first three learning types and the concepts behind them. An explanation of learning Types 4 through 8 will be presented in the following paragraphs.

Verbal Association (Type 4)

While most educational experts will not ignore memorization as a learning tool, it is typically not considered to be an important part of the educational process. The acquisition of knowledge, concepts, principles, and the ability to think logically are the primary focal points of educational programs today. However, the construction of our verbal utterances

Table 3.2 Gagné's eight types of learning.

1. Signal learning	This learning is a general diffuse response to a signal. The classical conditioning response discovered by Pavlov falls in this category.
2. Stimulus-response learning	The association of a single response to a stimulus situation followed by some consequence to the learner (i.e., operant conditioning as postulated by B. F. Skinner) represents learning of this type.
3. Shaping	This type of learning is represented by a chain of two or more stimulus-response connections. Gagné called this *chaining,* but we have used the term *shaping* to avoid confusion with other parts of the text.
4. Verbal association	A chain of two or more verbal associations characterizes this type of learning. Basically, it is the same as shaping but the use of language makes this a special type since internal links may be used from the individual's language capabilities.
5. Multiple discrimination	This type of learning occurs when the learner can make different but appropriate responses to different stimuli which resemble each other to a greater or lesser extent.
6. Concept learning	This is typically referred to as *generalization learning.* The individual acquires the capability of making a common response to a class of stimuli having some common characteristic or relationship, but otherwise differing more or less widely in physical appearance.
7. Principle learning	This type of learning is represented by a chain of two or more concepts characterized by the development of a formal logical relation between concepts similar to an "if A then B" formulation, where A and B are concepts.
8. Problem solving	This type of learning requires internal activity usually termed *thinking.* Two or more previously acquired principles are somehow combined to produce a novel (to the learner) capability which depends upon a "higher order" principle.

depends upon the ability to remember associations between the various units of our vocabulary. This is a key determinant of the ability we have to express ourselves in oral and written communication. Effective and original communication requires not only an understanding and application of the rules of grammar, but also the ability to recall a large base of verbal sequences or associations.

The basic foundation of verbal association is the pairing of a verbal response to an object or event in the environment. The mechanics behind this naming process are very similar to the mechanics of operant conditioning (Type 2 learning). One difference is that the stimulus (the perceptual image of the object) becomes internalized in terms of language. Thus, the word *horse* becomes associated with a stored image of the person's perceptual experience with animals of this type. Our perceptual experiences become labeled by internal codes (probably of an electrochemical nature) that are translated into the behavior we commonly know as language.

Of course, naming objects is not generally considered to be an indication of completed language development. Rather, it appears to be a necessary first step. Once this has occurred it then becomes possible to associate two or more of these language behaviors together. The consequences of chaining various language behaviors together will then enhance or discourage their use in the future. In this way, certain verbal sequences become memorized either intentionally or unintentionally.

Training implications Since the primary use of recalled verbal sequences is in the construction of communications that reflect the ideas and thought patterns of the person, an obvious use from the training perspective is that it serves as a means of measuring (or inferring) knowledge and ability that may not be readily or directly observable in the motor behavior of the individual. A manager, for example, makes decisions based on knowledge he or she possesses. Simply looking at the decision will not tell you very much about how knowledgeable that manager is. The skill and clarity with which the manager is able to describe the thought processes that led to the decision will indicate how knowledgeable the manager is. But, if the manager cannot communicate those thought processes, the focus of training should begin with language rather than with the content of the decision itself. Only after written and oral communication skills have been developed sufficiently can the trainer determine whether the content area within which the decision is being made also needs to be addressed in training. The identification of training needs in verbal communication is a part of the person analysis which must precede identification of training needs at higher levels of learning.

At this point, the reader is cautioned not to confuse the communication process with the thought process itself. Learning Types 1 through 4 are behavioral learning models. They describe the process of how behavior (both motor and language) patterns are developed. If a particular behavior pattern is evidenced, it indicates that learning has occurred. Learning may also have occurred even if the behavior pattern *hasn't* been evidenced. Lack of motivation or opportunity may have been the reason why the learning wasn't demonstrated. Where communication of thoughts is required for evidence of learning, a deficit in verbal association learning may mask principle or concept learning. While the person may have learned the principle or concept, he or she may be unable to express it in a manner that conveys learning to the trainer or to those in the job environment. Thus, the learning of verbal sequences that have common meaning both in the training and job environments has important consequences for the planning, evaluation, and generalization of training. However, in most cases, it is not sufficient simply to recall and express a verbal sequence. Rather, one must generalize to those stimulus situations in which it is appropriate and discriminate those from situations for which it is inappropriate. In this manner, the trainer is able to infer whether the "meaning" of the verbal sequence is understood. Understanding, in this case, refers to the degree of similarity in usage between the communicator and the recipient of the communication. This discussion leads us into the domains of Types 5 and 6 learning.

Multiple Discrimination Learning (Type 5)

The processes of *discrimination* and *generalization* can perhaps best be exemplified in the young child coming to terms with his or her environment. Suppose Amy is riding through the country with her mother and they pass a pasture with horses grazing in it. Mom stops the car and points to the horses, saying, "Look Amy, horses." Amy responds hesitantly, "Horsies?" Mom excitedly replies, "Yes, Amy, that's right, horsies!" As they continue driving they pass another pasture, but this one has cows in it. Amy jumps up in the seat and shouts, "Look mommy, horsies." Mom must now teach Amy the difference between cows and horses. If she does a good job, Amy will have two new words and two new concepts.

In reviewing the process, Amy began with no understanding of "horse" at all. When presented with a novel perceptual experience, a new category was created with the language label "horse" attached to it. The category may have been something like the following: "large, four legged, brown, moving thing." Thus, when Amy saw the cows, they fit very well into her horse category. This is the process of generalization—fitting things into existing categories or concepts. If Amy's mother did a good job of teaching Amy the differences between horses and cows, Amy will have learned to discriminate these two stimuli and attached appropriate language labels to them.

The developmental psychologist, Piaget, has labeled these cognitive processes *assimilation* and *accommodation. Accommodation* is the process of changing our construction of the world to correspond with our experience in it. In a sense, we are creating what Tolman called a "cognitive map of our world," and each accommodation process changes the map. Thus, Amy's first exposure to horses required her to modify her construction of the world to accommodate the existence of horses. When she then saw a cow, she ignored the differences between the two stimuli and assimilated or generalized the new stimulus into the existing category of horses. *Assimilation,* then, is the incorporation of our experience into existing cognitive categories. In terms of the cognitive map, assimilation doesn't change the structure of the map so much as it fills in the detail.

If Amy's mother hadn't corrected her, Amy would have completed the assimilation process by modifying her concept of horse to include the possibility of horns and udders (although she wouldn't have learned those language labels). The accommodation process then is one of creating new cognitive categories (or discriminating one from another), while the assimilation process is one of broadening or increasing the generality of the category. For instance, as Amy gets older she may acquire the concept "mammal" which will include the categories of horse and cow.

Most of our early years are devoted to the process of accommodation. As we mature and develop more and more categories, we begin to increase the degree to which we assimilate and decrease the amount of accommodation. What this means is that as we mature the likelihood that new information we accumulate will create new categories decreases and the likelihood that new information is integrated into existing categories increases. If the trainer is faced with a situation in which new multiple discrimination learning is required (i.e., the breaking down of an existing category into two or more separate categories or the creation of totally new categories, each with a different desired response pattern), it should be recognized that this will not be the form of information processing that is predominant in most of the adult trainees.

Training implications Suppose we are conducting a management training seminar for first- to middle-level managers. Since most of the evidence indicates that the effectiveness of a particular pattern of managerial behavior is dependent upon the situation the manager finds him- or herself in, we want to train managers to discriminate between situations and apply the appropriate behavioral pattern to each. In order to do this, we must first determine the managers' ability to name each part of the work situation that is relevant to making the discrimination (e.g., the structure of the work itself, the nature of the subordinates, etc.). Next, we must determine whether the trainee can name variations in each of the parts. For example, can the trainee recognize and appropriately label a job that is highly structured, one that is moderately structured, and one that is slightly structured? Essentially, we are asking, "Can the trainee discriminate different states of the category job structure." If not, we must establish the stimulus-response links referred to in Type 4 (verbal association) learning. That is, we must establish a stimulus-verbal response linkage in which the trainee becomes capable of recognizing and appropriately labeling the relevant stimuli. This is accomplished through repeated stimulus-response trials in which the trainee is reinforced for the appropriate response. Once we are satisfied that the trainee can not only recognize and label the relevant parts of the work situation, but also the variations in each of the parts, we can begin the process of multiple discrimination learning.

The entire set of stimuli that are to be associated with different response patterns must be presented to the learner one at a time so that the linkage to behavior can be established. Since this is not a chapter on leadership effectiveness we will only use two aspects of the work situation and two types of managerial behavior. For the former, we will use work structure and subordinate need for independence. For the latter, we will use initiating structure and participation. When task structure is high we want the initiating structure behavior of the supervisor to be low. When it is low (or the task itself is relatively unstructured), then we want the managerial initiating structure to be high. When subordinate need for independence is high, we want managers to engage in more participation in goal setting and the reverse when subordinate need for independence is low. As Figure 3.5

Subordinate Need for Independence

Work Structure		High	Low
	High	Low initiating structure High participation	Low initiating structure Low participation
	Low	High initiating structure High participation	High initiating structure Low participation

Figure 3.5   Supervisor behavior patterns recommended for various levels of two environmental stimuli.

indicates, we require the learner to discriminate not only between the environmental stimuli "task structure" and "subordinate need for independence," but also to discriminate within these categories high from low levels. The same is true of our response categories "initiating structure" and "participation."

Before we can hope to establish a desired response pattern to these stimuli, the trainee must first learn the concepts "task structure" and "need for independence." Before the trainee can learn the concept he or she must be able to discriminate between stimuli that are instances of the concept and stimuli that are not. If some characteristics of the work itself (e.g., the production process) are a part of the concept "task structure," then the trainee must learn to discriminate these stimuli from others in the stimulus situation. If we also consider the amount of discretion available to the individual in making work-related decisions to be an element of task structure, then the trainee must learn to discriminate decision-making stimuli from others that may exist in the stimulus situation.

For the moment, let us consider only the production process. Presenting stimuli (in isolation) that represent the production process and pairing them with the learner's verbal response "production process" will result in the learning of those S-R linkages if reinforced. When this is accomplished, the learner will have associated a number of stimuli with the phrase "production process." In order to establish discrimination learning, various stimuli need to be presented, some of which do represent the production process and some of which don't. The learner needs to discriminate those that do from those that don't. Once the learner has mastered this, the trainer must begin to teach discrimination between elements of the production process that increase and decrease the amount of task structure in the job. Reinforcement is no longer provided for simply discriminating production stimuli from other stimuli in the situation. Reinforcement now depends on discriminating the production process stimuli related to task structure *and* its relative level. Once the trainees have mastered this discrimination task, the trainer can say that the managers have learned to discriminate high and low task structuring stimuli in the production process from other stimuli.

The same learning must be achieved with stimuli associated with the need for independence, and the two response patterns. We must foster both stimulus and response discrimination learning in our trainees before they can learn the leadership principle we are trying to teach (i.e., the relationship between various types of leader behavior and the situation in terms of its effects on the leader's subordinates). This is true because principle learning requires concept learning as a prerequisite, and concept learning requires multiple discrimination learning as a prerequisite.

Concept Learning (Type 6)

Concept learning requires that a particular stimulus be categorized within a class of stimuli and a response learned to the class as a whole. Since multiple discrimination learning is the development of different responses to stimuli that are in some ways similar and in other ways different, concept learning might at first appear to be the opposite of multiple discrimination learning. However, this is incorrect since concept learning requires multiple discrimination learning in order to become a possibility.

If, in our example of management training, we want the managers to generalize the stimulus situations occurring in the training environment to the variety of situations they will face in their work environments, they will have to develop concepts for task structure and need for independence. Suppose supervisory jobs related to a manufacturing assembly plant had been used to demonstrate high and low task structure. Assembly line supervisors may have been used to exemplify a highly structured task because the technology of the work process, the programmed nature of their decision making, and the clarity of their duties pretty much determined their work activities. The production engineering supervisor may have been used to illustrate a less structured task, because the activities of this supervisor's subordinates are less interdependent, fewer of the work decisions are prescribed by the organization, and it is more difficult for the supervisor to determine what his or her role should be. While the trainees may be able to discriminate high from low task structure in the training environment, they may not when they go back to their respective jobs in word processing, personnel, sales, and information systems. Unless the trainer provides more than one stimulus situation in which the concept is present he or she will never know whether the concept has been learned or simply a stimulus-specific discrimination. By presenting a sequence of novel stimulus situations, the trainer can say that the managers have learned the concept task structure if the appropriate response is demonstrated consistently across the situations. In this case, the learner, presented with a variety of situations that differ widely in appearance, responds to them on the basis of some *common abstract property* (i.e., degree of task structure).

While trial and error learning may be used to establish a concept, it is not usually the best or most efficient method of doing so. Rather, the trainee usually has a large repertoire of categories and concepts coded in the form of language that the trainer can use as a base for building the new concept. For example, if the trainees are provided with a definition of the concept task structure, they can use the concepts associated with the verbal sequences in the definition to form an abstract foundation for the new concept. Suppose we define *task structure* in the following manner:

The degree to which the process of production, the rules of the work unit, and other factors outside the direct control of the worker determine what, when, how, and where the work will be done.

If the trainee can reliably associate the above definition with the verbal sequence "task structure," he or she has only learned a complex verbal paired association behavior (Type 4 learning). If he or she can consistently discriminate high from low task structure in a single stimulus situation and respond in the appropriate differential manner, the trainee can be said to have demonstrated multiple discrimination learning. If he or she can consistently discriminate high from low structure across multiple novel situations and respond in the appropriate differential manner, he or she can be said to have learned the concept task structure. The reader should not assume that simply providing the definition will be very effective in bringing about concept learning. Rather, the learner must begin with concrete examples that he or she can use to test the degree to which the concepts he or she has associated with the definition are shared in common with the trainer. In order to be useful tools for dealing with the world outside of the training environment, concepts must be referenced to "real" stimulus situations. These can be situations recalled from the past, hypothetical situations that are actually experienced (i.e., some case studies), simulations, or demonstrations. These provide the concept with an operational meaning that can come no other way.

To develop the learning of a concept, the learner must have already mastered the associations that are representative of the concept and that discriminate them from others that are not in the class. If these conditions are met, then the trainer must present the various stimulus associations that have previously been learned at the same time as the new stimulus. In this case, the previously learned associations linked to "process of production," "determine," "what, when, how, and where the work will be done" are presented simultaneously (visual presentation) or closely in time (oral presentation) with the new stimulus "task structure." Once this "abstract" linkage has been mastered, the trainee must apply the previously learned associations to a concrete stimulus situation that contains the elements of the concept to be learned. Following this, novel situations containing the elements of the concept as well as elements not included in the concept should be presented. The responses to these novel situations will indicate concept learning when the trainee is able to ignore elements unrelated to the concept and respond appropriately to elements in the concept consistently across the novel situations. At this point we are ready to move on to principle learning.

Principle Learning

Principles are chains of concepts making up what is generally called *knowledge.* The statement, "Low initiating structure in a high task structure work environment is effective," represents three distinct concepts: (1) low initiating structure, (2) high task structure work environment, and (3) effective. In order to learn this principle, the trainee must have already learned each of the three concepts. Again, the memorization of the verbal chain in no way implies learning of the principle, the concepts, or the discriminations. Learning of the principle is demonstrated by its appropriate use in specific situations. Thus, presenting the trainees with novel situations in which various factors are contributing or not contributing to the structure of a task, and asking them "what type of managerial behavior will be effective?" will demonstrate whether they have learned the principle. As always, reinforcement of the desired response pattern will strengthen the learning and reduce the likelihood of forgetting.

Problem Solving

Problem solving is the application of multiple principles to produce a novel response or capability that results in a higher order principle previously unknown to the learner. In our example, the trainer may have successfully fostered the learning of the task structure principle referred to earlier, as well as the following principle: "Participation in goal setting is an effective managerial behavior when subordinates are high in need for achievement." Suppose Mike, one of our manager-trainees, leaves the training site after learning these two principles and returns to his job. There he is confronted by an employee whom he knows is low in self-esteem. The employee tested out well in the selection process but hasn't been on the job long enough to evaluate in terms of performance. Nonetheless, the employee feels as if she is doing an inadequate job and is considering leaving the job for one that is not as demanding.

Mike thinks about his training program and realizes that neither of the principles is directly applicable to the situation. However, after thinking for a while longer he went directly to the employee and assured her that he believed she was doing a fine job and that he had every confidence in her that she would do a good job in the future. Mike had developed the higher order principle that "managerial behavior that compensates for discrepencies in the match between the subordinates' needs and the work environment is effective."

Training implications   When a problem has been solved, something has also been learned in the sense that the capabilities of the problem solver have been changed in a relatively permanent way. The higher order principle becomes a part of the individual's knowledge repertoire. Of course, higher order principles may be learned in the same fashion as regular principle learning. The difference is in the process of discovery, or the amount and nature of the guidance provided. In typical principle learning situations, the trainer will cue and even model the higher order principle in combination with differentially reinforcing trainee responses that more or less demonstrate acquisition. The problem solving type of learning occurs when the trainee is able to discover the new principle without help. Research evidence indicates that this latter type of learning produces a highly effective capability that is extremely resistant to forgetting (Ausubel, 1963; Gagné & Bassler, 1963).

Gagné's catagories can be described as a heirarchy of learning types going from the simple to the complex, with each successive step requiring competency at the preceding steps. A major implication of Gagné's perspective is that the training needs assessment must be complete. Identification of the performance deficiency is not enough. The behaviors that are essential for the targeted performance must be identified as well as what type of learning is necessary to acquire those behaviors. Only then can the learning objectives of training be stated.

ADULT LEARNERS

Since, for the most part, the training population within organizations consists of adults, it seems appropriate to focus on the learning processes of this group of individuals. A great deal of the research (Riegel, 1973; Jarvik & Cohen, 1973) on adult learning capabilities has suggested that intellectual functioning reaches a peak in young adulthood and then shows a steady decline. This period of decline was hypothesized to result from the inevitable biological breakdown of the human system due to illness, injury, and, in the latter stages of life, senility. More recently, researchers have challenged this interpretation of the data. An alternative view of the effects of aging on intellectual functioning (Baltes & Willis, 1976; Labouvie-Vief, 1977) has been put forward. This view suggests that what appeared at first to be deficits in intellect were nothing more than a different form of intellectual processing. The more recent evidence indicates that adults periodically go through episodes of reintegration, in which concepts or principles of longstanding are reevaluated in terms of experience. Knowledge of little functional value to the individual gets "lost" in these reintegration episodes, while more functional knowledge is discovered and integrated around practical experience. The processing of material (i.e., learning) becomes more experientially and personally based and less abstract.

As we pointed out earlier, the process of accommodation occurs less frequently in adults while the frequency of assimilation increases. This, of course, is due in part to the fact that adults have already accommodated quite a bit. Most adults have a fairly well developed "cognitive map" of the world that has served them "quite well, thank you," and thus, are reluctant to interpret new information as signaling a need for cognitive change.

Trainees enter our programs with elaborate and finely tuned maps about themselves, their associates, their job requirements, their organization, etc. Changing one part of that map affects many if not all of the other parts. To paraphrase R. R. Short (1981), director of a university-based human resource development program, we ignore that learning, like breathing, is one of the most natural processes we have. It is *unlearning* that is difficult. For, in learning a new concept or principle, we must unlearn or reintegrate all of those parts of the cognitive maps that relate to it.

In spite of all the problems associated with learning something new and upsetting to the status quo, the evidence indicates that adults engage in a great deal of learning on a continual basis. In a recent study (Tough, 1979), IBM salesmen were found to average over 1,100 hours a year involved in an average of 13 separate learning episodes. About two-thirds of these were job related. A *learning episode* was defined as a deliberate attempt to gain and retain some knowledge and/or skill for problem solving or changing in some way. Professors, by way of contrast, tended to spend more time (1,745 hours) on slightly fewer problems (an average of 12).

While children are more often characterized as learning for curiosity or for the sake of learning, adults are more oriented toward learning for application in the near future. Some of the specific tasks most frequently mentioned as the reason for adult learning episodes are problems on the job, preparing for an occupation, home and personal responsibilities, and improving some area of competence related to recreation or hobbies. Curiosity is one of the least frequent reasons given for adult learning. Thus, while adults are typically resistant to learning for the sake of learning, they are quite eager to engage in learning they see as being useful. Knowles (1978, 1984) suggested that the need to know and the readiness to learn are critical aspects in the success of adult learning programs. The "need to know" refers to the value of the knowledge to the learner. "Readiness to learn" refers to the amount of prerequisite knowledge the trainee posesses and the trainee's subjective opinion of his or her ability to learn the material. Both of these aspects of the trainee must be in alignment. It won't matter how useful the training is perceived to be if the trainee doesn't feel capable of learning. On the other side, it won't matter how ready the trainee is for learning if the training isn't seen as useful. For adult learners, then, the trainer must examine the relevance of the material to the trainee's goals and the trainee's readiness for learning the material.

Adults have been found to prefer to plan their own learning projects and to adopt a self-directed approach toward learning. This seems to derive from a desire to set their own pace, establish their own structure, and keep open the option to revise the learning strategy. This, however, doesn't mean that the adult isolates his or her learning from others. Frequently, the adult learner desires, seeks, and receives help from many others.

We have pointed out, and others agree (Baltes & Willis, 1976; Griffith, et al., 1980; Knowles, 1984) that adults walk into learning situations with a fairly well defined cognitive map. This map is based on their experience with the world, and the older they are, the more detailed their map is likely to be. Two very important training implications emerge from this fact. First, because experiences with the world differ considerably, there are likely to be a number of differences among the members of a training group in terms of their learning strategies. Second, these differences in experience can be seen as a learning resource. However, this requires a willingness to share those experiences on the part of the trainees. These two facts suggest that a learning approach that emphasizes both an individualized program and makes use of other group members as resources for learning will be most likely to succeed with adult learners. However, this is not always the most practical or cost-effective way to achieve HRD goals. The next chapter and the chapters on experiential and nonexperiential techniques explore these issues in greater depth.

The study of adult learning processes has only recently begun and much remains to be discovered about the ways in which adults learn. It would appear, however, from what we do know, that the role of the trainer of adults is one of supporting the natural energies and talents for learning possessed by the trainees. It would also seem that adults only grudgingly recognize that new learning is desirable or necessary. Typically, adults try to force incoming information into their existing cognitive map. They react to it in the ways they have in the past. And, if that fails to produce a satisfactory outcome, they do the same things all over again only louder or faster or with more tenacity. Yelling even louder at the deaf man only makes your throat hurt. And, it is usually only after our throat begins to hurt that we recognize that a new approach is required. If our communication with the deaf man is important enough, then we will set about learning how to communicate with him. It appears then, that the process of learning in adults is quite similar in the initial phases to the change model presented in Chapter 1. That is, learning is an activity that adults most often engage in when normal coping mechanisms fail to alleviate some problem that is important enough that it can't be ignored.

SUMMARY

In this chapter, we have presented a brief history of the theory and research related to learning. We would hope that you would now be able to discuss, at least in general terms, how Ebbinghaus, Thorndike, Tolman, and others have helped shape the way we think about learning today. We would especially hope that you could define the philosophical split that developed between the behaviorists and the cognitivists and understand how the very definition of learning contributed to this dichotomy of viewpoints.

We made a distinction between learning and performance in which performance could imply that learning had occurred but, that learning could occur in the absence of any observable behavior. We would hope that you would now be able to explain how motivation can intervene between learning and performance.

Observational learning (i.e., social learning theory) was presented and shown to integrate both the cognitive and behavioral approaches to learning. You should now be able to describe the various aspects of these learning processes and explain how they interrelate.

Finally, we presented some relatively recent insights into the characteristics of adult learners. You should be able to state how these new understandings contradict some of the stereotypes about intellectual capabilities and the aging process. You should also be able to draw implications for the development of organizational training programs from your understanding of these adult learner characteristics.

DISCUSSION QUESTIONS

1. What type of learning or conditioning can only be said to be learning in the sense that some reflexive behavior has been conditioned to occur in response to a novel stimulus?
2. How can a trainer demonstrate whether learning has occurred?
3. What is the basic unit of all learning?
4. What happens to the likelihood of a response being learned that is followed by positive outcomes?
5. A pattern of behavior can be learned (i.e., a combination of individual behaviors) if the original behavior in the stimulus situation is followed closely in time by the next link in the desired behavior chain and reinforcement is administered only for a combination of the behaviors in the desired order. The timing of successive stages in the training program is crucial in determining its effectiveness. What is this process called?
6. Language is the mechanism through which cognitive phenomena (e.g., ideas, thoughts, experience) are labeled and communicated. The verbal

sequences we use to describe our cognitive interpretation of the world are subject to the same learning processes as other types of behavior (e.g., motor). How is this knowledge of use to trainers?

7. What type of learning must be mastered prior to principle learning?

8. Training programs that include demonstrations and verbal instructions have been found to increase the effectiveness of training. What learning theory would best explain this?

9. What is the primary information processing strategy used by adults?

10. Why should training programs attempt to facilitate the "unlearning" of certain habits or ideas?

11. According to observational learning, what steps must occur before behavior can be learned?

LEARNING THEORY AND ADULT TRAINEES: AN INTERVIEW WITH GINO AND MARY DEANE SORCINELLI

Gino and Mary Deane Sorcinelli are residents of Bloomington, Indiana. Mary Deane is employed by Indiana University to assist faculty members in efforts to enhance their teaching effectiveness. Most of her time is spent conducting workshops with groups of faculty, consulting with individual faculty, and coordinating conferences on teaching and learning issues. Her husband, Gino, provides training programs for union members and leaders. He designs and coordinates courses, workshops, and seminars of various lengths and on a wide variety of topics all aimed at improving union effectiveness. He has worked with the AFL-CIO's education center, the UAW's education center, and Indiana University's Labor Studies Program. Both Mary Deane and Gino have completed doctoral work aimed at understanding the learning process of adult trainees so we felt that they would be ideally suited to answer our questions about the learning processes of adults.

Question: Much of the literature on learning theory has been developed by studying animals and/or classroom behavior of young students. How is learning different for adult trainees?

Gino Sorcinelli: What I've noticed is that the trainees I deal with bring a lot of experience to our sessions. Their experiences carry a lot of weight for them—much more so than espoused theories and research findings. As a trainer, it helps me when they describe examples that operationalize the concepts underlying the learning objectives of the training session. But, experience also creates habits and adds to some reluctance to consider new ways, new perspectives.

The biggest difference I have noticed about adult trainees (as opposed to young students in undergraduate courses) is that they tend to be *very* pragmatically oriented. If the material is directly related to their jobs as union representatives, they are very attentive, but their scope may be limited as a result. In order to promote learning, I am always challenged to produce examples directly tied to their union's situation. They are far more application oriented and generally demand more realism than undergraduates.

I might also add that training sessions remind adult learners of their school days. They may feel threatened if they weren't very successful in high school and grade school. Their fears of reliving those failures often show up in their tendency to underestimate their own abilities to learn and overestimate the trainer's knowledge, skills, and abilities. Reactions to the situation as well as the material must be dealt with in my line of work.

Mary Deane Sorcinelli: I have found that faculty members react as "adult learners" much in the same way Gino described. I think they demand examples—they may like theories but they appreciate case descriptions directly related to their own fields. I guess the key to working with adult learners is gaining their attention. I find that stimulating recall of previous learning and then relating those experiences to the present learning topic accomplishes two things: It provides recognition that the learners are not walking into the training session as blank tablets and it captures their attention. This can work with undergraduates too, but they often don't have as much experience to draw on and they tend to be more compliant than attendees at training sessions. Perhaps this occurs because, unlike adult learners, the primary motivation for many undergraduates is to pass their classes in order to obtain a degree. I have found that workshop formats designed to produce active involvement from adult learners tend to produce more learning than formats designed to deliver didactic lectures.

A lot of my work as a trainer involves delivering one- to three-day workshops. I typically have little chance to get to know my "trainees" before our sessions. I guess a more systematic means of assessing their needs might help me design sessions tailored to produce more learning. But, realistically, my "adult learners" come to me from so many different backgrounds and situations and from work-life styles that demand a great deal of their time that it would be difficult to gain a clearer assessment of their needs *a priori* to the training sessions themselves. This is where the activity orientation of the workshops serve the learning objectives again. I share the responsibility for learning with the participants and provide them with the opportunity to benefit from the experience base of their fellow trainees.

Question: Gino, do you feel that the fact that your trainees are union members and leaders presents special opportunities and problems compared to other groups of adult learners?

Gino Sorcinelli: That's true to some extent. On the one hand, virtually all my "trainees" are attending my sessions on a voluntary basis. They must have at least some interest in learning or they wouldn't have signed up for the program. The participants in my sessions are also quite used to working with groups of people. Discussion periods are rarely, if ever, a matter of pulling teeth. My unionists are generally quite willing to contribute to examinations of issues in group sessions.

On the other hand, the union leaders I deal with have so much going on that sessions often get interrupted. During breaks, they often need to call back to their headquarters to check on pressing problems. They receive phone messages generating further preoccupation. I also have the problems of conducting needs assessments that Mary Deane mentioned and, in addition, have a less clear hierarchical situation within the unions when I do try to assess needs from an organizational perspective. Other than that, I suspect union members and leaders are like many other groups of adult learners.

Question: Mary, do you feel that being a female trainer affects the learning processes of your adult trainees?

Mary Deane Sorcinelli: Not really—at least it's not obvious that there is a great difference. Research indicates that females are perceived as warmer and more interested in the trainees and males are seen as more knowledgeable. I am sure that a trainer's style accounts for these differences more than the fact that the trainer is male or female. I have found, however, that when I co-facilitate a workshop with a male colleague, male trainees tend to open up more to me than to my male co-trainer. When I have teamed up with Gino to conduct training with union leaders, I do have to work on establishing my credibility unless its predominantly a female union. I don't know if this is due to expectations that if I haven't worked in a shop then I can't help unionists with their training needs or if this represents some "macho" defense to receiving help from a female. Again, notice the theme of the importance of experience as a basis for adult trainees to learn from training sessions. It's been proven true in our experiences.

Question: Do either of you have any final comments regarding the topic of learning processes in adults?

Gino Sorcinelli: I would like to raise a point from my experience as a trainer and as a person who has studied learning theories. I think most theorists and researchers have focused on the material and the training designs in attempting to understand learning. My experience with adults has shown that these issues are important but that adults bring many other agendas with them to training sessions, especially residential sessions that involve staying at an education center. These trainees attend such sessions to meet people with similar interests and work problems as much as to learn about the topic of the sessions. "Networking," as it is referred to nowadays, can interfere with a trainer's well-planned time schedule and agenda. But, I believe this activity is an important benefit of training opportunities and we, as trainers, need to plan for this within our attempts to enhance learning. However, some other agendas of trainees attending residential training sessions not only interfere with efforts to achieve learning objectives but are a drag to deal with. I mean the agendas of some trainees who are interested in the training sessions primarily as an excuse to go drinking and carousing; to find out about the restaurants and shopping opportunities of such-and-such city; or merely as an excuse to get out of the house or to spy on someone from another part of their organization. It's no fun as a trainer to face a group on day three of an intensive workshop and find key people hung over and/or too tired or more interested in discussing their exploits in town than the topics at hand. Most of the time these are not serious problems but, when they arise, they can be frustrating for trainers of "adult" learners.

Mary Deane Sorcinelli: I would summarize by emphasizing that the age of the adult trainees in an audience may necessitate some special planning but most of the principles of learning discussed in your chapter seem to hold true across situations. Oh, age may deteriorate eyesight so that overheads may be harder to see but the adage that you can't teach old dogs new tricks certainly isn't true. Adult learners bring many habits and old ways of thinking that must be addressed before jumping into new approaches but such caution can be useful too. As long as the material can be shown to be relevant and pragmatically useful, adult learners not only understand but actually implement ideas more readily than younger undergraduate students. They are more typically in a position to be able to do so. I think that makes the jobs of trainers and adult educators both more challenging and more interesting.

Chapter 4

DESIGNING TRAINING FOR EFFECTIVE LEARNING

Several theoretical positions on human learning and some of the related scientific research were examined in the last chapter. The focus of that chapter was on understanding human learning. This chapter changes the focus from one of understanding to one of application. The difference in these two orientations is similar to the difference between the management scholar/scientist and the management practitioner/artist. The management scholar is trying to understand why certain managerial practices have the effects they do. The management practitioner is more concerned with developing skill in applying accepted management practices. While a person doesn't have to be an expert in both areas, managers who are familiar with both the science and art of managing are likely to be more effective.

This chapter will draw inferences from the research on human learning that are applicable to the development of training programs. These inferences will, by necessity, be general in nature. What is presented is more of a general philosophy of training program development than a cookbook for what to do in a specific situation. More specific prescriptions will be presented in the chapters covering the various training techniques. In addition, general steps in program development will be presented that should be followed regardless of the technique selected. Some of the questions this chapter addresses are listed next:

1. What is the role of the trainer in planning and designing training programs?
2. What are the differences among organizational, training, and learning objectives and how are they developed?
3. What role do individual trainee differences play in the design and development of training programs?
4. What are the basic components of a training program?
5. How can training be designed to have maximum impact on the learning processes?

Many approaches to the development of instructional programs have been proposed (e.g., Bass & Vaughan, 1966; Gagné, 1977; Goldstein, 1980; Mager & Beach, 1967). Very little empirical evidence exists to support one particular approach over another. The reason for this is that there are so many variables involved in a training program. The success or failure of a particular program will be influenced by the skill of the trainer, the type of learning technique selected, the intellectual capabilities and past experience of the trainees, the learning environment, the quality of the learning materials, and many other variables that are difficult at best to measure. Thus, it becomes very difficult to attribute the success or failure of training to any one aspect such as the design of the training. Obviously, if the desired result of training is not achieved, it can be said that something in the design of the training was inappropriate. The key question, however, is, "What part of the program was inappropriately designed?" The next chapter, covering the evaluation of training, will discuss this topic in greater length. This chapter presents the generally agreed upon components in the design of training programs. Within those components we have presented what we believe to be sound principles and practices that are logically derived from the research surrounding human learning. Attention to these will go a long way toward planning an effective training program.

One of the key aspects of sound human resource development is planning for change. In the design of training this means:

1. Developing and getting agreement on training goals.
2. Identifying and evaluating various approaches to achieve training goals.
3. Selecting an approach and doing the groundwork necessary for the approach to be successful.

Training is a change process and can be compared to the process of organizational change. Table 4.1 presents the corresponding stages of the change model presented in Chapter 1 and the stages of developing a training program. The close relationship between the two processes indicates that the trainer can be thought of in part as a change consultant whose role is to assist the organization and the potential trainee with the processes of diagnosis, development of alternative solutions, and implementation of the solution when the chosen alternative is training.

Table 4.1 Associated stages in the planned change model and training program development.

Planned changed model	Training program development
1. Stimulus for change is felt within the organization.	
2. The organization attempts to cope with the stimulus.	1. Perceived performance problems are identified.
3. A compelling need for change is established.	
4. The cause of the change need is diagnosed.	2. Training needs analysis is conducted.
5. Goals are developed and agreed upon.	3. Training and learning objectives are developed.
6. Alternative approaches are identified and evaluated.	4. Design of the training program is developed.
7. An approach is selected.	
8. The change idea is implemented.	5. Training is implemented.
9. The change effort is evaluated.	6. Training is evaluated.
10. The evaluation is fed back to the organization.	7. The evaluation is fed back to the individual and unit.
11. The change effort becomes becomes internalized.	8. Training becomes internalized.

THE ROLE OF THE TRAINER

The previous chapter described learning as a change in the cognitive structures and processes of the learner. At the same time, it was asserted that evidence of learning having occurred can come only from the learner's behavior. These two propositions create the basic parameters within which this chapter on instruction will operate. Taken together, these propositions suggest that the trainer can, at best, provide an environment that is supportive of the learner's knowledge/skill acquisition processes and that motivates the learner to engage in those acquisition processes. The trainer, then, must adopt the role of a change facilitator rather than the role of a director or controller (Lippitt & Lippitt, 1984). In many training programs, this issue becomes confused. The trainer is thought to determine the objectives, the knowledge required, and the manner in which it will be learned. In such a situation, it is the trainer's goals that are being pursued rather than the trainee's. Is it any wonder, then, that many training programs can be characterized by the apathy of the trainees? How motivated are you to pursue someone else's goals?

The above should not be interpreted to mean that the trainer abdicates all control and responsibility to the trainee. Rather, we are suggesting that the trainer should utilize his or her expertise to facilitate the trainee's learning processes. This means that the trainees must perceive the training to be of value to themselves and that the objectives of training are obtainable. The trainer also has a responsibility to insure that the outcomes of training are of value to the organization as well as to the individual trainees. Thus, the trainer must structure the training design in such a way that organizationally valued outcomes are achieved. At the same time, the effective trainer will recognize that very few if any of those desired outcomes will occur unless the trainees see that the learning is also of value to them.

As Table 4.1 indicates, the training needs analysis will have diagnosed the symptoms (proactive or reactive), creating a compelling need for change. If training is the accepted solution, the cause of the symptoms will have been identified as a lack of required knowledge/skill. This analysis should have identified those job incumbents whose performance deficiencies are a result of a lack of knowledge/skill or those whose developmental needs are in the knowledge/skill area. It also should have provided the trainer with a description of the job behaviors required for effective job performance. Thus, the total training population has been identified and the organizational training criteria (i.e., a description of the behavioral capabilities required to adequately perform some job or a particular aspect of that job) have been established. The trainer is now in a position to begin to develop the instructional program(s) necessary to meet the training needs.

LEARNING OBJECTIVES

After completing the needs analysis, the development of learning objectives can begin. Mager (1975, p. 5) defined *instructional objectives* as ". . . a description of a performance you want learners to be able to exhibit before you consider them competent. An objective describes an intended result of instruction, rather than the process of instruction itself." Laird (1978) suggested that useful learning objectives can be characterized by the fact that they contain an *observable action,* a *measurable criterion* (or criteria), and the *conditions of performance.* Michalak and Yager (1979), professional training consultants, suggested that a distinction be made between behavioral or task objectives and learning objectives. They contend that the *task objectives* are the ultimate behavioral goals of training and as such are more closely related to the job for which training is being given. *Learning objectives* are seen by these authors as intermediate or sub-objectives the trainee must master in order to become proficient at the task objectives. These learning objectives then are more closely related to the training itself.

There are useful concepts in each of the above descriptions and definitions. The development of learning objectives should begin with a description of what the intended result of training is. However, such a description is generally too broad to be of much help in the development of a set of procedures and activities that will lead to an effective learning experience. As pointed out earlier, an adequate needs analysis will have provided a statement of what the desired result of training should be. What is needed is a description of what learning outcomes are required in order to achieve the overall objectives. Refering back to Gagné's learning hierarchy, we need to specify the levels and nature of the learning steps required to reach the desired end state. Of course, the overall objective and the intermediate objectives are each learning objectives. What differentiates them is their chronological ordering in the training or learning sequence. Each of these learning objectives should be characterized by observable actions, measurable criteria, and a description of the conditions of performance. If they are, these formal learning objectives can be said to be behavioral or task descriptions that contain a standard verb. It is the verb that implies the type of capability or learning involved. Mager (1975) suggested, and we concur, that the selection of these verbs is critical for developing a clear and straightforward plan of action in training. The learning objective statements should avoid ambiguous or subjective verbs such as "understands," "feels," and "believes." Instead, action verbs that imply the type of capability involved, such as "discriminates," "solves," and "originates," should be used.

Advantages of Learning Objectives

It is possible to establish a good training program without developing a formal set of objectives for that program, just as it is possible for a business to be successful without establishing a formal set of goals or objectives. However, we and others (Gagné, 1977; Mager, 1975; Popham & Baker, 1970) suggest that the likelihood of developing an effective instructional program is greatly enhanced by going through the formal process of developing learning objectives. This process has several advantages associated with it other than simply documenting what the trainer is trying to do. Through the process of developing learning objectives, the trainer is able to identify and specify many of the criteria to be used in evaluating the training program. The process also allows the trainer to come to grips with precisely what is required in order to achieve the overall training goals. Perhaps most importantly, the learning objectives (if properly developed) should describe the relationship between the learning processes and the behavioral capabilities that training is trying to develop. As a result, the linkage between organizational outcomes and training experiences and results is clarified as are trainee expectations about what will be required of them. The job of "selling" training to line managers thus becomes much easier. To understand more completely how the development of learning objectives achieves these benefits it is necessary to first describe how one goes about developing them.

Using Domains of Learning to Develop Objectives

Before the trainer can plan the kind of activities that will be likely to facilitate the acquisition of the overall learning objectives, he or she must know what prior capabilities are required and what prior learning will act as support for or act to hinder the new learning. Once the overall learning objectives have been established, it becomes possible to identify the prerequisites and the supportive bases for learning.

Gagné (1977, 1984) found it convenient to think of learning as occurring in five domains: *intellectual skill, cognitive strategy, verbal information, motor skill,* and *attitude.* These domains have the potential to influence each other in the acquisition of new learning. A learning domain is a kind of capability. Gagné's basic types of learning occur in all of the domains. This represents an expansion of the three domains (cognitive, affective, and psychomotor) developed much earlier by Bloom (1956, 1964). What is important about these domains is that previous learning in each of them can act to support or inhibit new learning in the others. The trainer who is developing learning objectives must not only determine what types of learning are prerequisites for the new learning, but also what prior learning exists in the training population that will act to support the new learning. The basic data for this type of analysis should be available from the person analysis phase of the needs analysis. Once training has been accepted as a desirable course of action, a more detailed analysis of the training population will be necessary.

Let's go back to the managerial training example in the previous chapter. The organizational objective for this training program was for the manager-trainees to acquire the capability of producing the type of supervisory behavior that would be most likely to motivate the employee to pursue the organization's goals given the employee's needs and the existing work situation. As you may remember, certain types of verbal associations (information), discriminations, concepts, and principles (intellectual skills) were required before the trainees could be expected to learn desired relationships between the variables "employee characteristics and work characteristics" and "effective supervisory behavior." These capabilities can be said to be prerequisites for the overall training objective. However, to stop here would be to ignore certain motor skills that would also be considered prerequisites since the training is aimed at *both* intellectual skill and motor skill. Simply developing the intellectual skill will not ensure the behavioral skill. For example, by successfully completing a paper and pencil exam a trainee may indicate acquisition of the necessary intellectual capabilities for determining the appropriate supervisory strategy. The trainee may even indicate through this "exam taking behavior" that a thorough understanding of structuring behavior and what it consists of has been acquired. Yet, the trainee may still lack a great deal of skill in actually performing in a structuring manner. This could be the outcome of a training program if the trainer only focused on developing learning objectives in the intellectual domain. If, however, the trainer had adequately developed the specific learning objectives from the overall learning objective (i.e., the verb phrase "producing the type of supervisory behavior") the trainer would have seen that learning in the motor domain is a prerequisite.

Figure 4.1 presents the organizational and training objectives for the management development training program we were using as an example. The illustration shows that the organizational objective is more general and less behavior specific than the training objective. Another difference is that the organizational objective focuses on job behavior and outcomes while the training objectives do not. Obviously, trainers would like the new learning to transfer to the trainee's job behavior. However, as was discussed in the needs assessment chapter, there are many variables in the work environment that may inhibit the use of the new learning. Thus, motivational and opportunity factors in the work environment may restrict or prohibit performance of newly learned capabilities. Chapter 5 will discuss methods for determining when such a situation exists and provide alternative courses of action in dealing with it. For now, it is sufficient to note that the overall objective of training should describe what the criteria are for determining that the desired learning has occurred and how they are to be measured. In the present example, the criteria are the identification and production of the most effective managerial behaviors in five randomly selected, novel, employee-work situation scenarios. They will be measured in an assessment center (i.e., trained judges evaluating the assessee's activities in a simulated work environment). These criteria and methods are then used to evaluate the effectiveness of training activities. In this example, the degree to which trainees are able to successfully complete the assessment center process will provide some (but not absolute) evidence of the effectiveness of training.

The prerequisite learning objectives in Figure 4.1 are hierarchical in nature. Prerequisites 1 and 2 (P_1, P_2) were directly derived from the overall training objective. The prerequisites for P_2 have been developed to illustrate the process of deriving prerequisites from the next lower level of learning. As you can see, this set of prerequisites stops at the verbal association level. This implies that all of the trainees were competent at prerequisite abilities below this level. Perhaps you, the reader, might like to try your hand at

Organizational Objective

Managers will be able to interact with their employees in a manner that is effective in motivating the employees to pursue organizational goals.

Overall Training Objective

In an assessment center following the completion of training, the manager-trainees, when confronted with five, randomly selected, novel employee-work situation scenarios, will be able to identify and produce the type of managerial behaviors that have been identified as most effective for motivating the type of employee, in the type of work situation depicted, to pursue organizational goals.

Prerequisite Learning Objectives

P_1 Be able to produce all types of managerial behavior.

P_2 Match the appropriate managerial behavior to the various novel employee-work situation combinations (i.e., learn the higher order principle: effective managerial behavior compensates for discrepancies between employee characteristics and the work situation).

P_2a Recall each of the principles that stipulate which managerial behaviors are appropriate in the various employee-work situation combinations (i.e., learn all principles relevant to the proposition "if employee-work situation X,Y exists then managerial behavior A is effective").

P_{2b1} Identify all relevant employee characteristics in 15 novel presentations.

P_{2b2} Identify all relevant work situation characteristics in 15 novel presentations.

P_{2c1} Discriminate relevant employee characteristics from other stimuli.

P_{2c2} Discriminate relevant work situation characteristics from other stimuli.

P_{2d1} Associate the name of all employee characteristics with the description of the characteristics.

P_{2d2} Associate the name of all work situation types with the description of the characteristics of the type.

Figure 4.1   Objectives in a management development training program.

developing the prerequisites for P_1. The example in Figure 4.1 only identifies prerequisites in the motor and intellectual skill domains. The other domains must likewise be searched for prerequisites to the overall training objective.

Taking into Account Prior Learning

Besides identifying the prerequisites to the training objectives, the trainer should also determine what prior learning will act to support or hinder the new learning. For example, the manager-trainee's attitude about supervisor-subordinate interactions may act to make the new learning easier or harder. A manager who has a negative attitude toward his or her subordinates will have a harder time learning the new material than a manager who has a positive attitude toward them. This is because many of the employee-work situation combinations will require the manager to behave in a supportive or participative way with the subordinates. For the manager with negative attitudes toward subordinates, this behavior is contrary to existing attitudes. While the manager can still learn to identify and perform the appropriate behavioral style, he or she must develop a rationalization for why he or she is behaving in a manner contrary to his or her attitudes. This cognitive rationalization may take the form of denial, a change in beliefs, or several other forms of justifying the behavior. The point is that this cognitive activity takes time and energy which will detract from the time and energy that can be spent on learning. In planning the phases of a training program, the trainer needs to estimate how long training is going to take and what methods should be used to achieve the desired results. To do so, the trainer needs to consider the degree to which various factors in the five learning domains, which are not prerequisites, may act to inhibit or support the desired learning.

Individual Differences

As pointed out earlier, performance is a function of ability, motivation, and opportunity. This set of relationships is also applicable to learning. In order for learning to occur, the trainee must be motivated, be provided with an opportunity, and must have the ability to learn. Training will provide the opportunity, if planned appropriately. Thus, the degree to which the trainee is motivated to learn and the ability of the trainee to learn *with the methods available in training* can be considered to be measures of the trainability of the trainee.

After examining the training population, the trainer may discover that some of the potential trainees differ from others in terms of their skills, knowledge, and aptitudes. An *aptitude* can be thought of as any characteristic of the trainee that is related to his or her ability to learn. Cronbach and Snow (1977) suggested that, because of individual differences in backgrounds and heredity, differences also are likely to exist in the mechanisms individuals use for learning. Thus, some individuals may respond very favorably to a particular set of instructional materials and experiences while others are unable to learn much from them. The situation could theoretically be reversed if the trainer had chosen a different set of instructional materials and presentations. Figures 4.2 and 4.3 illustrate different types of *aptitude-treatment relationships*. In Figure 4.2, Treatment 1 has different effects for individuals with different aptitudes. The higher the aptitude, the higher the learning outcomes. However, Treatment 2 also has this relationship with the aptitude. Treatment 1 produces higher learning outcomes at every level of aptitude than does Treatment 2. A trainer who observed these aptitude-treatment relationships would correctly conclude that Treatment 1 (a particular training program) should be given to all the trainees. The implications of Figure 4.3 point to a different strategy. In this case, Treatment 1 again produces higher outcomes for individuals who have more of the aptitude. However, Treatment 2 produces higher learning outcomes for trainees who were lower on the aptitude. The implications here are that trainees who are high in this aptitude area should be trained with Treatment 1 while those who are lower in the aptitude should receive training with Treatment 2.

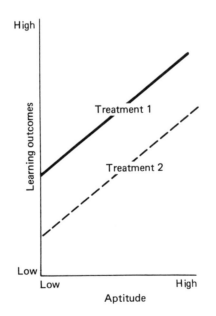

Figure 4.2   No aptitude treatment interaction effects.

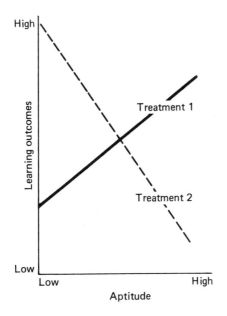

Figure 4.3 Aptitude treatment interaction effects.

In a review of the training literature, Goldstein (1980) found that aptitude-treatment interaction (ATI) effects typically have not been generalizable nor replicable. The aptitudes that most clearly seem to result in ATI effects are those dependent upon the trainees' prior learning. "Thus," "treatments work best for persons who have already experienced that particular type of instructional technique" (Goldstein, 1980, p. 149). Some relatively recent research seems to confirm this conclusion and provides some rather interesting aptitudes to examine in the trainee population.

D. Robey and W. Taggart (1981) suggested that human information processing can be dominated by either the left or the right hemisphere of the brain. The degree of hemispherical domination results in a differentiation in decision-making styles. These authors suggest that the typical left-hemisphere-dominant analytic style of information processing is only one of many possible styles, but is the one most instructional programs use. Measurement of information processing style can be conducted by physiological means (electroencephalograms), psychological tests (e.g., independent judges, Huysmans, 1970a, 1970b; the Embedded Figures Test, Witkin, et al., 1971) or self-description inventories (e.g., the Vasarhelyi Questionnaire, 1977; the Myer-Briggs Type Indicator, Myers, 1962). Certainly this could be an area in which the trainer might find that the trainee's characteristics (i.e., information processing style) interact with the method of training.

David Kolb (1981) proposed that learning is a four-stage process consisting of concrete experience, reflective observation, abstract conceptualization, and active experimentation. He suggests that people differ in their emphasis in using each stage. According to this perspective, people can be categorized along two bipolar dimensions of learning styles: active-to-reflective orientations and concrete-to-abstract orientations. Kolb speculated that the person characterized as an *abstract-reflective learner* is able to deal more effectively with theoretical models, inductive reasoning, and integration of disparate observations. *Concrete-active learners*, on the other hand, are predicted to have the opposite characteristics. This model has attracted a fair amount of supportive literature (Kirby, 1979), but requires considerably more before it can be regarded as sufficiently tested. Of particular interest for the purposes of this chapter is the fact that Kolb has developed an instrument for measuring *learning style* (Learning Style Inventory, Kolb, 1979, 1976). If his theoretical approach and measurement instrument receive enough empirical support, specific training programs can be developed to match the learning styles of the trainees.

While the speculations of Robey and Taggart and Kolb remain just that, speculatory, individual differences in trainees are still important in the development of training programs. Goldstein (1980) pointed out that many training programs have been able to validate trainability tests that predict the success of potential trainees in the training program. These approaches typically use a measure of learning performance on a sample of tasks relevant to the training program. The use of appropriate selection tests for determining who should and who should not enter the training program can substantially reduce the cost of training programs (Ross, 1974). In a training program in electronic switching systems, Reilly and Manese (1979) reported a cost of $25,000 per trainee over the six month course. A careful selection of trainees for this program could result in a substantial saving to the organization. Of course, the value (or utility) of a trainee selection procedure will depend upon the cost of training, the cost of developing and implementing the selection procedure, and the value of the training to the organization. One must be careful not to confuse the issues of selecting trainees who will be most likely to perform well in the training program and designing the training program to be maximally effective for the trainees who enter it. One can carefully select trainees so that each one will be likely to complete the program successfully. However, if the program is not related to the organization's needs, the program is a failure. What is needed is a careful mix of developing a program that meets the organization's needs and is designed around the capabilities of the trainees. The development of training and learning objectives, combined with a consideration of the supportive prior learning, will go a long way toward keeping the training focused on the organization's objectives. Utilization of learning methods and techniques that are compatible with the characteristics of the training population will help to maximize the learning experience for the trainees and to reduce the costly training failures.

FACILITATING THE LEARNING PROCESS

The social learning model presented in the last chapter is reproduced here as Figure 4.4. This model will be used as the point of origin for exploring instructional processes. The motivational component influences all the other cognitive components of the model and needs to be discussed in its own right and then in conjunction with the attention, retention, and behavioral reproduction processes.

Motivation

The expectancy model of motivation indicates that (1) the expectancy that effort will lead to performance and (2) the instrumentality of that performance for acquiring desired outcomes and avoiding undesirable ones will determine whether the effort is expended. The implications for training are that the potential trainee must believe that he or she can achieve the training objectives and that these objectives will result in outcomes that are, in the end, more desirable than the outcomes that would result from not achieving

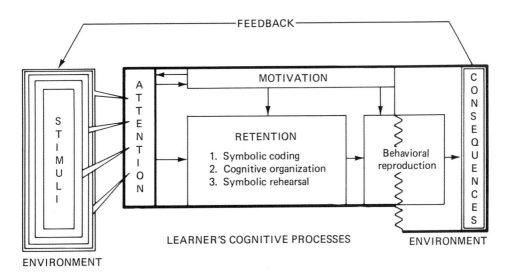

Figure 4.4   Graphic representation of the social learning processes.

the training objectives. While an employee may comply with an order to attend training, the learning that he or she achieves will depend only upon the effort to performance expectancies and the performance to outcome instrumentalities he or she perceives to exist. To insure positive instrumentalities and expectancies, the trainee should arrive at the training site having completed the following activities:

1. The trainee and his or her supervisor have discussed the trainee's job performance and job-related goals and have mutually agreed that the trainee needs to improve some set of skills/abilities in order to achieve those goals.
2. The trainee and supervisor have agreed that this particular training program is the best alternative available for achieving the desired skill/ability improvement.
3. The trainee and supervisor have agreed that demonstrated improvement in the identified skill/ability areas will result in desirable outcomes for the trainee.

In organizations with more sophisticated human resource management systems, this is usually accomplished through a training and career development performance review. This review, in its purest form, is based on the individual's regular performance review and any additional information from the training needs analysis that may be relevant. In less sophisticated organizations, however, the trainee arrives with only a part of the package at best. In these instances, even trainees who are performing below standards on their current job may not recognize that a change in their knowledge/skill repertoire is needed. Resistance to training, manifested in terms of absenteeism, lack of attention, and "goofing off" can be expected in these circumstances. The trainer can help to minimize this potential resistance by preparing the supervisor and the trainee for the training experience. Training must be perceived by both the trainee and the supervisor as leading to desirable outcomes. Since the trainee's supervisor may be the primary source of reinforcement and punishment during a normal work day, the trainer must make sure that the supervisor is supportive of training. If this is not the case, the supervisor may convey to the trainee that training is not likely to result in any positive outcomes back on the job. From expectancy theory we know that the positive value of performance outcomes must outweigh the negative or the desired behavior is not likely to occur. The trainee's supervisor can play a key role by indicating to the trainee ways in which training can result in positive consequences.

Gaining the Support of the Supervisor

The trainer can improve the likelihood of gaining the supervisor's cooperation by consulting with him or her before setting the times and dates of training activities. The trainer should take care to indicate what advantages the supervisor might expect as a result of his or her subordinates attending the training program. The supervisor will probably indicate to the trainer what the disadvantages are. These are nearly always stated in terms of lost work hours. The supervisor is responsible for seeing that certain things are accomplished in his or her domain of responsibility. If the supervisor's workforce goes to training, then the immediate tasks that need to be accomplished don't get done. This is one reason why the trainer needs to conduct a cost-benefit analysis of the training. The trainer needs to be able to answer the question, "Will the long-term improvements that result from training outweigh the short-term costs of conducting the training?" Methods for conducting such an analysis are presented in the following chapter. For now, it is important to consider several ways in which the costs can be reduced.

Determining when the peak workloads occur and avoiding those as dates for training is one way to reduce costs. For example, you wouldn't want to schedule training in the accounting area during the months of December to March since the time between the end of the tax year and the deadline for filing is typically very busy for this group of employees. The trainer should consider not only the time of the year, but also the time of the week and day. The trainer must also weigh the departmental advantages and disadvantages of training only part of the staff at a time over a longer period of time or training them all at once in a shorter time frame. The trainer in this activity is acting as a change consultant for the department. The supervisor should be given valid and useful information upon which to evaluate the various alternatives. The trainer should act as a resource person to assist the supervisor in making decisions about how best to provide the needed training to his or her staff. In this manner, the supervisor is making a free and informed choice and will be more likely to become committed to the training program.

Gaining the Support of the Trainee

While the importance of gaining the support of the trainee's supervisors shouldn't be underestimated, the focal point of training is on the trainees themselves. Although the trainer has, at this point, determined the organizational desirability of training and has garnered the support of the supervisory staff, the trainees have yet to be included in the commitment process. In order for training to be effective, the trainees must be motivated to attend training and participate in the learning process. That is, they must feel that their efforts will result not only in organizationally desired outcomes but also in personally desirable consequences.

In expectancy theory terms, the trainer needs to increase the effort to performance expectancy and the performance to outcome instrumentality.

The trainer must rely to some extent on the supervisor to accomplish the latter. However, the trainer can also point to the intrinsic outcomes associated with task mastery and intellectual growth. It is important to describe both intrinsic and extrinsic outcomes associated with the successful completion of training.

The ideal preparation for training would have the supervisor and potential trainee sitting down to discuss the employee's goals as well as his or her performance over the last review period. They would come to an agreement about what behavior needed to be acquired in order to achieve both the organization's and the employee's goals. The supervisor and employee must come to agree that the training program will ultimately result in outcomes that aren't currently available but are desired by both and that this training is the best alternative for achieving them. While the supervisor is important, this process is essentially a self-diagnosis by the employee (Kirby, 1980). This process will increase the trainee's motivation to pursue the training and to utilize the training back on the job. However, we also need to consider motivational factors that are applicable during training.

Attention

As indicated in the social learning model in Figure 4.4, motivation influences attention. People attend to the things in the environment that are the most important to them at the time. A trainer should try to structure the learning environment in such a way that the most important things are the materials for learning. One way to accomplish this is to remove motivational factors from the environment that act to distract attention from these materials. While the details for the design of a learning environment will depend upon the nature of the learning technique that is adopted, there are some general rules that apply to all learning environments. These rules, in general, are ways in which to keep the trainee's other need states (i.e., hunger, thirst, stimulation) from interfering with her or his learning activities.

The room in which learning takes place should be one in which the trainee is comfortable. The walls should be a neutral but pleasant color. They should be free of distracting objects such as posters, notices, and the like. Ideally, the room would be soundproofed and without windows. The room should also be removed from the workplace so the trainees can concentrate on the training. This means that the trainees are not subjected to interruptions by their boss, subordinates, or others to "just take a few minutes to look this over." The trainer is trying to create both a physical and psychological distance between the trainee and the everyday distractions of the workplace. This allows the trainee to concentrate on the learning without becoming distracted by what's going on back at the workplace.

The Xerox Corporation felt so strongly about creating the right kind of environment for learning that it built a center for training and development that took two and a half years and $70 million to complete. The center is a completely self-contained educational community that provides room and board, health care and recreation, as well as education for up to one thousand trainees (Xerox International, 1977). The idea behind the Xerox Center is to provide a place where Xerox employees can develop themselves to their highest potential. In order to do this effectively, they felt the need to develop a facility that would allow those employees the freedom from distraction necessary for effective learning.

Even training programs much less extensive than Xerox's can provide good learning environments by observing the following principles.

1. Do as much as possible to ensure that outside noise will not interrupt training. The interior of the room should be dead. By this we mean that the acoustics should be such that sound doesn't echo. Check interior machinery for excess noise.
2. Avoid visual distractors such as windows without blinds or curtains, busy wallpaper, or wall hangings that attract attention.
3. Make sure that the temperature in the room is independently controlled. Most adults seem to be comfortable at around 73° to 74° F and with the humidity level around 50 percent. Air movement at about 12 to 15 feet per minute with appropriate ventilation is desirable, particularly if people are smoking (McVey, 1971).
4. Use a dual lighting system or rheostatic controls so that lights can be dimmed but not eliminated during video or film presentations. Make sure that lighting is not so bright as to cause glare.
5. The seating should be such that the trainees will not become uncomfortable over a two-hour sitting period. At the same time, seating should not be designed for sleep. A comfortable, flexible, cloth covered chair with a place for resting arms and writing either attached or easily available (e.g., a table) should be chosen.
6. The scheduling of activities should be done with the following thought in mind, "The brain can absorb only as much as the seat can endure." Michalak and Yager (1979) suggested the following daily schedule:

   • Morning opening to break—short, light, easy, motivating learning. (Make sure water, coffee and tea are available.)
   • Break to lunch—heavy learning and input.
   • After lunch to break—short, heavy, and concentrated learning.
   • Break to close—participative and active learning (avoiding lectures, films, or readings).

These authors suggested that the lunch be kept light and avoid carbohydrates as they tend to make people drowsy after eating. Avoid alcohol until after the close of the day's training.

While the preceding discussion has indicated ways in which the learning environment can be controlled to reduce the number of distracting stimuli, the trainer must also attract the learner's attention to the learning events. As we have suggested, this actually begins before training takes place. Communications should be directed to the trainee that describe the nature of training and its intended on-the-job benefits. This may be accomplished by simply providing a detailed outline of the training objective(s) and the prerequisite learning objectives. Once the trainees arrive at the training site, these objectives should be clearly restated at the outset and again at strategic points throughout the training program. This helps to keep the focus of the training activities on the desired goals and helps the trainees focus attention on the training activities.

It is not enough for the trainer simply to state the training objectives and the prerequisite learning objectives, and to restate them periodically. The trainer must also make sure that the trainees have accepted those objectives. One way this can be accomplished is to have the trainees describe the ways in which accomplishment of the objectives will lead to the resolution of problems they face on the job. If the trainees can see how the objectives relate to their jobs and their job-related goals, it will not only increase their attention to the learning activities, but also will improve the degree to which the training will transfer back to the job.

Finally, the trainer must make sure the trainees feel that the objectives are obtainable. The objectives should be conveyed in a manner that suggests that they are challenging but achievable. The trainer should emphasize that the overall training objective is just the final step in a series of obtainable steps. Research on goal setting (Latham & Locke, 1979; Latham & Yukl, 1975; Locke, et al., 1981) suggests that following these procedures will result in increased trainee performance. In expectancy theory terminology, the above activities performed by the trainer will increase the expectancy that effort will lead to the desired performance outcomes and that these performance outcomes will lead to consequences that are desirable to the trainee. This cognitive linkage will result in increased attention to the learning activities.

On a more microscopic level, the trainee's attention needs to be focused on the critical aspects of each step of the learning experiences he or she goes through. Because the human perceptual mechanisms selectively filter information to be processed and permanently stored in memory (Lindsay & Norman, 1972; Klatzky, 1975), techniques for highlighting the important or critical learning points should be planned into the learning activities the trainees experience. Although the method of highlighting will vary with the training technique adopted (e.g., lecture, case study, etc.), the trainer must identify the key points to be emphasized. Ways to do this are discussed in the chapters covering the training techniques.

Retention

Once information has been attended to and selectively processed for retention, it is transformed from perceptual stimuli into a conceptual mode (Melton & Martin, 1972; Anderson & Bower, 1972; Bandura, 1977). Information seems to be stored as meaningful verbal codes similar to sentences or propositions. These codes are stored in long-term memory where they are called up when the appropriate cues indicate they are needed. The transformation process is called *encoding*. Gagné (1977) suggested that encoding can be facilitated by two processes. The first consists of stimulating the recall of the relevant prerequisites and supportive prior learning. The second process involved is the presentation or suggestion of an encoding scheme.

The management development training program we have been using as an example can help to illustrate these processes. Assume the trainer is attempting to facilitate the learning of the P_{2b1} prerequisite learning objective in Figure 4.1. (Identify all relevant employee characteristics in 15 novel presentations.) The trainer can stimulate recall of the prerequisites by saying something like, "You remember the names of the relevant employee characteristics and what things differentiate them from irrelevant characteristics." If the trainees all have some management experience, the trainer may call on this supportive material by suggesting, "Think back to the employees you've dealt with in the past. What were their relevant characteristics and how could you determine what was relevant and what wasn't?" The trainer may suggest schemes for encoding by using the technique of *guided discovery*. Guided discovery most often takes the form of statements followed by questions from the trainer. The statement is designed to stimulate retrieval of information from long-term memory. The questions ask the trainee to discover the appropriate rule from the cues provided in the question and preceding statement. In our example, the trainer may present a video tape of an employee in a discussion with his supervisor. Following the tape, the trainer might say, "Remember, certain employee characteristics are more closely related to how the employee approaches the work situation than others. What were the relevant characteristics you observed in the employee on the tape?" The questions the trainer asks shouldn't contain all the information needed to answer the question, but should suggest a strategy for discovering the answer.

Encoding can also be enhanced through the use of images. Anderson & Bower (1973), among others, have favored a dual-process model of retention. They suggest that visual images as well as verbal propositions are encoded and that these separate processes act to support the retention of each other, even though they are processed through different cognitive channels. The implication of this model is that figures, graphs, pictures, and other visual images can be used in training to provide concrete images supporting the verbal propositions that are to be retained. The organization of the material to be learned into the appropriate visual images will also provide important cues for retrieval of the information at a later date.

The principle of overlearning was discussed in the preceding chapter and will be discussed in more detail later in this chapter. Overlearning will also improve the retention of the material to be learned. The utilization of this procedure has several advantages. It reduces the likelihood of forgetting the material while at the same time increasing the number of cues that will stimulate recall. The increased number of cues will, in turn, aid in the transfer of the learning from the training site to the job situation.

ARRANGEMENT OF TRAINING ACTIVITIES

In designing a training program, every trainer is ultimately faced with the questions, "How much can the trainees realistically be expected to learn in one setting?" and "What is the best way to sequence learning units?" The answer of course is, "It depends."

The ordering of training activities can influence the degree to which trainees are able to retain the material. The total amount of practice, the manner in which the practice is distributed over time, the kind of practice, and the amount of material to be learned in one setting are major factors that will impact on retention.

The Amount to be Learned

If the learning task can't be logically divided into subtasks, the trainer has no choice but to present it as a whole. If it can be divided, then the trainer must decide whether to present it as separate parts or to present it as a whole. Wexley & Latham (1981) indicated that three basic strategies can be placed on a continuum from which all of the possible division strategies can be derived. The chart below illustrates the continuum of strategies for a learning task that can be divided into three distinct parts: A, B, and C.

Phase 1	A,B,C	A	A
Phase 2	A,B,C	A,B	B
Phase 3	A,B,C	A,B,C	C
Phase 4	A,B,C	A,B,C	A,B,C
	Pure whole training	Progressive-part training	Pure part training

At one end of the continuum is pure whole training in which all of the parts are presented in each of the learning units. At the other end is the pure part training strategy in which each part is taught in a separate learning unit and they are all brought together in the final learning unit. In the middle of this continuum is a strategy called *progressive-part training*. This strategy has the first part presented alone in the first learning unit. The next unit presents the first part again and introduces the second part. This progression continues until all parts are included.

Which of the above strategies is best will depend on the characteristics of the learning task, the trainees, and the type and amount of practice available in training. The more *complex* the learning task, the more effective a *part strategy* becomes (Naylor & Briggs, 1963). The more *interrelated* the parts of the learning task are to each other, the more effective a *whole strategy* becomes (Wexley & Latham, 1981). Use of the whole method becomes more advantageous when the intelligence of the trainee is high, as more practice opportunities are available, and when practice is distributed over time rather than massed (Bass & Vaughn, 1966). In most situations, some form of modified part training will be best.

The development of prerequisite learning objectives based on the learning hierarchy would predispose most learning tasks (other than the most simplistic or trivial) to a logical division into parts. We have suggested that it is important to make sure that learning has been mastered at each step before moving to the next level in the hierarchy and that the lower levels of learning are involved when mastering the higher levels. Thus, we would seem to be oriented toward the progressive-part training strategy. However, this really depends on the nature of the overall training objective. The objective may encompass several learning objectives that are so interrelated that they cannot be effectively separated. For instance, in our management training example, it would be very difficult to separate learning the names of the employee characteristics from learning the description of the characteristics for the prerequisite learning objective P_{2d1}.

Amount and Type of Practice

Next to developing the content of the training, planning for active practice of the learning tasks may be the most important thing a trainer does in the development of the training program. Since Ebbinghaus first developed the concept of overlearning at the turn of the century, it has become a firmly established principle of retention. This technique requires the trainee to first master the learning task and then to continue to practice it. In the early stages of learning, the trainee must be guided in *active practice*. By active practice, we mean that the trainee is actively doing something with the learning material; using it in some way, not just verbalizing what has been learned. *Guided practice* refers to the techniques utilized by the trainer to facilitate the encoding process (i.e., giving directions and suggestions, questioning, etc.) and the process of giving feedback. As the trainee becomes more proficient at the task, the trainer should decrease the amount of guidance and maintain the feedback. The feedback component is important and will be discussed in more detail shortly. For now, it is important to recognize that practice without feedback is most likely to be detrimental to learning and retention.

After the trainee has mastered the learning task, additional practice will result in overlearning and, thus, better retention. How much additional practice? That is difficult to say. Obviously, the more practice the better the retention. However, overlearning is subject to the law of diminishing returns. The first hour of overlearning will have more of an impact on retention than the last hour in a series of ten overlearning practice sessions. Since the amount of impact overlearning will have upon retention depends on the nature of the learning task, no hard and fast rule exists as to "how much is enough." The trainer will have to weigh the benefits of increased retention against the cost of additional training time.

Assuming the trainer has included a specific amount of time for practice in the development of a training program, how should that time be divided over the course of the training? Should it be distributed equally over the sessions or should it be massed at the end? In general, the research has shown that when a certain amount of practice time is distributed across time, with rest periods between, retention is better for motor skills than when that same amount of practice time is massed at the end of the training. The research on practice with factual, complex, and verbal material indicates that there may be an advantage in adopting a mixed strategy (Bilodeau & Bilodeau, 1961). The general results of experimental studies show that greater retention will result from distributed practice when the learning task is more complex, difficult, or extensive. The more capable and experienced the trainee, the more likely that massed practice can be utilized effectively. It is important to remember, however, that the amount of time between practice sessions will play a role in the effectiveness of distributed practice. If the interval is too long, the trainee may forget what was learned in the prior session. Thus, in the early stages of learning in particular, the interval between practice sessions should be short. Toward the end of training, these sessions can be more widely spaced.

While the advantages of distributed practice usually outweigh the disadvantages from a retention perspective, it does result in a longer training time until the trainees are up to the established standards. Wexley & Latham (1981) suggested that organizations become more creative in the ways in which they find for their trainees to practice. They report that a supermarket chain used the distributed practice strategy effectively by having their clerks work six hours a day on their regular cash registers and two hours a day on the new computerized cash registers they were being trained to operate. This is indeed a creative way for the organization to achieve the positive effects of distributed practice without the cost of additional "non-productive" training time. We would offer a cautionary note, however, as this particular procedure runs the risk of creating negative side effects which in the end may more than wipe out the advantages that were gained (e.g., negative transfer of training, interference with the learning process, lack of appropriate feedback and guidance, etc., are potential problems).

Transfer of Training

The material that is learned in training can result in several potential outcomes back on the job. The training could have no effect on job behavior (called *zero transfer*), a negative effect (*negative transfer*), or a positive effect (*positive transfer*). Zero transfer occurs when the material in training cannot be related to the cues that exist in the job environment. Negative transfer occurs when the material learned in training results in a decrease in job performance. This can occur when the material learned in training interferes with previously learned job behaviors that were acceptable. For instance, the managers in our hypothetical training program might go back to their jobs and spend all their time diagnosing the subordinate work situation and ignore their other management responsibilities. Thus, trainers need to make sure that the content and process of training doesn't interfere with parts of the trainee's job that are being performed satisfactorily. This can be accomplished, in part, by creating training programs that facilitate the positive transfer of training back to the job.

Principles for optimizing positive transfer are derived from two classical approaches to transfer of learning problems (Bass & Vaughn, 1966; Leifer & Newstrom, 1980). One approach is called the *identical elements* approach and the other, *transfer through principles*. The first approach stipulates that identical elements in the training and job situations must exist in order for positive transfer to occur. Thus, the more similar the training environment is to the job environment, the greater the positive transfer of training. The transfer through principles approach proposes that positive transfer occurs through cues that stimulate the recall of general principles or guidelines for behavior. Thus, once the principles are learned, the job problems related to those principles can be solved. However, it is implicit in this approach that the degree of similarity between the cues that stimulate recall in the job situation and those presented in the training situation will influence the likelihood of positive transfer. Utilization of the transfer through principles approach requires the trainee to learn not only the principles, but also the class of cues that signal its usage. The identical elements approach is most useful when dealing with motor or technical skills training, since most of the important elements required for learning (e.g., machine operation) are also present in the job situation (e.g., the machine). One must be careful here to examine the job requirements for stimulus situations that are highly similar but that require different responses. A good example of this is the person who learns to drive a car with a standard transmission and then finds himself driving an automatic and stomping a nonexistent clutch.

Under the reverse circumstances, the driver who is used to driving an automatic finds himself stalling the engine at every stop sign when driving the stick shift.

The principles approach to transfer is most effective with conceptual or administrative skills that are less objectively circumscribed (our management development program, for example). However, the trainer must build into the training program opportunities for the trainee to learn the cues in the job situation that signal when the principles should be applied. Leifer and Newstrom (1980) discussed a training program in which many of their participants reported that the examples used in training were not appropriate for their work situation. By rejecting the examples, the participants may have also rejected the utility or applicability of the principles.

Behavioral Reproduction and Feedback

The issues surrounding the practice of material being learned are related to both the retention and behavioral reproduction processes. Some authors in the training literature (e.g., Wexley & Latham, 1981, p. 61) have suggested that practice without evaluative feedback retards learning. While this is probably true for many if not most learning tasks, recent research by Decker (1982) suggested that repeated mental visualization of the learning task improves performance in the absence of any feedback. However, this type of practice is likely to be profitable only with tasks that are already well learned. For example, the novice golfer who practices his or her swing without an expert to observe and provide feedback will most likely reinforce the old bad habits or substitute new ones in their place. For most training situations, feedback is a vital component of the training program, both in the training environment and back on the job.

Figure 4.5 presents a model of the feedback process. The illustration indicates that three major factors influence the effects of feedback on performance: the source of the feedback, the characteristics of the feedback itself, and the characteristics of the feedback recipient. This parallels general communication models identifying the source, message, and receiver as major variables in the communication process. The model indicates that the feedback message must impact on three major cognitive processes before it can have a positive effect on learning and practice. The first process is the perception of the feedback. This refers to the accuracy with which the recipient perceives the feedback. Acceptance, the second process, is the degree to which the recipient believes the feedback to be an accurate reflection of his or her performance. The final process, motivation, refers to the recipient's willingness to utilize the feedback in performing the task in the future. What does the existing research tell us about the effects of the source, message and receiver characteristics on each of the above processes? Ilgen, Fisher and Taylor (1979) conducted an extensive review of this literature and the following paragraphs reflect their findings and conclusions.

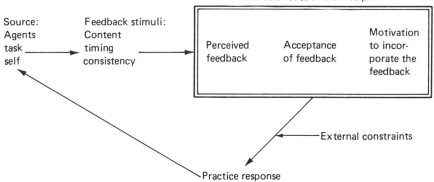

Figure 4.5   Model of the feedback process.

Recipients' Perception of Feedback

People generally rely on those who are psychologically closest to them for feedback. Thus, they most frequently rely on themselves, then the results of their activities (i.e., their task outcomes) followed in order by their supervisors, coworkers, and finally others outside the work group. Both the credibility and the power of the source will influence the above ordering. Generally, we believe ourselves to be more credible evaluators of our own performance than others. This can often lead us into difficulties, as when programming a computer. Many novice programmers are sure the machine has made a mistake when they receive their printed feedback that the program is in error. However, with time these programmers learn that the machine is a more credible detector of errors than they are.

In the training environment it is possible for feedback to come from any of the sources listed above. While developing the design of the training program, determine what sources of feedback are likely to be the most credible to the trainees. If the trainer is limited to one source (as with computer-assisted instruction), some time should be devoted to establishing the credibility of that source. In addition to the source, characteristics of the message are also important. It has long been believed that the longer the delay between performance and feedback, the less effect the feedback will have. While this is true for the most part, it is not entirely a correct generalization. Negative feedback has been found to have more positive effects when it is delayed some time after performance has occurred. Also, there is no loss in the effectiveness of positive feedback when it is delayed, provided that the trainee still remembers the performance toward which the feedback is directed.

Probably more important than the timing of the feedback is its positive or negative sign. Positive feedback is generally remembered more accurately than is negative, though this depends upon the characteristics of the recipient and the timing of the feedback.

In general, the more frequently feedback is given the more accurately recipients can recall the message. However, this generalization should be used with caution. When the task and/or the feedback is somewhat ambiguous, feedback should be provided less often so that the recipient can observe the pattern of the responses and the associated feedback.

Some individuals will respond better to certain kinds of feedback than others. For example, recipients who have an internal locus of control (i.e., believe they control events around them) do better with feedback from the task itself. Those with an external locus of control (i.e., believe they have little control over events) show better effects from feedback provided by the person in authority. Self-esteem is another recipient characteristic that influences the effects of feedback. Trainees who are high in self-esteem rely more on their own feedback and are less likely to model the trainer. They are also more likely to respond to positive feedback and less likely to respond to negative feedback than trainees with low self-esteem.

Recipient Acceptance of Feedback

The credibility of the source of feedback plays a major role in the willingness of the recipient to accept the feedback as an accurate reflection of performance. This credibility derives from the recipient's trust of the source or from the recipient's perception of the source's expertise, reliability, and/or intentions toward the recipient. Trainers are often asked to conduct training programs in areas where their perceived expertise is low. Take, for example, the trainer who is conducting a performance appraisal seminar for middle-level managers. The trainer may have a great deal of knowledge about the performance appraisal process but little or no actual experience conducting performance appraisals for lower-level managers. The trainer in this case must build his or her credibility in the areas of trust, reliability, and honorable intentions. This potential problem should be addressed in the planning and design stage of training rather than trying to ad lib it during the course of training. In this case, the trainer might develop his or her role as that of a facilitator (where expertise would be high) and utilize the trainees to provide feedback to each other (e.g., using the case study approach).

As with perception of the feedback, the sign of the feedback is important for its acceptance. People are much more willing to believe messages that say their performance was good rather than bad. This does not mean that negative feedback is not accepted at all. Rather, it means that negative feedback is not accepted as easily as positive and it has less of an effect on subsequent performance. Thus, whenever possible the trainer should attempt to phrase feedback in a positive manner. When this is not possible, the trainer should certainly use negative feedback rather than no feedback at all.

The characteristics of the recipient that are most likely to have an impact on acceptance of the feedback are his or her locus of control and age or experience. Recipients with an external locus of control (i.e., believe their behavior to be determined primarily by their environment) are less likely to accept feedback in general. This may be due to a feeling that they lack control over their behavior. This can be partially overcome by consistency and specificity in the feedback given to these individuals.

Younger workers have been found to be more likely to accept feedback than older workers. However, since age is correlated positively with experience, it is unclear whether it is experience or age that is the causal factor. Whichever is the case, the wise trainer will take special care with older, more experienced trainees to provide specific examples and documentation in their feedback and otherwise establish his or her credibility with the trainees.

Motivation to Make Use of the Feedback

Research evidence concerning the relationship between characteristics of the source of feedback and recipient motivation to use the feedback is extremely limited and no established generalizations can be formed. However, Ilgen et al. (1979) developed a logical argument for predicting that the power of the source will be more important than the source's credibility. This could result from the reinforcing and incentive properties of feedback.

Many writers have postulated that feedback per se is reinforcing (e.g., Annette, 1969; Hundel, 1969; Anderson et al., 1971). The rationale for this position begins with an assumption that feedback acquires secondary reinforcing properties through pairing with primary reinforcers over time. Then, applying Thorndike's "law of effect" (discussed in Chapter 3), the more frequently feedback is given for correct responses, the more frequently correct responses should occur.

While evidence exists supporting the above position (Anderson et al., 1971; Cook, 1968; Hundel, 1969; Ivancevich et al., 1970), this research has not examined the specificity or sign of the feedback. In some instances, the evaluative nature of the feedback is left up to the recipient to determine (e.g., Cook, 1968). It is probably the case that most feedback is positive. Thus, it is probably true that positive feedback acts as a reinforcer of the response. However, Wadc (1974) found that running totals of correct and incorrect responses improved performance, but over time performance dropped off more with only positive feedback.

The contention that feedback per se acts as a reinforcer is also challenged by studies that show that nonspecific positive feedback and indifference toward performance by the source person (Chapanis, 1964; French et al., 1966) produces little if any effect on performance. Nevertheless, feedback can be a form of reinforcement when it is applied appropriately. Appropriate positive feedback acts to increase the likelihood of the behavior that precedes it. Negative feedback acts as a negative reinforcer when it includes cues or directions as to the appropriate behavior. When the trainer uses both negative and positive feedback with trainees, the appropriate behavior receives twice the reinforcement that it would if only one or the other was used. When the trainee performs the behavior correctly, he or she not only receives the positive feedback, but also avoids the negative feedback. Negative feedback that does not include cues or directions for the appropriate behavior (e.g., "No, that's wrong" or "Try again, that won't do") is closer to punishment and should be avoided. Good programmed instruction and computer-assisted instruction programs have this reinforcing type of feedback built into them.

In addition to serving as a reinforcer, feedback's informational content may act to establish and maintain beliefs about the performance-reward contingencies. We know from expectancy theory that the motivational force to expend effort toward a particular performance goal depends on (1) the individual's belief that effort will lead to the performance goal (expectancy) and (2) that the performance goal will lead to a set of outcomes that are more desirable than the outcomes associated with alternative performance goals (instrumentality). If the feedback specifies how closely the trainee's performance is to the desired performance and contains information about what can be done to reach the performance goal, then feedback should positively influence expectancies. If feedback contains information about the rewards that can be expected as a result of correct performance, then instrumentalities will be positively influenced. Thus, when feedback is specific, contains information about how to improve performance, and links performance to desired outcomes, it will motivate the trainee to utilize the feedback in future responses.

The research evidence indicates that *intrinsically oriented individuals* (e.g., internals, high self-esteem, high in need for achievement or independence) desire feedback that indicates both competence and control over the task. These individuals have needs that are satisfied by mastery of the task. *Extrinsically oriented employees* (externals, low need for power or high need for affiliation) will prefer feedback that conveys information about extrinsic rewards. While we have already talked about how feedback can convey extrinsic reward information, feedback's role in intrinsic motivation needs to be discussed.

It was suggested earlier (with the appropriate caveats) that the more frequent the feedback, the more positive the effects on performance. Yet, if one is to experience a sense of control over, or mastery of, a task, then one must engage in the task without a great deal of assistance or interference from outside agents. Frequent feedback is likely to be perceived by intrinsically oriented trainees as a loss of control over the task and a removal of the rewards they desire. On the other hand, feedback is usually necessary in order to develop a sense of competence. Cues (feedback) from the task itself and from others often provide information about how well the trainee is performing even when not planned into the task. Fisher (1978) indicated that both personal control and competence are necessary for intrinsic motivation. These apparently contradictory (with regard to feedback) states can co-exist when feedback is primarily positive (increasing feelings of competence), provides information needed to improve performance (but not redundant), and derives from the task itself as much as possible (increasing feelings of personal control). If it is not possible to design feedback into the task, the trainer should take care to design it so that the recipient feels that he or she is controlling the task, not the trainer or the feedback source.

Feedback is a vital part of the training process and should be planned and developed as thoroughly as the presentation of the content of training. To do this, the trainer must attend to the perception, acceptance, and motivational components of the feedback process and how source, message, and recipient characteristics act to enhance or detract from the goals of feedback.

The final stage of the HRD design process is the development of the program evaluation. Since the next chapter covers this topic in depth, little discussion is needed here. However, the point to be made is that evaluation begins in the planning and design stage, not as an afterthought. Waiting until training has begun (or worse, ended) to begin thinking about evaluation makes a difficult task impossible.

SUMMARY

In this chapter, we have tried to present the components involved in developing an ideal training program. Those components are:

1. Development of the training and prerequisite learning objectives from the needs analysis.
2. Development of the instructional procedures for impact on:
   a. Motivation.
   b. Attention.
   c. Retention.
   d. Behavioral reproduction.

In discussing these components, we examined the concepts of:

1. Individual differences and treatment-aptitude interactions.
2. Supervisor involvement in the training process.
3. Reducing distracting stimuli and increasing attracting stimuli.
4. Encoding processes.

5. Arrangement of training activities.
6. Whole versus part learning.
7. Overlearning.
8. Massed and distributed practice strategies.
9. Transfer of training back to the job situation.
10. Feedback.

Some useful principles that can be derived from the material in this chapter are presented below:

1. Maximize the similarity between the training and job situation. The more similar the cues for recall in these two situations, the greater the transfer of the training to the job situation.
2. Identify and emphasize the important elements of the learning task. This helps the trainee focus attention on these elements and allows the trainee to distinguish this learning from similar learning that could potentially result in negative transfer of training.
3. Provide a wide variety of examples, contexts, and features of the learning in applied, active practice. The more broadly based the learning, (i.e., the more cues that stimulate recall) the more likely that it will transfer to the job situation. By focusing on application, the trainer is reinforcing both the transfer of the training and the utility of the training.
4. Provide as much experience as possible with the learning task. Overlearning increases retention. There is also evidence to indicate that adult learners retain more when learning is experientially based (Kirby, 1980; Saint, 1978) and when appropriate feedback follows the experiences.
5. Feedback to trainees should be designed to facilitate the processes of perception, acceptance, and motivation by taking into consideration source, message, and recipient characteristics.
6. Careful attention to the planning and design phase of the training process will identify potential problems before they become actual problems.

REVIEW QUESTIONS

1. How can positive transfer from the training situation to the job situation be increased?
2. What are the steps in developing learning objectives?
3. When should massed practice and distributed practice be used?
4. When should whole and part learning be used?
5. What are the motivational factors that need to be considered when developing HRD programs?

DESIGNING TRAINING FOR LEARNING: AN INTERVIEW WITH MARCEY ELLEN UDAY

Marcey Uday started her career by learning about human behavior as a teacher and family therapist (MSW) before becoming involved in training and consulting in the business world. She says that her counseling and teaching experiences provided her with the basis for understanding systems and becoming an organizational change agent.

In 1979, after 17 years in human service organizations, she founded Contemporary Learning Systems (CLS) in response to a need to develop a more effective means of helping unemployed workers find meaningful employment. By 1981, a second division of CLS was established. It was dedicated to the delivery of consulting services and training in human resources and organizational development. CLS now has three offices, two in Michigan (Southfield and Kalamazoo) and one in (Columbus) Ohio. There are 18 staff under contract to perform a variety of professional functions. CLS clients include several "Fortune 500" firms as well as smaller businesses and non-profit organizations. Although clients are primarily in Michigan and Ohio, some are in Oklahoma, Kentucky, and other states.

Marcey Uday is known by many for her enthusiastic and dedicated approach to helping organizations and their members address their training and development needs. She has (and still does) live up to her philosophy of work: "If you don't enjoy your work, you're in the wrong job." We chose Marcey to interview for this chapter because of her systematic approach to designing learning experiences.

Question: What steps do you use to design training programs?
Uday: We come to an organization as an outside change agent. That provides us with both an asset and a liability. The asset is that we have to do very little internal selling since the organization has already decided that, in some manner, training is desired. We can devote our effort to designing a quality program and delivering it rather than convincing someone that they need it. The liability is that, because we are from "the outside," we have to be doubly perceptive in ensuring that we clearly understand what the organization thinks they want.

What that means is that we get a call from someone who says, "Yes, I like that idea. We want to do something like that. We have the budget. Give us a program for 2 (or 3 or 5) days." We then go through what we call our seven-step process.

First: We explore what the desired outcomes are with the decision makers who have requested the training. Are they aware of the risks involved in the success of the training? Is the organization prepared to monitor and reinforce efforts made by trainees to make use of the results of the training sessions? What bottom line outcomes does the organization wish to gain from its investment in this particular training effort? Are they being realistic?

Second: We evaluate or re-evaluate the needs of the population to receive the training. Do they need awareness or skill building? How do their perceptions of their needs fit into the organization as we are aware of it from other sources? Can their needs or desires be realistically accomplished through training? Does goal accomplishment mean short-term programs or long-term organizational change?

Third: Any constraints on the project are surfaced and explored. Hidden agendas or preconceived attitudes are exposed, if possible, and dealt with sensitively but appropriately. Real and perceived barriers are brainstormed and plans are identified to overcome them.

Fourth: A curriculum outline is designed with benchmark objectives identified at each step of the program. Each concept to be covered is identified in three ways:

1. How it will be presented didactically.
2. How it will be related to the attendees real world of work.
3. How it will be experienced by the attendees (that is, what games, role plays, etc., could be used to get the points across).

Outcomes are identified for each activity and they establish the basis for the next step.

Fifth: A method of measuring the success of the training is identified based on benchmark and outcome accomplishment. Feedback systems are established with a clear means of utilizing their results.

Sixth: Logistics needs are identified. These include all areas from who will conduct the training, to what equipment and/or materials will be needed, to room location and set-up. These are all carefully thought out in advance and prepared as necessary.

Seventh: The program is piloted as designed. A detailed accounting is made of all activities, interactions, responses, etc. Materials, presentations, and activities are refined as necessary to more closely meet the desired results as identified in steps 1 and 2.

Question: It appears that you have a very well organized system for approaching the task of designing training for your clients. Would you further discuss the logistical issues that you feel deserve special attention in advance of training efforts?

Uday: We see the logistics issue as a three pronged concern: staff, materials and supplies, and facility.

Regarding the training staff, we believe trainers must be highly skilled in three areas:

1. Experienced and proficient in presentation skills.
2. Expert knowledge of the subject matter.

3. In-depth awareness of the industry in which the training is being conducted.

We believe that it takes all three of these qualities in a training staff to provide a meaningful program.

Materials and supplies must be easy to read, use, and understand. Ideally, they are made available prior to the program. Preworkshop materials allow attendees to prepare for lively participation and ease any apprehensions that may exist.

Facility logistics provide, in some cases, the greatest opportunity for mistakes: room arrangements—our preferred style is almost always a horseshoe; refreshments—if planned for; video or other equipment— must be checked out prior to the program; awareness of the room's entrance—we want it to be away from the front of the U; temperature and lighting; and we even check out whether the walls take masking tape for flip chart pages before the session.

Question: Finally, what additional features of designing training programs do you feel are important?

Uday: Designing training programs is both a skill and an art. For training to be truly effective, I believe it must be participant or learner centered rather than trainer or presenter centered. For that reason, the trainer must be highly skilled with the design and facilitation of each program. Although training is not designed to be entertainment, a trainer must be able to get and keep the audience involved. The attendees must want to learn, must see the need for changing their behavior or acquiring new behaviors or skills. That is really what training is all about—helping people change their behavior to something better, more effective, more successful or new.

Chapter 5

EVALUATION _____

Most management texts identify four basic management activities: planning, organizing, directing, and controlling. These four activities are particularly relevant to trainers. Within the training and development function, *planning* should occur for every component of the process. For example, at the needs analysis stage, plans are developed to address both the short- and long-term needs within the context of the organization's mission and strategic plans. *Organizing* occurs when the training program is designed and the various elements are put into place. *Directing* occurs when the program is "taken on the road." That is, the trainer directs and monitors activities that occur during the training itself. *Control* occurs through evaluating the program and feeding back the results of the evaluations. Unfortunately, many training and development departments give only a passing nod to the control aspect of their management responsibilities. The president of a human systems consulting and design firm described the state of training evaluation this way:

> Evaluation is to human resource development what losing weight is to the American middle class. No one denies its importance (who would dare?), almost everybody has plans to do it (or vague guilt about not having done it already), and the mere act of trying brings automatic approval. ... But like losing weight, the results of evaluation are rarely what one had originally hoped for. (Putnam, 1980)

Imagine a business concern that didn't examine its profits or return on investment. Imagine a job where no one looked at how well or poorly you've performed. Imagine paying someone to perform a service but not being able

130

to tell how valuable that service had been? If you can imagine these things then you can imagine what training and development is like without evaluation. In its ideal form, training evaluation will provide (1) information about the processes that have occurred, (2) the trainees' reaction to the training, (3) the amount of learning that has occurred, (4) the changes in job behavior that have resulted from training, and (5) the organizational outcomes that can be attributed to training. From this information, the training department can determine the return on the training investment dollar and the organization can evaluate its allocation of resources to the training department more intelligently. The training department can utilize the information to evaluate existing programs both in terms of outcomes and processes. Without this kind of information, training departments place themselves in a vulnerable position with respect to organizational resources. In spite of this potential hazard, many rationalizations continue to exist for not evaluating training. Some of these are examined in more detail below.

ARGUMENTS FOR AND AGAINST EVALUATION

No one really cares about evaluating training in my organization. What this usually means is that no one has specifically asked for, demanded, suggested, or otherwise indicated an interest in training evaluations. However, this doesn't mean that evaluations aren't being conducted. When top management makes budget decisions they rely on information available to them. This may be "hard" data or "soft" impressions. If the training department is doing a good job then it should want to demonstrate that effectiveness. Even under relatively good economic conditions, the fight for intra-organizational dollars is competitive. Those units in the organization that can document contributions to the welfare of the organization are more likely to realize their budget requests. Thus, even if no one appears to be concerned with evaluating training, you can be sure that some "evaluation" will occur. The question, then, is not whether it will be done but, rather, who will control the process. That is, who will determine the criteria, the methodology, and the design of evaluation? The training professional or the budget decision makers?

   The trainees and their supervisors will let me know how effective training was. Most certainly these individuals have their own opinions about the effectiveness of training. And, this is a valuable source of evaluation data. The problem is that these groups will rarely come forward with spontaneous feedback about the program. Even when they do, the hit and miss testimonials that result provide relatively little in the way of useful information. To know that a supervisor or two thought your training was "good" or "bad" isn't helpful by itself. What, for example, do they mean by "good"? Does it mean the trainees are more productive? Do they have higher quality work products? Are the trainees happy because they got a break from the daily routine? Did the trainees find it to be entertaining? Can the supervisors demonstrate the magnitude of the changes they have observed? Can those changes be translated into dollars and cents? Were all of the training components good or just some of them? Do all of the supervisors feel this way? How do the trainees feel? To answer these questions, a more systematic and formal assessment of training effects is needed. While the testimonials of a few supervisors may be gratifying to the trainer, it is not likely to wring many hard won dollars out of the corporate treasury.

Evaluating training is a waste of time since you can never "prove" what the effects of training have been. This rationalization for not evaluating training both misses the point and contains a kernel of truth. We will begin with the kernel of truth. The ways in which we come to "know" things determines how we define "truth" and what we consider to constitute "proof." Most of Western civilization has accepted science and its methods as the "official" or formally accepted way of coming to know something. However, other methods of "knowing" exist. Three tenuous but common methods are tenacity, authority, and intuition (Cohen & Nagel, 1934). These "ways of knowing" are more common in most people's everyday lives than the scientific. The difference between the scientific and the other methods is that for the other methods there is a high degree of subjectivity (evidence does not have to be reliable, observable, or measurable) and inflexibility (new evidence will not change the context or interpretation of old knowledge). In order to understand the advantages of the scientific method for conducting training evaluations, the various ways of "knowing" need to be examined in more depth.

Nonscientific Ways of Knowing

Tenacity occurs when we believe something to be true because we have always believed it to be true. These beliefs are acts of faith. Objective evidence has little impact on the truth or falsity of the belief. The "proof" of their truth is that they have been beliefs for long periods of time. Trainers are guilty of this when they continue to use techniques and content that haven't been evaluated because they "know" they are good.

Another form of "proof" comes from a reliance on respected others. This is called *authority reliance.* Reliance on experts is often the most reasonable course open to us in our daily lives. When the doctor tells us that our overeating is going to lead to heart trouble, our belief in that is not unreasonable. We may reasonably place more confidence in the "facts" about our health that come from our doctor than the "facts" coming from the latest diet book or health spa advertisement. While this is more flexible than tenacity, this authority reliance is extremely subjective. Who do you believe when the experts disagree? Every year economists make forecasts about the national economy. The number of discrepancies between the various forecasts often outnumbers the number of experts and bears a striking resemblance to the political ideologies of those "experts." Trainers sometimes make the mistake of assuming that other parts of the organization (e.g., top management) will rely on the trainer's expertise to tell them how valuable training is. Unfortunately for them, top management may rely on other "authorities" for this.

Intuition is a method of knowing that is based on the individual's insight into the meaning of his or her experiences. Thus, while "truth" may be evident to the individual intuitor, no objective evidence is available for others to verify. This method is flexible in that a new intuition may change what is known, but it is totally subjective by itself. If the intuition is put to the test it may then become an objective fact but, then, the reliance is on science rather than intuition. Intuition may be (and has been) a great help in advancing knowledge, but it can create new knowledge only for the person doing the intuiting. That person must then rely on science or some other method to convince others. Likewise, the trainer may intuitively know that a particular program was effective, but the trainer must convince others of this.

The reader may well ask, "Why all this to-do over the scientific method? Of course I expect those involved in the discovery of new knowledge to use scientific methods. But, what does that have to do with training evaluation? Is the trainer supposed to be a scientist also?" This is true only if the evaluation is designed to answer any question dealing with the relationship between training activities and some criteria. The trainer is then discovering knowledge that previously did not exist. Based on the discussion of the alternative ways of obtaining new knowledge, we would hope that both the organization and the trainer would prefer to use a flexible and objective method.

The Scientific Way of Knowing

While most of you who read this text will have at least a passing familiarity with the *scientific method*, it is probably useful to review its major components briefly. Essentially, this method consists of *observing events* in the real world, *formulating explanations* for those events, *generating predictions* about future real world events using deductive logic, and *verifying the predictions* through systematic, controlled observation. From the training perspective, this might be translated as follows.

The trainer is confronted with an organizational need that training might satisfy. The trainer here is utilizing his or her previous observations of the real world (i.e., the needs analysis data and training experience) to formulate an explanation for events (i.e., a lack of knowledge/skill has caused this organizational need). The trainer deduces an hypothesis (i.e., prediction) or two that certain types of training experiences will satisfy the organizational need. The trainer tests the hypothesis by conducting the training and observing the effects of that training in a systematic and controlled manner.

Thus, the trainer can be said to be engaging in the scientific pursuit of knowledge. However, just because the method bears resemblance to the scientific method doesn't mean that it is good science. The goodness or badness of the results, from a scientific perspective, will depend upon the degree of control the trainer is able to exert over the observations and measurements. Let's assume for the moment that the trainer was very sophisticated in the scientific method. Let's also assume that the evaluation results indicated that the training had the desired effects. The trainer still could not, from a purely scientific perspective, prove that training was effective.

The nature of science is such that statements about the world can never be proven. They can only be disproven. For example, we could never prove that humans need oxygen to live. The fact that no human to date has been able to survive very long without it merely gives the proposition a high likelihood of being true. A medical physiologist could show us how our vital organs utilize oxygen in the performance of their life-continuing functions. This would only increase the likelihood that the statement was true. We can never prove the statement because, at some point in the future, someone might be able to document the conditions under which a human could live without oxygen. A single instance would suffice to disprove the statement. The vast majority of us, however, having found no evidence to disprove the statement and quite a bit to support it, spend little time debating the point. We conduct our lives under the assumption that the statement is true and do quite well, thank you. Scientists, likewise, interpret the results of their research in terms of their confidence in the results. Their confidence in the "truth" of their observations is based on the degree to which replicated, objective observations of the same events yield consistent results. This is generally referred to as the *reliability* of the results. Even if the results are very reliable, the most the scientist can say is that they are *probably* true. The interpretation of the meaning of the results is another matter altogether. This will be discussed further under the heading of validity.

The difference between the pure scientist and the trainer is that the scientist is interested in "truth" for its own sake. That is, the scientist has been successful when new knowledge emerges from his or her activities. The trainer is also concerned with truth, but is even more concerned with usefulness. Thus, the trainer isn't interested in all the truths that the evaluation data may provide, but only with those truths that are useful. Few business organizations exist to provide the trainer with a laboratory in which to test hypotheses. Thus, the trainer must focus first and foremost on contributions to the organization's mission. This does not mean that the trainer should see only what he or she wants to see or that he or she should only look at data that show what he or she wants them to show. Rather it means that the evaluation should be designed to show truths that are useful and be conducted in ways that are meaningful to those who desire those truths. We will discuss this issue more at the end of the chapter. For now it is sufficient to note that even the scientist can't prove what the truth is and that there are similarities and differences between the goals of the scientist and the trainer. In either case, to say that we shouldn't investigate because we can't prove our results is begging the issue. The purpose of evaluation is not to absolutely "prove" something. The purpose is to provide information to the decision makers that they and the trainer can have confidence in so that the risk of making bad decisions can be reduced.

TYPES OF EVALUATION

Process Evaluation

Two basic types of evaluative analyses are conducted for training activities. Nearly all the professional literature advocates the use of an *outcome evaluation* in which a set of procedures is utilized to measure the results, or outcomes, of training. Alternatively, *process evaluation* focuses on what occurred during the development and implementation of training. While this evaluative procedure is less commonly referred to in the training literature, it is of equal importance for the development of a quality training department. Its importance arises because it allows the outcomes of training to be interpreted in light of what went on during training. It is not enough to simply record what effects training has had at various levels in the organization. Rather, the training department needs to know what is accounting for those effects. If, for example, learning is not what it should be at the end of training, the trainer needs to be able to analyze what had taken place so that appropriate changes can be made in the program. Even when the outcomes are acceptable, a process evaluation can provide the trainer with insights that may lead to even more desirable outcomes.

The basic methodology of process evaluation is the recording of what has occurred during the development and implementation of training. This can be done through training staff logs, films, video tapes, direct observations, or any other method of recording what has occurred. In general, the more methods used, the more valid and reliable the results. In particular, if observations or self-reports are used, multiple sources of data are recommended to reduce individual biases. The records of activities and procedures that actually took place are then compared to some ideal model of what activities and procedures should have taken place. If this is done to modify the training for future use, it is sometimes called *formative evaluation* (Goldstein, 1974; Scriven, 1967). This is because the evaluation forms the basis for the next implementation of the program. The idealized model must be developed within each organization, taking into account the constraints within which the program must operate. Thus, the model is an idealized *practical* model rather than a model of the "perfect" program. In many cases, the model is the course plan developed by the trainer combined with the diagnostic procedures utilized by the training department. The actual activities and procedures that were used in training are then compared to the model in much the same way that physicians conduct post mortems. Table 5.1 presents a set of questions that might be answered or at least considered in a process evaluation.

Outcome Evaluation

While process evaluation is important for the trainer and the training department, most people think of evaluating training as examining the effects training has had on people and their performance. This is termed *outcome evaluation* because its focus is on the identification and measurement of outcomes that training has produced. As we have previously indicated, training can affect many things within the organization. Kirkpatrick (1959, 1967) identified four criterion measures for evaluating outcomes which he sees as forming a hierarchy. He placed *reaction* at the bottom of the hierarchy. This criterion is designed to measure trainees' perceptions and evaluations of the training experience. Kirkpatrick placed this at the bottom of the hierarchy because he believes that favorable reactions to training are required before the appropriate learning events will occur. *Learning* is the criterion that follows reaction in the hierarchy. Learning is measured in terms of the prerequisite learning objectives and the overall training objective. The measurement of learning will depend upon the learning involved and the measurement technology available to the evaluator. Kirkpatrick indicated that positive trainee reactions lead to trainee learning which in turn leads to improved *job behavior.* Changes in job behavior will depend on the learning that takes place and will also be measured in terms of the objectives and measurement technology. Finally, improvements in job behavior will lead to what Kirkpatrick called *organizational results.* This is the highest level in the hierarchy and includes outcomes such as productivity, profit, turnover, absenteeism, etc. It has been suggested (Hamblin, 1974) that only by evaluating each level in the hierarchy will the trainer understand why training is successful (e.g., acquisition of knowledge/skill) or not. Thus, for evaluation to be meaningful at one level, the lower levels must also be evaluated.

The following evaluation scenario reflects the hierarchical nature of the Kirkpatrick model. At the end of a participative management program the trainer passes out a reaction questionnaire. This questionnaire measures the degree to which the trainees feel positive about the time and effort they invested in the total program and each of its components. Even if the trainees feel that something valuable has been learned, the trainer recog-

Table 5.1 Questions to be addressed in process analysis.

1. Were needs diagnosed correctly?
    a. What data sources were utilized?
    b. Was there a knowledge/skill deficiency?
    c. Was the need organizationally important?
2. Were needs translated into objectives?
    a. Was the organizational need translated into an organizational objective?
    b. Was the overall training objective derived from the organizational objective?
    c. Were prerequisite learning objectives derived from the overall training objective?
    d. Were trainees assessed to determine the number of prerequisite learning objectives they were deficient in?
3. Was an evaluation system designed to measure achievement of objectives?
4. Was a training program designed to meet the specific learning, training, and organizational objectives?
    a. Was previous learning that might support or inhibit current learning objectives identified?
    b. Were individual differences determined and taken into consideration?
    c. Was trainee motivation to learn assessed?
    d. Were steps taken to increase trainee motivation in the learning environment?
    e. Were steps taken to call attention to key learning events?
    f. Were steps taken to aid trainees with symbolic coding and cognitive organization?
    g. Was opportunity made for symbolic practice?
    h. Was opportunity made for behavioral practice?
    i. Was feedback available after practice?
    j. What steps were taken to facilitate positive transfer of learning back to the job?
5. Was there a match between the trainer characteristics, training technique, and learning objectives?
    a. Were trainer characteristics assessed?
    b. Was the training technique likely to achieve the learning objectives?
    c. What alternative training techniques were examined and why were they rejected?
    d. Were the trainer's lesson plans designed to maximize the positive effects of the technique used?
    e. Was the trainer's lesson plan designed to capitalize on his or her strengths and avoid his or her weaknesses?
6. Was the trainer able to follow his or her lesson plans?

nizes that the "right" learning may not have taken place. Therefore, a post-test of knowledge and skills is also administered and compared with pre-training and control group measurements. Assuming the trainees do know what they need to know about participative management and have acquired the skills to use it effectively, the trainer must determine if these will transfer back to the job. The trainer needs to find out if the leadership and decision-making styles of the trainees have changed as they should on the job. Finally, if the appropriate behaviors are being implemented on the job, the effects of these on the organization will need to be measured. Did productivity increase? Did satisfaction increase? Are turnover, absenteeism, and grievances down? Are higher quality decisions being made?

A recent examination of Kirkpatrick's hierarchy concept (Clement, 1982) found only partial support for it. Reactions were found to be strongly related to learning outcomes. Learning outcomes were somewhat less strongly related to improvements in job behavior. However, improvements in job behavior were not related to improvement in organizational results. These findings make intuitive sense when the reader considers the increasing amount of interference from outside factors as one moves up the hierarchy. The model in Figure 5.1 presents a revised description of the relationships between Kirkpatrick's four criterion domains. As shown, factors outside the control of the training department play an increasingly important role in determining the criterion outcomes higher in the hierarchy. Thus, in one sense the trainer is justified in factoring out these variables when evaluating training. That is, the trainer may legitimately state:

> This was a good training program. The trainees were very positive in their reactions, and the evidence indicates that they learned what we expected and wanted them to. If their supervisors had applied the right incentives back on the job I'm sure they would have achieved the improved job behavior objectives that we had set.

On the other hand, the trainer may be said to have an obligation to insure that the right incentives are in place prior to sending the trainees back to the work stations, or even before agreeing to conduct the training. By understanding the relationship between external factors and the interrelationships among the criterion domains, the trainer can deal with these intervening variables before the training actually takes place. This is why we have advocated that trainers view their function from an open systems perspective. Perceiving their role to be that of a change agent, and conducting activities accordingly, should result in greater organizational impact from training. When a more integrated training effort takes place, fewer qualifying statements need appear in the evaluation report.

While several criterion categories have been described, the practical question of actual criterion choice remains. Careful development of criterion measures is one of the keys to a successful evaluation. While many novice evaluators give this issue little attention, the professionals recognize its vital

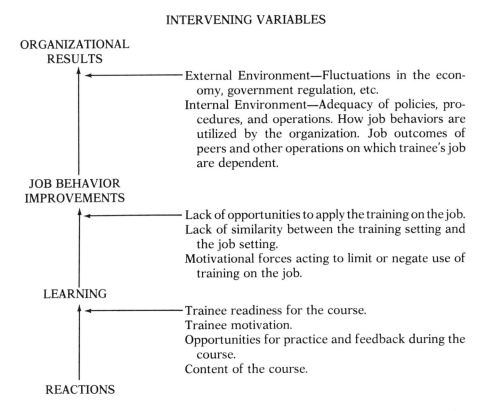

INTERVENING VARIABLES

ORGANIZATIONAL
RESULTS

External Environment—Fluctuations in the economy, government regulation, etc.
Internal Environment—Adequacy of policies, procedures, and operations. How job behaviors are utilized by the organization. Job outcomes of peers and other operations on which trainee's job are dependent.

JOB BEHAVIOR
IMPROVEMENTS

Lack of opportunities to apply the training on the job.
Lack of similarity between the training setting and the job setting.
Motivational forces acting to limit or negate use of training on the job.

LEARNING

Trainee readiness for the course.
Trainee motivation.
Opportunities for practice and feedback during the course.
Content of the course.

REACTIONS

Figure 5.1 External factors affecting relationships among hierarchical training criteria. (Modification of figure from R. W. Clement, "Testing the hierarchy theory of training evaluation: An expanded role for trainee reactions," *Public Personnel Management Journal,* Summer 1982, 176–184.)

impact on the total process. After reading the following section, you should have a better appreciation for just how difficult it is to develop good criteria. Our point is not to discourage trainers attempting to do this, but to point out the pitfalls so that they may be avoided without having to "learn the hard way."

CRITERION DEVELOPMENT

Evaluation by its very nature implies the existence of a *standard or criterion* against which actual events are compared. Thorndike (1949) differentiated between actual criterion measures and what he called the *ultimate criterion*. The ultimate criterion is what we would like to measure if we could. Instead, we typically must settle for what we are able to measure and make inferences from that about the ultimate criterion. For example, most training programs attempt to measure something called "learning." Yet, no one really measures actual learning because to do so would require a neurophysiologist, great advances in our understanding of brain functioning, and the consent of the trainee to open his head for a "look around." Instead, we settle for recordings of behavior (e.g., paper and pencil tests or assessment centers) from which we make inferences about whether learning occurred. In Thorndike's words:

> We are almost always thrown back upon substitute criteria which we judge, either in terms of rational analysis or in terms of empirical evidence, to be related to the ultimate criterion with which we are most fundamentally concerned. These criterion measures we may designate as intermediate or in certain cases immediate criteria. (Thorndike, 1949, p. 122)

Obviously, the skill with which we are able to develop these *intermediate* or *immediate criteria* will affect the value of the evaluation process. The closer the intermediate criteria are to the ultimate criteria, the more *valid* the intermediate criteria are said to be. The selection or development of invalid criteria will at best prove a waste of time and money. At worst, it could lead to decisions and actions that are damaging to the organization. The following discussion of criterion relevancy, contamination, and deficiency are of importance to the development of valid criterion measures.

Criterion Relevancy, Contamination, and Deficiency

Criterion relevancy is defined as the degree of overlap between the intermediate criterion and the ultimate criterion. The closer the relationship between these two criteria, the greater the relevancy of the intermediate criterion measure. But, if the intermediate criterion is real and the ultimate criterion is some idealized construct, how can one measure their degree of relatedness? Essentially, the evaluation of a criterion's relevance is a judgmental process. The judge must determine the degree to which changes in the ultimate criteria will be reflected in the intermediate criteria. If learning is the ultimate criteria, for example, the evaluator must determine the degree to which new learning will be reflected in paper and pencil tests given at the end of training. This, however, does not have to be a totally subjective process. If the intermediate criterion correlates* with other variables that the ultimate criterion should correlate with, this provides evidence for the relevancy of the intermediate criterion. On the other hand, if it correlates with variables that the ultimate criterion should not, this is evidence for criterion

---

*A *correlation* is a statistical relationship between two variables. That is, changes in one variable are associated with changes in the other. A *positive correlation* means that increases in one variable correspond to increases in the other. A *negative correlation* means that increases in one correspond to decreases in the other. Correlations range in value from 1.00 to −1.00.

contamination. Using learning again as the ultimate criterion, assume that filing procedures are the learning content area. Assume the intermediate criterion was the trainee's ability to correctly file ten labeled folders from the accounting department. If trainees have truly learned the filing procedures, scores on the intermediate criterion should be highly correlated with other abilities related to filing such as alphabetizing, identifying folders that are misfiled, and the speed with which a specific folder can be found in a correctly filed set of folders. To the degree that high positive correlations are found between the filing ability and the related variables, criterion relevancy is supported. To the degree that high positive correlations are found between the filing criterion and variables such as religious affiliation, number of friends in the personnel office, etc., criterion contamination is likely.

Criterion contamination occurs when variables that are unrelated to the ultimate criterion become a part of the intermediate criterion. Probably the most widely publicized example of criterion contamination in recent times occurred in the field of standardized intelligence testing. The ultimate criterion there was the construct "intelligence." The intermediate criterion, performance on the intelligence tests, has been shown to be correlated with performance in school, career success, and other variables that theoretically should be related to intelligence. However, other studies found these "intelligence tests" to be related to things like socioeconomic status, cultural background of the test takers, as well as the age, sex, and race of the test administrator (Chase, 1978). To the degree that these latter variables are unrelated to the construct "intelligence," they indicate that the intermediate criterion is contaminated. Awareness of which variables contaminate the criterion may allow the evaluator to eliminate their effects statistically. However, it is always better to develop criteria free of contaminants where possible.

Another problem in developing valid evaluation criteria is *criterion deficiency*. This occurs when the intermediate criterion doesn't encompass all of the relevant aspects of the ultimate criterion. For example, the use of a paper and pencil mechanical comprehension test would be deficient as the sole criterion for a training program in which the objective was to increase the ability of trainees to perform proper maintenance on various machines. Certainly, mechanical comprehension is relevant to the maintenance activities. However, the other aspects of performing machine maintenance such as knowledge and use of tools, knowledge of the specific machines, and the requisite behavioral skills are all missing. Thus, in this case the criterion would be relevant but deficient. It might also be contaminated if activities associated with the test such as reading and following instructions, translating two dimensional diagrams into three dimensions, etc., are unrelated to performing the desired machine maintenance.

Figure 5.2 depicts several relationships between the ultimate criterion and the intermediate criterion in terms of relevancy, contamination, and

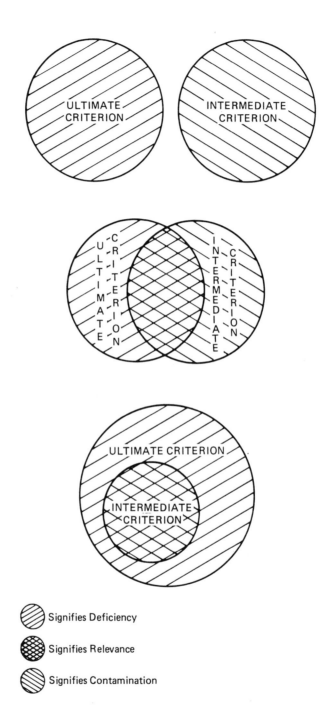

Figure 5.2 Potential relationships between ultimate and intermediate criteria.

deficiency. In Panel A, the intermediate criterion is irrelevant, deficient, and contaminated. The intermediate criterion in Panel B has become more relevant, less contaminated, and less deficient. In Panel C, the intermediate criterion is totally relevant, completely uncontaminated, but still somewhat deficient. In most cases, a trainer/evaluator must be satisfied with criteria that are similar to Panel B—that is, criteria that are somewhat relevant but that are also somewhat contaminated and deficient. Criterion relevancy, contamination, and deficiency are related to the validity of criterion measurement. The validity of criterion measurement is a part of the *internal validity* of the evaluation process. Threats to internal validity are examined below.

INTERNAL VALIDITY

Internal validity is concerned with the believability of the evaluation results. The internal validity problem that exists for training evaluation is to establish that some changes in the criteria have occurred and that training is responsible for those changes. Campbell and Stanley (1963) identified many variables that might cause the observed results rather than training. The following are threats to an evaluation's internal validity.

Threats to Internal Validity

History.   Events outside the training environment can produce changes in the criteria being measured. For instance, the occurrence of a racial disturbance in the work place may do more to influence trainee attitudes about race than the affirmative action training program they are attending. Thus, the program may not appear effective when in fact it may be. Alternatively, the informal "coaching" new employees receive may be the only factor related to improving their job performance criteria. Yet, the "New Employee Training" program would seem very effective using this criterion for evaluation. The *history of events* that are concurrent with training activities then pose one threat to the evaluation's internal validity. In this case, the criterion is measured correctly but the causal factors aren't identified.

Maturation.   Physiologically and psychologically, the trainees who emerge from training are different from what they were when they entered. Training is responsible for some but not all of these differences. Those changes that are unrelated to training but impact on evaluation criteria are threats to the internal validity of the evaluation. These are usually physical or emotional states of the individual that differ from pre- to post-training measurement such as fatigue, motivation, etc.

Testing.   Often training evaluations utilize some type of pretest to measure trainee characteristics such as knowledge or attitude. By doing so, this may sensitize the trainee to seek out information related to the pretest. If this is true, a question might arise as to whether it was training or simply pretesting that resulted in the trainee engaging in learning activities. Another problem in this area occurs when the pretest is the same as the post-test. In this circumstance, it might be argued that "real learning" hasn't occurred. Rather, trainees may have "just memorized" the correct answers or responses. While one might argue over the nature of "real learning," this situation contains enough problems to prove embarassing if the evaluation design doesn't control for this threat to internal validity.

Initial Group Differences.   Sometimes evaluation studies utilize comparison or *control groups.* That is, one group of people who receive training are compared to another group who do not. The logic here is that training can be said to be responsible for criterion differences between the groups at the conclusion of training. However, this is only true if the groups were identical prior to training. If they were not the same to begin with, then perhaps those differences are also related to differences in the evaluation criteria. Because critical factors affecting the criteria are not always known, it is both difficult and risky to try to match individuals in the groups on all of the relevant characteristics. However, obvious differences between groups that are related to the criterion (e.g., performance ratings) should be avoided.

Loss of Group Members (Mortality).   Occasionally, trainees will stop showing up for training and/or members of the comparison groups will no longer be available. These disappearances are to be expected in any organizational setting. People quit, get transferred, get promoted, or get sick. These are events that may make a person no longer eligible to be a participant in the evaluation. When one of the comparison groups loses considerably more people than the other, it calls the results of the evaluation into question. That is, perhaps if everyone remained in the group the results wouldn't have been so good (bad). The slower learning trainees may be more likely to drop out voluntarily. Because the trainees with higher learning abilities are left, it appears that a greater gain has been achieved than is actually the case.

Instrumentation.   Occasionally, evaluators will utilize different methods of gathering data. If different methods are used for different groups or at different times (i.e., pre- and post-tests) then the internal validity can be called into question. This is because changes may be due to the difference in measurement instrumentation rather than differences in training received.

Statistical Regression to the Mean.   Because measurements are not perfectly valid or reliable, some error in measurement can be expected. Assuming measurement error to be random, the average score for a group will not change because of this type of error. However, the variability of a group is likely to decrease across measurements. That is, those with very high and very low scores are likely to regress toward the middle (i.e., the mean). This is because the initial measurement of knowledge/skill that is high (low) is more likely to have errors that reduce (increase) the score on subsequent measurements. If training groups are composed of those who are very low to average on a pretest, as is typical, one would expect a certain increase of scores on the post-test due to "regression to the mean."

Methodological Precautions

By observing some rather simple procedures, many of the threats to internal validity can be overcome. However, the simplicity is deceiving. While the following procedures may be conceptually simple, in practice they may be very difficult to achieve.

Pre- and post-testing In order to determine whether any change has occurred, the evaluator must first establish a *baseline* (i.e., a measure of typical behavior). Some evaluators have attempted to avoid this by asking people to think back to a certain period in time and assess how much change has occurred since then. For example, they might ask the supervisor of trainees to tell them how much more productive trainees are after training than they were before. The obvious problems here are the unreliability of memory and the tendency of people to be selective in what they attend to. An additional problem is that the supervisor knows what you would like to hear. The supervisor may, under certain circumstances, be influenced to report more positive results or more negative results depending on what the advantages/disadvantages were seen to be. The point is that the measure is entirely subjective. We have already indicated that the more objectively measurable the training objectives are the better they are.

A true *pretest/post-test design* for training evaluation involves the collection of criterion data prior to training and again after training. Done appropriately, this provides evidence that some change has or has not taken place. It does not provide evidence of training's role in the change. Other procedures are needed to accomplish that. However, threats to validity involving testing, instrumentation, and differences in people are at least partially related to the pretest/post-test issue.

One solution to the internal validity threat posed by pretesting is to develop alternate forms of the test. By establishing the internal consistency* of each and the intertest correlation under nontraining conditions, the impact of the pretest on the post-test can be minimized. This will also minimize instrumentation arguments since the relationship between the two instruments has already been established. Finally, if control groups are to be used, pretesting is absolutely essential for establishing the similarity between the groups in terms of criterion levels prior to the training.

In addition to the methodological advantages of pretesting, Mezoff (1983) pointed out a number of practical advantages. Pretesting, with feedback, increases trainees' readiness to learn by objectively demonstrating

*This technique is described in the criterion evaluation section later in this chapter, under the heading *Reliability*.

what knowledge/skill deficiencies they have. In Kurt Lewin's terms, this unfreezes beliefs about self-adequacy by decreasing complacency and increasing anxiety. At the same time, the pretest can provide cues to the learner about what areas the organization sees as important. By struggling through a pretest (most of which the trainee shouldn't know or understand), the trainee has gone through a kind of initiation. The available evidence (Aronson & Carlsmith, 1968) indicates that having to undergo a difficult or stressful experience in order to gain entry into a group increases the value of the group to the individual. Having to take a pretest, then, can increase the value of training and training activities for the trainee. The pretest also can act to flag the important issues and topics to be covered in training. In terms of the social learning model, this should increase attention to and learning of these topics. At the same time, the pretest establishes a learning climate and creates expectations by trainees that training is being taken seriously. One final advantage of pretesting is that it keeps the trainer focused on the objectives of training.

Control groups   Pre- and post-testing alone does very little to eliminate threats to the internal validity of the evaluation. Simply establishing the existence of some change in the criteria is not enough. For example, measuring transfer of training (the ultimate criterion) through pre-post training changes in productivity (the intermediate criteria) may include contamination from changes in supervision and coworkers occurring during this interval. Thus, everyone's productivity has changed to some degree. The evaluator usually wants to separate transfer of training effects from these other effects. The use of control groups goes a long way toward accomplishing this.

A *control group* is a group of people who are as similar as possible to the trainees. Ideally, the two groups are treated identically with the exception of training. That is, the impact of factors other than training is the same for each group. Goldstien (1974) provided a good example of why control groups are necessary:

> In medical research, the placebo is an inert substance administered to the control group so that the subject cannot distinguish whether he is a member of the experimental or the control group. This allows the researcher to separate the effects of the actual drug from the reactions induced by the subjects' expectations and suggestability. In instructional research, similar cautions must be taken to separate the background effects sometimes employed . . . (p. 74)

As mentioned earlier, it is often difficult to anticipate and measure all of the variables that might eventually be relevant to changes in the criteria. Although often impractical, it is best, from a design standpoint, to randomly assign employees to training and control groups. When individuals are truly selected at random, no systematic differences are likely to exist between the training and control groups. This minimizes the "initial group differences" threat to validity. It will also reduce "statistical regression" and "loss of group members" effects since those in both groups are likely to be affected equally.

By treating each group identically in all respects but training, the history, maturation, testing and instrumentation threats to validity will also be minimized. Since each group is subjected to the same history, has the same amount of time for maturity, and receives the same tests and instruments, these variables cannot account for any differences that might exist between the groups at the end of training. Because the only thing that differed between the groups is training, differences in the criteria must be attributed to that.

WHAT'S A CRITERION DEVELOPER TO DO?

The first thing a criterion developer should do is to start at the beginning. That is, ask the question, "Who wants to know what about training?" Just as training should develop objectives that meet specific needs in the organization, training evaluation should also be aimed at meeting specific needs. Too often organizations that have shown conceptual wisdom by insisting on a formal evaluation of training have been made to look foolish by evaluations that are technically sound but practically useless. The only way for the training evaluator to insure that the evaluation will serve some practical purpose is to identify the audience and determine what they need to know and why they need to know it.

Identify the Audience

Potentially, there are three basic audiences for training evaluations, although any given evaluation may not include all three. Those audiences are (1) the trainer group, (2) the trainee group, and (3) the organizational decision makers. Broadly defined, the *trainer group* consists of the trainer, the training manager, and other training coworkers who might have a need for evaluative information about the particular training program under consideration. The *trainee group* consists of all those who were trained in the program and their immediate supervisors.

The *organizational decision makers* are, of course, those who control the operations and the purse strings of the organization (e.g., perhaps the vice-president of human resources and the vice-president of the functional area where training has taken place). Whether it is these individuals or others, the power brokers with an interest in the training program's outcomes need to be identified, not when evaluation begins, but when the needs analysis determines that training will take place for such and such a group (i.e., when the objectives of the program are defined).

Table 5.2 presents a matrix that provides a general description of what each group typically wants to know and why they need to know it. It can be

Table 5.2 Training audiences and their uses of evaluation information.

Criterion domains	Audiences		
	Trainer group	Trainee group	Organizational decision makers
PROCESS	*Trainer:* Determine what is useful and what is not. Modify and upgrade program. *Other Trainers:* Analyze process for applicability to other situations. *Training Manager:* Not very interested unless results poor in other domains.	*Trainee:* Guide choices during training. *Trainee's Supervisor:* Interested in process of proposed training, but not very interested in evaluation of process after training is completed.	Not very interested.
REACTION	*Trainer:* Modification and upgrading of professional and/or personal style when trainee attitudes and perceptions do not provide an appropriate foundation for learning. *Other Trainers:* Are reactions generally able to other groups? *Training Manager:* Evaluate trainee/ trainer effectiveness and, if positive, use to promote training program.	*Trainee:* Determine the similarity of trainee's reactions to those of other trainees. *Trainee's Supervisor:* Marginally interested, but little action taken on basis of this evaluation.	Not very interested unless training is just seen as a part of the benefit package.

Table 5.2   Training audiences and their uses of evaluation information. (*Continued*)

Criterion domains	Audiences		
	Trainer group	Trainee group	Organizational decision makers
LEARNING	*Trainer:* Determine the degree to which learning objectives are well achieved. *Other Trainers:* Determine the generalizability of results to other groups. *Training Manager:* Evaluate trainer effectiveness and, if positive, use to promote training programs.	*Trainee:* Serves as feedback for goal accomplishment. *Trainee's Supervisor:* Interested to the degree that learning objectives are translated into job behavior.	Not very interested.
JOB BEHAVIOR	*Trainer:* Determine effectiveness of process for transfer of training to the job. *Other Trainers:* Determine the generalizability of results to other groups. *Training Manager:* Evaluate the trainer on ability to promote transfer of training.	*Trainee:* Comparison with own past performance and with others. Answer the question, "Was training useful to me?" *Trainees Supervisor:* Most important part of evaluation. Basis for decision to provide training for others.	Interested to the degree that changes in job behavior are seen as critical to organizational goal accomplishment.

Table 5.2   Training audiences and their uses of evaluation information. (*Continued*)

Criterion domains	Audiences		
	Trainer group	Trainee group	Organizational decision makers
ORGANIZA-TIONAL RESULTS	*Trainer:* Not too interested. *Other Trainers:* Not too interested. *Training Manager:* Provide evidence of contribution of training to the organization's goals.	*Trainee:* Not very interested. *Trainee's Supervisor:* Basis for decision to provide training for others. Nearly as important as job behavior evaluation.	Most important part of evaluation. Basis for decision to allocate resources to the training function.

seen from this table that the trainer group and trainee group have evaluation needs in all five criterion domains. The organizational decision makers have needs in only some of the criterion domains. However, even within the same group, the kind of information that is needed within a criterion domain differs from member to member. Thus, if a given criterion domain is operationalized for only one person or group it may not satisfy others' informational needs.

Get Commitment to Criteria

The evaluation audience should be defined during the needs analysis and development of training objectives. Once it has been determined who the legitimate members of the audience are, a commitment to the measurement of certain criteria in a specified way should be established between the trainer group and the various audiences involved. The reason for doing it at this time centers around the training objectives. The careful development of objectives not only helps to focus the direction of training but also serves as the foundation for the evaluation. Because many of the objectives are either criteria for evaluation or influence the criteria, agreement must be reached as to their definition and measurement.

Because a substantial amount of time usually passes between the identification of objectives and the presentation of the evaluation results, some form of written documentation of the agreement referred to above is usually desirable. Supervisors and managers will be busy with their own affairs during this interval and time may distort, or they may forget, what they had agreed to. Likewise, the trainer group may lose track of what promises they have made to their various audiences. This agreement should specify what the criteria are, how and under what conditions they are to be measured, and why they were included. This is no different than what the trainer group would do in developing and operationalizing the training and learning objectives. What needs to be stressed here is that the trainer group works together with the various audiences to determine the criteria and objectives that are most meaningful to them (the audiences).

Work with the Audience

It doesn't do any good to do a classic quality control evaluation that generates solid data and illustrate it with curves and graphs if the audience is only interested in "How do the high performing, experienced employees feel about the new system?" You have to find out what kind of evidence counts with your audience. You may believe that "X" is a substantially better way to measure your criterion than "Y," but if your client doesn't trust "X," you better use "Y." A note of caution here: Just because the trainee's supervisor suggests the use of "Y" doesn't mean the trainer should roll over and play dead. The trainer should first establish what the trainee's supervisor is hoping to accomplish by sending the employee to training. Then, several alternatives should be developed by both the trainer and the supervisor. The advantages and drawbacks of these alternatives should be enumerated and then the supervisor should be allowed to choose the one he or she likes best. It still may not be the criteria or method of measurement you would have chosen, but the supervisor will be satisfied and you will have ample documentation of why that criterion was chosen. If the criterion the supervisor has chosen makes absolutely no sense in terms of the performance deficiencies identified, then chances are that some hidden agenda exists and that training aimed at the criteria won't solve the performance deficiency anyway.

CRITERION EVALUATION

The training group won't always be able to measure their criteria as precisely or design their evaluations as carefully as they might like to. They are likely, however, to be seen by others as the experts in these areas. Even if this is not the case, they should be able to explain in a rational, logical manner the advantages and disadvantages associated with various measurement and evaluation design procedures. One of the most basic considerations before the data can be utilized in a practical situation is to determine if the criterion measures meet two conditions. The first of these is that they must give *reliable measurement* so that the same result would be obtained if the same thing were measured again under similar conditions. Second, the measurements must really measure what they are intended to measure. This is called *validity*.

Reliability Estimates

Reliability is an estimation of the consistency of the measurement instrument. For example, if a trainer were to pretest trainees on their knowledge of bookkeeping, the reliability score of that test is a measure of the test's ability to give the same results on repeated testings of the trainees under similar conditions, regardless of whether the test had anything to do with knowledge of bookkeeping. The reliability of a measurement procedure is an empirical question and can only be answered through empirical testing.

If you were to sit down, put a standard hospital thermometer in your mouth, wait five minutes, and then begin to record the temperature reading every two minutes for an hour, you would probably obtain very consistent results. This would be true whether it was you or someone else who read and recorded the temperature. You could compare your recordings with others who made recordings and from this get a measure of the reliability of your measurement procedures. If you then removed all of the markings from the thermometer and repeated the process you would find much less consistency among your own measurements and between yours and others. Using the thermometer without the markings would be a less reliable measurement procedure. The extent of agreement between measures taken on different occasions or by different individuals can be computed by means of correlational techniques. The correlation coefficient for the agreement between repeated measurements under similar conditions constitutes an estimate of the reliability of the measurement procedure. This correlation coefficient is called the *reliability coefficient*. It can take on any value from zero to one. A value of zero indicates no reliability in the measurement process. A value of one indicates perfect reliability.

The most important factor in evaluating the reliability of a measurement procedure is the nature of what is being measured and the state of the art in measuring it. For example, we expect a great deal of reliability in our measures of physical length. If we were given an elastic yardstick to measure cuttings for a cabinet, we would quickly discard it for a more stable instrument. A distance measuring device that gives us reliability coefficients less than .99 would be considered poor by most of us. Yet, if we are talking about distances between galaxies, we might consider a reliability of .98 very good. On the other hand, a reliability coefficient of .75, which would be unacceptable in any modern distance measure, might be quite good for measurement of certain attitudinal dispositions. Virtually no measurement instruments used in the evaluation of training programs have perfect reliability. Few measures have reliability coefficients that range from .9 to 1.0; many have reliability coefficients ranging from .75 to .89. Some are acceptable with values that range from .65 to .74.

Because measurement error is an important issue in the use of evaluation results, investigations of measurement reliability should be conducted when new measurement techniques are used. There are several different methods of estimating the reliability of measurement techniques. However, the interpretation of the reliability coefficient is slightly different for each method used.

Internal Consistency

This method is used most frequently with paper and pencil tests, but can be used with any measure that has more than two items that are supposed to be measuring the same thing. For example, the consistency among raters (interrater reliability) is a form of *internal consistency.* Essentially, this reliability test measures the consistency among the various items by looking at the number of items and the average correlation among the items. The most commonly used form is known as *Cronbach's coefficient alpha* (Cronbach, 1960), also referred to as the *internal consistency coefficient.* While the mathematical explanation of this statistic is beyond the scope of this text, it is available in most texts on test theory (e.g., Nunnally, 1967; Magnusson, 1967). The result of this analysis provides an estimate of the degree to which the various components of the criterion are in agreement. Again, this number will range between zero and one and the higher the number, the more reliable the measure. This may be the most important measure of reliability since the common elements of a measure must be consistent among themselves before the composite can be consistent across time or across situations.

Other Measures of Consistency

The basic problem associated with reliability measures, other than internal consistency, is avoiding contamination due to changes in people and the environments. Consistency across time is usually measured in terms of *test-retest reliability.* That is, the variable is measured for the same people on at least two separate occasions. The correlation between the two measures constitutes the estimate of reliability. This type of reliability isn't recommended unless it can be shown that experience occurring between the first measurement and the later measurement has no effect on the variable that is being measured (Nunnally, 1967). This is because a reliable and valid measure (e.g., job behavior) can appear unreliable when changes in the work environment, occurring between testing periods, produce changes in the employee's performance. Correlations of before and after job performance ratings could be low even when the measure is in reality reliable.

The reader may correctly assume that reducing the time lag between measurements will reduce the likelihood of learning or environmental changes influencing the scores on the second measurement. There are, however, at least two problems associated with this strategy. The first is that the shorter the time span between measurements, the less confidence there is in the reliability estimate. If the time interval is very short people will remember the responses they've just made and will be likely to repeat them. If the interval is long enough for them to forget most of their responses (a few days to a few weeks) then changes in the individual and the environment are more likely to occur. The second problem has to do with two identical measurement instruments (particularly paper and pencil measures). Going through the first measurement experience can sensitize the person to the points of measurement. As a result, the person is likely to attend to events in the environment related to those points. Thus, the very act of measurement can stimulate the person to change.

A better approach for determining the reliability of a measure is to create *alternate forms* of measurement. For example, construct two different tests of bookkeeping knowledge and then administer them to the same audience on two separate occasions only a short time apart. In this way, the experience of taking the first test is not likely to affect results on the second. The short time period between administrations reduces environmental or maturation of the trainee effects on the second administration. By developing the alternative form, you have created a larger item pool and can better assess the reliability of each. One problem with this method is that the internal consistency reliability of one measure may be higher than the other. The correlation between the two forms is a measure of the reliability across measures. But, shouldn't you just use the one with the highest internal reliability? This is a question that can only be answered pragmatically. If you only need one measure, then use the one with the highest internal consistency.

Validity

In relation to training evaluation, the concept of *validity* has two meanings: It can refer to the design of the evaluation or to the measures of criteria that are used. In the first instance, validity is the degree to which your results can be said to be true for the evaluation itself and for other groups that are put into similar circumstances. When we speak of *measurement validity*, we are referring to the degree to which the measurement procedure actually measures what it intends to measure. That is, if we are trying to measure errors in bookkeeping, then the validity of our measures is how well we actually do that.

The earlier discussion of criterion relevancy, deficiency, and contamination deals directly with the issue of criterion validity. If a criterion is contaminated that means that it is measuring something in addition to what it was intended to measure. To the extent it does this, its validity is reduced. Similarly, the more deficient and irrelevant the measure, the lower its validity. The problem is how to measure these things in an objective fashion.

As discussed earlier, the best way to empirically examine criterion validity questions is to look at the correlation of the criterion with other variables. If the criterion correlates as it should with the things it should, and if it doesn't correlate with things it shouldn't, then it can be said to have demonstrated some degree of validity. However, no specific number can be logically assigned to a criterion as representative of its validity. Rather, the validity must be inferred from the pattern of relationships. One procedure for systematically examining this pattern of relationships is called the *multi-trait multi-method matrix* (Campbell & Fiske, 1959).

Assume you had several measures of both bookkeeping and communication skills. Assume further that these measures had demonstrated reliability. To the degree that bookkeeping measures correlate with each other they demonstrate what is called *convergent validity*. Likewise, the convergent validity of the communication measures is determined by their intercorrelation. Table 5.3 presents some hypothetical correlation coefficients that illustrate the concept. The correlations contained in the upper left triangle represent the convergent validity of the bookkeeping measures; those in the bottom right triangle are for the communication measures. Examination of these correlations shows that the test of bookkeeping has the highest average correlation among the measures.

Table 5.3 Hypothetical multi-trait, multi-method matrix.

	Test of Book-keeping	Supervisor's Rating of Book-keeping	Coworker's Rating of Book-keeping	Test of Communi-cation	Supervisor's Rating of Communi-cation	Coworker's Rating of Communi-cation
Test of Bookkeeping	.85	.75	.70	.20	.30	.10
Supervisor's Rating of Bookkeeping		.80	.65	.20	.70	.30
Coworker's Rating of Bookkeeping			.75	.05	.05	.50
Test of Communication Skills				.85	.70	.55
Supervisor's Rating of Communication Skills					.80	.40
Co-worker's Rating of Communication						.70

The degree to which a measure does not correlate with variables it should not is called the *discriminant validity* of the measure. The discriminant validities of the bookkeeping and communication measures are contained in the square at the upper right of the table. The bookkeeping test has an average correlation of .20 with the communication measures. The average correlation of supervisor's and coworker's ratings of bookkeeping with measures of communication are .40 and .20, respectively. It would appear, superficially, that the test of bookkeeping and the coworker's rating of bookkeeping have equal discriminant validity. However, closer examination shows that the coworker's ratings do not discriminate well from each other. The determination of discriminant validity rests first on the ability to discriminate different variables (sometimes called *traits*) using the same measurement method. In the example, both the supervisory and coworker ratings do a poor job of this. If, as with the tests, there is high discrimination (i.e., low correlation) between concepts within a method, then discriminative ability is examined across measurement methods. Of course, what we are looking for is a measurement procedure that gives us both high discriminant validity and high covergent validity.

The reader may have noticed the correlation coefficients not contained within a triangle or a square. These represent the reliability of the measurement procedure. These numbers place an upper limit on the validity of a measure. That is, a measure can never be more valid than it is reliable. The reliability must always be equal to or greater than the validity. This makes intuitive sense. How can a measurement procedure truly measure what it purports to if it isn't measuring something consistently? If the supervisors' rating of bookkeeping performance is only consistent in its measurement about 64 percent of the time, how could it truly be measuring bookkeeping 70 percent of the time? Because the validity of measures is difficult and costly to demonstrate, many times only the reliability is calculated. This will at least indicate the maximum level of validity possible with a given measure.

DESIGNING THE EVALUATION

Once the criteria have been developed and a measurement procedure is agreed upon, a plan is designed for collecting the data. This plan is called the *evaluation design* and is as important as the development of the criteria. The manner in which the data is collected will have as much to do with the credibility of the evaluation results as the kind of data that is collected.

The purpose of training evaluation is to provide evidence of the degree to which training activities have achieved their objectives. As was pointed out earlier, different audiences are interested in different objectives. The design of the evaluation, as well as the measurement of the criteria, should be developed with the audience in mind. Because the training group is interested in all of the objectives (i.e., criterion domains), this group should be most concerned with the validity of the design. By validity of the design, we refer to *both* the internal validity and the external validity of the evaluation study.

External Validity

The *external validity* of the training evaluation is characterized by its ability to show that the results of the training program are *generalizable to* other groups and situations. Training departments usually aren't interested in just finding out if the training worked one time on one group. They would like to be able to say that the program would work with similar groups. To do this, the evaluation must be externally valid. For an evaluation to have external validity it must also be internally valid. If the results can't be assumed to be valid for the group being studied, they can't possibly be valid for other groups. In general terms, the more representative the evaluation and training program are, the greater the external validity. The threats to external validity discussed below are slight modifications of those listed by Campbell and Stanley (1963).

Pretesting reactivity Pretesting can sensitize trainees to give more attention in training to material that was on the pretest. Because of this, the training itself may not be effective with groups that don't receive the pretesting. The solution to this problem, however, is quite simple. Just make sure that all the groups who receive training are pretested. This makes sense for all the reasons discussed previously in the section on pretesting.

Interaction of selection and training The characteristics of the particular group that went through training may have made this particular type of training more or less effective. For example, a time management course that was very effective for secretaries may fall flat on its face with scientists from the research and development department. On the other hand, it might work very well, but you won't know it until some scientists become participants in the program. In general, the external validity of the evaluation is limited to the characteristics of the population from which the training sample was selected.

Reaction to evaluation Tests, observations, recordings, and other evaluation procedures reinforce feelings in the trainee that he or she is being "observed." These feelings can and often do lead to changes in behavior that wouldn't occur if the trainee were not aware of the evaluative nature of his or her participation. The results of the evaluation, then, are not generalizable to groups that wouldn't be exposed to the evaluation component. In many organizations where large numbers of people need to be trained, evaluation is only conducted on the initial training programs. Once the usefulness of training has been established, evaluation is curtailed. In situations such as this, the evaluative procedures should be as nonobtrusive as possible. The effects of reaction to evaluation can be measured to some extent by the use of appropriate control groups. If the reaction interacts with the training, however, it can't be controlled for.

Interaction of training methods Results from trainees who receive many different methods of training in a particular order can only be generalized to other trainees who receive those same treatments in the identical order. For example, assume an evaluation showed that trainees were exposed (in order) to lectures, case studies, and role plays. Significant changes in job behavior only began occurring after the role-play training. It would be invalid to conclude that only the role-play training was effective. It may be true that only the role-plays were effective but there is no evidence to support it. The evidence only supports the conclusion that a progression from lectures to case studies to role-plays results in significant changes in job behavior.

Types of Evaluations

It has been reported (Wexley & Latham, 1981, Bass & Vaughan, 1966) that the two training evaluation designs most often used are the post-test only and the pretest/post-test. This is unfortunate since both of these designs suffer severe threats to their internal validity. Table 5.4 presents the major evaluation designs for training. They are characterized in terms of whether they contain control groups, pre-, and post-testing, and how employees are assigned to the group(s).

Post-test only Because this design has no measurements prior to the onset of training, no factually supported statements can be made concerning the effect training has had on the outcome criteria. The only thing that can be known from this evaluation is that, by the end of training, the trainees were at a certain level of proficiency. Whether training had anything to do with that level of proficiency is anyone's guess. The point is that no one can tell whether any change has taken place. The trainees may have entered the program at the same level of proficiency or even higher, in which case training had either no effect or a negative one on the outcome criterion. Of course, it's possible that training did have a positive effect, but this design gives us no way to find out.

This design is useful for one of the criterion domains, however. When assessing trainee reactions to training, it would make no sense to measure these before training has taken place. For assessing reactions to a specific program, this design will suffice. However, the results may be rather difficult to interpret unless some comparisons are available. When the program is given more than once, reactions can be compared across courses. When multiple sections of the same course are unavailable, it may be possible (but risky) to compare the results to other training courses that are similar in content and process. Assessing trainee reactions is the only purpose for

Table 5.4   Types of evaluation designs.

Design	Groups	How Assigned	Pretraining Measurement	Post-training Measurement
Post-test only	Trainees	Random or Representative	No	Yes
Pretest/ Post-test	Trainees	Random or Representative	Yes	Yes
Post-test only,	Trainees	Random	No	Yes
Control Group	Controls	Random	No	Yes
Pretest, Post-test,	Trainees	Random	Yes	Yes
Control Group	Controls	Random	Yes	Yes
Soloman 4-group	Trainees-A	Random	Yes	Yes
	Trainees-B	Random	No	Yes
	Controls-A	Random	Yes	Yes
	Controls-B	Random	No	Yes
Time-series Control Group	Trainees Controls	Random Random	Several	Several
Multiple Baseline	Trainees		Several— Multiple Measures	Several— Multiple Measures

which the post-test only design should be used. If, for example, interest is focused on determining whether general opinions and attitudes about training have changed as a result of participation in the program, a more sophisticated design would be necessary.

Pretest/post-test design   This design should not be used in a formal evaluation of training because it provides no evidence of training's effectiveness. While it will show whether the criteria have changed over time, it can't show that training was responsible for that change. History, maturation, testing, possibly instrumentation, and statistical regression to the mean are all threats to the internal validity of this design. If trainees are not randomly or representatively selected for training, initial group differences between those being trained and those not will also be a likely problem. The lack of an appropriate control group makes any or all of these factors a possible explanation for any changes that might be observed in the trainees.

Perhaps the following story will illustrate the deficiencies of the pretest/post-test design.

A psychiatrist was conducting research on the causes of schizophrenia. It was his hypothesis and firm belief that this mental disorder was caused by certain chemicals produced in the body and carried in the blood stream. He wanted to show that the injection of blood from schizophrenics into a normal organism would produce schizophrenic-like behavior. His problems were many. He certainly couldn't use normal humans for his study, for if his beliefs were correct, he would be creating schizophrenics. He also wanted objective evidence of the abnormal behavior, if it should occur, but how do you tell when an animal is schizophrenic? He finally hit upon a solution that seemed to have merit. He would use black widow spiders and compare the design and geometry of their webs before and after injection of the blood. He chose these spiders because of a great deal of documentation concerning the symmetry and structure of their webs.

After procuring the spiders and waiting a few days, he photographed their webs. Comparing these photographs to the documentation, he found striking similarity. These were indeed normal spiders. He then proceeded to inject, with a microscopic needle, a small amount of the schizophrenic blood into each spider. He placed each spider in a new container and waited for them to begin spinning their webs.

The results were startling. The webs were bizarre in every imaginable sense. Some were incomplete, all had gaping holes and no symmetry. Satisfied, he disposed of the spiders and wrote his article for publication. As it happened, a biologist with some knowledge of these spiders happened to read the article and immediately penned a letter to the editor of the journal. The gist of that letter was that these spiders were terminally allergic to human blood. What the psychiatrist had observed was not spider schizophrenia, but rather, the web weaving of mortally injured spiders.

The psychiatrist in this story could have avoided professional embarassment by simply using control groups. Those groups could have been constructed as follows:

1. Randomly assign spiders to one of the four groups.
2. Group 1 would be the treatment group and receive the schizophrenic blood.
3. Group 2 would be a control group that received normal human blood.
4. Group 3 would be a control group that received an injection of inert solution.
5. Group 4 would be a group that received no injections at all.

Comparison of groups 1 and 2 would show whether changes were due to differences between the schizophrenic's and normal human's blood. Comparisons among groups 1, 2, and 3 would show whether it was the blood or the injection that produced the effect. Group 4 would show whether other factors in the environment were producing the effect. Groups 3 and 4 allow the psychiatrist to determine whether the procedures of treatment and environment might be masking the effect he was looking for. That is, if spiders in all groups began weaving bizarre webs, the psychiatrist would know that something in the environment was causing the disturbance. He could then reconduct the experiment in a better environment. If only groups 1, 2, and 3 showed the effects, the psychiatrist would know it was probably the injection procedure that produced the effects. He could then reconduct the experiment using a better method of injection. In both of the above instances, the original hypothesis is still viable since the environment or injection effects could have masked the effect of schizophrenic blood. Obviously, there are still alternative hypotheses that could explain the results. However, the obvious ones have been eliminated.

In order to show that training has had some impact on the criteria, the training evaluator, like the psychiatrist, needs a control group. The more control groups the more alternative hypotheses that can be eliminated and the greater the confidence that can be placed in the results. However, at least one is necessary and, for the purposes of most training evaluations, probably sufficient. Going back for a moment to our spider example, group 2 can serve as a sufficient control group without creating the other control groups. If groups 1 and 2 both showed the same effects, we would know that it wasn't the schizophrenic blood that caused it. We wouldn't know what caused the effects, but we would know that our hypothesis wasn't supported. Making the analogy to training, the only hypothesis we're interested in is the one that states that training program "X" improves the performance of employees in "A," "B," and "C" criterion domains. If we appropriately create a single control group, this hypothesis can be adequately tested. If the trained group is significantly higher on the relevant criteria, then we've supported our hypothesis. If there are no significant differences, then we will regret having only one control group. With a single control group, if we can't support our hypothesis, we won't know why. Perhaps for many of the evaluation audiences, the question "why" is unimportant. For the training professionals, however, it is very important. At this point we would be unable to show that training worked. Alternative hypotheses that explain why will remain untested in the single control group design.

Post-test Only Control Group

As shown in Table 5.4, measurements are only taken at the end of training with this design. The assumption is that randomizing assignment to the training or the control group will equalize pretraining levels of performance on the criteria for the two groups. A process called *matching*, in which pairs of workers are found who are alike on relevant variables such as age, sex, experience, etc., can be used to increase the probability that the two groups only differ in terms of the training they receive. However, pretraining equivalency can only be demonstrated through measurement prior to training.

This design is most useful when training needs to be implemented rapidly and time is not available for the collection of premeasures. A cost is paid, though, in terms of a reduction in knowledge. At the end of this evaluation, you will know whether a difference exists between trained and untrained employees and their respective levels of criterion performance. You will not know for sure how much impact training has had. This is the consequence of not knowing what level the two groups started out at. Imagine, for example, that the control group was somewhat higher on the criterion measures prior to training. At the end of training, if training has done what it was supposed to, the training group will have higher scores on the criterion than the control group. But, the difference between the two after training will underestimate the impact of training. Similarly, if the training group was initially higher on the criteria, this design would overestimate the effects of training.

Pretest, Post-test Control Group

This evaluation procedure corrects the deficiency of the previous design. Ideally, employees in the training population are assigned randomly to the control and training groups. By so doing, the conditions that pose threats to the internal validity of the evaluation are controlled. That is, the maturation, history, testing, etc., are the same for both groups. Since training is the only factor that differentiates the groups, training must be responsible for any differences in the post-training criteria measures. The only problem with this design, and it is minor, is that the effects of pretesting can't be known. While improvements in criterion scores may be related to exposure to the premeasures, is that bad? Only if your concern is to determine the impact of training itself. The following design takes this problem into account.

Soloman Four-Group

This is the most sophisticated evaluation design presented in this text. The design allows the evaluator to assess the effects of training and the effects of pretesting. As shown in Table 5.4, a training group and a control group are measured on the criteria both before and after training. Another training group and control group are measured only after training. Thus, this design combines the Pretest, Post-test Control Group and the Post-test Only Control Group designs. By comparing the pre- and post-criterion scores, the effects of training and pretesting are mixed together. By comparing the post-measures of those who were pretested and those who weren't, the effects of pretesting can be estimated. These effects can then be subtracted from the training effects to get a "purer" measure of training's impact on the criteria.

Time Series Analysis

The previous designs all have the slight disadvantage of requiring at least ten people per group. This requirement arises from the mathematical properties of statistical procedures used to compare group scores. In order to get a reliable estimate of the average criterion score for each group, at least ten people per group are needed. Since most training is conducted for larger numbers of trainees, this is typically not a problem. Occasionally, however, training will be required for groups of less than 20. For these occasions, the time series analysis is a viable alternative.

This design establishes a baseline of performance prior to training and subsequent to training. Cook and Campbell (1976) indicated that the number of pre- and post-training measurement points should be sufficient to ascertain all variations in the pattern of performance. Once a pattern of behavior has been established prior to training, deviations from the pattern can be attributed to training. However, it is possible that some other event affecting the training criteria has occurred concurrently with training. Because no control group exists, it is impossible to untangle the effects of one from the other.

A control group can be added to this design, making it a much more powerful evaluation tool. Because multiple measures are obtained (making the composite more reliable) on the pre- and post-training measurements, fewer people are needed in each group. The inferences one makes about training effectiveness can be much clearer when this approach is used.

For example, assume you were conducting a training program for quality circle group facilitators. The company had previously launched a so-called quality of worklife process (see Chapter 10) and the groups have been chosen and facilitators identified. You had monitored these facilitators for several months prior to training through questionnaires completed by the group members. The same method was used to monitor their effectiveness after training. Figure 5.3 depicts the results. A gradual increase in effectiveness can be seen by the facilitator's leading up to training. This could be expected as the facilitators became more familiar with their roles and the other group members. By the time they enter the training program, they are moderately effective. Looking only at the solid line, representing those who received training, performance levels out and remains steady. If no control group existed, the conclusion that training was ineffective would be quite compelling. An argument could even be made that training had a negative impact since it "flattened out" an upward trend. However, the existence of a control group shows that training prevented a rather dramatic drop in

Ratings of effectiveness

High

Low

12 11 10 9 8 7 6 5 4 3 2 1   Training   1 2 3 4 5 6 7 8 9 10 11 12

Weeks before training   Weeks after training

————— Training Group

------- Control Group

Figure 5.3   Time series line for quality control group facilitators.

effectiveness. This drop in effectiveness might be expected, for example, when management becomes aware of the program's impact on traditional roles. The training evaluation presented in Figure 5.3 not only prevents an inaccurate conclusion being reached about the training program, but provides documentation of a trouble spot in the quality of worklife program.

Multiple Baseline Design

The basic logic behind this design and the time series design is very similar. A baseline of behavior is established through multiple measurements. After establishment of the baseline, training is conducted followed by establishment of the post-training baseline. The difference, however, is that start times of the training are staggered across groups. Figure 5.4 illustrates the nature of this design. In this example, the same training (stress management) is given to each of three groups, but the training is provided at different times. Criterion data are being collected from each group on a weekly basis.

The advantage to this approach is that every group receives training. The staggered starting times allow for comparisons of trained and untrained groups. By examining the pattern of change for each group, the effects of training can be determined. In the example, a large increase in the percentage of weekly goals accomplished occurs during the second week in the first two groups and during the third for the third group. The rise in goal accomplishment continues until a peak of 85 to 90 percent is reached. Once this peak is reached, performance is maintained almost uniformly. It would

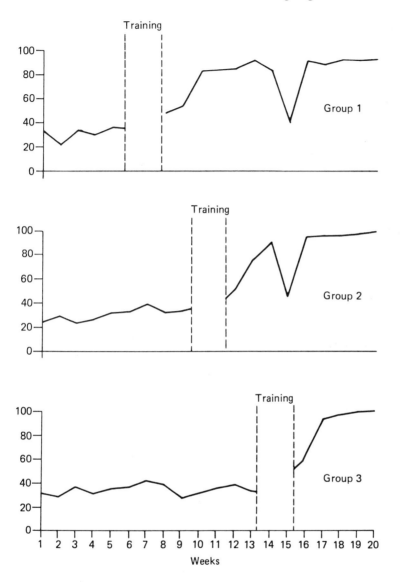

Figure 5.4 Multiple baseline evaluation of a time management training program.

be extremely difficult to argue against the effectiveness of training, given these data.

This is a very powerful approach for evaluating training programs. While the example in Figure 5.4 used multiple baselines across groups, it can also be used across behaviors within a group. For example, a management development program may span a period of 12 weeks. The first four weeks may be devoted to oral communication, the next four to delegation, and the last four to planning and organizing. Baselines can be established for each of the three categories for the five weeks prior to training, the 12 weeks of training, and five weeks subsequent to training. Since the presentation of topics is staggered, changes in the criteria associated with each should also be staggered. That is, changes should occur in the criteria only after that component of the training has been presented. When changes in the related criteria are concurrent with or immediately follow the training component, a causal inference can be made between training and those changes. Obviously, if those changes occur prior to training, something other than training must be the causal agent.

One of the advantages to this design is that the effects of training are examined at different points of time. In our example, a significant drop in goal accomplishment occurs during the 15th week. If training had only been evaluated at this time, it would have appeared as if training was ineffective. As it is, however, it can clearly be seen that some external event (perhaps a major crisis) occurred that reduced the total effectiveness. The following week shows a return to the previously high levels of goal accomplishment.

The major disadvantage to this design is the requirement for repeated collection of data. If data can be collected unobtrusively, from records or documents, this doesn't pose a serious problem. However, for other criteria such as supervisory evaluations, behavioral observations, and the like, severe limits may be placed on the trainer's ability to acquire the information. Before adopting this design, the trainer should carefully evaluate the ease with which data can be collected across multiple points in time.

Several different ways of demonstrating the effects of training have been presented. Some of them have very limited capabilities while others are quite sophisticated. The more sophisticated designs are better able to pinpoint the changes that training is responsible for. However, they present practical problems (e.g., randomizing assignments to training and control groups) that may limit their usability in pure form. The following section addresses this in more detail.

PRAGMATIC RESTRICTIONS ON EVALUATION

I recently went to a personal computer retail outlet to investigate purchasing my own microcomputer system. I had seen several advertised prices that appeared to be within my reach. One system in particular was advertised at just under $2,000. However, discussion with the salesperson revealed that the advertised price only covered the basic computer. If I wanted a "hard copy" of my output I would need to purchase a printer. I would also probably like to purchase some disk drives to save data files and other important information and to increase the memory capabilities of the system. Speaking of memory capabilities, I should really get a plug-in module that would increase the "RAM." Oh, would I need to have any graphical information output? Well, I shouldn't get just the regular printer, but one with graphic capabilities in four different colors. Of course, I will also need about $500 in software to start out. There was more, but I think the point has been made. The basics were affordable to me but at some point the utility of the increased sophistication ran out.

Observing the three methodological precautions (pretesting, control groups, and random assignment) outlined previously seems a small price to pay for increasing the validity of the evaluation. However, like the personal computing system, one must make sure that the costs of the system don't outweigh its benefits. Most organizations require the assessment of costs and benefits. Top executives must decide the relative value of alternative courses of action based on probable outcomes and the risks involved. Evaluation documents the effects of past actions. The value of this information is that it serves as a measure of progress and as a guide to future courses of action.

The more accurate the information received by managers, the lower the risk involved in using that information. However, increased accuracy goes along with increased cost. The cost as well as the validity of information increases proportionately with the sophistication of the data gathering process. The evaluator must make reasonable assumptions about how valid the information needs to be for a decision maker. Science has set up fairly rigorous standards for the validity of information it considers valuable. Business can afford to take bigger gambles since it is not concerned with matters as weighty as "THE TRUTH." Thus, the cost of the evaluation must be weighed against the value of the information.

The preceding pages have described various ways of designing and conducting evaluations. We make no claim that there is one best way. Rather, we suggest that the right design and procedure depend on the nature of the information needed by the organization. We would suggest that no outcome evaluation at all is preferable to an evaluation without pretesting or some form of control group. Since evaluations without these precautions are without validity the company might as well save the money. At the same time, only rarely will the knowledge that the pretest had a certain effect on the post-test be worth the cost of a full blown Soloman Four-Group design.

One further step is needed to complete the evaluation process. After determining the effects of training, the evaluator needs to translate those effects into a return on investment for the organization. The following section discusses how to translate training effects into dollars and cents.

RETURN ON THE TRAINING DOLLAR INVESTMENT___

Taking an excessively simplistic view, the basic objective of a business is to make a profit. Therefore, a key factor in top management's evaluation of the functional areas is their role in contributing to the profit or loss of the business. As stated earlier, trainers and training managers are often guilty of failing to document training's contribution to the profit picture of the organization. While the documentation of training's effects on job behavior is important, it falls short of providing the kind of information that would be most valuable and understandable for the business' executives. Documentation of the return on the training dollar investment is the kind of information these decision makers need.

Contributions to profit can accrue through increasing revenue or by decreasing expenditures. The basic formula for calculating profit, shown below, should be familiar to even those without a business background.

Revenue − (Costs + Expenses) = Pretax Profit

Training can contribute to increased revenue through improving the job performance of revenue-producing employees. Increased sales that can be attributed to a sales training program would be one example. Likewise, improving the job performance of employees so that costs and/or expenses are reduced will also contribute to the profit of the business. An example of this would be training that resulted in less scrap by production employees.

Translating Behavior into Money

In order to demonstrate training's contribution to the organization's profit, the evaluator must translate changes in behavior into dollars and cents. Many complicated approaches to this task exist (e.g., Cascio, 1982; Hunter & Schmidt, 1983; Johnson, 1980; Ryan; 1980). While these are, for the most part, beyond the scope of this text, we believe there are some relatively simple concepts common to them all. First, some measure of individual productivity must exist. Roche (1982), for example, reported using a "standard costing" method for determining the dollar worth of a production employee to the company. Time study procedures were used to establish the time it took a competent operator to complete one piece of work. A performance ratio was then computed by dividing actual production per day by "standard production" per day. A ratio of 1.0 would signify that the employee (or group) was performing at the "standard" rate. A ratio above 1.0 indicates performance above standard.

In a competitive market, a company's pricing strategy will normally incorporate the cost of materials, production, sales and marketing, overhead, and profit in relation to some estimate of demand and market share. Given that the company can sell a certain number of the product, it will price the product using a cost plus profit formula. A part of the cost of production involves the cost of labor. This cost is based on a calculation of standard performance. If the company builds a 20 percent profit into the price of the product, a worker performing at standard can be said to be contributing a 120 percent return on the company's wage investment. This is true because the cost of that employee is built into the cost of the product and consequently reflected in the price of the product. If training can improve the performance ratio of the employee it can directly improve the profitability of the product by reducing its cost (fewer employees are needed to produce the same number of pieces) or increasing revenue (more pieces can be produced in the same amount of time) or both.

However, the increased profitability comes at a cost. The cost of the training now becomes a part of the cost of the product. Thus, the increase in profitability must be reduced by the cost of the training. Table 5.5 presents a list of cost factors associated with various training activities. While overhead is listed separately, in truth it is a cost factor in all training activities. All of these cost factors added together represent the company's investment in the training program.

Typically, the rate of return on investment refers to the ratio of additional net income (generated by the investment) to the cost. If a new

Table 5.5 Factors contributing to the cost of training.

Activities	Costs
Developmental	
1. Need Analysis	Labor
2. Objective Determination	Materials
3. Course Content and Process	Travel (?)
4. Evaluation Instruments and Procedures	Accommodations (?)
5. Course Tryout and Revision	
Course Implementation	
1. Trainer(s)	Labor
2. Trainees	Facilities
	Materials & Equipment
	Travel (?)
	Accommodations (?)
	Food & Drink (?)
	Trainee Time/Lost Production
Evaluation	
1. Data Collection	Labor
2. Data Analysis	Materials & Equipment
3. Report Preparation	Travel (?)
4. Feedback	Accommodations (?)
Overhead	
1. Staff and Clerical Support	Labor
	Office Space
	Utilities
	Other (?)

machine generates $4,000 of income above that produced by an old machine, the additional net income would be the $4,000 minus the additional taxes on the income (say $1,000) and the depreciation (say $2,000), or $1,000. If the new machine cost $8,000, the yearly return on investment would be $1,000 divided by $8,000, or 12.5 percent. The example below uses the same logic for determining the rate of return on the training investment.

Muffy's muffler repair makes a profit of $5.00 on each muffler installed. Muffler installers are paid $7.00 an hour. The cost of worker benefits comes to $3.00/hr., making the cost of this labor $10.00/hr. The installers average 14 installations a day and it takes about a half hour for each installation. If an installation is done improperly, it takes a half hour on the average to make repairs. On the average, each of the 100 installers in district A will make 1 bad installation out of 7.

Because the company guarantees both labor and parts on muffler installations, the district training director has developed a program he feels will reduce bad installations to 1 in 28. The trainer has gotten approval to take the installers off the job for the four-hour training program. Subsequent evaluation revealed that training did reduce bad installations to 1 in 28, on the average.

To calculate the return on investment for the example above, it is first necessary to determine the additional net income resulting from training. To do this, we must determine the increase in profit due to the reduction in muffler installation errors. For this we will assume 250 working days a year.

(14 installations) $\times$ (100 installers) $\times$ (250 days) = 350,000 installations
(350,000 installations) $\times$ ($5.00 profit) = $1,750,000 profit

The calculations above show that if all installations were performed correctly, Muffy's should make $1,750,000 in yearly profit. However, 200 per day are incorrectly installed. This means that, on the average, the workers are performing two jobs a day for free. This labor cost must be subtracted from the profits. One must also subtract the lost profit that could have been made, but was not because the installer was doing work that had already been paid for. The yearly cost of the installation errors is calculated below.

(2 bad installations) $\times$ (100 installers) $\times$ ($15.00 labor & lost profit) $\times$ (250 days) = $750,000.

Nearly 43 percent of the potential yearly profit was being lost to bad installations prior to training.

Since training reduced bad installations to 25 percent of their pre-training level, multiplying the pretraining cost of bad installations by 25 percent will provide the post-training cost of bad installations. The post-training cost of bad installations is $187,500. Subtracting the post- from the pretraining cost of bad installations provides the additional gross income attributable to training. This figure is $562,500. Assuming a 20 percent tax on this additional income, the additional net income is $450,000. Thus, training can be said to have generated an additional yearly net profit for the company of nearly a half million dollars. However, the cost of training has not yet been calculated.

The costs associated with training are detailed below.

Developmental Costs:

1. 20 days of Director's time at $40,000/yr.	$ 3,200
2. 5 days of trainer time at $25,000/yr.	500
3. Travel	300
4. Materials	500
Subtotal	$ 4,500

Implementation Costs:

1. 5 days of trainer time at $25,000/yr.	500
2. Training facility rental; 5 days at $100/day	500
3. Materials and equipment	2,000
4. 100 trainees for 4 hours at $10.00/hr.	4,000
5. Lost profit (potential profit—cost of bad installations for 4 hrs.)	2,000
6. Travel (mileage reimbursement)	1,200
7. coffee, juice and pastry	500
Subtotal	10,700

Evaluation Costs:

1. 8 days evaluator time at $25,000/yr.	800
2. Materials and equipment	1,200
3. Travel	300
Subtotal	2,300

Overhead

Using company policy for calculation	4,500
TOTAL TRAINING COST	$22,000

Based on these figures, Muffy can be said to have invested $22,000 in training and received a $450,000 return in one year. This translates into a 2045 percent return on a one year investment. It was achieved by improving employee performance a little more than 13 percent.

While the example above may be a little unusual in terms of the magnitude of the return on investment, we do not feel it is at all unusual for a competent training department to generate an average return on investment of 200 to 300 percent. While we have no evidence to support this claim, we feel that it is reasonable. Yet, without knowledge of the impact training can have on profits, the hypothetical district manager of Muffy's might have balked at a $22,000 budget for a four-hour training program.

SUMMARY

Arguments against evaluating training have been examined and found to be inadequate. The fact is that training will be informally evaluated by others in the organization and it is to the training department's advantage to have input into the process. While the evaluation process is a search for truth (as is science) about the effectiveness of training, differences between the needs of the organization and the needs of science exist. The organization can take greater risks about what it considers proof than can science. This does not mean, however, that the organization should abandon logic in favor of reliance on authority, tenacity, and intuition. The principles of the scientific method should be adhered to but more flexibility can be granted in their application.

One of the most difficult tasks in training is the translation of objectives into measurable criteria for evaluation. Kirkpatrick's four criterion categories were presented followed by a discussion of how to develop valid criteria by avoiding threats to internal validity. Procedures for empirically evaluating criteria provide the trainer with some evidence of the degree to which the criteria are relevant, free from contamination, and encompass the concept of interest. Reliability and internal validity measures are used to accomplish this.

Once the criteria have been developed (and perhaps evaluated), a design must be developed to demonstrate the external validity of the evaluation. Threats to external validity are to a greater or lesser extent minimized by various evaluation designs such as the Soloman Four-Group and the multiple baseline. The value of minimizing the threats to internal and external validity must be examined in terms of increased costs and other pragmatic restrictions faced in an organizational setting.

Once the behavioral and organizational effects of training have been determined, they should be translated into a return on the organization's financial investment. Some methods for doing this and an example are presented in the final section of this chapter.

DISCUSSION QUESTIONS

1. What methods of minimizing threats to the internal and external validity of training evaluation would seem most reasonable in the organization you belong to? What are the factors that seem the most important to you in making this decision?

2. How would you determine the return on training dollar investment for a service organization such as a government agency or an accounting firm?
3. How would you go about conducting a process analysis for a management development program?
4. What are the various types of training criteria and their relationships to each other?
5. Describe the relationship between criterion contamination, relevance, and deficiency and criterion validity.
6. What are the differences in the kind of criteria that trainers and organizational decision makers are interested in?

EVALUATION OF TRAINING EFFORTS:
AN INTERVIEW WITH LAURITA THOMAS

Laurita Thomas is the Manager of Human Resources Development for the University of Michigan Medical Center. After 14 years of specialist positions in virtually every area of personnel administration, she now has a generalist position heading up this major department of a large health care organization. She has also held two other management positions in her distinguished career.

Ms. Thomas has a Bachelor's degree in Political Science and is completing a Master's in Business Administration. She is accredited in Personnel Management by the American Society of Personnel Administrators. Laurita is the President-Elect of the Ann Arbor Chapter of ASTD and a board member of the Michigan Society for Health Education and Training. She has published several articles and was recently named "Boss of the Year" by the American Business Women's Association.

We chose Laurita Thomas as the interviewee for this chapter because of the leadership she has provided in the area of training evaluations for her organization.

Question: Is evaluation of training really necessary? Why is it so important?

Thomas: There are many reasons to conduct evaluation of training programs. For one thing, as professionals we want to know if our training efforts made a difference. We also need the feedback to know what to keep and what to change when we run the program again. The feedback provides reinforcement. It is a key link in the process of education.

   The organizations we work for also need to have their training efforts evaluated. In my own case, I know that health care organizations must think more about themselves as a business. As trainers we need to demonstrate to our leaders that our product can be measured. Such information assists the decision making processes involved in budgetary and other planning endeavors.

   I also need evaluation data to help me evaluate my staff. You can see that evaluation of training programs has all kinds of benefits.

Question: But aren't there costs also involved in conducting evaluations?

Thomas: Yes, of course, but the costs are really dependent on the approach taken. Probably, the biggest cost is time. It takes time to design appropriate evaluation efforts and time to develop the skills needed to use those designs properly. We are also allocating monies to acquire the computer support to carry out the level of evaluation that we feel is needed. In today's organizations, trainers need more than a gut sense of what is working. We must demonstrate our value in a way business recognizes.

Question: What kind of evaluations are being conducted at your organization?

Thomas: About four years ago our department was given the mandate to conduct more thorough evaluations of our training efforts. I was in another position at the time but I well remember the frustrations my predecessor went through to establish rigorous research approaches to evaluation. A program evaluation consultant was hired who conducted a two day training program for us. Then we contracted with public policy analysts with experience in evaluation. They attempted to gather data simultaneously on control groups and our training population. After over two years of very hard work, the staff was frustrated to find limited proof that we made a difference on our population. The more we looked at it, the more it became clear that the methodologies used by program evaluators for places like the Public Policy Center weren't terribly appropriate for settings like ours. They had huge samples observed over long time frames and we didn't.

   When I moved into this position, I suggested that we switch to more pragmatic approaches of evaluation. We used a consultant, a principal with "Partners In Change," Pittsburgh, Pennsylvania, Dana Gaines Robinson and she helped us apply what she calls the "Training for Impact" or Tracking for Change model. The key to this approach is to carefully contract in advance of training. We work with the trainees and their supervisors and choose specific variables to track across time. We attempt to get our clients to define what success in this training effort would look like. We urge them to set the objectives in very specific and observable terms. We then attempt to measure our efforts against these standards by gathering data at several points in time and by including the observations of several sources for each variable. We also track variables in the work environment to help determine whether these elements are hindering or facilitating the successful use of our training.

   We now have some results to show our leaders. It took us awhile but we can now track level 3 and level 4 of Kirkpatrick's evaluation scheme that you mention in your chapter. For example, we were able to identify a $60,000 cost savings in one group that was directly attributable to changes in the participants' skill levels. We have also been able to document behavioral changes in trainees attending the time management, guest relations, telephone, complaint resolution, and management development programs.

Question: What do you see other organizations and trainers doing in the evaluation arena?

Thomas: My activities with ASTD and with colleagues in the health care field has provided me with a few glances of what is occurring elsewhere. Most are using self-report forms filled out by the participants immediately after a training program. Nearly everyone still uses the "happy sheets" (immediate feedback forms) but few feel this is where to stop. Very few are using control groups and I don't think that's so bad. I have some professional concerns regarding their use within the organization. How do you select participants in the control group and control for the other influences? Certainly those training programs that include computer-assisted instruction have built in feedback mechanisms. It is clear at the end of these programs whether the participants have learned something (Kirkpatrick's Level 2). We are also interested in professional peer reviews and will be exploring this concept in the next year.

We experience most of the same problems in conducting evaluation as other organizations do. It's very difficult to conduct a cost-benefit analysis in any service industry when it is difficult to define the costs and very frustrating to identify the standards expected of the employees. It is quite difficult to get the managers of trainees to put on paper what their evaluation is of our participants' progress. We need to do a lot of persuasion with these managers to get them to trust the use of the data and to perceive the value of filling out our forms. The time commitment required to observe the trainees and evaluate the level of accomplishment across a variety of variables is something very difficult for most managers to make.

Question: What do you feel is necessary to make evaluation data really useful?

Thomas: I believe you should reach an agreement that not everything should be evaluated. We now only evaluate about 10 percent of our programs plus any of our new offerings. We had to evaluate about 30 percent of our programs over the last couple of years to get to this stage but now we have thorough information on key offerings and don't burden the system down with too many duties. Other programs still contain some self-report evaluations in order to maintain the feedback loop to our trainers. Some programs that may be described as "fun courses" or career exploration courses probably shouldn't be evaluated . . . at least not at the Kirkpatrick 3 or 4 level.

Probably the key to making an evaluation effort useful is to gain "buy-in" from the supervisors of the trainees. Agreements must be reached a priori regarding the use and access to the evaluation data. Like I said before, much of our job requires being a persuasive communicator.

Question: Is evaluation more of an art or more a science?

Thomas: You warned me that you were going to ask me that question, so I have been thinking long and hard on it. I have concluded that it's not an either/or situation. Evaluation requires hard analysis, systematic development, and thinking and that's the science part. The art part includes the development of the language necessary to specify objectives in behavioral terms. That is difficult and requires creative thinking for many of the more "ethereal" training offerings. I think the art part also shows up in the tough work of gaining cooperation, interviewing participants and their supervisors and in being insightful observers. I guess if I were forced to decide, I would say that evaluation is more of an art than a science.

Question: How should people interested in careers as trainers prepare themselves to be able to conduct useful evaluations?

Thomas: I gained my own analytical skills on the job as the manager of compensation and organizational analysis. Conducting surveys for this organization taught me a lot about data collection, analysis and feedback. I would urge people to consider taking courses in project management, survey research design, task analysis and descriptive statistics.

I would hope that people entering the field would find it exciting to see if their training efforts make a difference. We all need strokes to keep going in our professions. Recognize that evaluation is right up front in the process of training. When you establish clear objectives before the sessions begin, you will be able to track the differences you are looking for.

Question: Do you have any final comments?

Thomas: I just hope trainers don't forget to build in the fun involved in conducting evaluations. Don't make it more of a headache than it's worth. Working with others on these matters often helps keep it all in perspective.

Chapter 6

NONEXPERIENTIAL TRAINING TECHNIQUES _____

The first portion of this book focused on the training system and its components. This section (Chapters 6 and 7) will focus on training techniques. As noted in Chapter 4, if we truly are referring to methods of instruction, and not ways that people learn, there are relatively few unique alternatives available. Basically, these alternatives involve telling, showing, and/or allowing the trainee to practice in some manner. There are many techniques that use some combination of these instructional methods. One of the most difficult aspects of organizing this book was developing a method of categorizing them. Unfortunately, there is no perfect categorization scheme. One or more of the techniques always seem to fit in more than one category, no matter what method is used. Nevertheless, categorization is important since it is helpful in comparing and contrasting the different techniques. Thus, we have selected a method of categorization that distinguishes between what we refer to as *nonexperiential* techniques in this chapter, and *experiential* in the next. It would be inappropriate to consider *nonexperiential* synonymous with the term *passive*. Many of the techniques to be described in this chapter suggest that the trainee take an active role in learning. The term *nonexperiential* was chosen for these techniques because they are more cognitively than behaviorally oriented. Stated another way, these techniques attempt to stimulate learning through their impact on thought processes, rather than as a result of the trainee's behavioral actions.

The techniques included in this chapter are the lecture, audio-visual approaches, programmed instruction, and computer-assisted instruction. For each technique, we will attempt to answer the following questions:

1. What factors should be considered in deciding whether to use this technique?
2. What planning should take place prior to implementation?
3. How should the technique be implemented?

Unfortunately, as Goldstein (1980) noted, the literature on training techniques is "mainly at a stage which must be described as nontheoretical and nonempirical" (p. 257). A more recent review (Wexley, 1984) echoes this thought. Thus, our recommendations for utilizing these techniques are often derived primarily from what we and other writers believe to be appropriate rather than solid scientific evidence. We will, however, attempt to supply research findings where they are available.

LECTURE: DEFINITION AND FEASIBILITY _____

Broadwell (1980) noted that the lecture, in its simplest form, is merely "telling somebody something" (p. 11). However, writers on this topic (e.g., Brown, 1978; Bligh, 1974) have noted several variations of the lecture format. A key variation focuses on the role the trainee should play in the lecture process.

One approach to lecturing has been called the *straight lecture* (Broadwell, 1980). With this type of lecture, the trainer presents the material and the trainee's only role is to absorb the information. In our opinion, this form is very rarely, if ever, an effective method of instruction within organizations. Research has shown that attention fluctuates throughout a one-hour lecture. After approximately 20 minutes there is a decline followed by heightened attention just before the lecture ends (Johnstone & Percival, 1976; Lloyd, 1968; Maddox & Hook, 1975). The decline is less likely to occur if the trainee is active.

It was noted earlier that adults prefer to take an active role in their learning. Trainees can actively learn from lectures by listening, observing, summarizing, questioning, and note-taking. Understanding may occur directly as a function of the lecture process or later as a consequence of examining notes. A straight lecture eliminates the possibility of understanding by questioning. Questioning is beneficial not only because it directly enhances learning through greater understanding but also because it keeps trainees active and more attentive. Thus, we feel that (ideally) the *lecture method* of instruction should be a two-way flow of information in which knowledge is transmitted from trainer to trainees. The method or way in which information is transmitted may need to be modified based on feedback regarding trainee understanding.

Prior to planning a lecture, it is important to conduct an analysis to determine whether the lecture method is a feasible strategy to address the specific training need. What we are really asking is whether the lecture approach is the optimal instructional technique for this particular problem. The first step in this process is to analyze information obtained from the training needs assessment. As noted in Chapter 2, training is (typically) only effective for resolving deficiencies that arise due to a lack of knowledge or skill. Knowledge is information; skill is the application of information. Since a lecture is designed to transmit information, it is best suited for those problems that arise due to a lack of information. If the deficiency arises due to a lack of skill, one of the experiential approaches described in the next chapter would probably be more appropriate. Finally, if the deficiency is a result of a lack of both skill and knowledge, then the lecture approach may be appropriate in conjunction with a more experientially based technique.

Given that the training needs assessment reveals a deficiency that is at least partially due to a lack of knowledge, three additional factors must be examined before the lecture can be considered a potentially useful technique. One factor is the *lecturer*. Some type of analysis (either by the training manager or possibly a trainer's self-assessment) must be conducted to determine if the potential lecturer possesses the basic skills required for lecturing. Table 6.1 provides a description of some of these skills. If only a few of these skills are possessed, there is a low probability of effective training by lecture.

Another determinant of whether a trainer will be an effective lecturer is his or her expert power (French & Raven, 1959). *Power* is the ability to influence; *expert power* is the ability to influence as a function of perceived knowledge. In order to be effective, a lecturer must be perceived by trainees to have information worthy of assimilation. A large portion of this ability may be a result of the quality of information and the manner in which it is presented. However, some portion of this power should be a function of the perceived expertise of the lecturer. This point was brought home to a trainer we know in his first training assignment as part of a corporate training staff. An (apparently) accurate training needs assessment was conducted along with detailed preparation. The topic of the course was "nonfinancial methods of motivation." All participants were first-level supervisors with several years of experience. What could have been a very effective training effort failed miserably. The failure was (according to the trainer's perspective) a result of a question generated after only ten minutes into the first session/lecture. The question was, "Sonny, have you ever supervised the kind of (unskilled) employees we do?" The answer was no, with the clarification that the trainer's supervisory experience dealt with professional staff. This led to several knowing smirks around the room. It was clear that the

Table 6.1   Basic lecturing skills.

Skill	Description
1. Orientation	Presenting information such that trainees understand the direction the lecture is headed.
2. Explaining	Providing information in such a manner that trainees understand the lecturer's intent.
3. Organization	Providing information in such a manner that transitions between major points appear logical to trainees.
4. Giving directions	Providing information in such a manner that trainees can use the information to appropriately carry out a procedure or solve a problem.
5. Illustrating	Providing examples of how information can or has been applied appropriately or inappropriately.
6. Comparing and contrasting	Providing information that presents the similarities and differences or advantages and disadvantages of various perspectives.
7. Enthusiasm	Providing information in such a manner to attract and maintain trainee attention.
8. Varying trainer activities	Providing information using several of the skills described in this table as well as encouraging trainees to take notes, reflect on key points, and ask questions.
9. Questioning	Obtaining feedback as to whether trainees comprehend the information provided.
10. Summarizing	Providing information that links topics or ideas together.

trainer's credibility was destroyed and the rest of the program was received with little attentiveness or enthusiasm. This example illustrates that an effective lecture depends not only on appropriate information and a skilled trainer, but on how the trainer is perceived by the trainees.

   This example is not meant to imply that only individuals who have had the same types of experiences as the trainees are appropriate as trainers. Rather, it is meant to show the necessity for being aware of and developing a plan to deal with how one may be perceived by trainees. In the example just described, a more sophisticated trainer might have anticipated this question and responded in the following manner:

   Before I answer your question, let me ask you why you think that's important? Are unskilled employees different from any other type? If so, how? (Assume the trainee notes some differences.) Weren't you an unskilled employee at one time? Were you that way? If not, why not?

The questioning process noted above tests several of the implicit assumptions of the trainee's question. Leading the trainee to recognize the fallacy of his or her assumptions should increase the trainer's perceived expertise as well as serve as a lead into the training topic.

Another factor to consider in assessing the feasibility of lecturing is the characteristics of the *trainee population*. Two trainee characteristics influence the feasibility of the successful use of lectures. The first is the communication skills of the trainees. As noted earlier, trainees can learn from lectures as a result of questioning, listening, and/or note-taking. These are basic communication skills and, of these, "listening skills" are the key since information must be perceived before it can be retained. If the trainees do not possess such skills, even a well prepared and presented lecture will fail. The second characteristic is the heterogenity of the trainees' intellectual abilities. If there is considerable variability in trainee abilities, the lecture may very well be over the heads of some of the audience yet too elementary for others. A major problem with the lecture is that it cannot compensate for *individual differences*. While this must be a judgment, a general rule to follow is the greater the difference in ability levels between trainees, the less the value of the lecture.

The final factor to assess in determining the feasibility of using the lecture method is the trainer's *access to necessary resources.* On a very basic level, some facility (e.g., a room) in which to conduct the training must be available. The more conducive this facility is to learning, the more feasible the lecture method becomes. Logically, an appropriate facility will have good ventilation, acoustics, and lighting. Seating should be ample and comfortable, considering the length of the training session. Seating should also be arranged in a manner that allows trainees to take notes easily. All of these factors should be examined as a basis for deciding whether or not to use a lecture approach. Similarly, logistics/scheduling must also be examined. A lecture (as we have defined it) requires assembling trainees at one point in time (typically) at one location. The practical problems of accomplishing this may reduce the feasibility of using a lecture. The investigation of logistics should also include an examination of the costs to the trainee and his or her immediate supervisor of taking the employee off the job. If trainees are concerned about what is going on "back at the office," their total attention will not be focused on the lecture and learning may not occur.

Figure 6.1 summarizes the factors to consider in examining the feasibility of using the lecture as a training technique. If the response to the first question is negative, one of the experiential techniques described in Chapter 7 is the type of approach needed. If a negative response occurs somewhere in response to questions 2 through 6, one of the other techniques described in this chapter may be appropriate.

1. Is the training need a result of a lack of knowledge? → Yes 2. Is the trainer skilled in the lecture method? → Yes 3. Does the trainer have expert power? → Yes

4. Do the trainees have the communication skills to learn from a lecture approach? → Yes 5. Are the trainees relatively homogenous in intellectual abilities? → Yes 6. Are there appropriate facilities? → Yes

7. Can logistics be coordinated? → Yes Lecture is feasible

Figure 6.1 Factors to consider in examining the feasibility of using the lecture technique.

Lecture Planning

Assuming the lecture method is chosen as the instructional technique, plans must be formulated regarding the way in which to implement it. This involves going back to the training needs assessment and examining the discrepancy between the trainees' current level of knowledge and the specified instructional objectives. Chapter 3 described the process of learning. Earlier in this chapter, we described the types of trainer skills involved in lecturing. Table 6.2 illustrates the effect particular trainer actions have on the process of learning.

Prior to beginning instruction, a plan should be developed indicating the type of action(s) that will be undertaken to remove the knowledge deficit. This plan goes under a variety of names (e.g., *lesson plan, lesson guide*, etc.). It should contain specific trainer and trainee activities as well as the objectives to be obtained by each. In Chapter 4 we described several key issues to consider in developing such a plan. These include determining the impact of a trainer's action on trainee attention, retention, and motivation. Yet, how does one actually put such a plan together? The place to begin is with the training objectives. The lesson plan should outline the procedure(s) by which these objectives will be obtained. In examining the objectives, the trainer should ask, "What does the trainee need to know to perform in the manner outlined in the objective?" This question should be answered in terms of the level(s) of learning described in Chapter 3. A blueprint should be developed, beginning with the highest level of learning required and working backwards through the prerequisite lower levels. This plan should be such that, if it is appropriately implemented, the desired objective(s) will be obtained. Once this is done, the next step is to determine where the trainees fall in terms of their current level of knowledge. If this information

Table 6.2 Relationship of trainer actions
to learning processes.

Trainer Action	Impact on Learning Process
Orientation ──────────▶	Attention/motivation
Explanation ────────▶	Encoding
Organization ────────▶	Storage/retrieval
Directions ────────▶	Encoding
Illustration ──────▶	Encoding/transfer
Comparison ──────────▶	Storage/retrieval
Enthusiasm ──────────▶	Attention/motivation
Varying activity ──────▶	Attention
Questioning ────────▶	Attention
Summarizing ────────▶	Retention/transfer

is not available from the person analysis of the TNA, steps should be taken to obtain it as soon as possible. This could be done by pretesting trainees the first day of training or earlier, if feasible. Obviously, not all trainees will be at the same level of knowledge and the trainer must decide whether to bore some through remedial work or force others to catch up on their own.

As noted earlier, considerable variability in trainee ability indicates that the lecture is not the optimal training method. Once the decision of a starting place is made, the trainer is ready to plan how to develop this learning through classroom activity. Trainers unsure of what types of trainer actions are needed to produce certain levels of learning should review Chapters 3 and 4. The point raised here is that several different ways to achieve any particular level of learning should be developed since all of them will not work. The final aspect of the lesson planning process is to develop some indicators that a trainer can use to signal that he or she should progress to the next higher level of learning desired. This might involve developing several sets of questions that, if trainees can answer correctly, indicate the information has been transmitted. Figure 6.2 summarizes the entire lesson planning process.

One additional point should be added in regard to the process of lesson planning. As described and typically implemented, the process focuses on the trainee. We have noted that (typically) training needs to take a wider perspective. This is illustrated by the classic Fleishman (1953) study. This study indicated that an otherwise well prepared training program failed because the supervisory reactions to the training content were not considered. This point should not be overlooked in lesson planning. Plans should

1. List the   →   2. Place trainees →3. Develop sets of →4. Develop some
   levels of   along this   activities for   criteria to
   learning   continuum.   each level of   indicate that trainees
   required   Start from   learning   can progress to
   from highest   this point   along the   the next
   to the   and progress   continuum.   highest level
   lowest to   to the   of learning.
   obtain the   highest level.
   training
   objective.

Figure 6.2   The lesson planning process.

be developed to assure effective *implementation* of the information. As Fleishman has shown, the trainee's supervisor may be a major impediment to effective implementation. One way to reduce this is to involve the (trainee's) supervisor in the lesson planning process. A short interview, in which the supervisor is asked to contribute ideas and/or approve lesson content, will go a long way toward developing supervisory commitment and support of training. As we have noted throughout this book, training effectiveness can be improved if trainers are willing to broaden their focus beyond the classroom.

Lecture Implementation

No matter how much time and effort are put into planning, learning will not occur unless the plan is appropriately implemented. We have already outlined many of the skills of an effective lecture (see Table 6.1). In addition to these points, the following tips should be considered when lecturing:

1. *Present an outline to the trainees.* This is not only an aid for organization but also gives the trainees an idea of the direction the lecture will take. It may also help trainees see the interrelationship among the various components of the lecture, which should aid learning. If possible, the outline should be displayed (e.g., on a chalkboard, overhead, or a handout) so that it can easily be seen. When you've completed a major point on the outline, announce it and check it off. This will be helpful in coordinating trainee attention on the same issue. While handouts are also an important tool of the lectures, these will be discussed in detail in the next portion of this chapter.
2. *Observe the trainee's behavior.* By examining the difficulty (or ease) with which trainees are taking notes, you can gauge the appropriate speed of your lecture. Puzzling looks from trainees are also an important clue that information is not being received appropriately.

3. *Encourage and use questions.* During the lecture, it is important for the lecturer to obtain feedback on its effectiveness. Written tests do not accomplish this since they take place after the instructional process. By asking and encouraging questions, a lecturer can assess whether learning is taking place. Rather than simply asking "What have you learned?" a lecturer can state something that is incorrect or contradicts an earlier statement. If trainees are attentive and have understood the material, the error or contradiction should be noted. If not, the lecturer should clarify the incorrect statement and review the material with which it deals.

4. *Use humor and self-assess your platform skills.* Much earlier in this chapter we noted that trainee attention can slacken during a lecture. Humor is a tool the lecturer can use to maintain attention. It may also create a loose, congenial learning atmosphere. While a lecturer should not be presenting a comedy routine, every effort should be made to make the lecture as interesting as possible. Without attention, retention is impossible but attention alone is not sufficient. Humor can gain attention but should be used to promote retention as well. In a similar vein, a good presentation/delivery cannot overcome bad material, but a bad one can ruin good material. It is tough to judge whether it's worse to listen to a monotone, unenthusiastic lecturer or the continuously intense "machine gun" delivery. Both should be avoided.

Table 6.3 lists some typical *platform errors* that lecturers make and steps that can be taken to correct them. To use this information, the trainer must be aware of his or her own faults. This can be accomplished by asking for anonymous trainee feedback on the effectiveness of the instructional *process.* Comments from a trainer/colleague who's observed your training techniques are also helpful. Finally, lecturers should also self-assess their ability (perhaps by observing video tape) and incorporate actions into their lesson plan that capitalize on their strengths and compensate for their weaknesses.

Lecture Evaluation

Ideally, this section should contain a summary of the research studies that have indicated which aspects of the lecture approach are most useful in organizational training. Unfortunately, such research does not exist. Research that is available has focused on comparing the lecture method to other training techniques rather than determining the optimal situation or method of administering a lecture. The problem in comparing any two training techniques is that the comparison must be made in terms of a learning objective for which both techniques are appropriate. For example, it is unfair to compare the relative effectiveness of the lecture versus sensitivity training for developing interpersonal skills, since the lecture is not designed

Table 6.3 Typical platform errors and ways to avoid them.

Errors	Ways to avoid
Talking while writing on the blackboard	If considerable blackboard work is required, use overheads.
Using highly technical words and complex sentences	Provide definitions prior to making your point.
Providing irrelevant examples and asides	Rather than explaining how the particular example illustrates a point, ask trainees to determine this themselves.
Reading rather than lecturing	Prepare an outline of key points rather than lecture notes that contain every sentence you plan to say.
Monotone voice	In everyday conversation, practice raising and lowering the tone of your voice. Listen to radio and TV announcers and analyze how and when they change the level of their voices. Also plan for pauses within your lesson plan.
Distracting gestures	If possible, videotape one of your lectures to help you recognize and correct these errors.

for skill enhancement. This point should be considered in examining the classic Carrol, Paine and Ivancevich (1972) study. These authors surveyed the training directors of several large companies regarding the relative effectiveness of several training methods for various training objectives. Three of their six training objectives are appropriate criteria for evaluating the lecture method. These are knowledge acquisition, knowledge retention, and participant acceptance. Of the nine training techniques used in the study, the lecture was rated as least effective for knowledge acquisition and eighth in effectiveness for the latter two categories. This does not mean the lecture is ineffective. Research studies (Stovall, 1958; Schramm, 1962; Nash, Muczyk, & Vettare, 1972) have shown that, for knowledge acquisition, the lecture is just as effective as TV courses, group discussions, or programmed instruction. The latter technique was rated as most effective for knowledge acquisition by the training directors, in the Carrol et al. study.

The studies (e.g., Stovall, 1958) that actually examined how well trainees learn from lectures are more reflective of the true value of the lecture as a training device. Yet, training director perceptions (which is what Carrol et al. measured) are probably the best reflection of how the directors will act (i.e., use techniques). A more recent study complicates this issue further. Neider (1981) attempted to update the Carrol et al. study (1972). She distributed a survey similar to that used by Carrol et al. to a sample of members of a professional training association. In her study, the lecture was rated the third most effective technique for knowledge retention and participant acceptance. It was also rated the second most effective technique for knowledge acquisition. It is difficult to assess whether the discrepancy between the Neider and Carrol et al. findings is a function of changing perceptions or differences in the characteristics of the samples used in the two studies. Regarding the latter point, perhaps Neider's sample contained more trainers (as opposed to training directors) who, as a result of their everyday training experiences, have a clearer understanding of the value of the lecture approach. Alternatively, perceptions may have changed. Further research is needed on this issue to give us a better understanding of whether the training professional's perceptions reflect the empirical evidence on the value of the lecture approach.

AUDIO-VISUALS: DEFINITION AND FEASIBILITY

Audio-visuals (AV) is the term used to describe all nonprint media and special equipment that aid in learning and instruction (Casciero & Roney, 1981). This may seem to be an overly restrictive definition unless one is aware that typically only books and periodicals are classified as *print media*, where media requiring the use of special equipment to be seen or heard (e.g., overheads, records, films, and television) are classified as *nonprint media*. Under this definition, computers can be considered audio-visual media through their video-displays. Computers also play a very important role in the development and use of the various types of nonprint media noted above. However, our discussion of computers will take place later in a separate portion of this chapter, as well as in the next chapter under the topic of simulation.

Table 6.4 illustrates the variety of ways organizations have used AVs within their training programs. Although we may think of them as a byproduct of this high technology age, AVs have played an important role in learning for a long time. For example, in 1870 a prototype slide projector was invented and used in Germany (Merril & Drob, 1977). Today, audio-visuals are sometimes used as an instructional method by themselves. More typically, they are used in conjunction with other techniques. In this section, we will discuss both approaches, but focus more on the former.

We have found from our own experiences that (whenever feasible) it is good to use AVs to complement another technique (e.g., the lecture). The AV may be a welcome change of pace from the other technique and, therefore, heighten attention. They may also be more effective in cuing or focusing the trainee's attention on a key issue. Many researchers in the education field have recommended multisensory teaching approaches (e.g., Lerner, 1976; Valett, 1978). Whether AVs are used individually or in conjunction with another method, the first step in the instructional process is to determine whether an audio-visual is suited to deal with the training at hand.

Table 6.4 Examples of how organizations use audio-visuals in training.

Organization	Description/Comment	Reference
1. Pitney-Bowes—a mail equipment firm	Uses AVs in conjunction with lectures as part of two-day seminar.	(Luongo, 1980)
2. USAir—airlines	Uses a sound/slide program that can convey more information (in the same time frame) than a lecture. Has found AVs three times more effective than the lecture for conveying certain types of information.	*Training,* 1982
3. General Motors—automobile producer	Uses video-discs to train dealer sales staff.	(Sullivan, 1982)
4. Cleveland Twist Drill—parts manufacturer	Uses a combination of audio-visual tapes, computer terminals, and printed material to train over 6,000 people in North America.	*Training,* 1981

Audio-visuals can be helpful in resolving performance deficiencies that are due to a lack of skill and/or knowledge. In the former instance, they are often used to create a simulation of the work environment where the trainee learns by observing and/or practicing the needed skill. Police training illustrates this usage. In some police departments, a film is used to visually place the trainee in the position of an officer searching for a suspect. The trainee must make decisions about if and when to shoot at appearing objects. Chapter 7 discusses the role of simulation in more detail. For now, we will examine the use of AVs for deficiencies that are (at least partially) a result of a lack of knowledge.

As they have been defined, AVs merely represent the use of one or more nonprint channels of communication. Yet what, if anything, do they add beyond other methods of instruction (e.g., the lecture)? Examination of the various types of AVs suggests the additional factor is the representation of an object in the form of a picture(s) or diagram.

Gagné (1977) suggested that the use of pictures (e.g., in a movie, slide, filmstrip, television show, or overhead) offers two instructional advantages. First, the picture may represent the object with which the trainees will be *directly involved* as a result of the learning. Second, the use of objects or pictures should allow the trainee to acquire the *visual* images that are useful in memory encoding and storage. This occurs because the image that is formed and stored is retrieved in its specific form. If, as part of a lecture, a trainer states "picture this situation," the trainee must mentally construct it. The picture that is constructed may differ depending upon the particular characteristics of the trainee. However, if a particular situation is depicted in a film, that situation should be retrived with the same characteristics existing when originally perceived. Although differential loss of information and detail may occur across trainees, what is retrieved is the initial perception of the same (common) object. If a variety of pictures are shown, all pertaining to the same issue, trainees have a wide base of common cues to use in retrieving the information associated with the pictures.

Wexley and Latham (1981) noted that AVs also offer the unique capability of demonstrating how procedures should be followed over time. For example, through time-lapsed photography a film can illustrate the consequences of improper maintenance on a particular machine. Similarly, split screen photography can simultaneously show the effect of a particular action in diverse settings. Finally, technological advances such as slow motion and close-up photography may provide the opportunity to observe events not normally observable by the human eye.

The discussion above illustrates the advantages of using AVs but does not describe those situations for which AVs are feasible as a self-contained training technique to solve a knowledge deficiency. There are several factors that must be examined in making this determination. Two of the factors must be considered jointly. These are trainee characteristics and resources/logistics. Regarding *trainee characteristics*, it's important to remember that

AVs (as we defined them) are a one-way communication process. Given this one-way flow of information, trainees do not have the benefit of acquiring understanding through questioning the instructor. Trainees should, therefore, have more difficulty with understanding information presented solely by AVs when:

1. Information presented to the trainees is difficult and/or complex.
2. Trainees are not experienced or skilled in learning solely from AVs.

To the extent that these factors exist, trainee understanding will suffer from the lack of opportunity to ask questions. In such a situation, the feasibility of AVs as a sole training technique is correspondingly decreased. However, this effect will be moderated by the availability of the AVs for re-use by the trainees. Issues may become clear after a second or third viewing/listening session. Although one of the advantages of AVs is that they can be re-used, certain *logistics* must be coordinated for this to be possible. For example, films can only be re-used by trainees if the viewing room, projector, screen, and skilled operator are available at the same time as the trainee. If these can be coordinated, the disadvantage of the lack of opportunity to ask questions in AVs is somewhat reduced since the trainees may learn through repeated use. Regardless of trainee characteristics, a resource analysis should always be conducted prior to determining the feasibility of using AVs as the sole training technique. One often cited advantage of this type of training is the capacity to use it on an organization-wide basis for training large numbers of employees. However, this is only true if the resources needed to implement the AV are available throughout the organization. Not only must the appropriateness of equipment be considered, but also whether desired instructional objectives can be obtained within the learning environment that will be provided (e.g., the room).

Figure 6.3 summarizes the factors to consider in determining the feasibility of using AVs as the sole training technique for a knowledge deficiency. The question as to whether the deficiency is at least partially due to a lack of knowledge is not listed, since this approach may resolve skill and/or knowledge deficiencies. Affirmative answers to each of the questions in the figure does not indicate that AVs are the optimal choice, only that they are a feasible training technique for the situation.

1. Is the information of the   Yes   2. Are the appropriate resources   Yes   3. Can the AVs
   nature that trainees will   ——→   and logistics available to   ——→   be re-used by
   not need to learn through   use the AV?   the trainees?
   questioning?

Yes   ——→   AV is feasible as the sole training technique

Figure 6.3   Factors to consider in examining the feasibility of using AVs as the sole training technique.

Planning AVs

Assuming that AVs have been determined to be not only a feasible technique but the desirable training mechanism, a decision must be made as to what type or combination of AV media should be used. Romiszowski (1974) provided a guide for deciding what type of verbal or visual media is most beneficial for the task at hand. This guide is reproduced in Figures 6.4

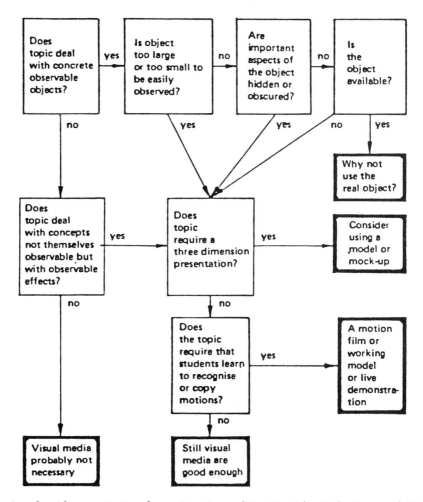

(Reprinted with permission from Romiszowski, A.J. *The Selection and Use of Instructional Media.* John Wiley and Sons, New York, and Kogan Page, London, 1974, p. 72.)

Figure 6.4   Decisions for selecting visual media.

and 6.5. As the figures indicate, the first factor to consider is the extent to which the topic deals with *observable events* (for considering visual media) or the extent to which verbal communication is the *main objective* (for verbal media). Earlier we mentioned that AVs can aid instruction; however, they should not be merely thrown in, but added for a specific instructional purpose. For visual media, factors to consider are (1) the size of the object, (2) the extent to which it is hidden or obscured, and (3) the importance of depth and motion. For verbal media, major factors to consider are (1) whether the topic is complex or abstract, (2) can the material be developed as a script, and (3) how often will it be used?

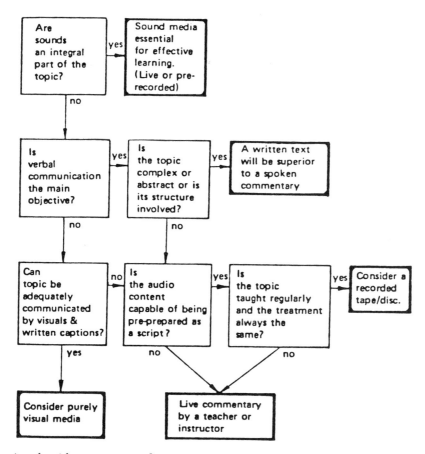

(Reprinted with permission from Romiszowski, A.J. *The Selection and Use of Instructional Media*, John Wiley and Sons, New York, and Kogan Page, London, 1974, p. 73.)

Figure 6.5 Decisions for selecting verbal and sound media.

Figure 6.6 illustrates the factors to examine in deciding *between* visual or verbal media. As shown in the figure, in certain situations, both may be needed.

Once the decision has been reached on the appropriate media or media mix, a lesson plan should be developed to help organize the presentation. The plan should be formulated along the lines previously described. Instructional objectives should be specified for each media used. This activity will increase the probability of effective instruction as well as play a useful role in the evaluation process.

Once media have been selected, the next step is to acquire or develop them. While we will not discuss these processes, several sources are available to aid the trainer in these types of activities. These include the professional journals *Training* and *The Training and Development Journal* which often run relatively straightforward "how-to" articles on media development. *Training* also typically publishes articles on recent advancements in AV technology (e.g., new cameras or sound equipment).

Even AV material of the highest quality will not serve its instructional purpose if presented inappropriately. Before the materials are developed or purchased, the trainer should investigate the room conditions in which they will be used. For films or opaque projectors, the trainer should check to be sure that any windows in the room have shutters or blinds so that the light can be blocked out. The accessibility of electrical outlets should also be investigated.

If one wall is an off-white color and free of objects, it may serve as a projection screen. If not, the trainer must select a screen. Screens can be categorized into three basic types of screen surfaces: *matte white, glass beaded,* and *silver lenticular.* Each of these is most appropriate for a particular viewing condition (Casciero & Roney, 1981). The matte white screen has a smooth, nongloss surface and will diffuse light evenly over a large surface area. It can reproduce a picture with good detail if used when the projection light is strong (e.g., with an overhead projector). Glass beaded screens have excellent picture sharpness and good color rendition when used in a very dark environment. The surface of a glass beaded screen is several times brighter than the matte white variety and has a narrow viewing angle. Because of this, the image is brightest and sharpest when viewed directly, rather than at an angle. Finally, the lenticular screen provides an extremely sharp image, even in partially darkened environments. Its major advantage is that it's designed to control horizontal light reflections.

Sound is another factor that must be considered. Most projectors have a built-in speaker system that will have at least the three watts needed for the average meeting or classroom (O'Sullivan, 1976). However, whenever possible, it is preferable to place a remote speaker near the screen for improved fidelity.

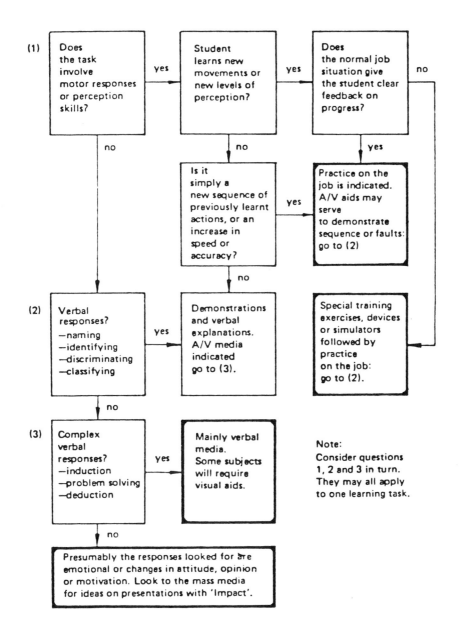

(1) Does the task involve motor responses or perception skills? — yes → Student learns new movements or new levels of perception? — yes → Does the normal job situation give the student clear feedback on progress? — no

no ↓ (from first box)

no ↓ (from second box)

yes ↓ (from third box)

Is it simply a new sequence of previously learnt actions, or an increase in speed or accuracy? — yes → Practice on the job is indicated. A/V aids may serve to demonstrate sequence or faults: go to (2)

no ↓

(2) Verbal responses?
—naming
—identifying
—discriminating
—classifying
— yes → Demonstrations and verbal explanations. A/V media indicated go to (3).

Special training exercises, devices or simulators followed by practice on the job: go to (2).

no ↓

(3) Complex verbal responses?
—induction
—problem solving
—deduction
— yes → Mainly verbal media. Some subjects will require visual aids.

Note:
Consider questions 1, 2 and 3 in turn. They may all apply to one learning task.

no ↓

Presumably the responses looked for are emotional or changes in attitude, opinion or motivation. Look to the mass media for ideas on presentations with 'Impact'.

(Reprinted with permission from Romiszowski, A.J. *The Selection and Use of Instructional Media.* John Wiley and Sons, New York, and Kogan Page, London, 1974, p. 71.)

Figure 6.6 Decisions for the matching of learning task to media characteristics.

AV Implementation

As mentioned earlier, trainer characteristics need not be examined in considering AVs as the sole training technique since the AV is the trainer. However, someone must take responsibility for running and/or setting up the AV. For visual media (e.g., slides, overheads, films, or TV) two of the most important considerations are seating arrangement and screen placement. Regarding the latter, the screen should be placed with its back to the window. This should prevent light from "flowing" over the screen and "distorting" the projected image (Casciero & Roney, 1981). If the screen is viewed from an oblique angle, it will result in a "keystone" appearance of the image. A *keystone* is a distorted image that makes one side of a rectangular or square area appear shorter than its opposite. This can occur when an image is projected on a screen that is not parallel to the projector's plane. It can easily be corrected by tilting the screen. This principle applies to all types of projector equipment.

On a logical basis, a screen should be placed where it can be easily seen. Chairs should be arranged to leave a clear path for the projector's beam. Since this may be difficult, a more desirable approach is to set the projector on a stand so that the beam will project above the heads of the audience. A projector set up on a four-foot stand will project a beam that will not interfere with a person of average height on a normal chair. For viewing a relatively large television screen, it is typically recommended that the minimum viewing distance be 5 to 6 feet. The maximum distance should be based on a ratio of one inch (of television screen) to one foot of viewing distance. Thus, seating should not be arranged more than 24 feet from a 24-inch television screen.

Some additional logical considerations involved in implementing an AV presentation are to:

1. Bring along extra accessories (e.g., bulbs, cable, extension cords, etc.). To slightly modify Murphy's Law, the more important the situation, the more likely whatever can go wrong will. It is wise to be as safe as possible.
2. Check to make sure all visuals are right-side up. One upside down slide can ruin a training session by reducing trainee attention and trainer credibility.
3. Be prepared to train when the lights go out. Films should be prethreaded. An overhead should be on the screen when the projector is turned on. Small issues such as these make a big difference in the perceived professionalism and acceptance of the material you present.
4. Have a dry run (i.e., practice presentation). This type of activity is not a waste of time since it can be very beneficial in pointing out many things you might have overlooked.

Although the discussion above focuses on AVs as the sole training technique, clearly they are more commonly used as a supplement to other methods. Although data is not available, the AVs most typically used in this

Table 6.5   Guidelines for using overheads and handouts.

1. Be careful not to overload overheads or handouts with information. Keep them simple (i.e., include major points) so trainees will be able to attend to and retain the information.

2. Overheads and handouts can divert attention from other training activities that are taking place (e.g., a lecture). To try to reduce this by using the "revelation technique" for overheads. This involves revealing information one line at a time. Handouts should typically be passed out at the end of a lecture, unless trainees will need to follow along the handout during the learning process or the information cannot be presented in an overhead. If handouts will be passed out after a lecture, trainees should be informed at the beginning of the lecture that they are coming. These activities will control the educational pace and maintain audience attention.

3. Overlays can be used to provide a depth dimension.

4. Dual projectors are useful in comparing and contrasting the information depicted in two overheads.

5. Don't forget to turn off the projector after you're done with an overhead or when positioning another. This will return trainee attention to the trainer.

6. Pretest your overheads and handouts in the training environment to make sure they're readable. Obtain trainee feedback as to how they could be improved.

7. Set objectives for your overheads and handouts. Specify what you want to accomplish with them and, based on trainee feedback, determine if this is taking place.

manner are most likely overheads, handouts, and films. Table 6.5 lists some basic guidelines for trainers to follow when using overheads and handouts. Table 6.6 lists some considerations for the selection and use of training films.

AV Evaluation

Just as with the lecture, research on AVs has focused on comparing this approach to other techniques. Data from the Carrol et al. (1972) study cited earlier indicates that training directors rated televised lectures fifth (of nine techniques) for knowledge acquisition and lowest for participant acceptance and knowledge retention. Films were rated fourth for knowledge acquisition, and fifth and seventh for participant acceptance and knowledge retention. Neider (1981) reported basically similar findings, with the exception of films which dropped to seventh in terms of knowledge acquisition.

Again, professional perceptions differ from the empirical evidence. Studies indicate that AVs are just as, if not more, effective than live lectures in terms of the amount of knowledge acquired (Schramm, 1962; Chu & Schramm, 1967). A considerable amount of data also suggests that television

Table 6.6   Guidelines for selecting and using films.

1. Choose a film that depicts situations that the trainees can relate to or identify with. Don't show a film about an executive decision situation to a group of first-level managers.
2. Choose a film that fits the ability and experience of the trainees. In previewing a film, check for jargon that trainees might not be familiar with. If you decide to use this film, clarify these terms *prior* to showing the film. Also, be careful not to choose an over-simplified film for highly sophisticated and experienced trainees.
3. In previewing a film, check for points that will contradict issues that you plan to raise in training. Point out and resolve these discrepancies before trainees raise these issues. Failure to do so may reduce your credibility.
4. Pick a film for its educational value not just because it offer a break from the training routine. Set objectives for your training film.
5. Evaluate whether your film accomplishes your objectives. One way to do this is through a discussion with trainees regarding their perceptions of the major points the film tries to make and how trainees will behave on the job after seeing this film.

can contribute to cognitive development (Solomon, 1979). Caution must be used in applying these findings to industrial training since the majority of this work has been with children. Goldstein (1974) noted that the effective use of motion pictures is contingent upon the use of good training techniques. He also pointed out that research studies have focused on AVs as the sole training technique, while in industry they are typically used in conjunction with some other technique. Thus, it is difficult to generalize the findings cited above to the typical industrial training situation when multiple techniques are used.

PI AND CAI: DEFINITION AND FEASIBILITY

Since both programmed instruction (PI) and computer-assisted instruction (CAI) operate on several, common principles, these techniques will be described simultaneously. However, this should not lead one to believe that they are synonomous, since there are several crucial differences between them. These differences will be outlined in the discussion that follows. First, it is important to understand the concepts on which these instructional techniques operate. Table 6.7 describes these principles. The format of this table utilizes the programmed instruction approach. Thus, this example can be thought of as a PI on PI. To get a feel for this method of instruction, the reader should work sequentially through the questions. A piece of paper can

Table 6.7   A programmed instruction on programmed instruction.

1. Many people think that it is impossible to learn without making a large number of *errors*. Learning by making errors is called trial and ___ learning.

answer = error

2. Yet, most people don't like to make errors. When people make errors they don't enjoy themselves and might lose their *desire* to learn. Trial and error learning will probably (increase-decrease) _____ someone's desire to learn.

answer = decrease

3. Not everyone feels that errors must occur for learning to take place. Some people feel if material is *programmed* (i.e., prepared) in a certain way, people can learn by making few errors. This material has been prepared so you will make few errors. It has been ___ .

answer = programmed

4. Programmed learning operates on the concept that if learning progresses in very small steps, few errors will occur. This material will progress in ___ steps so that few ___ will occur.

answer = small—errors

5. The idea that learning that progresses in small steps results in few errors can be called a *principle*. Another principle of programmed instruction is based on the idea that people will learn more if they are given immediate *feedback* regarding the appropriateness of their actions. This principle is called immediate ___ .

answer = feedback

6. Another principle of programmed instruction is that learning is enhanced if the trainee is active in learning. Requiring trainees to respond makes the trainee take an (active/passive) _____ role.

answer = active

7. The final principle we will discuss is the idea that people learn at different rates. People will learn best when they move at their own learning pace. In moving through this material, you can progress at your own pace. That is because we are trying to illustrate the principle of _____ learning.

answer = self-paced

8. Programmed instructions also review often so that trainees will not forget what they have learned. We will now review the four principles of programmed instruction.

The principle that learning should try to reduce errors is called the principles of ___ ___ .

answer = small steps

Table 6.7 A programmed instruction on programmed instruction. (*Continued*)

The principle that people should be told immediately about the appropriateness of their action is called immediate ____ .

answer = feedback

The principle that trainees should not be passive in their learning is called ____ responding.

answer = active

The principle that trainees should move at their own pace of learning is called _____ learning.

answer = self-paced

be used to cover the answer column. The reader should only uncover the answer to the question after an answer has been placed in the space provided.

PI is a method of self-instruction that uses the basic principles of reinforcement (Silverman, 1960). A PI is defined by the principles used to construct it, rather than the media used. Thus, PIs can come in book, machine, record, or any other format. We will define *computer-assisted instruction (CAI)* as the application of PI through the use of a computerized format. In a literal sense, this is incorrect since computers assist instruction in a variety of ways. After analyzing studies dealing with the effectiveness of computer-based (college) instruction, Kulik, Julip, and Cohen (1980) developed the following categorization of computers in instruction:

1. Tutorial—where new information is presented to the trainee.
2. Managed—similar to tutorial except that the trainee's strengths and weaknesses are evaluated and instruction is designed to correspond to the former and correct the latter.
3. Simulation—where the trainee learns through the use of models that simulate aspects of social and physical reality.
4. Programming—where the trainee learns through programming computers to solve problems in a particular area.

There are many similar classifications. Goldstein (1974) and others (Bork & Franklin, 1979) have classification schemes that add a category called drill and practice. This refers to learning by repeated exercise of a particular procedure or formula application. From our view, this is very similar to the use of computers as simulators. For example, drilling a trainee in addition problems is an attempt to simulate what the trainee has to do when facing an "on-the-job" math problem. If the computer is used to *teach* the trainee how to add, this is an example of the tutorial mode. If this instruction is designed to capitalize on the trainee's strengths, it would be in the "managed" category. Often, although not always, the design of computer instruction in the tutorial or managed modes is based on PI principles. Therefore, we will use the term *computer-assisted instruction* throughout the remainder of this text to refer to the use of computers in either a tutorial or managed mode.

To complicate matters further, there is more than one category of PI. Table 6.8 illustrates the *linear programming* version of PI. In this version, all trainees work sequentially, one step at a time, progressing to a common end goal. In a *branching program*, an appropriate trainee response to a frame (i.e., segment of the program) refers the trainee to the next frame. If the response is inappropriate, the trainee is referred to a branch of the program

Table 6.8 An intrinsic program example.

Our discussion of the lecture technique began by examining when this was a feasible approach to training. We noted that since it is a method of transmitting information it is useful for those problems that are *at least partially* due to a lack of knowledge. We also noted that the feasibility of a lecture technique depends on certain characteristics of the trainee population. One important group of characteristics are the trainee's communication skills. The greater the ability of the trainees to take notes, listen, and question, the more feasible the lecture approach. Second, the greater the difference in trainee intellectual abilities, the *less* feasible is this approach.

Question 1: Based on the above, lectures are feasible for solving performance deficiencies which are:
    A. Totally due to a lack of knowledge
    B. Partially due to a lack of knowledge
    C. Either A or B
    D. Neither A nor B

Question 2: Based on the above, lectures are feasible as a training technique when:
    A. Trainees possess certain communication skills
    B. Trainees differ considerably in intellectual abilities
    C. Both A and B
    D. Neither A nor B

Answers

Question 1: If your answer was:
    A. You're partially right but re-read page 180
    B. You're partially right but re-read page 180
    C. You're correct.
    D. We suggest you read page ____ *very* carefully.

Question 2: If your answer was:
    A. You're correct.
    B. Read page 182
    C. Read page 182
    D. Read page 183

that provides more detailed information regarding the basis for the designated correct answer. When the trainee completes this branch, he or she is directed back to the main program.

An intrinsic program (Crowder, 1960) utilizes branching as well as a larger frame than typically found in a linear program. After the longer frame, the trainee's knowledge is tested through the use of a multiple choice question. Again, based on appropriateness of the chosen alternative, the trainee is referred to a particular location, where additional (remedial) information is provided. Table 6.8 provides an example of an intrinsic program that one could develop based on the information presented so far in this chapter. By definition, PI and CAI are designed to provide information and, therefore, are helpful in resolving "lack of knowledge" performance deficiencies. However, other factors may limit their usefulness. One such factor is the length of time between the identification of the perceived training deficiency and when the PI or CAI can be developed and ready for use. One of the negative aspects of both of the techniques is that they require considerable preparation time which results in a high developmental cost. Both must be designed in line with the principles previously described and this will require some lead time which is not always available. This problem is more acute with CAI since both appropriate instructional and computer principles must be followed.

If time is a factor and financial resources are available, the trainer may wish to buy a previously developed PI (often referred to as *off-the-shelf programs*) or hire an expert to develop one. If either of these routes is chosen, care must be taken to assure that the instruction provided is appropriate for the particular performance deficiency. One very important concern is whether the examples from materials developed outside the organization will be perceived as relevant by the trainees. This is especially a problem for off-the-shelf programs. Thus, this program should be pretested (i.e., previewed and evaluated) by a group of trainees as well as trainers before a purchase decision is made.

Another important issue in determining the feasibility of using PI or CAI concerns the *characteristics of the trainees.* One advantage of PI and CAI is that they recognize and attempt to deal with *individual differences* of the trainees. PI and CAI allow a trainee to move at his or her own pace. If the program is from the "managed" mode, it is designed to utilize the trainee's strengths and correct weaknesses. However, if these advantages are to take place, two things must occur. First (excluding audio forms of PI), the trainees must be capable of reading the information provided. If trainees find this difficult, their motivation to use this method may be decreased. This is an important factor to consider when developing PIs. They should be designed according to the reading level of the trainee population. If trainees cannot read, an audio version of PI is the only feasible format.

The second trainee characteristic to consider is their *receptivity* to the use of PI or CAI. Some people are simply afraid of computers and don't want to use them. This should be more of a problem with trainees who have had no previous training and/or a negative experience with computers. From the opposite perspective, some individuals may find the PI format so simplistic as to be demeaning. For example, a manager who makes large financial decisions on a daily basis may perceive it to be beneath his or her dignity to progress in the small steps noted in the previous PI examples.

The final factor in determining feasibility applies only to the CAI method of instruction. An often cited advantage of PI in any media is the notion that trainees do not have to be gathered in one central location for instruction. Thus, this is typically considered an advantage for training employees in diverse locations of the organization. This advantage applies to CAI to the extent that employees have access to a computer. To the extent that access to a computer is limited, the feasibility of using CAI is correspondingly decreased. The increase in the number and the decrease in cost of personal computers may make this less of a concern in the future.

Figure 6.7 summarizes the types of issues that should be examined in determining the feasibility of using PI or CAI. A negative answer to any of the questions indicates that either technique is inappropriate for the particular situation. Just as in the previous sections, affirmative answers to these questions only indicate that PI and/or CAI is feasible but not necessarily the optimal technique(s).

1. Is there sufficient   Yes   2. Do trainees have the   Yes   3. Will trainees   Yes
   time or resources   skills (e.g., reading   find the use
   to develop or buy   ability) to use   of this tech-
   a PI/CAI?   PI/CAI?   nique accept-
                                                                        able?

   PI is feasible   4. Is access to   Yes   CAI is feasible
                                      computer readily
                                      available?

Figure 6.7   Factors to consider in examining the feasibility of using PI or CAI.

PI/CAI Planning

If PI is chosen as the instructional technique, the first issue in planning for this approach is to determine what media the PI will use. Many of the factors that influence this decision have already been addressed. For example, if trainees cannot read, the trainer has no choice but to use an auditory media. The issues raised in the audio-visual portion of this chapter should also be considered. Figures 6.3 through 6.5 (presented earlier) illustrate the decisions that must be made in matching the learning task to media characteristics. As noted earlier, CAI methods of instruction must be excluded from consideration if computers are not readily available. If this is not a concern, the other major considerations for CAI are the number of people to be trained and the stability of the information. It is (typically) not cost-beneficial to develop CAI for only a few employees on information that will be changing fairly quickly. However, this also depends on how important it is to resolve the performance deficiency.

After the media has been selected, a decision must be made on whether to develop the program internally or buy one off the shelf. Internal development of this type of material requires considerable skill. Trainers should carefully self-assess their ability in this area before undertaking such a project. Regarding CAI, Reynolds and Davis (1983) noted the following points to consider when buying a computer-based learning system:

1. No single system can do everything a modest size organization wants to do.
2. Training in the use of the system should be bought as part of the package.
3. Choices are narrow for the unsophisticated user.
4. Growth potential of the system should be considered.
5. Hardware quickly will become the smallest part of the investment in most systems.
6. There is a low probability of finding existing courseware for developing specialized skills or dealing with specific equipment and techniques.
7. The use of the mainframe computer is typically not desirable due to:
   a. Security issues.
   b. Loss of access/response time during peak hours.
   c. The fact that data terminals generally make poor teaching terminals.

There is considerable debate among experts regarding several of the issues noted above and technology is rapidly changing. Nevertheless, these illustrate the range of factors to consider when buying a CAI system.

PI & CAI Implementation

If the decision is made to write the program internally, much of the trainer's role in "training" is in developing the program. The first step in this as in any training effort is to develop the instructional objectives (see Chapter 4). This will be helpful for developing and sequencing the learning frames appropriately. Although a variety of formalized methods have been suggested for organizing frames (Mechner, 1961; Evans, Homme, & Glaser, 1962), we would suggest that information be ordered in line with the principles of learning outlined in Chapter 3. Thus, verbal association must be developed prior to concept and principle learning.

PI & CAI Evaluation

PI was rated as the most effective technique for knowledge acquisition and retention in the Carrol et al. (1972) survey of training directors as well as in the Neider (1981) study. Surprisingly, PI was rated relatively low (sixth) in terms of developing problem solving skills in both studies. This is surprising since the format of PI and CAI not only presents information but gives the trainee practice in using this information (e.g., decision making). Participant acceptance was also rated as relatively low (seventh) in both studies.

In reviewing the PI and CAI literature, Goldstein (1980) noted that many of the studies "have at least preliminary data supporting positive trainee reactions and learning effects" (p. 261). While comparative studies tend to show few differences between PI and other methods, the time saved in instruction is typically greatest in PI (Nash et al., 1971). Researchers have also warned about the high cost of CAI systems (Dallman & DeLeo, 1977). However, Seltzer (1971) noted the unique advantages of CAI relative to their cost. In a recent review of the CAI literature, Wexley (1984) noted, "At this point it seems clear that computer based instruction requires less time than more conventional methods to teach the same amount of material, and that there are usually no significant differences in achievement scores between trainees taught by the two methods" (p. 536). However, Wexley also reviewed a study (Hall & Freda, 1982) that compared CAI to conventional group-based instruction and concluded that each method had its respective advantage for certain types of tasks and students of certain ability levels.

One (potentially) negative aspect of PI and CAI is that trainers may perceive their responsibility as over once the program has been developed. Yet, student reaction data (Patten & Stermer, 1969) tends to indicate that trainees prefer PI in combination with some other method of instruction. Although PI and CAI allow for considerable individual differences, they do not allow trainees to learn as a result of questioning. Therefore, trainers should make themselves available to trainees using these methods of instruction to give them the opportunity to learn as a result of the questioning process. Dossett and Hulvershorn (1984) argued that trainers can devote more time to student needs when using CAI as compared to conventional instruction.

The field of OD suggests that care be taken in accepting high technological methods of training (such as CAI) since it may not necessarily mesh with the social system of the organization. The sociotechnical approach to OD recognizes that negative consequences may occur when technology is not compatible to social needs (Trist & Bamforth, 1951).

One advantage of training is the opportunity for trainees to present ideas and receive feedback from colleagues regarding the appropriateness of certain actions. One can also meet new friends or contacts in training (i.e., network). As a function of their design, PI and CAI technologies eliminate this social aspect of the training process. While some trainees may enjoy this, others may see PI and CAI as significantly reducing the value of the training effort.

SUMMARY

The empirical literature suggests that any of the nonexperiential techniques discussed in this chapter are effective if they are implemented correctly. The question of how one picks between the various techniques then arises. Table 6.9 attempts to address this issue. As depicted in the table, if one has to

Table 6.9 A comparison of nonexperiential techniques—conditions in which the technique is most appropriate.

Contingency	Lecture	AV (Sole technique)	PI	CAI
Nature of performance deficiency	Must be at least partially due to a lack of knowledge	Either knowledge or skill deficiencies	Either	Either
Trainee characteristics	Good communication skills and relatively homogenous in intellectual ability	Somewhat familiar with material	Can read at level of PI	Same as PI but also not afraid of computers
Trainer characteristics	Strong platform skills, perceived expert power	If financial resources are not available to buy "off the shelf," trainer must be skilled in principles needed to develop these techniques		
Major implementation concern	Centralizing employees at location and time	Availability/centralizing of resources (e.g., screen) and appropriateness of training location	Maybe viewed as too simplistic	Availability of computer
Time constraints	Not a major concern	Long lead time for development		
Cost	Small developmental cost but also small number of trainees taught per instructor, relative to the other techniques	High developmental cost but capacity to teach large number of students in diverse locations		
Major advantages	Trainees learn by questioning, content easily modified	Standard image presented to all trainees	Concern for individual differences	
Major disadvantages	Lack of capacity to deal with individual differences	Lack of easy adaptability/cost		

choose between techniques, the decision is typically between the lecture versus one of the other techniques listed. While the lecture offers relatively easy adaptability and the opportunity for the trainees to learn through questioning, the other techniques offer advantages such as a common image (AV) and concern for individual differences (PI and CAI). Thus, the ideal training course would attempt to use as many of these techniques as possible in an attempt to utilize their respective advantages.

DISCUSSION QUESTIONS

1. Certainly, all of us have had instructors/trainers who we thought were effective or ineffective lecturers. Think of the best lecturer you've ever seen. What made him/her so good? Don't use words like he/she "could communicate." Try to describe in specific behavioral terms (i.e., ones that others could observe) the specific actions that made this person such an effective lecturer.
2. Now do the same thing for the most ineffective lecturer you've ever seen. Again, the focus should be on behavioral actions.
3. Think of some training topics that PI and/or CAI would be useful as the chosen instructional method. Think of some where PI or CAI would be inappropriate. Explain the rationale for your answers.
4. Audio-visuals can obviously be useful to instruction. Can they be harmful? If so, how?
5. Make a list of your own strengths and weaknesses as a lecturer. Get feedback from others to see if they agree with your assessment.

TRAINING STYLES AND TECHNIQUES:
AN INTERVIEW WITH JOYCE MORGAN _____

Joyce Morgan is a staff development associate for the University of Michigan. Her duties include training and development programs for all managers and supervisors. She is also responsible for providing internal consultation services on a variety of organizational issues ranging from office procedures to long-term strategic planning. Prior to her employment at the University, she was an independent consultant and trainer working in both private and public sector organizations in Colorado and in Michigan.

Joyce is actively involved in several HRD-related professional associations including being the president of the Ann Arbor chapter of the American Society for Training and Development (ASTD).

We selected Joyce to interview for this chapter because of her constant exposure to the whole gamut of training styles and techniques.

Question: How do you decide which training style to use?

Morgan: I think of styles as essentially formal or informal. Most of the formal styles might be labeled nonexperiential while the informal styles are more experientially oriented. The choice of which style to use should be primarily a function of the objectives, content, and audience involved. The objectives should be determined by an analysis of the knowledge, skill, and attitude needs of the potential pool of trainees. If the knowledge needs predominate, a formal, nonexperiential style could fit the bill. If skill needs predominate, I would favor a more experiential style. I rarely feel comfortable with attitude needs being labeled as the primary objective in a training session so I can't really recommend one style over the other in these cases.

The key to choosing which training style to use is a matter of deciding which style is most likely to enhance your credibility and trust-worthiness. Personally, I have a strong preference for co-facilitating training sessions. With more than one trainer, we are highly likely to meet the style needs of the audiences we face.

Question: We described many "nonexperientially" oriented training techniques in the chapter that will precede this interview. How would you rate the general effectiveness of the various nonexperientially oriented training techniques, assuming they are used in situations that require a more formal approach?

Morgan: The most common technique, the lecture, generally doesn't deserve a high rating. It's really only good to impart knowledge and I believe that adults have short attention spans—20 minutes or so. Thus, the lecture method appears quite limited to me.

Films are another common nonexperiential technique that I don't see as generally effective. They seem more available nowadays and the technical quality of the film is clearly better. However, I bet I review 20 poor training films for every good one. Slides and video tapes that are generated in-house seem to me to be somewhat better methodologies because they provide so much more flexibility, often without as much cost.

The self-paced learning materials, much of which are computerized nowadays, can be quite useful. In fact, these materials can be designed to address skill and attitude objectives as well as knowledge needs. Still, adults tend to need interaction so I don't think many programmed learning efforts succeed without adding the benefits of group discussions, "real world practice," or the opportunity to receive coaching and clarification from the trainer of the material.

Formal one-on-one coaching can clearly be effective. The instant feedback thus provided can be quite powerful. However, this approach is quite labor intensive and thus not practical in situations where there are many trainees.

Question: Do you think trainers really adapt their styles to match the needs of the trainees they face?

Morgan: I would estimate that 60 percent of all trainers have some form of a canned program. They use and re-use essentially the same content and delivery methods with virtually every audience. Tailoring their programs to match a given audience's needs is more a matter of remixing canned parts. In their defense, they are leaving well enough alone based on previous successes. Let's face it; there are quite a few successful trainers who use a canned approach. The other 40 percent of trainers really attempt to develop a match between the needs of the audience and their personal style. However, not many trainers can effectively utilize all training styles. Some trainers lecture well and some don't. Some trainers can't manage group discussions well; they lose the focus provided by the stated objectives to the comments provided by the most verbal participants. I think trainers should periodically try styles that may be outside of their "comfort zones" but I wouldn't recommend choice of style to be solely determined by trying to satisfy the audience's preference. Comfort and competency issues must be considered.

Good trainers, in my opinion, are capable of using more than one style. They roll with what's working with an audience. They are capable of switching styles in midstream. I remember one trainer who I observed in a "train the trainers" session on "how to increase innovativeness." I thought he was going to be great. He had slick but useful materials and everything was cruising along just fine until the audience disrupted his pattern by asking a lot of questions, most of which were not covered in his hand-outs. He became flustered and couldn't really switch his style at this point. The session went downhill from there on.

Question: Based on your field experiences, what tips would you offer on how to enhance the effective use of the various training styles and techniques?

Morgan: Maybe I should offer a couple of general ideas and then tackle the more specific techniques. I believe any style is greatly enhanced by building in as much feedback as you can provide the trainees. Use of video tape equipment can assist this by providing a means of experiencing some information or exercise without interruptions and then providing detailed feedback as the tape is replayed. It's a method that's hard to beat because it can be used so objectively.

Another general comment I would like to make is that virtually any audience we face as trainers will have more cumulative experience than any of us individually. We need to facilitate the use of that 100–150 years experience or whatever it amounts to. Use of their experience will lessen resistance to almost any training technique. It provides the audience with some control and recognition that liberates the learning process in a powerful way.

Regarding the use of flipcharts, overheads, and other visual aids, I am concerned with a trend toward putting too much detail on these devices. They are sometimes overused or used in a matter not unlike underlining every sentence in a book rather than highlighting the key words or phrases. Variety is important but too many flipcharts confuse trainees with stimulus overload.

I must admit I have never felt good about programmed instruction and computer-assisted instruction methods. These methods rely too much on the motivation of the trainee and fail to provide the human interaction so crucial for adult learning to take place. I think some trainers fall in love with the jazzy technology. They become blinded by the medium and fail to notice some crucial elements of the training process. Trainers must never lose track of the objectives. We can't allow ourselves to be seduced by the glitter of video equipment or computers. We could end up doing more harm than good. Technical training requires effective use of relevant technology but we, as trainers, remain the key human link in the process of adult learning.

Chapter 7

EXPERIENTIAL TRAINING TECHNIQUES _____

EXPERIENTIAL LEARNING PHILOSOPHY _____

One of the basic ways we learn during our lives is through experience. The process of operant conditioning (described in Chapter 3) explains how we learn from experience. Trainers have attempted to take advantage of this natural learning process by designing training programs that focus on concrete experiences. It is assumed that active rather than passive processes promote more effective learning, especially for adult learners. The notion is not a new one. Centuries ago Confucius stated, "I hear and I forget. I see and I remember. I do and I understand." The potential for "learning by doing" is clear but the importance of trainers transmitting knowledge and abstract concepts has also been demonstrated throughout this book. Trainers need to be skilled in the techniques described in the previous chapter but need other methods to tap the potential of "learning by doing."

> There is a need for learning to include both active, personal experiences and general concepts, both theory and action. Theory gives a person some general principles to guide action, but if there is no opportunity to test theories in action, the theory remains just theory and does not become part of the person. (Hall, et al., 1982, p. 1)

This chapter will explore the following questions:

1. What are the assumptions of experiential learning theory?
2. What experiential training techniques are commonly used by trainers today?
3. When should a trainer consider using experiential training techniques?
4. What plans should be developed before using experiential training techniques?
5. How can the implementation of experiential learning techniques be enhanced?
6. What evidence exists concerning the effectiveness of the various experiential learning techniques?
7. What implications from the field of OD exist regarding the various experiential learning techniques?

We do not always learn or benefit from our experiences. As George Bernard Shaw put it, "If history repeats itself, and the unexpected always happens, how incapable must man be of learning from experience." If trainers are expected to manage the learning process in a way that promotes the learning of knowledge and skills, a theory is needed to help explain how learning from experience occurs when it does. Kolb (1971) developed an *experiential learning theory* which suggests that learning is a cyclical process involving four steps (see Figure 7.1). He suggests that we have many experiences that we fail to reflect upon and thus fail to learn from. If we observe our experience and identify the elements of that experience, we can then attempt to formulate a concept that explains what occurred by relating

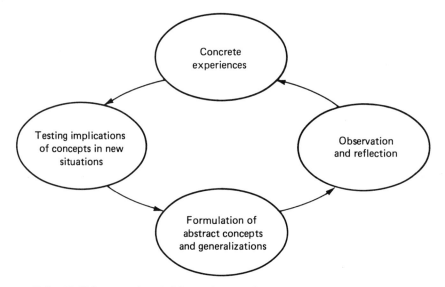

Figure 7.1 Kolb's experiential learning cycle.

it to previous experiences. Now that we have explained what happened, we can attempt to predict whether similar consequences are likely to recur if we repeat certain behaviors in other situations. Learning is not complete until we test out these notions in the other situations. This testing behavior constitutes another concrete experience, thus beginning the entire cyclical sequence again, allowing us to refine and expand our learning. Note that this explanation of learning is not unlike the models of the training process (Figure 1.1) and the cycles of organizational change described in Chapter 1.

Trainers using the techniques described in the previous chapter often manage the learning process by controlling the flow of information to an audience that is passive. The role of the trainer is basically that of provider of learning. The role of a trainer utilizing experiential techniques is different in degree, if not in kind. He or she shares with the trainee the responsibility for and control over the learning process. The trainer orchestrates an *opportunity* for the trainees to have a relevant experience, then encourages reflection and open discussion by the trainees. He or she also attempts to arrange for the trainee to try out the behaviors associated with the conclusions derived from such discussions. Thus, the trainer facilitates/guides the learning process as a collaborative effort. His or her expertise must include a thorough understanding of the process involved in achieving the training objectives but may also require expert knowledge of the content involved in the training experience. The trainees attempt to discover the underlying principles and master the necessary behaviors through active experimentation. The training design provides for more interaction between trainer and trainees, resulting in the opportunity for more personalized learning. Following is a list of five basic assumptions of the experiential learning approach. While these assumptions may not hold true in all situations nor with all trainees, they are the keys to designing some powerful training techniques.

1. Learning is more effective when it is an active rather than a passive process.
2. Problem-centered learning is more enduring than theory-based learning.
3. Two-way communication produces better learning than one-way communication.
4. Participants will learn more when they share control over and responsibility for the learning process than when this responsibility lies solely with the group leader.
5. Learning is most effective when thought and action are integrated. (Hall et al., 1982, p. 3).

Experiential learning is not without its critics. Freedman and Stumpf (1980, 1981) argued that there is little or no evidence of the validity of Kolb's theory. Their major concern is with the *"Learning Style Inventory,"* an instrument developed by Kolb and utilized as a means to identify preferences for various learning experiences and as the foundation for research to back the theory. Perhaps the major problem faced by trainers who utilize experiential approaches is that trainees can become so involved/excited/ intrigued by the experience that they miss the point of the training. They enjoy the game but fail to reflect upon the concepts that the training session was attempting to exemplify (Green & Taber, 1978; Hall, et al., 1982). Green and Taber (1978) also pointed out that, if the trainees do not have keen observational skills, they won't know what to look for and are likely to miss the point of the exercise. They suggested using the structure of the scientific method of inquiry as a means of putting the particular training sessions into a familiar, systematic framework and thus facilitating learning from subsequent experiences. Specific suggestions for enhancing the likelihood of training effectiveness will be included in the descriptions of experiential training techniques that follow.

> On the basis of need assessment techniques, it should be possible to determine what tasks are performed, what behaviors are essential to the performance of those tasks, what type of learning is necessary to acquire those behaviors, and what type of instructional content is most likely to accomplish that type of learning. Unfortunately, these steps remain the most elusive aspects of the design of training systems. (Goldstein, 1980, p. 235)

It is difficult to prescribe precisely when a trainer should use experiential, rather than nonexperiential, training techniques. It is particularly difficult to prescribe just when a specific experiential technique should be utilized. However, as a general rule of thumb, we suggest that if the results of the training needs assessment indicate that a skill deficiency exists (more than a knowledge deficiency), experiential training techniques should be strongly considered. One might safely assume that, if a trainee must learn how to operate a forklift truck or how to administer life saving CPR techniques, lectures and multiple choice formatted program instruction techniques will be inadequate. In addition to enhancing the skills of trainees, well developed experiential training programs have been known to increase self-awareness and to impart knowledge of principles through guided self-discovery.

Schein (1964), in his article on how companies should break in newly hired college graduates, suggested choosing experientially oriented techniques over lecture-style training. He pointed out that college graduates have received lectures throughout their college coursework and are anxious to gain the "hands on" opportunities offered by their new jobs. As a management trainee, he or she will be anxious to prove him- or herself, to verify that the effort expended in obtaining a degree was worth it. Schein maintained that a steady diet of nonexperientially oriented training sessions is likely to lead to higher turnover rates among newly hired college graduates.

Experiential training techniques also deserve special consideration when conducting training in an organization that is attempting to cultivate a leadership philosophy of participative management. The use of a participative training style to promote a participative management style provides an integrated perspective that should aid change efforts. In fact, to conduct management development training through a lecture on participative management promotes a "Do what I say not what I do" message. Of course we are not suggesting that lectures and other nonexperiential training techniques are never appropriate in "participative" oriented organizations or with newly hired college graduates. The decision of when to use an experiential method must be based on the needs of the trainees and of the organization, the skills of the trainer, the time and facilities available, the costs involved, and the number of trainees who require training.

Research on the effectiveness of simulations, business games, case study methods, role playing, incident methods, behavior modeling, and sensitivity training will be cited along with the descriptions of these experiential training techniques. It should be noted, however, that most of the literature on these techniques is still nontheoretical and nonempirical in nature. The few evaluation studies that have been published often failed to use reliable and valid measures of effectiveness and/or failed to use appropriate research designs. The literature of the last decade shows some improvement but still suffers from these problems.

SIMULATION

Experientially oriented trainers have designed training programs that provide an experience by simulating basic processes and features of actual on-the-job behaviors in order to allow trainees to practice skills or discover principles. Simulation/experiential training techniques include equipment simulators, business games, the in-basket technique, the case-study method, role playing, behavior role modeling, and T-groups. These exercises provide trainees with a safe opportunity to develop and learn. A novice attempting certain behaviors or applying certain theories on the actual job may make costly mistakes and/or create dangerous situations and/or distract the other employees during initial attempts. The cost of developing the simulation may be well worth it in terms of the costs that a company may accrue through damage to the equipment, scrappage of products, reduction in productivity rates of novice and interdependent coworkers, injuries to the novice or coworkers, and loss of customers. Furthermore, equipment simulators, role plays, cases etc., can provide a chance for trainees to practice what they would do in nonroutine, emergency situations in case they are ever confronted with such circumstances in subsequent job experiences. In addition, games provide a safe environment to experiment with new behaviors that might never have been tried because of their potential for embarrassment. Managers don't want to look "stupid" in front of their subordinates but may feel freer to experiment in a training session filled with supportive strangers. Thus, well developed simulation exercises can prevent nonproductive job behaviors as well as develop productive ones. The remainder of this chapter will provide the reader with a comprehensive view of what we feel are the major experiential training techniques utilized by practitioners today.

Equipment Simulators

As the name indicates, *equipment simulators* involve the use of machinery that requires trainees to use the same procedures and movements that they will have to use in order to operate the actual equipment assigned to them on the job. Equipment simulators have been developed to train airline pilots (Killian, 1976; Thorpe, et al., 1978), air traffic controllers (Killian, 1976; Parsons, 1972), battlefield officers (Erwin, 1978), taxi drivers (Edwards, et al., 1980), cashiers (Killian, 1976), maintenance workers (Fink & Shriver, 1978), telephone operators (Barrett, et al., 1981), and ship navigators (Paffet, 1978), just to name a few.

When planning training programs involving the use of equipment simulators, we recommend that the training equipment be designed to resemble the actual equipment as closely as possible in order to maximize the likelihood of positive transfer of learning. Furthermore, replication of the psychological conditions under which the real equipment will be used (noise levels, time pressures, pressures of being watched, etc.) deserves consideration. The author of this chapter well remembers feeling confident while being trained to ring up various types of sales in the training room of a large department store a number of years ago. My ability the following day to ring up actual sales on a machine that had key buttons in a different location than the simulation machine, together with a long line of unhappy waiting customers, made me feel that my training was a waste of my time and the company's money. I had to unlearn the habits gained from the training and learn to deal with impatient customers.

Some research literature addressing the effectiveness of equipment simulators as training devices does exist but should be considered as evaluations of specific machines not of the method as a whole. Killian (1976) reported that the use of flight simulators saved the airlines money since pilots in the evaluation study who had been trained on flight simulators had not experienced a crash of the planes to which they were eventually assigned and they used less fuel than pilots who had been hired years before when the airline had used a different training system. He also suggested that the use of equipment simulators should increase learning efficiency since the task could be "frozen" in order to point out very specific feedback concerning a trainee's actions. He did not provide any empirical evidence on this point, however.

On the negative side, Miller (1974) and Adams (1978) criticized the literature for failing to validate the principles involved in transfer of learning from simulation to actual experience. Thorpe et al. (1978) pointed out that they could not find any research on the long-term retention of knowledge/skills gained via equipment simulation training. And Edwards et al. (1980) reported finding no correlation between scores on two of the most frequently used driving simulators. Furthermore, no correlation between scores on either simulator and subsequent on-the-road performance was found for the 360 taxi drivers in their study.

The initial cost of developing equipment simulation is often high and the "cost" of storage can also be a problem. However, since the equipment is reusable, the volume of trainees that must be trained helps determine the cost effectiveness of investment. Furthermore, when human lives will be at stake, provision of simulation training may be deemed necessary.

The literature associated with OD and the behavioral sciences may provide trainers who use equipment simulators with some insights. For example, writings concerning the "sociotechnical" approaches to OD provide guidelines for the design/redesign of plant equipment (see, for example, Trist et al., 1963; Davis, 1977; Walton, 1975). The guidelines are very applicable to trainers attempting to design equipment simulators as well. In particular, the suggestion to involve the employees who will be using the equipment and the supervisors of those employees should aid OD efforts and should improve training programs dependent on the acceptance of equipment utilized. Such involvement should reduce resistance to change and promote "ownership" of the equipment to be utilized. Furthermore, the behavioral science literature of psychophysiologists, human factors psychologists, and perception theorists should also aid members of the training field. Behavioral science research on fatigue and field dependency provides but two examples of factors that should be considered in efforts to develop training devices likely to produce learning.

Business Games and Functional Simulations

Campbell et al. (1970) described this training method as a system that attempts to represent the functioning (usually economic functioning) of an industry, company, or organizational subunit based on a set of relationships, rules, and principles derived from theory and/or research. Trainees are provided with information regarding a situation and are asked to make input decisions. The system then provides feedback on the impact of the decisions made on the firm's outputs. Since the advent of computers, these systems can be very sophisticated and realistic.

Two basic types of systems exist: *games and functional simulations.* When a training program is described as being a game, one should expect that an element of competition is being introduced into the learning situation (Delamontagne, 1982). The competition may be between the individual trainee and the system or between trainees with win-lose decisions being made by the system. Functional simulations (such as "Strike or Settle," a collective bargaining simulation) may also involve an element of competition or may be a problem-solving exercise relevant to a particular business function.

The use of games as an approach to business training was first seriously introduced in 1957 by the American Management Association (Zemke, 1982). The AMA developed a game for its executive development program that divided participants into five teams in competition to capture a market. Quarterly decisions were made by each team for 12 rounds and a computer was used to calculate the outcomes of the decisions. A summary discussion session was held to compare the results with the various strategies used. This discussion is a key element of the learning process since it forces the participants to articulate what they learned from the experience as well as provides a forum to learn from the perspectives of others.

With advances in game theory (the quantitative study of decision-making behavior under conditions of uncertainty about the intentions of competitors; see Von Neumann & Morgenstern, 1944) and computer technology, there has been a virtual explosion of games available for use by trainers. Espoused objectives of various business games include:

- To strengthen/reinforce top managerial skills.
- To improve decision-making skills.
- To improve problem-solving skills.
- To apply theory.
- To demonstrate principles.
- To expose trainees to an integrative systems approach.
- To integrate training program subunits into a meaningful whole.
- To increase awareness of the impact of decisions on other subunits.
- To solve complex organizational problems in a safe, simulated setting.
- To explore attitudes and values of self and of others.
- To teach the need for coordination among members of a management team.
- To train managers in crisis management.

(see, for example, Groth & Phillips, 1978; Standke, 1978; Zemke, 1982). If this list includes an objective derived from your training needs assessment procedures, then shopping for an appropriate business game should be considered.

Business games have been used as a training technique by a wide variety of companies including banks (Goudy, 1981), the military (Van

Hemel et al., 1981), the entertainment industry (Zemke, 1982), and insurance companies (Ancipink, 1981). They have been used to train managers, supervisors, entrepreneurs (Lessem, 1979), industrial engineers (Lindenmeyer & Chrisman, 1980), and negotiators (Veglan et al., 1978) to name just a few.

Several authors (see, for example, Gentry et al., 1982) have offered suggestions on how trainers can enhance the effective use of business games. Guidelines include:

- Try the game yourself and read the players' manual.
- Make sure the game requires participants to make their own decisions rather than merely recall the opinion of an expert.
- Assess the compentency of the computer you may be using in conjunction with the game.
- Have contingency plans established in case of a computer crash.
- Arrange for participants to operate from several perspectives during the course of the game.
- Provide and discuss feedback from the instructor and fellow trainees in addition to the feedback provided by the game itself.

The literature also suggests that business games/simulations have some advantages over some other training techniques. Games are re-usable and thus their cost can be spread across the number of trainees who need such training. Playing a game, rather than sitting through another lecture or reading another policy manual, is usually an appealing proposition. The competition engendered and the gimmicks utilized by business games (especially realistic ones) tend to result in participant involvement and enthusiasm. In fact, this sometimes has been a problem for trainers since some trainees get so wrapped up in the activity or spend so much energy trying to "beat the system" that they fail to learn the principles and/or skills the game was designed to produce (Zemke, 1982).

Games that simulate entire companies or industries provide a systems perspective that few other training techniques can. As the trainee discovers how the parts are interrelated and how decisions he or she made have impact on other subsystems, a clarification of "the forest from the trees" can occur. Thus, while learning various decision-making skills, the trainee is also provided a broader view of an economic system. This is a major dividend to companies that want managers who can juggle a great variety of variables while producing a coherent, overall strategy. Furthermore, these games teach content such as rules, regulations, and jargon related to the industry or company while providing training in the processes of decision making, problem solving, and strategic planning.

Business games, like their equipment simulator counterparts, allow trainees the opportunity to make mistakes (and hopefully learn from them) in the safe confines of the training situation rather than in the costly arena of the real business environment. Reactions to simulated emergency business situations can be explored and quick, objective feedback (based on a game's programmed scoring system) concerning the impact of the decisions can be provided. In this and other ways, business games can compress time and expedite the learning cycle.

Not all games provide the advantages described above and most can suffer from the overzealousness problem previously mentioned. In addition, some games lack realism and virtually all must limit the range of issues/ variables addressed in ways that reduce their absolute fidelity to "real world" situational counterparts (Veglan et al., 1978). Since the scoring system is designed to account for a finite number of possible decisions, some games may stifle creativity by penalizing or failing to reward innovative responses.

Research evidence on the effectiveness of business games is limited and evaluations should be conducted on a game-to-game basis. Boocock and Schild (1968) claimed research evidence that simulation games produce real learning with measurable effects, but they failed to share that evidence with readers. Carroll et al. (1972) reported that training directors rate games and case studies as the best approaches for developing problem-solving skills and that participants find games more acceptable than most other methods. However, Raia (1966) and Rowland et al. (1970) provided evidence that the use of business games does not always produce positive reactions to the training effort. Finally, Frank H. Rosenfeld of Rutgers University is quoted by Zemke (1982) as having reviewed the evaluation literature on gaming and concluded that games are good for cognitive skill acquisition but not so good for fact and figure learning. He also claimed that there is a vast difference between participants' perceptions of the effectiveness of games as a training device and actual measures of behavioral change over time. He even found some negative impact on trainees who have trouble coping with ambiguity. Furthermore, he documented the moderating influences of age, I.Q., and educational background. He reported that the better the game is at teaching technical specifics, the less effective it is at teaching problem solving and decision making. Again, the effectiveness of the technique varies from game to game and one group of trainees to another. However, in general, the more realistic the game, the more effective it will be as a training device. The face validity of many games and the enthusiastic involvement of many trainees boost the hopes of trainers seeking program designs (Zemke, 1982).

As was pointed out in Chapter 1, the field of OD advocates taking a systems perspective. Comprehensive business games, perhaps more than any other training technique (with the possible exception of integrative case studies), utilize a systems perspective. The use of business games as a training method may be of particular efficacy to organizations interested in launching or reinforcing OD/HRD activities or for organizations with a need for improved coordination between departments/divisions. Since games can compress time, the short-term versus long-term impact of decisions can also be explored through this training technique.

IN-BASKET TECHNIQUE

A popular training program known as the *in-basket technique* provides trainees with a packet of memos, phone messages, and other written requests to simulate the types of written stimuli that managers/administrators might have to address in a given day. The primary purpose is to assess and/or develop the participants' decision-making skills (Otto & Glaser, 1972; Zoll, 1969). In-baskets can also be used to develop skills in report preparation, customer relations, disciplinary procedures, and time management.

Typical procedures include (1) describing the managerial role the trainees are to play, (2) providing the trainees with in-basket packets of written materials to which each must respond in writing in a given period of time (usually 2 to 4 hours), (3) a group discussion of the process the trainees used to go about the task guided by the trainer (Did anyone organize the memos according to subject matter? How did trainees decide the order in which they addressed the materials? etc.), (4) a group discussion of the trainees' responses to the materials, and (5) a discussion of how to utilize what was learned in training back on the job. A common variation of this procedure involves providing four interrelated in-baskets for every group of four trainees. The trainees are allowed to discuss the memos provided on a one-to-one basis over a telephone or may meet as a team in a designated conference room. The purpose of this variation is to provide training in team-building skills and to emphasize the interrelatedness of decisions made in organizations. The in-basket technique is also often used in conjunction with the Kepner-Tregoe method to develop rational decision making (see Kepner & Tregoe, 1965).

Although no research evidence of this specific simulation method was found, several authors (Otto & Glaser, 1970; Zoll, 1969; Campbell, et al., 1970) suggested that the method has the potential advantages of being relevant (sampling actual work behavior), easy and inexpensive to construct (just save actual memos, correspondence, etc., transmitted within a company, edit and produce a relevant packet) and is usually stimulating to the participants involved. Some of the drawbacks of this method include (1) the need to keep the number of trainees small in order to provide enough personal feedback, (2) the time involved in reading all the responses generated by the trainees, (3) unrealistic responses may be generated since no past history between the source of the in-basket materials and the trainee exists, and (4) the anxiety many trainees exhibit over having to write out their responses.

CASE-STUDY METHOD

Looking back in history we find Aesop (through fables) and Jesus Christ (through parables) demonstrating a method of teaching principles. Combine such a method with Socrates' approach to guiding a discussion and you have the basic procedures used to teach law and business principles at

Harvard University since the beginning of this century. The *case study* "provides an alternative type of simulation which is less costly, both in terms of time and facilities, but which may induce a considerable element of experiential learning" (Simmons, 1975, p. 185). It is a "system of instruction built on the premise that people are most likely to retain and use what they learn if they reach understanding through 'guided discovery'" (Kelly, 1983, p. 46).

Trainees are typically provided a written description of the history, key elements, and problems of a real or imaginary (but realistic) organizational situation. Often the case is written from the perspective of top management or an outside observer; although recently more cases describing problems faced at lower levels have appeared (Kelly, 1983). Trainees are expected to identify the decision issue, organize the documentation and data provided, determine a diagnosis, derive a solution with a statement of rationale, and develop an action plan to implement the solution. This analysis is usually worked on by teams of trainees (sometimes referred to as *buzz groups*) of five to eight members. In a subsequent, larger group discussion of the case, the trainer is to encourage maximum possible involvement of the trainees. He or she is to act as a catalyst by calling on trainees to state their views, by encouraging other trainees to confront elements of those views they do not support, and by fending off requests for the trainer to reveal his or her opinions of the case situation. The trainer is to promote the notion that there are no right or wrong answers, that cases are incomplete, and so is reality (Argyris, 1980). These procedures put the responsibility for learning on the shoulders of the trainees. It is hoped that the trainees will discover their own principles of business practice; demonstrate, refine, and apply their analytical skills to the solving of complex problems; and develop group discussion skills.

The keys to utilizing the case study training method successfully are the selection of the right case and the skills of the trainer. A "good case" is one that is detailed and complex yet contains no right or wrong answers to its problems (Kelly, 1983). Case studies describing actual situations are preferred because fictitious cases often contain inconsistencies that may frustrate or discourage trainees. Ideally, the case studies should be write-ups of the very organization the trainees are members of (Argyris, 1980). Trainers should act in accordance with the espoused principles of the case study method. They should emphasize double-loop learning (i.e., not only learn what the likely consequences of their decisions would be but why and how they behaved as they did) and emphasize during later discussions how the learnings discovered by analyzing the case can be applied to "back home" situations (Argyris, 1980).

Case-study methods are used by nearly all business schools and by many executive development programs. Leimberg (1980) reported the use of this training technique to develop estate planners and Broom and Ferguson-DeThorne (1978) reported the use of the case method to promote public relations.

A number of articles can be found in the literature describing the potential benefits that can be derived through the use of the case study approach. For example, Simmons (1975) stated that the method provides an intellectual/cognitive exercise that includes an opportunity to assess one's attitudes. He feels that case-study analysis sharpens the power of one's thinking, imparts knowledge about a particular industry, and develops inter-personal skills by encouraging trainees to verbalize their opinions. Kelly (1983) felt that decision-making, problem identification, and problem-solving skills are developed in addition to increasing the trainees' awareness of their own thinking processes. Leimberg (1980) touted case studies as an excellent technique for intermeshing several disciplines needed to solve problems. However, Campbell et al. (1970) pointed out that the method's emphasis on self-discovery leaves the trainer with no control over the teaching of princi-ples and thus trainees may draw inappropriate conclusions based on their examination of a single case. They, Carroll et al. (1970), and Goldstein (1980) all pointed out that very little research proof exists substantiating the bene-fits of the case study approach—especially research in organizational settings.

Research conducted by Butler (1967) did find that members of a class taught by the case method scored higher on achievement tests than a class taught by lecture and discussion. Castore (1951) found that interest in cases dwindles over time, although Carroll et al. (1970) reported that training directors of Fortune 500 companies feel that the case method is a more acceptable training technique than most other methods. They also reported the directors as feeling that cases and business games are the best methods for developing problem-solving skills.

Argyris (1980) conducted one of the few systematic evaluations of the use of the case-study approach in executive development programs. He found the trainers frequently violate the espoused principles of the approach. Not only did behaviors vary from trainer to trainer but the same individual frequently varied his or her behaviors in different situations. They fre-quently dominated rather than facilitated discussions, used set procedures while espousing that there was no one way, contradicted the principle that there are no wrong answers, and failed to relate the learning gained from a particular case to their back-home work situation. Trainees responded by looking for cues on how to succeed in the sessions.

> The result is a series of games and camouflaging of the games. For example, the theory of learning espoused by the faculty members is significantly differ-ent from that implied by their actions. However, the discrepancy between their theory and their actions is never discussed because the faculty members give cues that it is not discussable. Executives and faculty members evaluate each other covertly but they do not make the evaluations public and hence subject to test. The faculty and the students assert that education must be applicable in their work situation, yet they limit the applicability to technical concepts and exclude the concepts that are related to executives and organizational learning in the work setting (pp. 295–296).

Berger (1983) pointed out that Argyris' criticisms are based on a study that contains methodological and conceptual flaws and may be too harsh. Nevertheless, the point that Argyris makes regarding the fact that behaviors exhibited by advocates of the case-study method often varied from their espoused procedures deserves special attention.

The face validity of the case method has great appeal to some trainers. The time-honored procedures for conducting the sessions should be adhered to so that the true impact can be assessed. The field of OD has also many published case studies and so a link between the fields of training and OD may in fact lie in the training of OD change agents. The research of behavioral scientists on the discovery of insights may prove useful to trainers in their efforts to use the case-study method. In particular, the problem of translating insight into action has been of concern to psychotherapists for years. For example, Carkhuff and Berenson (1967) pointed out that psychotherapy has "been plagued with insight therapy approaches with patient products who have 'understood' but have been unable to act upon their understanding" (pp. 16–17). They go on to describe methods for change agents (therapists) to systematically develop action programs that flow from systematically developed insights. Parallel approaches seem appropriate for trainers who wish to use the case-study approach but want to insure that the learning accrued translates into action.

THE INCIDENT METHOD

A variation of the case study method deserves a short note. In this method, instead of providing all the details of a complex case, the trainees are given only a short history and a few details. Then the trainees are supposed to draw out the rest of the key points from the trainer by asking questions. The trainer is to reveal only what has been asked about. The interested reader should consult Pigors and Pigors (1961) for a more detailed description of the procedures and the rationale of the incident method. They felt that the questioning behavior utilized in this approach is the key to developing successful decision making for managerial positions. Trainers who use the incident method often supplement it with role playing and conference methods.

ROLE PLAYING

Role playing is another frequently used simulation technique. Utgaard and Davis (1970) reported that role playing is used by 15 to 20 percent of companies that conduct in-house training programs.

> Role playing may be defined as an educational or therapeutic technique in which some problem involving human interaction, real or imaginary, is presented and then spontaneously acted out. The enactment is usually followed by a discussion and/or analysis to determine what happened and why and, if

necessary, how the problem could be better handled in the future. (Wohlking, 1976, p. 36-2)

There are two basic types of role plays: the *structured* role play and the *spontaneous* role play. In the structured role play, the trainees are provided with descriptions of the characters they are to play, their attitudes/perspectives on a problem, and the situation that brought the characters together. This type of role play is used to train people in basic human relations skills such as problem solving, conflict resolution, and communications. In the spontaneous role play, one trainee plays him- or herself and the other plays a character that the first trainee recently encountered or soon will encounter. This second style is used to acquire insight into the behavior, attitudes, and style of oneself and/or others rather than skill development per se (Onder & Tuma, 1980).

The presentation of these two types of role plays typically occurs in one of three formats: the *single* role play, the *multiple* role play, and the *role rotation* method. In the single role play method, one example is played for the rest of the training group to observe, analyze, and learn from. This format provides the advantages of a focus on a specific interplay and shared feedback from a skilled observer—the trainer. It does have disadvantages in that the trainees involved in the role play itself may be embarassed by all the attention given them by the rest of the trainees who are placed in a rather passive role. Also, the example upon which the role play is focused might not exemplify the desired skills.

In the multiple role play all trainees are placed into role play groups and simultaneously carry out the exercise. This provides the advantages of participants feeling less embarassed about being put on the spot as well as getting more people actively involved. The subsequent discussion of the experiences of the various role playing groups points to how a variety of conclusions can be developed from the same stimuli. However, the multiple role play has the disadvantages of some pairs/groups finishing before the others and then having to sit and wait for the others. This may also inhibit others from delving more deeply into the situation. The post role play discussion may be richer for the variety of experiences the method produces but the discussion itself will be more difficult to manage. The method also has the drawback of not having a skilled observer available for each set of role players, thus reducing an important source of feedback.

In the role rotation method, a single example of the role play is initiated for all trainees to observe but the trainer frequently interrupts the role play for the group to discuss its progress; then different trainees are asked to replace the original players and pick up where they left off. The advantages provided by this approach are that examples of various styles will be viewed; it helps examine the developmental stages of issues and styles; it keeps trainees more active than the single role play; and it provides for feedback from a skilled observer. Its disadvantages include the fact that the interruptions add to the artificiality of the role play technique and that the trainees may feel inhibited to critique the focus example or may be embarassed to act as the example in front of the others.

As was mentioned previously, role playing can be used to train people in human relations skills and to investigate/modify attitudes. Wexley and Latham (1981) reported the use of role playing to train people in how to handle grievances, how to conduct performance evaluation feedback sessions, how to lead group discussions, how to listen more effectively, how to resolve conflicts, and how to discipline employees. Other recent descriptions in the literature of uses of role playing include training managers to be more assertive (Paul, 1979), training women for managerial roles (Baron, 1980), training salespersons in selling techniques (Horn, 1980; Skolnick, 1981), training supervisors and managers on how to handle sexual harassment incidents (Deichman & Jardine, 1981), training employees in listening skills (*International Management*, 1981), and training insurance agents to sell and to handle claims (Saint-Paul, 1982).

Shaw (1967) suggested that role playing can accomplish four types of learning: (1) learning by doing, (2) learning through imitation, (3) learning through observation and feedback, and (4) learning through analysis and conceptualization. Thus, role playing can be used to accomplish content and process objectives and can be used to supplement other training techniques so that trainees learn how to implement newly learned ideas.

The fact that role playing can be used to train people in such a wide range of topics and processes is not its only advantage. Otto and Glaser (1972) pointed out that role playing sessions tend to be very stimulating; they activate trainees to practice skills (such as listening, persuading, communicating, etc.) that are very transferable and useful back on their jobs. Role playing involves experiential as well as cognitive learning and it is expected that this should aid the transferability of the training session. As Maier et al. (1957) put it in their classic manual on role playing, "Seeing's believing but feeling's the truth." A trainee may see the logic of a theory through a lecture, see the application of that theory through a film, but has the opportunity to feel the personal utility of the concept when practicing its application in a role playing session. In fact, Solem (1960) pointed out that a basic characteristic of role playing is its emphasis on feelings as a source of human behavior. Since much of the human relations activity of the business world is conducted in face-to-face encounters, role playing allows an excellent (and less risky) opportunity for trainees to practice skills needed to deal with feelings and business-related issues.

Despite its many advantages and applications, role playing does have several limitations and can easily be misapplied. As Wohlking (1976) pointed out, a trainer using role playing techniques must be skilled at setting a conducive atmosphere, observing subtle elements of human interaction behavior, feeding back observations in a constructive manner, and leading group discussions that draw out the principles underlying the actions observed during role play sessions.

The potential for success with the role playing technique can also be limited by the trainees. Some trainees fail to take the role playing sessions seriously. They may take actions in the exercise (e.g., firing an employee) that they would not have used or used so quickly in a real job setting. Some trainees show off in order to entertain observers rather than using the session to practice what they actually would do in the situation. On the other hand, some trainees display acting anxiety (Onder & Tuma, 1980). They feel awkward taking on a role unfamiliar to their own situation especially under the watchful eyes of observers. Some trainers fail to sufficiently "warm up" the participants which adds to the artificiality of the training session as the trainees feel self-conscious and unprepared.

Another source of restriction on the successful use of role playing is the limited description of the case/situation provided to the participants and used as the framework of the role playing session. Wohlking (1976) pointed to three common errors prevalent among the prepared cases readily available to trainers. First, some cases present problems that would not or could not actually be solved by the roles represented in the role play. An example of this is a role play depicting a problem-solving session between a supervisor and a subordinate on a problem that really would require intervention by a higher level manager. Second, some written descriptions of the roles to be played are incomplete or misleading. One player may be told about a previous event but the other player may not. Finally, Wohlking pointed out that many of the available situation descriptions build in too many sources of conflict between the players. This results in an inconclusive session since that many conflicts cannot really be resolved in the time typically allocated. In fact, the whole issue of time consumption represents a general limitation of the role playing technique, especially if the benefit of trained observers is to be utilized (Campbell et al., 1970). Only a few trainees can be processed at a time and most available cases are written such that only one trainee is really "on the hot-seat" while the other role(s) merely provide the stimulation for that trainee to react to and learn from.

A number of actions can be taken by trainers to reduce the impact of the problems described above. Several authors have emphasized the importance of the trainer establishing a positive, conducive atmosphere (Otto & Glaser, 1972; Wohlking, 1976; Onder & Tuma, 1980). Very early in the session, the trainer should clarify the objectives of the training program and the connections between these objectives and on-the-job behaviors in order to develop motivation in the trainees. Some trainers provide a brief lecture on the desired behavior or attitudes while others prefer to have the trainees discover this element and reserve such a mini-lecture for the post role play enactment discussion. Some reduction in the "acting anxiety" levels of the trainees can be facilitated by clearly describing the situation, allowing the participants sufficient time to study their roles, allowing the participants to privately ask the trainer questions concerning their roles before the enactment, clarifying the time allocated for the enactment (typically 10 to 12 minutes unless more than two people are involved in the situation or if designed to develop problem-solving skills), and by encouraging the trainees to enjoy themselves and to be open to learning from their mistakes. Ideally, information regarding the situation and the roles should be provided to the trainees in advance of the training session. Trainees should be encouraged to heighten the reality of the role play by using their own personalities within their assigned roles and be discouraged from reading their role or situation description sheets during the actual enactment.

Again, it is important for the trainer to set a constructive atmosphere for the post-enactment discussion. Participants and observers should be discouraged from dwelling on mistakes and should be encouraged to point out what behaviors the role players displayed that helped as well as hindered the situation. Wohlking (1976), in particular, emphasized having the role player who was "on the hot-seat" (had the skill burden) process the activity first. This allows that trainee to acknowledge his or her own deficiencies and explain what strategy was being utilized. The trainer has a responsibility to structure the discussion of the role so that the focus is on the skills or conceptual model the session was designed to address. When using a multiple role play format, a data round-up, organized on a visible chart, aids reporting from each group and aids the process of comparing the results between groups. If trainees have been used as observers in the various role play groupings, those observers should have been provided with a structured observation report form in order to help them look for the emergence of behaviors/attitudes/issues relevant to the training objectives of the session.

Some trainers have used video-tape equipment in order to enhance the feedback process. The replay is carefully reviewed by the trainer and trainees and may be stopped at any point to emphasize an observation or ask the role player what motivated a certain comment. Wohlking (1976) recognized that the use of such equipment can indeed be very helpful but felt that it is frequently misused as a glaring reminder of embarassing mistakes the trainee made. In order to better use the video-tape technology, he recommended that a fixed rather than roving camera be used to record the session in order to reduce distraction. He suggested allowing the role players to initiate most of the discussion. He reminded trainers to stop the tape to exemplify positive/appropriate behavior as well as to point out mistakes. Finally, he stressed that the trainer should clarify what will happen to the tape after the session so that the role players won't worry about who else will see it.

While many articles boast of successful uses of role playing as a training technique, very few provide empirical support and fewer still report the use of sound research designs. This is due, in part, to the fact that role playing is rarely used alone, but rather, in connection with other training techniques (Goldstein, 1980). Carroll et al. (1972) reported that training directors view role playing techniques as more effective than lectures, games, and films at changing attitudes and developing interpersonal skills. They also cite a half-dozen references containing some empirical evidence that role playing can change attitudes. Ingersoll (1973), however, raised doubts over whether attitudes were really changed or whether the trainee responses indicated that they had been sensitized as to how to respond on post role playing questionnaires. Since very few follow-up studies have been conducted, he wondered whether behaviors and attitudes remained changed outside the role playing sessions.

Kidron (1977) provided the most thorough review of the research literature on role playing. He reported that several studies (Janis & King, 1954; King & Janis, 1956; Solem, 1960; Hoffman et al., 1962; Maier & Hoffman, 1965; Colgrove, 1968) that used control groups and found significant gains by groups trained by the role playing technique. He also reported five other reasonably well-designed studies that only provide mixed results on the efficacy of role playing (Lawshe et al., 1959; Janis & Mann, 1965; Gardner, 1972; Gray & Ashmore, 1975; Ingersoll, 1973).

Several studies compared the impact of role playing to other training techniques. Solem (1960) reported that both the case-study method and the role playing method helped participants develop solutions to problems but role playing was more effective at training participants on how to gain acceptance for their solutions. He also reported on seven other studies that showed role playing to be effective in developing problem-solving and solution implementation skills. Colgrove (1968) reported that role playing a case can produce more creative responses than the traditional case method. And Gardner (1972) found role playing more effective than lecture for teaching behavior modification skills but lecture more effective for teaching the theoretical underpinnings of behavior modification. It should also be mentioned that, like virtually any other training technique, the effectiveness of role playing is moderated by the composition of the trainee population, the specific procedures used by the trainer, and whether reinforcement for changed behaviors/attitudes is subsequently provided back on the job (Kidron, 1977).

As was suggested in Chapter 1, OD interventions are more likely to be successful when they address a felt need, are appropriately planned, and involve voluntary but active participation of organization members. Parallel procedures have been found to enhance the effectiveness of role playing (see, for example, Janis, 1968). Efforts to use behavioral science literature as a basis for improved role playing procedures has led to the development of other training techniques such as behavior role modeling.

BEHAVIOR MODELING TRAINING _____

Based on the notion that we learn most behaviors by observing models, practicing our imitation of those models, and then repeating those behaviors that receive reinforcement, a training technique known as *behavior modeling* (sometimes referred to as *behavior role modeling*) has received increased interest in the last decade. In fact, in the 1970s, it has been used to train over 500,000 people per year (Robinson & Gaines, 1980). Behavior modeling attempts to address systematically the weaknesses of several of the training techniques that have been previously described in this book. Byham and Robinson (1976) felt that it is better than on-the-job training (OJT) because supervisors are usually not ideal models and sometimes don't even recognize the mistakes they are making themselves. Thus, the trainee may never discover a good way of handling a difficult situation on his or her own. Additionally, learning by making mistakes can lower one's self-confidence.

Byham and Robinson also suggested that behavior modeling improves upon the role play training session since role plays typically give trainees the opportunity to view a number of negative illustrations of how to handle a situation without a clear idea of how to do it right. Trainees thus learn how to criticize what was done wrong but not necessarily how to go about it correctly. And, finally, while the lecture method may provide a detailed explanation of a behavioral theory, behavior modeling only stresses the key action learning points that the trainee is to recall about the theory. It is thought that, by stressing and repeating these learning points, the trainee is more likely to remember and act on the important features of a relevant behavioral theory.

What exactly is the behavior modeling technique? Several authors provide descriptions of the steps involved (Goldstein & Sorcher, 1974; Huegli & Tschirgi, 1980; Goldstein, 1980; Wexley & Latham, 1981; Zemke, 1982; Sims & Manz, 1982), although the number of prescribed steps and details differ across authors. Following is our summation of the steps of behavior modeling:

1. Define the key skill deficiencies.
2. Provide a brief overview of relevant theory.
3. Specify key learning points/critical behavioral steps.
4. Model demonstrates appropriate behavioral approach.
5. Each trainee practices appropriate behavioral approach through a guided role play.
6. Trainer and other trainees provide social reinforcement for appropriate attempts to imitate the model's behavior.
7. Trainee's supervisor reinforces attempts to apply critical behavioral steps on the job.

As step 1 infers, the technique emphasizes skill development over attitude modification or insight enhancement. It is based on Bandura's social learning theory (1977) not on Skinner's reinforcement theory. Thus, it is not a behavior modification technique that is only dependent on behavioral responses under various reinforcement contingencies. Instead, behavior modeling advocates the belief that learning can occur vicariously through imitation and/or through reinforcement, therefore acknowledging a cognitive as well as a behavioristic element. (See Locke, 1977; Gray, 1979; and Locke, 1979 as well as Chapter 3 for the debate surrounding this issue.)

Steps 2 and 3 reveal the cognitively oriented features of the technique, 4 and 5 the behavioristic, and 6 and 7 the importance of reinforcement to integrate such learnings. Suggested guidelines for enhancing the effective implementation of these steps will be discussed later in this chapter. A training module consisting of all seven steps is developed for each specific skill deficiency as well as one overview workshop for organization members not involved in the actual modules. For example, a commonly used package marketed under the title of "Interaction Management" consists of 20 two-hour skill modules presented once a week plus an introductory overview module, a review module, a diagnosis module, and a 1½ day workshop for managers of supervisors to be trained (Byham & Robinson, 1976).

Behavior modeling has been commonly used to improve the interpersonal skills of supervisors (Goldstein & Sorcher, 1974). It has also been used to train salespersons (Smith, 1976), job interviewees (Huegli & Tschirgi, 1979), and managers (Sims & Manz, 1982). Other applications have been reported in Burnaska (1976), Byham, Adams, and Kiggins (1976), Moses and Ritchie (1976). Recently, Sorcher and Spence (1982) applied the behavior modeling technique to change racial attitudes and related behaviors between white supervisors and black employees in several companies in South Africa.

Although this system of training seems to hold much promise, it is not without its critics, problems, or drawbacks. Some have complained that behavior modeling is direct manipulation of human relationships. Sorcher and Spence (1982) answered that claim by stating that it may be manipulation but it is not deceit. It does manipulate people to explore and practice alternative means of behaving in the training session but the decision regarding whether to use these alternatives on the job is left in the hands of the participants and their respective supervisors.

The most common problems associated with using behavior modeling center on the program's administrator. This person must be quite skilled in the behaviors being taught as well as in the areas of time management, feedback provision, and confidence building. Byham and Robinson (1976) reported that the most common problems with administrators are (1) skill deficiencies in group leadership and the use of positive feedback, (2) a lack of training in this specific technique, and (3) an inability to sustain enthusiasm for the procedures after the newness of the approach wears out.

The method has other limitations as well. A model or videotape of a model properly displaying the appropriate behaviors in relevant settings must be identified. Time must be allocated for each participant to practice the proposed behaviors under the guidance of a skilled observer/trainer. Behaviors learned in the training session must be reinforced by supervisors back on the job. Thus, the method requires that an organization have members who are skilled at providing reinforcement and a high degree of coordination between those in charge of training and line management. Limitations of training time, trainer's skill, and training load must, therefore, be addressed.

A number of authors have provided suggestions on ways to enhance the likelihood of successful implementation of the behavior modeling training technique (Goldstein & Sorcher, 1974; Byham & Robinson, 1976; Rosenbaum & Baker, 1980; Robinson & Gaines, 1980; Borinstein, 1982; Decker, 1982; and Zemke, 1982). Suggestions include:

1. Carefully select the trainer/program administrator who will set up and conduct the sessions. He or she must be skilled and experienced with this technique.
2. Carefully consider whether this technique will meet your needs within your constraints of time and money. Unless you can identify specific skill deficiencies, present a positive model of the appropriate behavior, provide the time for each trainee to practice the behavior under the watchful eye of the trainer, and arrange for reinforcement from the manager of each trainee back on the job, you probably shouldn't select this training technique.
3. Identify real skill deficiencies in advance of training and involve the potential trainees and their bosses in this identification process. As mentioned in Chapter 4, this will gain the key people's attention and gain their ownership of the objectives of the training sessions.
4. Break the skills that have been identified to be in need of development into small behaviors. Build a module around each small behavior and progress one step at a time, starting with a simple behavioral element, in order to gain confidence. This is also in accordance with the advice on developing training objectives provided in Chapter 4.
5. Do not emphasize more than seven learning points during any one training module.
6. Models used to demonstrate the correct way of behaving/handling a certain situation should have enough status in order to be credible yet easy for the trainees to identify with.
7. Use of a videotape of a model performing the correct behavior insures that all groups of trainees will see a positive example and may reduce

costs since it is re-usable. However, this improvement may be negated since it is difficult to find a model and a situation that is likely to be highly relevant and identifiable across diverse groups of trainees.

8. Before trainees actually practice the desired behavior, have them verbalize the behavioral cues the model demonstrated and then have them visualize their pending performance. Decker (1982) found this does not enhance trainee reactions to the training process but does improve generalization and use of the behaviors in new situations.

9. A supportive climate that encourages experimentation must be established for the practice sessions. Emphasis on positive reinforcement rather than criticism increases self-confidence and learning.

10. After each session, some behavior modeling experts provide a wallet-sized card that outlines the key learning points' critical steps. This is to act as a security blanket for the trainees so that they can rest assured of knowing the crucial features as they attempt to apply the training back on their jobs.

11. Conduct a review session after several modules have been completed in order to reinforce the learning points and to demonstrate the progress that has been attained by the trainees.

12. Manage the consequences of attempting the newly trained behaviors in the actual job situation. Work with the managers of the trainees to insure that they set attainable goals for their trainees, remove obstacles that may prevent trainees from attempting the new behaviors, and provide incentives for such attempts.

Research on the effectiveness of behavior modeling is more plentiful than on many other training techniques. For example, Moses and Ritche (1976) found that behavior-modeling (BM) trained employees at AT&T were much better at handling problem discussions than a control group (84 percent rated exceptionally good or above average compared to 33 percent). Burnaska (1976) found BM-trained subjects at General Electric handled assessment center situations significantly better than untrained control group subjects. However, he reported that there was no significant difference in the perceptions of the subordinates of these trained and untrained managers in their ability to handle on-the-job behavior. On the other hand, the turnover rate of difficult-to-employ employees whose supervisors had BM training was significantly lower than the control group of untrained managers. Smith (1976) reported a significant increase in sales for BM-trained teams compared to a decrease during the same period for the untrained teams.

Despite the encouraging news presented by the above three studies, McGhee and Tullar (1978) pointed out serious flaws in the research designs, leaving the question of the effectiveness of BM unanswered. However, a study conducted by Latham and Saari (1979) corrected these flaws and has been labeled by many (see, for example, Goldstein, 1980) as one of the best designed research studies of a training effort ever conducted. Forty first-line supervisors were randomly assigned to a behavior modeling program or to a control group. The BM subjects experienced two-hour sessions once a week for nine weeks. Each session had the segments listed below:

1. Introduce the topic.
2. Present film demonstrating effective behavior and present three to six learning points immediately before and after the film.
3. Group discussion of the effectiveness of the model's exhibition.
4. Actual practice in role playing the desired behavior in front of observers.
5. Feedback on demonstration by trainee.
6. Copy of learning points provided trainees.
7. Trainees report successes and failures of attempts to apply previous week's training.

The following lists the topics of the nine sessions:

1. Orienting a new employee.
2. Giving recognition.
3. Motivating a poor employee.
4. Discussing poor work habits.
5. Discussing a potential disciplinary action.
6. Reducing absenteeism.
7. Handling a complaining employee.
8. Reducing turnover.
9. Overcoming resistance to change.

The group of supervisors who experienced the behavior modeling sessions demonstrated greater improvements in all four evaluation categories (Reaction, Learning, Behavior Change, Results . . . see Chapter 5 and Kirkpatrick, 1977) immediately after training and several months later. Furthermore, the control group was subsequently provided the BM training and demonstrated the same improvement pattern. More recent research efforts have substantiated the positive findings of Latham and Saari (1979). For example, Decker (1980, 1982) demonstrated the added effectiveness of symbolic coding (verbalizing the cues demonstrated by the model) and symbolic rehearsal (visualizing the practice session prior to the actual session) in the use of the behavior modeling technique. And, Sorcher and Spence (1982) reported dramatic improvements in interracial attitudes and behaviors between white supervisors and black employees as measured by structured interviews. Finally, it should be noted that many successful applications of social learning theory have been reported by Bandura (1977), although most of these were in nonorganizational settings.

Behavior modeling techniques parallel the prescriptions for enhancing the effectiveness of organizational development techniques. When properly administered, BM programs are planned to address felt needs and open system notions by including more than one level of the organization's structure. BM programs are also firmly based on behavioral science theories and research. While it is not applicable to all training situations and has definite time and cost drawbacks, behavior modeling represents a systematic experiential training technique that has the demonstrated potential to change individuals and ultimately the organizations employing those individuals.

T-GROUPS, SENSITIVITY TRAINING, AND LABORATORY EDUCATION

While training techniques such as role playing, business games, and case studies use "artificial" experiences as the source of stimulation for experiential learning, T-groups have trainees focus on the stimulus of merely being together and relating to each other as the source for experiential learning. A *T-group* (T stands for "training" as in "human relations training" or "sensitivity training") may be briefly defined "as an intensive effort at interpersonal self-study and an attempt to learn from the raw experience of participation in a group, how to improve interpersonal skills and to understand the phenomena of group dynamics" (Shaffer & Galinsky, 1974). More has been written about T-groups than perhaps any other training method. It also represents the first major force to examine training from an organizational development perspective. Its "heyday" was the 1950s and 60s. Even as late as 1970, it was virtually the only OD technique in widespread use. It fell in disfavor because of misuse, lack of criteria for who should be allowed to lead T-groups, and lack of screening of potential participants. While most people left T-groups with a sense of having developed insights into their interpersonal relationship styles, few felt they had the opportunity to apply what they learned back on the job.

Today, the use of the pure unstructured T-group is quite uncommon. However, quite a few companies still send managers to the National Training Laboratories in Bethel, Maine, the center of T-group activity in the U.S. Other trainers use methodologies resembling the T-group but they are likely to call them "Human Potential Seminars," "Interaction Laboratories," or "Teambuilding Skill Training." In addition, these sessions are typically far more structured and far more likely to use intact work groups than was the practice in the earlier days.

Since this technique is no longer commonly used by trainers in business settings, we will not discuss it further in this chapter. However, because much can be learned from the history of this intervention, we have included an in-depth review and analysis of T-groups in Appendix A the end of the book.

SUMMARY ──

Education in the United States has been characterized as being action learning oriented with an emphasis on pragmatism (see John Dewey's writings, for example). The methods described in this chapter attempted to capitalize on these tendencies. The methods tend to take considerable time, require different skills for trainers, and require considerable planning in order to encourage transfer of learning from the training situation to on-the-job situations. They typically provide less control for the trainer than more didactically oriented approaches since the responsibility for learning is shared with the learner. However, research on "learning through discovery" indicates the potential for long-term retention of such learning. The interest, enthusiasm, excitement, and anxiety typically produced by the use of experiential methods add to their appeal to trainers. Certainly, trainers capable of using these techniques are in a position to address some very important training needs.

Throughout this chapter, we have attempted to stress that merely providing trainees with some sort of experience is insufficient to insure that learning will take place. Trainers must be skilled at encouraging reflection about the experience in a way that results in trainees' discovery of some concept or generalization. Furthermore, the trainer must help the trainee structure a plan for using his or her newly discovered concept back on the job.

We expect the reader to realize now that experiential techniques (simulations, games, case studies, role plays, behavior modeling, T-group, etc.) can be powerful training devices but also have certain drawbacks. We have attempted to prescribe procedures to increase the likelihood of successful use of the various techniques. However, practical considerations such as the type of facilities available, budget allocations, number of trainees to be involved, and time requirements will often limit a trainer's ability to use experiential techniques for a given training assignment. These factors, as well as the skills of the trainer and the needs of the trainees, must serve as the basic guidelines for using certain training techniques. It is our hope that our exposition of the procedures and our provision of additional references for supplemental reading will enable the reader to make rational decisions regarding the selection of these techniques.

DISCUSSION QUESTIONS ──────────────────────────

1. What do you see as the advantages of experiential learning? What are the disadvantages?
2. Of all the experiential techniques described in this chapter, which would you feel the most capable to implement as a trainer? Which would you feel least capable to implement? Why?

3. Why do you think T-groups are no longer as popular as they once were?
4. In Chapter 4 we talk about an aptitude by treatment interaction. What kind of aptitude would maximize the impact of the training (i.e., treatment) techniques discussed in this chapter?
5. How would you evaluate the effectiveness of experiential learning (see Chapter 5)?

TRAINING STYLES AND TECHNIQUES: AN INTERVIEW WITH EDWARD COHEN-ROSENTHAL AND CYNTHIA E. BURTON ——————————

Edward Cohen-Rosenthal is a recognized authority in the U.S. and abroad on union-management relations. His professional life has been dedicated to finding new ways that labor and management can work together for mutual benefit. He is president and founder of ECR Associates, established in 1979. Cohen-Rosenthal was formerly Associate Director of the American Center for the Quality of Work Life in charge of union liaison and training. He has consulted and provided training for a large number of organizations in private industry, government, labor unions, and education.

Cynthia E. Burton has been Vice-President of ECR Associates since June, 1980. She has been involved in designing and delivering training for over 15 years, beginning with her participation in the civil rights movement and continuing through the peace and women's movements. Currently, she uses training to assist union and management partners in quality of working life programs, to work with staff to make women's organizations more effective, and to resolve conflicts within and between community-based organizations.

Together, Ed and Cynthia have been involved in developing and implementing comprehensive quality of working life efforts at CONRAIL and the Milwaukee Road Railroads. Also, they have assisted the AFL-CIO and the United Paperworkers International Union in the development of comprehensive training programs.

We selected Ed and Cynthia to be interviewed for this chapter because they are well known for their use of experientially oriented training techniques. We also wanted to gain their insights regarding training style issues when co-facilitating training efforts.

Question: How do you and other trainers you know go about choosing training style?

Burton: Trainers choose styles that they are comfortable with. I don't think we could say that the trainers we have seen really adapt their style to the situations they face. Most seem to have found an approach that worked and they stick with that approach until or unless it fails them. Styles seem to evolve across time but I must say that, unfortunately, the trainers we see seem to be of only one of two camps. Either they are very structured and didactic and control time within their sessions very strictly or they are very "loosey-goosey," providing almost no structure or input. Neither of these extremes are likely to address all of the broad range of problems and issues that arise in training sessions.

Question: Which style have you chosen for yourselves?

Burton: We consciously selected an experiential approach for our training sessions but we do provide some time structure, clear statements of expectations for the exercises we use, and some input regarding the subject matter of the session. We train adults so we know from the research on learning principles and theories that experiential approaches to training should help us achieve our objectives. In addition, since much of our work involves the development of joint union-management problem-solving teams, the experiential approach is best because of the emphasis on group interaction and collaboration. Effective participation is something people learn by doing not by hearing lectures about it. Also, since we have worked so much in the rail industry, and since they have used on-the-job, hands-on approaches to training for decades, it just makes sense that we choose an experiential style. To be honest, we also choose this style because we enjoy it. It provides for stimulating and effective sessions. It allows us, as trainers, to learn as well as contribute and this keeps us fresh and better prepared for future assignments.

Question: Ed, are you also an experientially oriented trainer?

Cohen-Rosenthal: Yes, I am. It is clearly my personal preference. We have seen it work for us and it fits the kind of work and clients we deal with. That's not to say that Cynthia and I have identical styles. While we both are biased toward experiential methods, our different personalities show up in the way we lead these sessions. We don't try to modify this—in fact, we even point out some of our differences to groups of trainees because we want them to value diversity. Many union-management task forces need a model of collaboration between people of differing personalities and ideas. We try to provide that model, although we don't have to "try" very hard because we naturally disagree on some issues. In addition, we find our differing perspectives help convince trainees that there are different ways of doing the same thing. When a group truly learns that there are many ways to skin a cat, that unleashes a powerful source of creative energy that serves them well in their efforts to resolve problems.

Question: What other effects have you experienced as a result of co-facilitating your sessions rather than being solo trainers?

Burton: First, we should point out that we do sometimes "solo," as you put it. But, to answer your question, I think cofacilitation promotes planning. You feel a responsibility to completely think things through and share that thinking with your partner. So the styles witnessed by trainees are a result of our spending time designing the training sessions together. We try to think through a style that reflects and capitalizes on our differences as well as ways that we can reinforce major elements related to the objectives of our training efforts.

I also think that group activities go better when co-facilitating. I may pick up things that Ed might miss and vice-versa. We are more effective process consultants as a result. It also helps us manage the group activities in a more effective manner.

Cohen-Rosenthal: I think Cynthia and I are both better trainers as a result of working together so often. Getting reactions and feedback from trainees helps but getting that feedback from an experienced professional really adds some important learning and growth. Co-facilitation is also less boring for the trainers and the audience. It gives the audience some variety and provides each of us opportunities to recoup our energies and study audience reactions to the material while the other person is "on." This allows us to provide a more intense experience for our trainees.

I want to add that I also like co-facilitating with Cynthia because it gives us an opportunity to promote nonsexist values. We switch leads on activities and demonstrate equality rather than just talking about it.

Question: What do you think the impact of having a male and a female co-facilitation team is, Cynthia?

Burton: We believe that modeling behaviors and values is an important role to be filled by trainers. We model teamwork and equality in a manner quite different from patterns typical in most industrial settings. We hope this counters the traditional white male dominated perspective. Even though many of our clients send mostly males to our training sessions, our model has been well received.

As you know, not all female trainers use the same style and we don't all receive the same reactions even when we do use similar styles. Likewise, all male trainers are not alike either. I do perceive some trends, however. I think a higher percentage of male trainers as opposed to females take on the role of "expert." Some clients want and encourage this role because they are seeking some sort of "hired gun" or "savior." A woman using the same role may be perceived as threatening and may increase defensiveness on the part of her clients.

Sometimes, when no females hold jobs similar to those held by a group of trainees, I feel the audience question my credibility. "How can she know what it's like on my job?" is what they seem to be asking sometimes. I think that may be another reason why the experiential style of training is appropriate for us. We don't tell them how to do their jobs. We structure learning opportunities so that we manage the process and they are responsible for the content. As we clarify that with our audiences, I feel that my credibility becomes enhanced not downgraded.

It's hard to generalize, but I would also venture to say that trainees may open up more to a female than a male. Perhaps we are perceived as a less competitive threat. Whatever, it has provided us with more information that ends up helping us keep our training sessions relevant.

Question: During this interview, you have often spoken of the effectiveness of experientially oriented training styles and techniques. Do you see all experiential techniques to be equally effective?

Burton: No, nor do we use all of them with equal frequency. We have chosen our techniques on the basis of the responses we have received on evaluation forms or reactions expressed by our clients. We have found structured games to be most useful. We use simulations probably next most often. We see the value in role playing exercises but frankly don't use them very often. Case studies can be useful but it seems that groups tend to just analyze decisions rather than truly build decision-making skills. We feel you need to prepare structured questions relevant to the objectives of training to best utilize case studies. Finally, I would say we never really use unstructured, "T-groupy" approaches anymore. I wouldn't make a blanket statement that this method has outlived its usefulness; it just needs to be reserved for the appropriate situation. In fact, in general, the usefulness of any of the experientially oriented techniques depends on its match with the situation in which it is used.

Chapter 8

TECHNICAL
TRAINING

The first two sections of this book dealt with the specific components of the training system along with an examination of various training techniques. The third section examines three major content areas of training: technical training, management development, and training within OD efforts. This chapter focuses on technical training. We define *technical training* as any effort designed to provide an employee with the knowledge and/or skill necessary to perform a nonmanagerial job. Technical training is by definition job related, but only to those individuals who hold or manage that particular job. Some training issues are related to individuals who possess different jobs. For example, certain management skills are common to both the data processing and engineering manager (see Chapter 9), while the nature of training provided to someone who worked as a programmer or engineer would be a function of the specific job duties of the respective positions. This chapter focuses on the latter category of training.

The most common ways of providing technical training will be examined first. This will be followed by a review of more recent and innovative approaches. Finally, ways of improving technical training will be discussed. Specifically, this chapter is designed to answer the following questions:

1. What are the typical methods for training employees how to perform the techniques of their jobs?
2. What are the most recent and innovative approaches and ideas in providing technical training?
3. What does research suggest for improving technical systems and training?

TYPICAL APPROACHES TO
ON-THE-JOB TRAINING

Coaching

While most of the remarks in this book are directed toward the formal training staff, a great deal of training goes on outside the training department's umbrella. Many employees receive their training through their immediate superior or their coworkers. Although the terms *coaching* and *on-the-job training* have been used on occasion to mean slightly different things, they will be used synonymously here to refer to training conducted at the work station, by a senior member of the work group (including the supervisor), usually on a one-to-one basis.

While equipment simulators, business games, in-basket exercises, case studies, role playing, and behavior modeling provide trainees the opportunity to learn from simulations of job experiences, coaching is a training technique that utilizes the trainee's actual job experiences as a source of learning.

> *Coaching* serves a number of important functions within an organization. It (1) lets subordinates know what their supervisors think about how they do their jobs; (2) enables supervisors and employees to work together on ways in which employees can improve their performances; (3) improves communication and collaboration between supervisors and employees, and (4) provides a framework for establishing short- and long-term personal career goals. (Wexley & Latham, 1981, p. 114)

In addition to being a useful training technique in and of itself, coaching can complement and supplement virtually every off-site training approach. Rackham (1979) pointed out that knowledge can be gained from off-site training efforts through lectures, role plays, simulations, etc. But, he suggested that such efforts often feel very artificial, especially to experienced trainees, and there is rarely enough training time available for trainees to repeatedly practice the application of their new knowledge. When a trainee attempts to try a new skill on the job, he or she feels awkward. Without a supportive, observant environment, many trainees drop efforts to try to practice what they learned. Coaching, thus, can serve the purpose of refining and reinforcing the new skill.

Despite the potential beneficial purposes coaching may serve, many supervisors are uncomfortable and/or unskilled in such a role (see, for example, the study of coaching practice at General Electric by Kay, Meyer, & French, 1965). The heart of this problem seems to be that supervisors feel that to expect them to be coaches as well as supervisors creates a conflict of roles. It sets them up to be helpers, which requires openness and the tolerance of mistakes, while they still are in a position to judge the employee and report his or her evaluation of that employee to the organization. This later role may cause employees to hide or cover up their mistakes, thus making the helper role more difficult.

Wexley and Latham (1981) presented a review of this problem and the research that has been conducted on efforts to facilitate the blending of the roles of coach and evaluator. Several researchers suggest a key to improvement is to have the supervisor and employee mutually set very specific goals for improving performance (Wexley, Singh, & Yukl, 1973; Latham & Yul, 1975; Latham et al., 1978; Burke, Weitzel, & Weir, 1978). However, Hillery and Wexley (1974) found a directive approach where the supervisor sets the goals may be more effective with inexperienced new employees. Regardless, clarification of goals should aid the employee in determining how to use his or her training in a way the organization approves of and should aid the supervisor/coach by pinpointing what actions need observation and what standards are appropriate for subsequent judgment of progress. By providing feedback and reinforcement on the employee's behaviors as well as on the results of those behaviors, the employee has a clear picture where he or she stands and what needs correcting in order to improve that standing. The description of reinforcement theory provided in Chapter 3 suggests that these feedback and reinforcement sessions should be held almost continuously at first in order to shape new behaviors and then on a variable schedule afterward in order to maintain long-term retention of the behavior.

The very nature of change requires some risk taking. Thus, supervisors who display considerate, supportive behaviors are more likely to encourage employees to try out the new behaviors (Nemeroff & Wexley, 1979). Research on social learning theory (Bandura, 1977) suggested that modeling behavior is a powerful source for learning. Thus, supervisors who "practice what they preach," by modeling the very behaviors they expect their subordinates to demonstrate should be more effective coaches.

Research on coaching is not limited to goal setting and performance appraisal interview studies. Kondrasuk (1979) presented evidence that off-site seminar-type training was more effective than on-site coaching, but he used a very small sample and his measure of effectiveness was limited to a knowledge test. Rackham (1979), on the other hand, reported a study by Xerox Corporation that estimated that 87 percent of skill changes brought about by an off-site training program is lost if coaching is not provided when trainees return to their jobs. He also reported a study that demonstrated that a coaching program was far more effective than an off-site program in developing salepersons for Xerox.

If your job has very limited contact with other departments of your organization, the person you report to will be a key individual in any efforts to change (improve) your job behavior. Unless he or she is supportive of such changes, the likelihood that you will apply what you learned in off-site training sessions is quite low. Practitioners in the field of OD have known that a climate conducive/ready for change is generally a prerequisite for successful intervention. Likewise, trainers need to assess how conducive/ ready for change are the managers of the trainees in order to increase the likelihood that the skills/knowledge transmitted through training will be effectively applied. The willingness and ability of such managers to act as coaches should be cultivated. In addition, trainers should assist those managers in developing a plan of action for their coaching activities. They should help to develop a set of goals and criteria for evaluating progress to those goals. A set of prerequisite skills should be developed and procedures developed for transmitting those skills. In short, the "coach" should have a carefully designed program as a trainer. Unfortunately, most coaches, (e.g., supervisors/managers) don't have the training necessary to develop such programs. If the organization is going to rely heavily on the coaching method to develop its employees, that organization should probably have a training program for the coaches.

Job Instruction Technique (JIT)

One way to provide formalized training for coaches and assure trainees learn in a standard fashion is to use the *job instruction technique (JIT)*. The JIT is a systematic approach to training developed during World War II (Wickert, 1974). Although there are variations in format (McCord, 1976), the JIT often consists of five major steps that one performs in sequence. Table 8.1 lists these steps and the actions that trainers should take when implementing each step.

Table 8.1   Steps in the job instruction technique.

17-Steps	Action
1. Prepare to Teach	Decide what should be taught. Gather tools and supplies. Arrange the workplace.
2. Prepare the Trainee	Put trainees at ease. Determine trainee knowledge and motivation.
3. Train the Trainee	Describe and demonstrate. Question trainee to assure learning. Repeat demonstration if needed.
4. Trainee Performs the Job	Observe trainee. Correct errors.
5. Trainee Becomes a Regular Worker	Check to assure performance is acceptable.

In step 1, the trainer prepares to teach the job. This involves deciding what the trainee needs to be taught. Efficiency, economy, and safety are major factors that are examined. The trainer must also gather the appropriate tools and supplies and arrange the workplace in proper order. Step 2 is preparing the trainee. This involves attempting to put the trainee at ease, determining what he or she knows about the job, and motivating the trainee to learn the appropriate way of performing the job. When this is accomplished, the trainer moves to presenting the information (step 3). The trainer is supposed to describe and demonstrate the desired action and question the trainee to assure that learning is taking place. Guidelines caution the trainer to speak slowly, clearly, and completely. Through questioning, the trainer is supposed to determine if the trainee comprehends. If not, the trainer is expected to "patiently repeat the process." Once learning has occurred, the trainer moves to the next step. This step consists of the trainee performing the job. While this takes place, the trainer should observe the performance, correcting errors and repeating instructions if necessary. The trainer should also ask the trainee questions beginning with why, how, when, or where to assure that the trainee comprehends his or her actions. The final step of the JIT requires the trainer to check frequently on the trainee to assure instructions are being followed. Based on trainee performance, these "follow-ups" are reduced as the trainee demonstrates the capacity to work under normal supervision.

Before the JIT is implemented, the trainer (typically the employee's supervisor) is trained on how to follow the JIT approach. The steps and key points of the approach are also written on cards to give the supervisor/trainer a guide to follow when implementing the training.

To use the JIT in teaching someone how to use a computer terminal, a trainer might take the following steps. First, a training needs assessment would be conducted (see Chapter 2) to determine the particular performance deficiency and its source. Assuming the problem can be resolved by training, the trainer would then gather the necessary training materials. This might involve reserving a terminal for training purposes.

The trainer would then "prepare the trainee." This could be accomplished by explaining why the trainee needs to learn this ("All our files are being computerized."), asking what the trainee knows ("Have you ever used a computer terminal?"), and motivating the trainee ("This should really eliminate a lot of the problems in your job."). This would then be followed by a demonstration that might involve the following trainer actions:

1. Turning a switch on the terminal to the on position.
2. Hitting the return key on the keyboard.
3. Typing in a five-digit password then hitting the return key.
4. Typing in a five-digit identification code.

The trainer would ask the trainee if he or she understood this four-step process. If not, the trainer would repeat it. Once the trainee felt capable, he or she would perform the four steps. The trainer would ask the trainee to explain why each step needs to be performed. The trainer would then check back with the trainee occasionally to assure the task was being performed appropriately.

Apprenticeships

Another major source of technical training is through apprenticeships. *Apprenticeship* training involves a combination of off- and on-the-job training. It is a descendant of the craft guild system of the Middle Ages. In America, prior to the Industrial Revolution, an apprentice typically lived in the house of a master craftsman while learning the craft. These apprentices received no wages but were given room and board (Beach, 1980). Currently, the government regulates apprenticeship training. The major law is the Apprenticeship Act of 1937, popularly known as the Fitzgerald Act. The act reorganized and enlarged the Federal Committee on Apprenticeships. This committee has suggested the following as elements of an effective apprenticeship program (*Apprenticeship Training*, 1956, p. 6).

- A minimum starting age of 16.
- A schedule of work experience supplemented by at least 144 hours per year of related classroom instruction.
- A progressively increasing schedule of wages.
- Proper supervision.
- Periodic evaluations of the apprentice's work.

The program is administered through the Bureau of Apprenticeship and Training (BAT) of the Department of Labor. Several states also have state apprenticeship councils (SACs). Graduates of programs that meet BAT or SAC standards are given certificates of completion by the appropriate agency. However, there is no requirement to conform to state or federal standards for various trades (Beach, 1980). Thus, there is no guarantee that apprentices within the same trade have received the same quality of training. Since unions (especially in the skilled trades) take an active interest in apprenticeship programs, it is the specific labor agreement that will have the greatest impact on the nature of the apprenticeship program. Such agreements typically deal with the following aspects of apprenticeship training (Holley & Jennings, 1984):

- Standards of acceptance into the apprenticeship program.
- The nature of apprenticeship committees. Such committees often consist of an equal number of union and employer representatives.
- Number of apprentices to be accepted.

- Standards and nature of training.
- Employment rules (e.g., wages, probationary period, certification, etc.).

Approximately 46 percent of labor agreements have provisions governing apprenticeship programs, although this varies considerably with the nature of the industry (Bureau of Labor Statistics, 1981). In 1981, 395,000 people were in registered apprenticeship programs, 130,000 of which were new apprentice registrations. Apprenticeships account for three percent of the civilian labor force in the United States (Holley & Jennings, 1984). The proportion of workers in apprenticeships in many other countries (e.g., Germany) is considerably higher (Briggs, 1981).

Although research has shown that apprenticeship training can be superior to simply training someone on the job (Franklin, 1973), it has also been criticized (Strauss, 1971). Such criticism has typically focused on nepotism and discriminatory practices in selecting apprentices. While a full discussion of this issue is beyond the nature of this text, recent efforts by organizations such as the National Urban League and agencies of the Federal government have resulted in progress in this area (Wexley & Latham, 1981).

Summary of On-the-Job Training

Providing technical training on the job through the use of coaching, JIT, or apprenticeship programs offers several advantages. First, it is clearly a beneficial method of skill enhancement since trainees are actually applying their knowledge. For this reason, *transfer of training* from a "class" to the workplace is not a concern. Second, trainees may be more attentive and motivated since it is easier to see a direct relationship between training and job performance. Third, these methods have some cost advantages since trainees produce while learning and a full-time trainer does not have to be hired.

However, there are also several possible negative aspects of using these methods. These can be classified into two areas. The first concerns the competency of the trainer. As noted earlier, for a supervisor or peer to be an effective trainer, he or she needs ability, motivation, and opportunity to effectively perform this job. Unless someone possesses all three of these qualities, effective training will not occur. Often we make the assumption that someone who is capable of performing the job is capable of effectively teaching someone else. This is not necessarily true. We have described some characteristics of effective trainers in Chapter 6 and we will expand on these characteristics later (see Chapter 11). Finally, we wish to re-emphasize that anyone who conducts training must be rewarded for this effort and have this function included as part of their defined job responsibilities.

The second concern with on-the-job training deals with the climate of learning that may arise as a result of providing training in this location. Individuals who are trained on the job may not be able to devote their full time to learning, since there will be some pressure to fulfill job requirements. Similarly, the cost of errors in this type of training is considerably higher and it may lead to products or services of inferior quality as well as machine damage. Finally, trainees' learning may be retarded due to a reluctance to ask questions before knowledgeable peers. If these issues are of concern, an off-the-job approach may be a preferable strategy.

OFF-THE-JOB TECHNICAL TRAINING

Chapters 6 and 7 describe off-the-job training techniques. At this point, we will examine factors to consider in using these techniques in technical training. One factor is the rate at which the organization's *technology is changing*. A rapidly changing technology requires training to be constantly updated and modified. This reduces the cost/benefit of techniques such as computer-assisted instruction (CAI) and programmed instruction (PI) due to their high developmental costs. For example, in the computer industry, technology is changing at such a rapid pace that CAI or PI developed training materials may be obsolete before they can be properly produced (Lee, 1983). For such volatile technologies, often the traditional classroom or workshop is the most practical training approach. The rate of change in technology should also be considered when assessing whether to develop the training program from outside the organization. A rapidly changing technology typically suggests a required level of expertise that organizations may not be able to acquire or generate. Given such a situation, professional conferences, seminars, and university programs may prove to be the most desired source of training.

A second factor to consider in selecting a technique for technical training is *trainee safety*. When safety is a concern, simulators (see Chapter 7) are a viable training technique. Pilot and driver training are two areas where simulators are often used (Williges, 1982). *Vestibule training* is a term often used to refer to training someone how to operate a particular machine in a simulated environment. There are two major criticisms of simulators. The first concerns the extremely high developmental costs. For example, flight simulators for pilot training can cost as much as $10 million each (Shannon, 1981). However, this cost must be compared to the savings (e.g., fuel and maintenance) in not having to actually fly an aircraft.

The second criticism of simulators deals with the issue of realism. A simulator can be developed that perfectly represents the actual physical working environment. This is called *physical fidelity*. However, it is impossible to have perfect psychological fidelity. *Psychological fidelity* is the extent to which the training environment simulates in the trainee the feelings and emotions that would actually be experienced on the job. Trainees on a flight simulator know that if they make an error they will be able to walk away from the simulator. The same statement does not always apply if one receives training on a real aircraft. Thus, flight simulator training provides physical but not psychological fidelity.

In summary, there is no perfect technical training technique. Each has its respective advantages and disadvantages. The appropriateness of a technique will depend upon the particulars of the situation. A key for effective technical training is a careful analysis of the characteristics of the situation prior to technique selection.

INNOVATIVE APPROACHES: SOCIALIZATION

Our focus now turns to examining more innovative approaches and ideas for training employees in the techniques of their jobs. Since employees typically receive some training when they first enter a job, we begin with an examination of training issues for new employees.

Breaking in the New Employee

The process by which an employee "learns the ropes" has been referred to as *organizational socialization*. More precisely, it is the process by which an individual acquires the social knowledge and skills necessary to assume an organizational role (Van Maanen & Schein, 1979). The specifics of the process may vary greatly (Wanous, 1980), ranging from extensive training programs to reading the employee handbook (Jones, 1973).

The importance of effective socialization stems from the *success spiral syndrome* that several people have suggested (Hall, 1976; Schein, 1978). This is the notion that success breeds success. Therefore, an employee who initially succeeds in his or her organizational role should also be more successful in other job assignments. Socialization is a major determinant of initial job success. Later we will see that training can play an important role in effective socialization.

There are several models of the socialization process (Van Maanen, 1975, 1978; Schein, 1978). One of the most comprehensive was developed by Feldman (1981). Feldman recognized the importance of socialization by suggesting that, if done effectively, it should lead to a worker who:

1. Carrys out work assignments dependably.
2. Remains with the organization.
3. Is innovative and cooperates spontaneously.
4. Has high general satisfaction.
5. Has high internal work motivation.
6. Is involved in his or her job.

Obviously, these are desirable goals for the organization. The key question is how does one socialize an employee to produce these effects?

To create the desired results, one must understand what an employee faces during the socialization process. Feldman developed three major categories of employee concerns. *Task mastery* is the extent to which the employee has the skill knowledge and ability to perform the job. When an employee is confident and capable of performing his or her job assignments, task mastery has occurred. An employee must also resolve any conflicts that arise from the demands of taking a new role as a member of an organization. Feldman stated that the *role demands* are resolved when the employee agrees with the work group on the priority and nature of tasks to be performed. Mutually agreeable methods of resolving conflicts between personal and work life and intergroup conflict are also part of this resolution process. For example, a trainer for a large organization who accepts the fact that he or she will have to spend some percentage (often as much as 50 percent) of his or her time "on the road" conducting training at different divisions of the company has moved toward resolving the role demands of this position.

Finally, a new employee also has a new work group to deal with. Groups have norms and values. If the group's norms and values are similar or at least acceptable to the new employee, *adjustment to the group* should not be a problem. However, when the employee's norms and values are considerably different than the group's, the employee may feel left out. For example, a new employee who has a norm or standard of higher productivity than other group members may be distrusted and even harrassed by colleagues. Feldman feels that adjustment to group norms and values has occurred when an individual feels liked and trusted by peers. An understanding of group norms and a feeling of satisfaction with the group climate is also part of this process.

To summarize, Feldman's model suggests that effective socialization should lead to several positive organizational outcomes. For these results to occur, the socialization effort should result in the employee (1) mastering the task, (2) resolving role demands, and (3) adjusting to the work group norms and values. Figure 8.1 provides a more comprehensive view of this model. At the bottom of the figure are the previously described outcomes of effective socialization. The three factors that influence these outcomes (e.g., task mastery) are listed in the middle of the figure. Factors that influence task mastery, resolution of role demands, and adjustment to work group norms are listed at the top. The three factors in the far left column of the figure are what Feldman believes to be the three phases or stages of socialization. Phase I is labeled *anticipatory socialization* and refers to the learning that takes place before an individual actually joins an organization. It includes the knowledge the individual acquires through association with friends, neighbors who may work at the firm, newspaper reports about the firm, etc. Phase II is the *encounter phase*. The individual is now an employee of the organization and, therefore, has a better understanding of it. As a result of this knowledge, some change should take place in the individual's values,

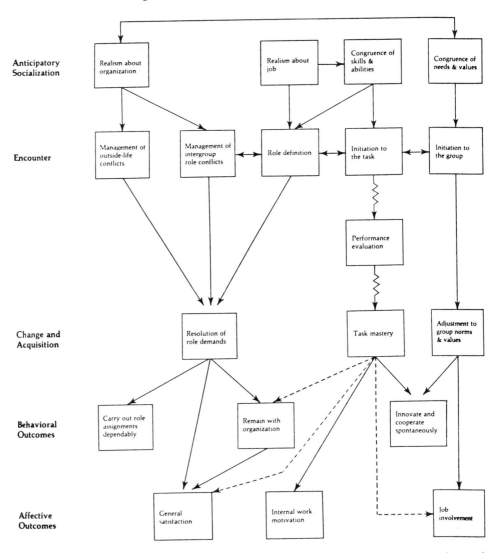

(From Feldman, D. C. The Multiple Socialization of Organization Members. *Academy of Management Review*, 1981, 6, 309–318.)

Figure 8.1 Feldman's model of the socialization of organization members.

skills, and attitudes. However, the most long lasting change will take place in the third phase. It is in this *change and acquisition stage* that the individual attempts to become proficient in the skills needed for effective job performance and adjust to his or her work group and role demands.

Beyond describing the process, Feldman's model also illustrates some actions that can be taken to create effective socialization. These actions concern (1) increasing realism and (2) enhancing job skills. Our focus now turns to these issues.

Realism

Figure 8.1 suggests that, in order for the change and acquisition phase to be effective, individuals must resolve role demands, adjust to work group norms and values, and master their task requirements. For these processes to take place, the individual must acquire realistic information about the organization, job, and coworkers during anticipatory socialization. This will help the individual when he or she actually joins the organization (i.e., enters the encounter stage) and must manage issues such as outside life and intergroup conflicts.

Realism can prove useful in several ways. First, it may allow certain individuals to recognize that they lack skills and abilities required for effective job performance or that organizational demands conflict with other priorities (e.g., too much travel) (Wanous, 1980). These individuals may self-select out and decline to join the organization. Thus, those that remain should be more capable as well as more aware of the skills and demands required for the position.

A second advantage of realism was noted by Dugoni and Ilgen (1981) who suggested, "If employees are made aware of problems to be faced on the job, they cope with such problems better when they arise, either because they are less disturbed by the problem or because they may prerehearse methods of handling them" (p. 580). Research on stress (Finkleman & Glass, 1970) provided some support for this notion in that problems are less stressful when people are aware of the nature of the problems they'll face.

Given the above, the question arises as to when one should provide realism. In line with Feldman's model, realism should be provided during anticipatory socialization. Wanous (1973, 1980) has long been an advocate of providing such information as part of the recruitment process. He noted that the traditional approach to recruitment relies on trying to select employees based only on the organization's interests rather than in terms of the balanced interests of both the company and the employee. Wanous argued that a *realistic job preview (RJP)* should be balanced and include information about the job and organization that typical employees find satisfying and dissatisfying.

Although it is widely accepted that RJPs reduce dissatisfaction and turnover (e.g., Reilly, Brown, Blood, & Maliteston, 1981), Schwab (1982) suggested that there is little evidence to support this notion. Breaugh (1983) has noted that this may be due to methodological deficiencies in studies that have examined this issue. We will discuss this point in more detail later in this chapter. For now, it is sufficient to say that although conceptually RJP should lead to more effective socialization, there is little scientific evidence to support this point.

In other portions of this book (see Chapters 2 and 10), mention was made of an OD technique that goes under the titles of *job expectation technique (JET)* and/or *role analysis technique (RAT)*. Briefly, this technique involves group meetings during which members reach agreement on everyone's prescribed and discretionary roles. Although JET and RAT are often used with existing work groups, Huse (1980) found these techniques helpful in bringing new members into an organization. Dayal and Thomas (1968) found that RAT was useful in decreasing worker concerns about their identity and alienation. Although it clearly requires a large time commitment, the RAT/JET techniques would seem to be another useful method of organizational socialization.

Matching Individual Skills and Job Requirements

Feldman's model also suggests that the congruence between the individual's skill, knowledge, and ability (SKA) and those required for effective job performance will impact the socialization process. The obvious impact of this congruence is on task mastery. The less obvious influence is on role definition. Feldman (1981) suggested that, since people bring their own personalities to their job, they emphasize those tasks at which they feel most competent and which they prefer. Similarly, Dunnette, Arvey, and Banas (1973) found that the inability to use one's skill was a major cause of employee turnover in one location.

One way organizations can attempt to maximize the congruence between the SKAs of the individual and the job is to develop valid selection systems. Considerable evidence now exists that suggests that valid selection systems have a positive impact on productivity (Cascio, 1982; Schmidt, Hunter, & Pearlman 1982). The positive impact such systems would have on socialization (i.e., increasing task mastery through a congruence between skill and job requirements) increases their utility. The relationship between the organization's selection system and socialization also reinforces a point stated much earlier in this book. Organizational subsystems must work in conjunction in order to be effective.

Skill development can also be provided through job-related training. One way for training to enhance skill development is to provide an orientation training program that trains individuals on the nature of the organization's business and the various functional responsibilities. An employee who is hired into the personnel department will probably be provided with information as to how personnel functions, but may never be given quality information as to how the organization and other areas actually operate. However, this type of background information may be very useful in solving problems within the personnel area. If this type of training cannot be provided, reference material (e.g., an organizational chart indicating who to call for what type of problem) should also prove useful.

Feldman's model suggests that an individual's task initiation (i.e., how one learns new tasks) will influence task mastery. There is evidence to support this point. Berlew and Hall (1966) and Feldman (1981) provided evidence that individuals who encounter initial challenge and success on the job tend to be more successful performers in the long run. One of the biggest influences on an employee's initial job success is the employee's supervisor. As Feldman (1981) noted, "there is virtually no aspect of the socialization process that the supervisor cannot sabotage or smooth, depending on inclination and talent" (p. 191). It is the organization's responsibility to make sure that the supervisor has both the inclination and talent to smooth the path for the employee. The fields of training and OD would suggest several ways to do this. First, supervisors must become committed to effective socialization. One way to accomplish this is to involve supervisors in the planning stages of employee socialization. Supervisors will be more likely to "own" a program that they helped create, rather than one developed by the training department. Second, supervisors must be provided with the skills needed to effectively socialize their employees. One crucial skill is providing quality feedback. New recruits will need more feedback than the more experienced employees. The feedback will need to be timely, more descriptive than evaluative, and at least initially will need to emphasize the positive aspects of performance. (See Chapter 4 for a more detailed description of feedback.) Although these feedback concepts are relatively straightforward, supervisors will need to develop skills in applying them if they are to positively contribute to the socialization effort. Third, supervisors will need to get rewarded or punished based on the quality by which they socialize their employees. Efforts must be taken to make socialization part of the supervisor's job responsibilities. This can be accomplished by incorporating it into the supervisor's job description and performance appraisal. The above comments also apply to peers and anyone responsible for socializing employees.

Summary of Socialization

The issue is no longer whether organizations should formally socialize employees but how socialization can best be accomplished. Feldman's (1981) model provides an excellent framework for understanding the stages and processes of socialization. An examination of his model indicates that socialization occurs in stages, the first of which takes place even before the individual actually joins the organization. It also suggests that socialization involves adjustments to job skill requirements and appropriate role and work group behaviors.

Perhaps the most important implication of Feldman's model is that it illustrates that socialization is a complicated series of events, all of which must operate effectively for socialization to lead to positive organizational outcomes. This is illustrated by the contribution of realistic information to effective socialization. Although, conceptually, such information should lead to more effective socialization, research evidence is not overwhelmingly supportive of this notion. Part of the reason for this lack of support may be due to other weaknesses in the socialization effort. For example, we doubt whether realistic information would lead to more effective socialization if an individual is assigned a supervisor who is neither motivated or talented in utilizing the skills described earlier (e.g., providing quality feedback). Our point is that socialization must be viewed as a system that requires all components performing their function in order for the desired outcome to occur.

It is also our feeling that many organizations fail to provide realistic information on many of the issues that concern employees. Examples of such issues include (1) workload (hours per week), (2) job transfers, and (3) travel.

More important is the new employee's insensitivity to the political environment and ignorance of the true evaluation criteria (Webber, 1976). Organizations that are sincere in their concern for providing quality realistic information need to anonymously survey recent recruits for information they needed but lacked when they were introduced to the job.

Finally, in addition to the issues noted above, it would be inappropriate to consider socialization as something that applies only to new employees entering the organization. A person's career, even within the same organization, often involves transitions from one position to another (Van Maanen, 1978). Departmental socialization is involved in each movement (Van Maanen & Schein, 1979). Therefore, if effective socialization is to occur it needs to be viewed as a continuing "process" of the organization rather than as a program that begins and ends for new employees.

THE TECHNICAL TRAINING SYSTEM

This section of the chapter is designed to examine the different components of the technical training system. The process of technical training is basically the same as any other type of training in that it should adhere to the model and principles described earlier in this book. There are, however, some factors that can refine and advance this type of training.

Training Needs Assessment

Just as with any training effort, the initial focus should be on conducting a training needs assessment. The following discussion assumes that an organizational analysis has been conducted (see Chapter 2) and indicates the need to address the perceived performance deficiency. The focus then shifts to an analysis of the job and incumbent.

In studying a job to assess technical training requirements, one should attempt to analyze the various task and ability requirements. This effort would be relatively easy if clear task and ability taxonomies existed along with corresponding measurement instruments that related to training content and techniques. Unfortunately, such is not the case (Goldstein & Buxton, 1982). There are, however, certain aids available to assist trainers who are familiar with the literature.

Probably the two most useful task taxonomies are derived from Fine's (1963) *functional job analysis* and the work conducted by McCormick and his colleagues (McCormick, 1976; Mecham & McCormick, 1969a, 1969b) on the *position analysis questionnaire* (PAQ). Both instruments have been described earlier (see Chapter 2). At this point, only the PAQ will be examined in more detail.

The major emphasis of the PAQ is on physical and perceptual work activities that are typically associated with skilled and semiskilled blue-collar jobs, although some coverage is provided for more white-collar-type activities. Several research studies that have statistically analyzed the instrument have arrived at similar dimensions of task behavior (Peterson & Bownas, 1982). While this categorization may provide a valuable reference, Goldstein and Buxton (1982) noted that there is a lack of research indicating the usefulness of this information for determining training needs. They suggested that the best strategy is to "analyze each job individually by considering each task required for performance and the frequency, importance and difficulty of the tasks" (p. 150).

The above information simply refers to ways of describing the tasks involved in job performance. The needed abilities for those tasks must also be categorized. Such a categorization would need to include the necessary cognitive abilities, psychomotor and physical proficiencies, and personality characteristics. Work is progressing in these areas. Individuals interested in a research-based taxonomy of cognitive abilities should consult the work of Ekstrom and his colleagues (Ekstrom, French, & Harman, 1975). Although this is one of many such taxonomies, Fleishman and his associates (Theologus, Romashko, & Fleishman, 1973) have conducted extensive research on basic psychomotor and physical abilities. Finally, categorizations of basic personality attributes also exist (Peterson & Bownas, 1982) although there is considerable debate as to whether "personality" measures account for a meaningful portion of the variability in human performance.

The final step in this portion of the process is the development of a task by ability matrix along with the creation of accurate methods of measuring the respective abilities. Although some progress has been made in the latter area (Peterson & Bownas, 1982), a great deal of progress is still needed (Dunnette, 1982). Nevertheless, it is our hope that the type of information provided above will be useful as a general guide in technical job analysis.

In addition to an understanding of task and ability requirements, a technical training needs assessment should answer questions such as:

1. To resolve the performance deficiencies, does the trainee need technical knowledge, skill, or both?
2. Does the trainee have any familiarity or experience with the technical area (i.e., is the focus on introducing totally new and unfamiliar information or merely updating a base of knowledge)?
3. To what extent is the work environment and work process structured in a way to maximize productivity?

Question 3 is obviously relevant to the issue of technical training, but requires extremely specialized knowledge. Individuals trained in human information processing and engineering psychology have the skills needed to answer this question (Kantowitz, 1982). If there is any evidence that this may be a concern, individuals with these capabilities should be consulted to help redesign the work environment.

The answers to questions 1 and 2 will provide useful information for the selection of an appropriate training technique. Earlier (see Chapters 6 and 7) we noted that certain techniques are more effective for knowledge deficiencies while others are best suited for deficiencies that arise from a lack of skill. We have also noted that a person's knowledge or skill level, prior to training, is an important factor in the selection of a training technique. We now turn our attention to a more detailed analysis of the people who will be receiving the technical training.

Person Analysis

One factor that will influence how an individual views training is that person's perception of his or her current and future job positions. The series of positions that one holds throughout his or her lifetime is typically referred to as a *career* (Super & Hall, 1978), although there are many different meanings attached to this term (Hall, 1976). Similarly, there are a variety of perspectives from which careers are viewed (Milkovich & Anderson, 1982). From an *individual perspective,* the focus is on career choice and the problems encountered in the path required by the career. Alternatively, the *organizational perspective* views careers both as characteristics of individuals and attributes of organizations (Anderson, Milkovich, & Tsui, 1981). A major concern of this perspective is how careers can be planned and developed to simultaneously fulfill individual and organizational needs. The following discussion is based on this latter perspective.

A variety of models have been developed that categorize careers into *stages.* (Hall, 1976; Dalton, Thompson, & Price 1977; Schein, 1978). Table 8.2 lists Schein's categorization as well as the general issues he suggests need to be confronted in each stage.

Table 8.2 Stages and tasks of the career cycle.

Stages	General issues to be confronted
1. Growth, fantasy, exploration (age 0–21) (Roles: student, aspirant, applicant)	1. Developing a basis for making realistic vocational choices 2. Turning early occupational fantasies into workable realities 3. Assessing the realistic constraints based on socio-economic level and other family circumstances 4. Obtaining the appropriate education or training 5. Developing the basic habits and skills needed in the world of work

Passage into an Organization or Occupation

2. Entry into world of work (age 16–25) (Roles: recruit, entrant)	1. Entering the labor market—getting a first job that can be the basis for a career 2. Negotiating a viable formal and psychological contract to ensure that own needs and those of employer will be met 3. Becoming a member of an organization or occupation—passage through first major inclusion boundary
3. Basic training (age 16–25) (Roles: trainee, novice)	1. Dealing with the reality shock of what work and membership are really like 2. Becoming an effective member as quickly as possible 3. Adjusting to the daily routines of work 4. Achieving acceptance as regular contributing member—passing the next inclusion boundary
4. Full membership in early career (age 17–30) (Roles: new but full member)	1. Accepting the responsibility and successfully discharging with duties associated with first formal assignment 2. Developing and displaying special skills and expertise to lay the groundwork for promotion or lateral career growth into other areas 3. Balancing own needs for independence with organizational restrictions and requirements for a period of subordination and dependence 4. Deciding whether to remain in the organization or the occupation or to seek a better match between own needs and organizational constraints and opportunities

Table 8.2 Stages and tasks of the career cycle. (*Continued*)

Stages	General issues to be confronted
5. Full membership, mid-career (age 25+) (Roles: full member, tenured member, life member, supervisor, manager) (person may remain in this stage)	1. Choosing a speciality and deciding how committed to become to it vs. moving toward being a generalist and/or toward management 2. Remaining technically competent and continuing to learn in one's chosen area of specialization (or management) 3. Establishing a clear identity in the organization, becoming visible 4. Accepting higher levels of responsibility, including work of others as well as one's own 5. Becoming a productive person in the occupation 6. Developing one's long-range career plan in terms of ambitions, type of progress sought, targets against which to measure progress, etc.
6. Mid-career crisis (age 35–45)	1. Major reassesment of one's progress relative to one's ambitions—forcing decisions to level off, change careers, or forge ahead to new and higher challenges 2. Assessing one's career ambitions against more general aspects of mid-life transition—one's dreams and hopes vs. realities 3. Deciding how important work and one's career are to be in one's total life 4. Meeting one's own needs to become a mentor to others
7(A). Late career in non-leadership role (age 40 to retirement) (Roles: key member, individual contributor or member of management, good contributor or deadwood) (many people stay in this stage)	1. Becoming a mentor, learning to influence, guide, direct, and be responsible for others 2. Broadening of interests and skills based on experience 3. Deepening of skills if decision is to pursue a technical or functional career 4. Taking on more areas of responsibility if decision is to pursue general-management role 5. Accepting reduced influence and challenge if decision is to level off and seek growth outside of career or work

Table 8.2 Stages and tasks of the career cycle. (*Continued*)

Stages	General issues to be confronted
Passage through Inclusion and Hierarchical Boundary	
7(B). Late career in leadership role (may be achieved at early age, but would still be thought of as "late" in career) (Roles: general manager, officer, senior partner, internal entrepreneur, senior staff)	1. Using one's skills and talents for the long-range welfare of the organization 2. Learning to integrate the efforts of others and to influence broadly rather than making day-to-day decisions or supervising closely 3. Selecting and developing key subordinates 4. Developing broad perspective, long-range time horizons, and realistic appraisal of the role of the organization in society 5. Learning how to sell ideas if in individual contributor or internal entrepreneur role
8. Decline and disengagement (age 40 until retirement; different people start decline at different ages)	1. Learning to accept reduced levels of power, responsibility, and centrality 2. Learning to accept and develop new roles based on declining competence and motivation 3. Learning to manage a life that is less dominated by work
Passage out of the Organization or Occupation	
9. Retirement	1. Adjusting to more drastic changes in life style, role, standard of living 2. Using one's accumulated experience and wisdom on behalf of others in various senior roles

Reprinted with permission from E. H. Schein. *Career Dynamics: Matching Individual and Organizational Needs.* © 1978 (Reading, Mass.: Addison-Wesley, 1978), pages 40–46.

Given this blueprint, organizations might wish to provide training and developmental activities that correspond to the needs of the various stages. Examples of such activities might include job rotation in early stages, career counseling for re-assignment in middle stages, and the development of mentoring skills/roles in later stages.

However, there has been little research that has tested the various models of career stages. That which has been done has not been overwhelmingly supportive (Rush, Peacock, & Milkovich, 1980). Finally, there is little agreement regarding whether career stages are age-linked. This makes the operationalization of the stage notion more difficult.

In their review of this literature, Milkovich and Anderson concluded that

> There is reason to believe that there are stages in individual careers and that understanding these stages may help one understand workers' behaviors and attitudes. However, the theoretical frameworks of career stages and their associated characteristics and tasks need to be more fully developed . . . (p. 374)

In addition to concern for career stages, there are a variety of other activities that organizations can undertake to help plan and develop careers. Figure 8.2 lists these activities. As noted in the figure, these are "matching processes" that benefit both the individual and the organization. To the extent that such activities are undertaken, the probability of effective technical training is correspondingly increased. However, these types of activities will not have any benefit if a lack of skill is not the source of the technical training problem. We now turn to the issue of skill assessment.

Skill Level

Earlier (see Chapters 2 and 4) we noted that training will not succeed if the trainee's poor performance is not due to a lack of skill or knowledge. The easiest way to assess whether these are concerns is to ask the employee to perform the task in question and/or describe his or her knowledge of the issue you are trying to assess. To the extent that the trainee illustrates knowledge or skill, training is not the appropriate solution to the problem.

When conducting a job analysis for a training needs assessment, it is often beneficial to ask the following types of questions:

1. Have you ever known anybody who was very ineffective or effective on the job?
2. What did this person know (or not know) that distinguished him or her from everybody else?
3. What could this person do (or not do) that distinguished him or her from everyone else?
4. How do you know that this person was effective or ineffective?

Answers to the types of questions noted above can be a useful source of data for developing a test of skill or knowledge. If you find that the trainee does lack the necessary skill or knowledge, decisions must be made as to the optimal process for providing training.

Implementation

Chapters 3 through 6 talk in great detail about the process of training. This section will focus on the issue of who should be the trainer. Often, this comes down to a choice between someone skilled in the job (the technical expert) versus the professional trainer.

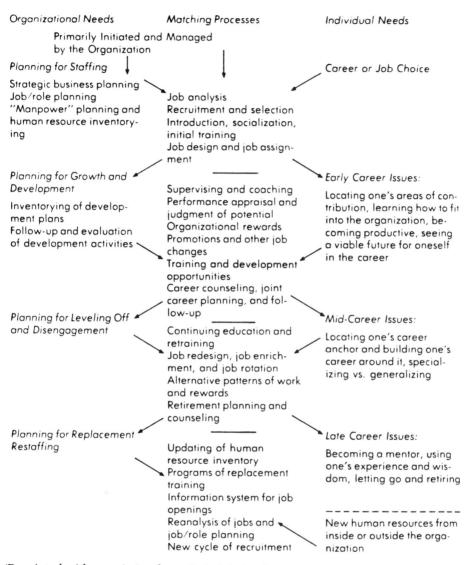

Organizational Needs   Matching Processes   Individual Needs

Primarily Initiated and Managed
by the Organization

Planning for Staffing   Career or Job Choice

Strategic business planning
Job/role planning
"Manpower" planning and
human resource inventory-
ing

Job analysis
Recruitment and selection
Introduction, socialization,
initial training
Job design and job assign-
ment

Planning for Growth and
Development

Inventorying of develop-
ment plans
Follow-up and evaluation
of development activities

Supervising and coaching
Performance appraisal and
judgment of potential
Organizational rewards
Promotions and other job
changes
Training and development
opportunities
Career counseling, joint
career planning, and fol-
low-up

Early Career Issues:

Locating one's areas of contribution, learning how to fit
into the organization, becoming productive, seeing
a viable future for oneself
in the career

Planning for Leveling Off
and Disengagement

Continuing education and
retraining
Job redesign, job enrich-
ment, and job rotation
Alternative patterns of work
and rewards
Retirement planning and
counseling

Mid-Career Issues:

Locating one's career
anchor and building one's
career around it, special-
izing vs. generalizing

Planning for Replacement
Restaffing

Updating of human
resource inventory
Programs of replacement
training
Information system for job
openings
Reanalysis of jobs and
job/role planning
New cycle of recruitment

Late Career Issues:

Becoming a mentor, using
one's experience and wis-
dom, letting go and retiring

New human resources from
inside or outside the organization

(Reprinted with permission from E. G. Schein. *Career Dynamics: Matching Individual and Organizational Needs.* © 1978 (Reading, Mass: Addison-Wesley, 1978, p. 201.)

Figure 8.2 Human resource planning and career stages.

Although it is difficult to generalize to all situations, we suggest that the more sophisticated the nature of the technology, the greater the need for a technical expert to provide the training. Such an expert can handle the detailed questions that often arise on training. However, it is also our feeling that technical expertise alone is insufficient for an effective trainer. Hopefully, you are also aware (at this point in the book) that both the content and process must be effective in order for training to be effective. A way of dealing with these dual needs is to have a professional trainer train the technical expert (i.e., "train the trainer") on effective instructional techniques. Professional trainers should be aware that technical experts often feel that their knowledge of the subject matter (alone) qualifies them to be capable trainers. One way to deal with this issue is to have (very early on) the technical expert provide a "practice training session." The practice session can be assessed for participant knowledge and/or reaction. If these are a problem, the "professional trainer" can offer some "helpful hints." Obviously, the approach just described is very costly (i.e., some bad training occurs). An alternative might be to have the technical expert practice or observe training being performed in several ways. These actions or comments of observers may illustrate to the technical expert the value of providing training in a more professional manner.

Evaluation

One of the problems with technical training is that it often relies on what is refered to as "face validity." *Face validity* means something looks like it's doing what it's supposed to do. Stated another way, we often assume that, since the content area is relevant to the job, the specific content is also. This can be illustrated by a situation where programmers are given training on a new programming language. Obviously, the content *area* is relevant to the job. Programmers need to program, but will this specific programming training session accomplish what it is designed to? Will programmers make fewer mistakes with this language? Will they program faster? These points must be considered in comparison to other types of technical training that could be provided. The point is that training should not be judged based on whether it looks relevant to the job, but based on an evaluation of whether stated objectives were obtained (see Chapter 5).

In summary, the comments in this section have dealt with factors to consider in improving the needs assessment, implementation, and evaluation of technical training. As we have advocated throughout this book, if training is to be effective it must also examine factors outside of the development and delivery of training. Ways that OD can help deal with these broader concerns are outlined in the following section.

Technological Change and OD

Personal computers and robotics are examples of the many ways that technological advancements have impacted the workplace. The field of OD offers several suggestions as to how these new technologies can be effectively incorporated into organizations. In fact, the whole area of sociotechnical approaches to OD focusses on this issue. Williams (1983) noted several principles that should be considered when dealing with new technologies.

First, he suggested that, instead of allowing technical experts to design technical systems as a function of their own knowledge and experience, top management should allow the people affected by the new technology to *play an active role in planning* for the change. Besides reducing resistance to change, these individuals can make valuable contributions to successful design based on their knowledge and experience with the work system. Given new technologies, such as computer programming languages in standard English, organizations are more able to capitalize on the knowledge and experience of the users of their systems and are less dependent on external technical experts.

Second, Williams noted that new technical systems should *not be designed to reduce employee control* over their own work. He argued that the focus should be on the interface between people and the technical system to create what he refers to as *joint self-management*. For example, as a result of advancements in computers/information technology, individuals in physically remote locations can share information and, as a result, can jointly reach higher quality decisions than they were previously capable of.

Finally, Williams pointed out that the assumption is often made that, if a system is technically sound, organizational and behavior adjustments will follow as a matter of course. Such an assumption can lead to severe problems. He suggested that the design and implementation of new work systems be *viewed as a learning process* that must evolve through stages and be open to modification in any aspect of the system. Stated more simply, there may be a situation where it is wiser to change the technological design of the system rather than require people to attempt to behaviorally adjust to it.

Williams (1983) felt that adherence to the principles described above will increase the probability that a new technology will lead to a more effective work environment. It will create the desired productivity gains while at the same time improving the quality of work life for the workers who will use it. The introduction of new technology thus represents an excellent opportunity for human resources and organizational development.

SUMMARY

This chapter has focused on the process of providing technical training. The first type of technical training employees receive is when they are socialized into the organization. We have noted that:

1. Socialization takes place in stages, the first of which occurs even before the prospective employee joins the organization.
2. Socialization involves the development of skills needed to perform the job along with adjustments to job demands and work group values.

3. Effective socialization can result in positive, affective, and behavioral outcomes.
4. Effective socialization should occur if the new recruit receives realistic information and the socializing agents have the skill, motivation, and opportunity to socialize the employee.
5. Socialization is a system that requires all of the components working in synchronization for it to reach its desired goals.

We have suggested that the process of providing technical training is basically the same as providing any type of training. However, we have also noted:

6. An effective training needs assessment for technical training requires the development of a task by ability taxonomy. Although progress has been made in this area, considerable refinement is still needed.
7. The concept of career stages and the utilization of career development activities are factors that can increase the effectiveness of technical training.
8. On-the-job training techniques such as the JIT and apprenticeship methods are valuable training techniques but require careful attention as to whether the trainer has the appropriate skill, motivation, and opportunity. The environment in which OJT is conducted may also be a concern (e.g., is it conducive to learning?).
9. The appropriateness of off-the-job training techniques for technical training will be influenced by factors such as the rate of technological change and concern for trainee safety.

Finally, the field of OD has noted factors to consider when implementing technological change. These include:

10. Allowing the employee who will be using the new technology to take an active part in system design.
11. Using technological advancements to enrich rather than simplify the nature of work.
12. Having an openness to system modifications in new technologies to conform to organizational and behavioral needs.

DISCUSSION QUESTIONS

1. Describe how you were socialized for your current job or a job you've previously held. What do you see as the advantages and disadvantages of how you were socialized?
2. Describe several jobs you would not want people to be trained for by the on-the-job training approach. Are there any common characteristics about these jobs?

3. Many people resist the implementation of new technologies. Often people do not want to be "retrained." Why do you think this is so? What can organizations and trainers do to deal with it?
4. What can an organization do to assure that supervisors will be effective coaches?
5. How is technical training similar to other types of training? How is it different?

TECHNICAL TRAINING: AN INTERVIEW WITH LISA SELLARS

Lisa Sellars is the manager of in-plant continuing education programs for the Society of Manufacturing Engineers (SME), a professional society serving the training needs of the manufacturing community. Ms. Sellars' responsibilities include assessing the needs of client companies and providing the appropriate short course or series of courses to update technical skills. She has been involved in the design, administration, and evaluation of courses covering everything from basic machining operations to computer-integrated manufacturing. Client organizations of SME include Ford Motor Company, General Motors Corporation, The United States Army, IBM Corporation, and Westinghouse Electric Corporation. Prior to her work with plant site training, Ms. Sellars spent two years developing short courses for the Society that were marketed to a nationwide audience. Ms. Sellars is in progress with a Master of Science in Organization Development at Eastern Michigan University (EMU). She received a Bachelor of Science degree from EMU with a major in speech communication and a minor in business management.

We selected Lisa's interview to appear after this chapter because of her active involvement in technical training for professionals.

Question: What do you see as the technical training needs of managers and professionals?

Sellars: In order to maintain its position in the world economy, U.S. manufacturing industries have increased their use of automation. Investments in these technological innovations require a top down approach to technical training. Management needs to know the big picture, not the details. The manager of a drafting department must know what a new computer can do, not how to get the computer to design a solid model. Management needs to understand the scope of the capabilities of new technology rather than the skills needed to run it. Professionals need the skills to use the technology as a tool to advance and/or apply their knowledge bases. The manufacturing sector is beginning to look more and more futuristic. Trainers are needed to help to plan the maximal use of all these technological advancements.

Question: Some professionals I see seem to resent the computer invasion of their offices. How can trainers reduce resistance to technological change?

Sellars: The major step I take through my position at SME is to meet the trainees on their own ground. In-plant training sessions may be less exotic but they do provide familiar surroundings and this seems to reduce some resistance.

Using in-house trainers rather than ones from the big automation companies helps too. Increasing the use of automation generally raises job security fears even among professionals and managers. If a company is expecting no layoffs to occur, it should reassure its employees on this matter. Such reassurance will help reduce resistance to training in at least some trainees.

Question: Let's reverse our perspective. Has increased technology affected professional trainers themselves? For example, how has the proliferation of computers in the business world changed the training profession?

Sellars: In my job, I see the hardware and the software impact that computers are having on how we conduct training. First, it requires a whole new skill level requirement. Trainers must know how to use the equipment. Since each system has its own nuances, this can be a real problem for external trainers. This is another reason why the sessions should be held on-site. That way trainees learn on the actual equipment they will be using to conduct business.

In addition, computers have opened up so many more options for self-paced training programs. Such programs provide much greater flexibility to the company and to its employees. Scheduling worries disappear and the need to select a group of trainees all at the same skill level no longer remains a concern. We have seen many companies using Control Data's Plato system. It may be expensive now but it does provide some advantages.

An impact of all this on trainers is the need to spend our time designing software rather than working on our presentation skills. Automation won't replace all trainers, but clearly the same displacement issue that worries employees of manufacturing companies is a real issue for trainers too. The new technology may eliminate some "old" jobs but generates some "new" ones—not only software development jobs, but the jobs of training people on the maintenance of computer systems and the security procedures needed to protect company information.

We are all moving from the industrial age to the information age. Trainers must make this step too. Trainers must plan greater coordination between training programs. This integration is needed not only to enhance comprehension of information but to think through the compatibility needed to run different programs on different systems.

Question: What training style and design issues come to mind when you think about technical training for professionals?

Sellars: The overriding issue for us at SME is to provide hands-on experience during the training programs we offer our clients. It's so important to receive "feedback" from the machine itself. We find our hands-on orientation is highly preferred by the participants. When people are actively working on a variety of experiences, they remain interested in the training session. This is especially important for those in need of updating their skills but who have not been in a classroom for a while.

As a result, the more skills-oriented our sessions are, the fewer trainees we can handle per session. If only an overview is needed by a group of upper-level managers, we can increase the number of people per session. We still prefer to give them some active, hands-on experience but do use demonstrations and videotapes to familiarize them with the whole process.

Question: How should technical training programs for professionals be evaluated?

Sellars: It's a very similar process to any other type of training. In some ways it may be easier to evaluate technical training because the outcomes are easier to observe and test than the outcomes of "management style" or "communication skills" training programs.

No one will ever use a perfect system for evaluating training programs but some things could be done that would improve the meaningfulness of the evaluation data we receive. In particular, companies need to do a better job of assessing the need level of individuals before they come into training. Clearly the differences in need levels could affect evaluation results.

Question: What do you foresee as the future of the field of technical training?

Sellars: The field is growing by leaps and bounds and will continue to grow. The rapid pace of technological change will continue in the manufacturing sector and has also invaded office settings and service industries. People are changing jobs on a more frequent basis and, even if they remain in their same position, they are finding their job requirements to be changing. This will mean a steadily increasing demand for competent technical trainers. It's a great field to be in. It's right with the times.

Chapter 9

TRAINING AND DEVELOPING MANAGERS _____

WHY MANAGEMENT DEVELOPMENT? _____

This text has already described many training techniques and covered the topic of technical training. Why a special chapter on management training? Don't the previously described techniques work for managers? Is there a process difference between training activities for managers and nonmanagers? Actually, the techniques and processes are equally applicable for both groups. We chose to emphasize managerial training because of the importance of good management to the success of the organization, the scarcity of good managers, and the difficulty of developing truly good management development programs.

The importance of management to the success of an organization becomes clear when examining differences in effectiveness among companies competing in the same market. Most companies within a given industry have roughly the same potential access to resources. Yet even the casual observer can detect significant differences in the operations and results of these competing firms. While potential access to resources may be roughly equal, actual access differs markedly. Careful analysis will inevitably show that it is differences in the management of the organizations that allowed some of them to acquire more than their share of the desired resources while others fared less well (Peters & Waterman, 1982). Because managers are responsible for the planning, organizing, and controlling of activities, they are ultimately responsible for the effectiveness of the organization. It is management, for example, that is responsible for seeing to it that employees have the knowledge and skill required to perform their jobs properly. It is also management's responsibility to see that appropriate motivational systems are in place and that barriers to employee performance do not exist. Thus, if employees don't perform up to expectations, it is ultimately management's fault.

All but the most successful firms complain about the lack of effective management. In attempts to satisfy this need, public and private organizations seem to have developed insatiable appetites for new managers (Miner, 1974; Sayles, 1979). It is obvious that the better managed organizations will be able to attract more of the most talented new prospects. Many of these prospects, however, will not realize their potential in that organization. Some of those will change employers and blossom into "good managers." Thus, it becomes apparent that the nature of the organization and its internal environment have a lot to do with management effectiveness. This is why the field of organizational development has stressed the importance of matching the managerial processes and behaviors in an organization with its internal structure and design components.

The apparent shortage of "good" managers may actually be a symptom of the organization's lack of understanding or clarity about what, for it, constitutes good management. Thus, determination of the appropriate managerial processes and behaviors for *this particular organization* is the first step of any well-constructed management development program. It is also one of the biggest problems since to do it requires a very clear understanding of the organization *and* of leadership/managership research. While it is much simpler and more comforting to believe that there is one best way to manage, the evidence quite clearly contradicts this (e.g., Fiedler & Chemers, 1974; Vroom & Yetton, 1973; Steers, 1977; House, 1979; Kerr & Jermeir, 1978).

This chapter is designed to answer the following questions:

1. What is the nature of a manager's job?
2. What are the common bases of knowledge and behavioral skills that managers need?
3. What kinds of training programs have been developed to meet managerial knowledge and skill requirements?
4. What are the alternatives to developing an in-house program, and what are the associated advantages and disadvantages?

THE NATURE OF THE MANAGERIAL JOB

Ideally, the components of a management development program will reflect those factors that have been shown to be predictive of managerial success.

John Miner (1968) pointed out that any approach to the identification of these factors must be closely attuned to the value and reward structure of the particular organization. The development of training programs to enhance managerial effectiveness must, therefore, look to the often complex interaction between the characteristics of the individual manager and the characteristics of the organization.

Given the fact that what may be effective managerial behavior in one organization (or at one level within an organization) may be ineffective at another, how can general statements be made about managerial duties and responsibilities across different industries? Actually, there is no real contradiction. The issue is not so much differences in the activities that managers engage in but the style and frequency with which they are performed. In fact, the empirical literature shows that there are more similarities than differences across managerial jobs in different industries (Campbell et al., 1970; Dowell & Wexley, 1978; Nealy & Fiedler, 1968).

Henry Mintzberg (1975) integrated much of his own and others' research on managerial activity into *roles* that can be "customized" to fit into a particular position in a particular organization. Figure 9.1 illustrates the relationships among these roles. Mintzberg's definition of a *manager* includes anyone who is in charge of an organization or one of its subunits. The roles that managers are required to assume derive directly or indirectly from their *formal authority*. Mintzberg described the roles as shown in Table 9.1.

Mintzberg pointed out that these roles form an integrated whole. To remove one from the total framework changes the nature of the others. As a result, training must provide not only the knowledge/skill required for each of the roles, but also that required for their integration. While individual

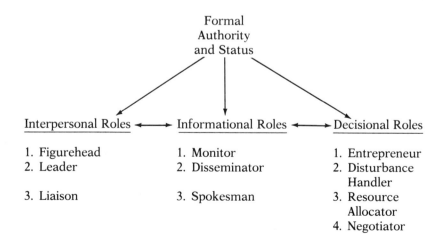

Figure 9.1   Mintzberg's managerial roles.

Table 9.1 Description of managerial roles.

Roles	Activities
Interpersonal	
Figurehead	Meeting the routine, obligatory social and legal duties required of the head of a unit. Examples would be attendance at social functions, meeting touring politicians, and lunching with buyers or suppliers.
Leader	Maintaining, developing, and motivating the human resources necessary to meet the needs of the unit.
Liaison	Developing and maintaining a network of individuals outside the unit in order to acquire information and actions of benefit to the unit.
Informational	
Monitor	Searching for and acquiring information about the unit and the environment the unit exists in so that the manager becomes an information center for the unit and the organization. Derives from liaison and leader roles.
Disseminator	Distribution to others within the unit or organization, selected information, some of which has been transformed through integration with other information.
Spokesman	Distribution to others outside the unit or organization, selected information regarding the plans, values, activities, etc., of the unit.
Decisional	
Entrepreneur	Proactive development and adjustment of the unit to take advantage of existing opportunities or meet anticipated changes in the environment. Actions are based on inferences and conclusions drawn from the evaluation and integration of information gathered in the monitor role.
Disturbance Handler	The reactive development of responses required to meet the immediate demands of the units' environment. Examples of these demands would include a wildcat strike or the loss of a major customer or supplier.
Resource Allocator	Evaluating and choosing among proposals, integrating activities, and authorizing activities and resource utilization.
Negotiator	Bargaining to acquire the resources to meet the needs of the unit and the organization.

managers may give more or less attention to particular roles, the roles remain inseparable. Elimination or neglect of one role has direct consequences on performance of other roles and, ultimately, on managerial effectiveness.

Mintzberg also provided more detailed descriptions of the managerial job which, though less systematic, provide more of a day-to-day flavor of managerial work. Some examples of these descriptors are:

- Brief, varied, and discontinuous activities.
- Unrelenting pace.
- Performs numerous regular duties, as well as handling the exceptions in the routine and exceptions in subordinates' routines.
- Communication is primarily verbal.
- Most decisions are made on the basis of judgment and intuition.

Leonard Sayles (1979) identified the following contradictions managers face on a day-to-day basis:

- Subordinates need to be given a clear understanding of their jobs and their boundaries, yet jobs inevitably overlap and boundaries are blurred.
- Managers need to establish routine and regularization to obtain efficiency, yet routines and stability must be purposefully sacrificed to introduce change.
- Controls destroy the validity of information, but no manager can function without controls or valid information.
- Organizations are indisputably hierarchical but, in larger institutions, most managers spend a majority of their time coping with lateral relations.
- Managers need to be decisive, but it's often difficult to know when a decision is made, and many decisions must be reconsidered and remade.
- Managers must have a strong need for achievement yet receive little sense of "closure" or completion (not unlike the homemaker's problem of starting over each day).
- Rules and standards are important constraints that can't be ignored but, inevitably, they are also inconsistent, and the manager must be able to violate or ignore some to meet others.

Obviously, the descriptions above do not indicate that managers sit down and carefully plan and organize their unit's activities and then logically and rationally direct and control the unit's activities. The manager's job is quite simply to get the unit's work accomplished and keep it productive. Because the organization itself produces a dynamic internal environment, management must constantly act to meet the challenge of new circumstances. In other words, management must be prepared to quickly exercise responses that meet the unique demands of each new situation. Subunits of the organization must not only adapt to the new circumstances, but also coordinate their adaptation to other subunits that are themselves adapting.

There is typically little time for careful reflection and planning. Those plans that have been carefully thought out may not reflect the new challenges.

Managers must have at their fingertips the knowledge and skills necessary to meet these challenges as soon as they arise. This is not to say that careful, reflective analysis and planning are not necessary for organizations. It's just that managers typically have little time for this important activity. That is why so many organizations have staff units whose activities compose much of the long-term planning and organizing functions of the company (e.g., corporate or organizational planning, organizational analysis, and research departments). A typical manager, however, must be able to quickly diagnose a situation, develop a response that is appropriate to the situation and consistent with organizational plans, implement it, and move on to the next task. To do this, the manager must understand the organization, the function, and level of his or her job, the situation, himself or herself, and have the skills to implement the solution. The following section discusses the knowledge and skill requirements for meeting these demands.

KNOWLEDGE AND SKILL
REQUIREMENTS OF MANAGERS _____

Research into the nature of the managerial job has provided some insight into the kind of knowledge and skills the manager must possess. However, as was pointed out in the chapter on needs assessment, an inferential leap is required to go from the job analysis (e.g., an understanding of the job) to the identification of the knowledge and skills required to perform the job. The length of the cognitive leap can be shortened somewhat in this case by examining the empirical literature to see what kinds of knowledge and skills are predictive of managerial success. Combining this with the results of some organizational needs analyses and examining the curriculum of established management education programs should provide a fairly clear picture of the things a manager must know and be able to do.

Categories of Requirements

The results of assessment center research (Bray, 1973; Bray & Grant, 1966; Bray, Campbell, & Grant, 1974; Byham, 1980; Thornton & Byham, 1982), managerial needs analyses (Niehoff & Romans, 1982; Starcevich & Sykes, 1982), examination of the curricula of professional and educational management development programs (Bricker, 1981), and the contents of several management texts (Griffin, 1984; Koontz, O'Donnell, & Weihrich, 1984; Scanlon & Keys, 1983) can be organized into four major knowledge/ skill categories. These categories are *administrative, technical, interpersonal* and *personal.* It should be pointed out that these areas are not independent of one another. One's personal characteristics and interpersonal skills will obviously have some effect on technical and administrative activities. In fact, it is most probably the integration of these categories into a coherent whole that determines the degree of success a manager will find. The technical and interpersonal categories might be considered subcategories within the administrative area since they each deal with a specialized part of the administrative process. The technical area deals with the functional responsibilities of the unit while the interpersonal category covers the human relationships and interactions necessary for managerial plans and directives to be carried out. Nevertheless, it is both convenient and useful to consider them separately for the time being.

Administrative Administrative knowledge and skills are those qualities that are required to effectively run an organizational unit, but that are not a part of the technical or interpersonal requirements. These are the knowledge and skill requirements for performing the managerial functions common to all (or nearly all) management positions. Listed below are some of the most frequently cited examples of the knowledge and skill requirements in this category.

Planning and decision making
● Knowledge of decision-making alternatives.
● Setting priorities.
● Forecasting events.
● Knowledge of organizational policies, procedures, and objectives.
● Knowledge of and skill in applying management science tools.
● Knowledge of legal, social, and political environment.
Organizing
● Knowledge of organizational structures.
● Coordinating activities.
● Scheduling activities.
● Allocating resources.
● Integrating unit activities into organizational plans.
Controlling
● Knowledge of control systems.
● Developing control systems.
● Communicating in writing.
● Initiating activities.

Technical Technical knowledge and skill consists of that which is required to meet the specialized functional demands of the managerial position. In the functional area of marketing, for instance, knowledge and skills in advertising, direct sales, and consumer psychology are examples of technical knowledge and skill. There seems to be general agreement that all managers, regardless of level in the organization, need to have some in-depth technical knowledge of the functional area within which they are managing and some basic technical knowledge of the other functional areas in the organization (e.g., human resources administration, production management, finance and accounting, marketing, etc.). Also, within the technical area are knowledge and skills related to the technical aspects of managing in any functional area. The most frequently mentioned of these are financial analysis, budgeting, and forecasting; managerial accounting; understanding of micro/macro economics; and marketing goods and services. The reason for including these in the technical category is that they are techniques and areas of technical information that apply only to a specific aspect of managerial activity. Administrative knowledge and skills are more broadly based.

Interpersonal   In this category are the managerial skills and knowledge that are used most frequently. These are what provide the manager with the ability to communicate with, understand, and motivate individuals and groups. As Mintzberg's research indicates, managers spend most of their time interacting with others. The manager's skills and knowledge in this area will be the primary determinant in influencing others and developing necessary information networks. The knowledge and skill elements most frequently mentioned are:

Leadership
- Understanding human behavior.
- Motivating subordinates.
- Managing performance.
- Developing subordinates.
- Team building and team leadership.
- Managing conflict.
- Intra- and inter-group development.
- Behavioral flexibility.
Oral communication
- One-to-one and in groups.
- Presentation skills.
- Listening.
- Awareness of social cues.
- Maintenance of social objectivity.

Personal qualities   This category is conspicuously different from the preceding ones. The elements in this category are not skills or areas of knowledge. Rather, they are qualities of the individual—the characteristics or personality traits, if you will, of the manager. While leadership studies have consistently failed to identify personality traits that predict successful leaders (Bass, 1981), the assessment center research cited earlier has isolated some individual traits that do. The reader should be aware that a personal trait that exists early in a manager's career may change markedly over the course of the career. The traits identified here are those that predicted later success when measured early in the manager's career (often prior to having even a first-line supervisory position).

The reader may wonder why personal traits and characteristics are being discussed in terms of training and development. If these are relatively stable characteristics, tendencies and temperaments that have been significantly formed by inheritance, social, cultural, and environmental factors (Maddi, 1980, p. 41), then don't we just have to accept them as given? Even if we know what traits and temperaments are most predictive of managerial success, what can training and development do about it if someone doesn't have any or all of them? Isn't this a selection issue rather than one that training needs to consider? Let's take these questions in order. Yes, we pretty much have to accept existing traits and characteristics as given. It's unlikely that a training department would have the time or skill required to effect changes in personality (not to mention the dubious ethics of such an action). However, just because someone may not have some or all of the traits doesn't mean they aren't or they can't be an effective manager. Remember, these are predictors not requirements. Just because intellectual ability predicts scholastic success doesn't mean that hard work and attention to detail won't produce scholastic success in spite of some intellectual deficiencies. After all, that's the definition of the "over-achiever."

The management and leadership literature clearly indicates that different personal styles and characteristics are more or less effective in different situations (e.g., House & Baetz, 1979). Training can help the manager understand the situational contingencies that make his or her personal style more or less effective. Alternative strategies can be developed for situations in which that style is less likely to be successful. This approach is one of changing behavior rather than personality. While the predictive ability of traits and characteristics is a selection issue, the traits and characteristics that get selected are a training and development issue. At the very least, knowledge of these will help the trainer understand what the majority of the managers who attend management development activities will be like. Jon Bentz, Director of Psychological Research and Services at Sears, Roebuck & Co., has used personality assessment for selection and development purposes for many years (Bentz, 1984). The intellectual and personality factors used by Sears are very similar to those identified by the assessment center research referred to earlier. These traits and characteristics can be segmented into two subcategories—intellectual abilities and personality traits—as shown below:

Intellectual
- Scholastic aptitude including numerical and verbal reasoning.
- Conceptual ability: ability to understand cause/effect relationships and how the parts must fit to create the desired whole.

- Diagnostic ability: ability to deduce from the nature and location of symptoms the causal agent(s) of those symptoms.
- Analytic ability: after understanding the nature of a system, the ability to determine the parts that will exert the most influence on the whole or any other part of the system.
  Personality
- Stability of performance across situations
- Work-oriented motivation
- Career orientation
- Likeability
- Independence of others
- Resistance to stress
- Initiative

Integrating the Job and the Requirements

If we now compare the four knowledge, skill, and ability categories to the managerial roles indentified by Mintzberg it is possible to determine role requirements. Table 9.2 presents what seems to us a reasonable matching of roles and requirements. The meeting of obligatory ceremonial duties clearly calls for awareness of social cues, oral communication skills, and probably human relations skills and behavioral flexibility. Of course, the manager's

Table 9.2   Knowledge/skill requirements for managerial roles.

	Administrative	Interpersonal	Technical	Personal
Interpersonal				
Figurehead		x		x
Leader		x	x	x
Liaison	x	x		x
Informational				
Monitor	x		x	x
Disseminator	x	x	x	
Spokesman	x	x	x	
Decision Maker				
Entrepreneur	x	x	x	x
Disturbance handler	x	x	x	x
Resource allocator	x	x	x	x
Negotiator	x	x		x

personal qualities, particularly resistance to stress and likeability, will determine the kinds of situations and kinds of behaviors the manager is most
comfortable with. On the other hand, it seems unlikely that the manager's
technical or administrative knowledge and skill will be very important in this
role. Using a similar logic, we have filled in the rest of the table. We make no
claims that this table is inviolate. Rather, we hope that it can serve as a
heuristic device for relating managerial skills and knowledge to various
aspects of managerial jobs.

While the roles and their associated skills are common to most
managerial positions, it is important for trainers to realize that the precise
nature of the roles and skills will differ somewhat from organization to
organization. It is also clear that, even within the same organization, the relative *importance of the roles will differ from level to level in the hierarchy*
(Pavett & Lau, 1983). *Lower-level managers* primarily coordinate and super-
vise the work of others who are not managers. They are usually in daily
contact with their subordinates and other first-line supervisors and are
responsible for the day-to-day operations of their unit. They depend primarily on their interpersonal and technical skills (Coleman & Campbell,
1975). Their roles are primarily leader, monitor, disseminator, disturbance
handler, and negotiator. Some amount of resource allocation may also be
required but often these decisions will have been made by the middle manager. *Middle managers* coordinate the activities of lower-level managers.
This means that, in addition to the roles identified for the lower-level managers, they must fill the roles of liaison, spokesman, entrepreneur, and
resource allocator. Technical and interpersonal skills are still important but
emphasis on interpersonal increases in relative importance. Administrative
skills assume much more importance at this level. *Top managers* coordinate
the activities of the organization through middle managers. Administrative
skills are much more important at this level, particularly as the entrepreneur
role becomes more dominant. Other decision-making roles are typically
delegated. Informational and interpersonal roles (particularly liaison and
figurehead) usually increase in importance as one moves from middle to top
management.

The data from the assessment center research indicates that *administrative skills* are most important for predicting managerial success, followed
by *interpersonal skills.* Of the personal qualities, intellectual ability, stability
of performance, and work-oriented motivation seem to be the most predictive. Of course, technical skills and knowledge would not be predictive since
the functional area of a lower-level or nonmanagerial assessee will not
usually have much correspondence to the functional area of the manager
nearly a decade later. However, it is interesting to note that administrative
and interpersonal skills developed very early in an employee's career are
predictive of success that far in the future.

SOURCES OF KNOWLEDGE/ SKILL ACQUISITION

Examination of successful managers' backgrounds, as was done by Max Ways (1978) in his article "The Hall of Fame for Business Leadership," shows that most acquire their skill from education and experience. Business schools and colleges provide one type of knowledge and skill development, while experience provides another. Professional management development programs (such as the AMA management course) and in-house programs fall somewhere in the middle.

Most managers would agree that managerial proficiency can't be acquired just through listening, observing, and reading. More than just practice in the training or educational environment is needed to develop the broad range of knowledge and skills that have been shown to be required of the successful manager. An opportunity to apply knowledge and skills over a period of time in a "real" setting and to observe the results is of vital importance to the development of a proficient manager. And yet, some listening, observing, and reading is also vital as both a foundation for further development and to avoid the most obvious and frequent managerial errors. For example, one review of management performance (Couch & Strother, 1971) discovered that managers without formal management training learned primarily from their mistakes. Managers with training in formal management concepts were found to utilize the training to organize both their success and failure experiences in a realistic manner. For this and other reasons, few of today's companies are willing to leave the development of their management to on-the-job experience alone. The following example describes the process one company went through in deciding how to approach the development of their managers and executives.

Company growth and expansion led Phillips Petroleum to recognize the need for providing a large number of employees with formal management training (Starcevich & Sykes, 1982). While university-based educational programs for managers have existed since the mid-1940s, Phillips wasn't convinced that this was the answer to their problem. Analysis of the characteristics of about 25 of these university-based programs revealed that the average cost of tuition, room, and board was about $900 per person, per week. That figure is similar for nonuniversity-based programs. For example, the AMA course for 1984–85 is advertised at between $2,200 and $2,750 per person for tuition and course materials but room and board are not included. The average length of a program was 6 weeks, ranging from 4 to 14 weeks. The most frequent instructional methods were the case study followed by lecture/discussion and small group work projects. The goal of the programs (and most were very similar) was to "broaden and expose participants to new horizons and to enlarge their outlook toward events taking place around them" (p. 28). The concepts most often stressed were new methods of analysis, decision making, and strategic planning.

While several advantages to a university-based program were noted (e.g., exposure to current thinking and theory in management, removal of organizational constraints in exploring novel approaches to problems, and others), it was felt that the limitations of these programs were too significant to ignore. Those disadvantages included:

- The inconsistency of faculty effectiveness both within and between programs.
- The vagueness of purpose and expected outcomes both for specific subject areas and complete programs.
- The length of time required off the job.
- The inability to handle large numbers of trainees from a single company at the same time.
- The inability of these programs to facilitate on-the-job reinforcement of concepts and skills learned in the classroom.

Thus, Phillips decided to develop their own internal advanced management programs.

Phillips is not the only company that has opted to build their own management development program. General Electric, IBM, Motorola, Shell Oil-USA, Marathon Oil, and St. Regis Paper all have their own tailor-made programs. Why have these companies rejected the university in favor of building their own programs? Probably for many of the same reasons as Phillips. The university draws to its executive and management development programs employees from vastly different corporations. Because of this diversity, teaching general concepts that are applicable across most situations does the greatest good for the greatest number. While the faculty may encourage students to apply the concepts or principles to their own situations, there is little the faculty can do to assist the student in "making it work" at Phillips or Shell. Unfortunately, the general good may not provide anyone with what they and the sponsoring company really need. If the traditional university-based program is used, it must be supplemented with training back at the company in terms of its applicability and use.

Another problem with the traditional university-based executive development program (as well as many commercial programs) is that it usually focuses on what to do and what results should be achieved, but not on how to do it. That is, the development of the behavioral skills necessary for implementing the newly learned management strategies is given, at best, only superficial attention.

A model of managerial skill development has been put forth (Waters, 1980) in which the behavioral specificity of the skill is combined with the amount of time it takes to learn the skill. This model is presented as Figure

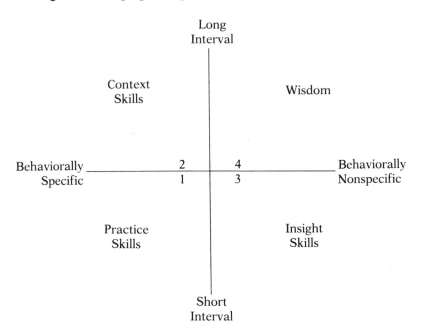

Figure 9.2   Managerial skills framework, from Waters, J. "Managerial Skill Development." *Academy of Management Review*, 1980, *5*, 449–453. Reprinted with permission.

9.2. Traditional university education may be said to rest in quadrants 2 and 4. That is, it takes a relatively long time to learn the skills, some of which are readily specified (e.g., work planning, designing controls, and introducing change) while others can't be described with much precision (e.g., gaining power, allocating resources, strategy formulation) and perhaps aren't skills as much as applied knowledge.

Internal training programs, on the other hand, are likely to fall into quadrants 1 and 3. These are skills that are learned in a relatively short time and which may or may not have readily describable behaviors. Practice skills include things like active listening, report writing, and managing conflict. Insight skills include empathizing, creativity, building trust, and negotiating. Thus, while university programs may tell you what to do, but not show you how to do it, internal training programs may show you how to do it, but do not provide an understanding of why it's done.

The ideal internal management development program will, of course, depend on the nature of the organization, its resources, and its commitment to management development. However, assuming conditions are favorable, where would ideal internal management development programs fit on

Waters' graph? According to the Phillips research, they fit just about in the middle. The programs are developed to be conceptual but not abstract. They are aimed at understanding of or appreciation for the subject matter, but not for providing expertise. They are designed to make individuals aware of where they need to develop themselves and how those areas fit into the company's needs. The target population being aimed at is high-potential, practicing managers, early in their careers.

There are some obvious advantages to developing an internal management development program. The company has control of the curriculum and can shape it to meet company needs and values. The organization can emphasize its commitment to management development and the importance of "continuing education" for managers. Everyone can get the same training. Training is more convenient for managers as it can be scheduled more appropriately and travel time should be less.

There are disadvantages to internal training programs as well. Costs can become considerably higher than externally based programs. Phillips' program ended up costing about $3,300 per participant. Finding appropriate faculty for the training program can be burdensome. The organization is not likely to employ experts in international macro-economics, human behavior, or decision strategies. If they do, there is no guarantee that these people will have the required skills to train others. Thus, outside trainers must be brought in and familiarized with the organization, keeping them in tune with what the participants need to know. If more reputable and experienced faculty/trainers are recruited (and this is desirable) they may have their own ideas about what the participants "should know."

Even though the organization has control over the curriculum, matching that to the needs of the company is still a difficult proposition. No blueprint of the ideal management development program exists. The nature of the subject matter can now be fairly well articulated. However, the proportion and definition (e.g., depth of coverage) are still problematical. Pressures within the organization may discourage training in some areas or methods while encouraging others. Though this may reflect "political reality" within the organization, it may act for the detriment of the participants and ultimately the organization.

Observing the advantages and disadvantages of university-based and internal management development programs leads to the conclusion that both are of some value. To the degree that they can be coordinated, the value of both increases. Universities are most suited for conveying wisdom, some context, and some insight skills. This is the "what should be done" and "why should it be done" forum. Training and development departments are most suited for practice skills, some insight skills, and some context skills. This is the "how can it be done" and "how does it fit in" forum.

MANAGEMENT DEVELOPMENT PROGRAMS AND TECHNIQUES

A description of all the different types of management development programs would require a separate text. New programs and techniques are constantly being developed as is evident by examination of professional publications such as *Training and Development Journal* and *Training/HRD*. There are, however, some relatively well established management development programs and techniques the trainer should be aware of. While the trainer will need to explore these in more depth than can be provided here, Table 9.3 has organized many of them by the knowledge or skill area they primarily address. The reader will notice that no technical training programs are listed. Most of the techniques related to technical training for managers are covered in Chapter 8. Colleges and schools of business provide broad-based general management programs at the undergraduate and graduate level. These programs include specialized concentrations and courses in all of the technical areas except engineering. Professional associations and commercial training companies also offer broad-based as well as more specialized training programs. While the cost is typically higher, in some cases the curriculum can be modified somewhat to more closely reflect the needs of the organization.

Other more general techniques such as on-the-job training, simulations, and T-group (or laboratory training) are referenced with the chapters in which they were discussed in this text. This list is not intended to be exhaustive, nor to indicate the authors' support or endorsement of the programs and techniques. Many important management development topics are not included (e.g., goal setting) while a few that are included may be of questionable value. The only purpose of the list is to provide students and new practitioners with a glimpse of the diversity of programs and techniques available for management development. Those wishing to probe deeper into this area might begin with the references provided in the table.

When selecting techniques and programs, the training department must attend to its match with the total system. One of the downfalls of early T-group training was due to precisely this error. While training departments were busily sending managers off to Bethel, Maine, and Big Sur, California, researchers were discovering a distinct lack of organizational impact. Ultimately, the cause of this failure of transfer of training was attributed to differences in the training and organizational environments that should have been readily observable. Thus, it is important to answer the following questions in the affirmative before adopting a particular technique or program:

1. Does it meet an identified need?
2. Will the underlying values be supported on the job?
3. Will the resulting behavior conform to existing policies, procedures, and norms?
4. Will the individuals realize any personal benefit (intrinsic or extrinsic)?

Table 9.3 Examples of management development programs and techniques.

<u>Administrative</u>

1. Management/business games and simulations (Chapter 7).
2. On-the-job training: Included in this are understudy training and junior boards. In understudy training, the manager is appointed as an assistant or adjutant to the executive. The manager learns by observing the executive and completing assignments of gradually increasing complexity and responsibility (Chapter 8). Junior boards combine simulation and on-the-job training techniques. A junior board of directors is created and staffed with promising middle managers. This board is presented with critical aspects of the company's business and asked to make recommendations to the senior board. (Mintzberg, 1973; Roberts, 1974)
3. Vroom and Yetton decision-making model: This program is based upon the participative decision-making literature and involves the manager's matching the appropriate decision-making style to the situational characteristics (also might be considered under leadership training). (Vroom & Yetton, 1973; Vroom, 1976)
4. Managerial role theory: This approach is based on Mintzberg's research. Basically aimed at understanding of what managers are doing and why. Through self-observation and understanding of one's management roles, effectiveness is said to be increased. This program might also be relevant to the other categories of knowledge/skill. This program is similar to the critical incident technique (Latham & Wexley, 1981). (See Mintzberg, 1973 and 1975)
5. Case Study (Chapter 7).
6. Rational manager training: This training is aimed at providing managers with good problem-solving and decision-making skills through practice in a simulation. (Kepner & Tregoe, 1965)
7. Conference method: This is similar to rational manager training except it is done in a group setting. Thus, group problem-solving and decision-making become the focus. (Lerda, 1967; Maier, 1963, 1982)

<u>Interpersonal</u>

1. Leader match: A program based on Fiedler's "Contingency Model of Leadership" which trains managers to diagnose their situation and themselves to determine the fit. Since Fiedler believes managerial style to be relatively unchangeable, he suggests ways in which the situation can be changed to match the style. (Fiedler & Chemers, 1974; Fiedler, Chemers & Mahar, 1976)

Table 9.3 Examples of management development programs and techniques. (*Continued*)

Interpersonal

2. Grid management: This program is based around a theory that proposes that the two most important managerial characteristics are concern for people and concern for the task. It is proposed that managers who are strong in both of these areas are the best managers in all situations. Training focuses on increasing managers' abilities to display these characteristics simultaneously. (Blake and Morton, 1978; also see Wexley & Latham, 1981)

3. Path-goal theory: No developed training programs for skill development. A basic theoretical model that is used to help managers understand their role in forming linkages between subordinates' effort, performance, and outcomes, as well as the linkages that exist for themselves. (Evans, 1970; House & Mitchell, 1974)

4. Social learning theory and behavior modification: Theoretical and technique-oriented approaches to help managers understand the behavior of their subordinates. (Chapters 4 and 5)

5. Interactive skills training: Provides trainers with interactive experiences in a number of simulated situations with feedback from observers and participants of the exercise. It's designed to point out differences between self and others' perceptions of interactions, ways of more accurately interpreting others' behavior, and more clearly conveying our messages. (Rackham & Morgan, 1977)

6. Role playing (Chapter 7).

Personal Qualities

1. Role motivation: The object of this program is to develop six motivational states in managers and help them deal with employee work deficiencies. It is based on a theory of managerial motivation developed by Miner. It is included in the personal qualities section because of its emphasis on self-examination, but could also be included in interpersonal. (Miner, 1974, 1975, 1978)

2. Need for achievement: This program of self-study, goal-setting, and case-study applications is designed to provide managers with an understanding of their own needs for achievement and to develop that need so that it is focused on constructive behavior. Based on McClelland's need achievement theory. (McClelland, 1961, 1965; McClelland & Winter, 1969; Miron & McClelland, 1979)

Table 9.3 Examples of management development programs and techniques. (*Continued*)

Personal Qualities

3. Laboratory (T-group) training (Chapter 7).
4. Transactional analysis: The theory underlying this type of training suggests that problems in interpersonal relations stem from unhealthy interactions in which people who should be interacting on a responsible adult basis adopt parent/child roles instead. The training focuses on understanding the model and improving the manager's ability to adopt adult-to-adult interactions with subordinates and superiors. (Berne, 1964; Harris, 1969)

SUMMARY

Much of the evidence indicates that a scarcity of good managers has plagued organizations for some time. It was suggested that the apparent scarcity might be more a function of a failure to develop managers to meet the needs of a particular organization rather than a general lack of managerial talent. This means that management development programs need to focus on the management needs of the particular organization, as well as the knowledge and skills that encompass managerial jobs in general.

Nevertheless, a basic understanding of the managerial job and the requisite knowledge and skills is the foundation upon which more organizationally specific programs must be built. Managers were shown to have various interpersonal, informational, and decision-making roles that form an integrated whole. Since managers typically have little time for careful conceptualization, diagnosis, and planning, these skills must be so ingrained as to be almost instinctual.

Examination of the published literature in the areas of managerial selection, developmental needs analysis, and developmental program curricula shows four major categories of knowledge/skill emerging: administrative, interpersonal, technical, and personal. It was suggested that general management knowledge and some skill areas might best be provided by university-based programs or perhaps by commercial training firms. More specific skill development can probably best be provided by the organization or the organization in conjunction with outside agents.

Finally, a sampling of management development programs and techniques was provided to illustrate the diversity of approaches available. The training department needs to make sure that the programs or techniques adopted match the norms and values of the organizations.

DISCUSSION QUESTIONS

1. How are the specific knowledge/skill requirements for meeting the demands placed on a manager determined by the training department?
2. How might the emphasis on particular management roles change relative to level in the organizational hierarchy and functional area?
3. What are the roles of a manager that can be generalized across organizations and levels of management?
4. What are the relative merits and weaknesses of internal and external management development alternatives?
5. Describe the types of knowledge, skill, and abilities required of managers.

MANAGEMENT DEVELOPMENT: AN INTERVIEW WITH JON M. HUEGLI

Jon M. Huegli is the Vice-President for Human Development for Spring Arbor Distributors, Ann Arbor Michigan. For the past 17 years, he has been actively involved in virtually all elements of the HRD and OD fields. Prior to his taking the position at Spring Arbor, Jon was, for 8 years, the administrator for Management and Organization Development, the Detroit Edison Company. He has also served as a consultant to over 120 organizations including government agencies, volunteer associations, and private sector businesses. He holds a doctoral degree from Indiana University. We wanted to interview Jon because of his strong conviction that management development and organizational development are hand-in-hand partners for organizational health and growth.

Question: What trends do you see in training directed at managerial level employees?

Huegli: Let me address that question at three levels.

First, training and development activities being offered to senior-level managers, CEO types, tend to emphasize strategic planning and thinking. I have seen a lot being offered in the areas of "environmental scanning," organizational assessment, and understanding, expressing, and reinforcing corporate culture. I also believe that more is being provided in the humanities area to these senior-level people since they are so often expected to serve in the community. It's hard to get these folks into classroom settings. So much of the so-called training is provided on the job through coaching and consulting. I have also seen a trend toward providing personalized, individualized lists of readings and the use of microcomputers to allow for self-paced learning opportunities.

The second level—middle management—is being bombarded with all kinds of training efforts. Many organizations feel that too many clones have been produced and stuck into middle management positions. Training and development activities appear to be emphasizing the need for these people to look externally rather than within their own departments or divisions. Courses in creative problem solving, goal setting, coaching, written and oral communications, meeting management, and performance (appraisal) skills seem quite popular right now. The thrust seems to be toward broadening this group beyond its technical backgrounds. I have also seen an emphasis on getting these people to develop more collaboration with their peers and manage their subordinates in a more participative fashion.

The other group of managers receiving management development training is the first-level supervisors. The trends here haven't changed that much over the last few years. The primary focus of the offerings seems to be people needs. Sessions in developing leadership, project planning, performance appraisal, grievance handling, and delegation skills are typical. The sessions tend to be more situation-specific especially for those just entering supervisory positions. However, there also appears to me to be a trend toward offering these people courses to prepare them for future, higher-level jobs. In fact, much of the thrust in management development today is on how to prepare people for the rapidly changing organizations of tomorrow.

Question: What kinds of managers are most difficult to train and how do you overcome the barriers they present?

Huegli: I would say managers who have been successful with one style who now have been promoted to another position that requires a different style are the most difficult to work with. Actually, as I think about it, most middle- and upper-level managers exhibit some dissonance about being assigned to management development or training. They have received many messages through their title or salary grade level that say "You're good," "You've made it." So there is a natural reluctance to face the "training" needs the person may have. They are also so busy that they find it difficult to reserve time to attend training.

I must also say that managers who have been technically trained in the hard sciences are frequently a resistant lot. They have been programmed to mentally argue the postulates of any proposition or theory. Since being a manager is still more of an art than a science, many of them have difficulty receiving management development assistance.

Question: How does management development differ from technical training provided to hourlies?

Huegli: For one thing, the number of technical training activities far exceeds the number of management development offerings. At Detroit Edison, we had five times as many trainers assigned to provide programs for hourly employees, including skilled trades, as we had management development trainers.

In general, technical training places greater emphasis on today's job and on certifying people on a given technique. Management development is more likely to emphasize tomorrow's job, be more cognitively complex, and stress more generalizable techniques that could be used across various situations. So when conducting a needs assessment as a technical trainer, you look for more specific components and step-by-step procedures. In general, it's easier to use the observation method to conduct the assessment. Doing a needs assessment as a management development trainer, you look more globally for combinations of behaviors and you need to consider the situations under which the behaviors are elicited. Thus, it's harder to observe and you need to rely more on self-reports from the potential trainees and their managers.

I think most techniques of training can be applied to either technical or management development training. However, I believe many of the programmed learning methods are more amenable to technical training. You also have to use more visual techniques rather than relying only on words. Taped or live demonstrations and hands-on practice sessions are more likely to be necessary for successful technical training, although these techniques obviously can be helpful to management development too.

When it comes to evaluation, it's easier to assess the impact of technical training because measurable, observable behaviors are the clear outcomes of successful efforts. When managers attempt to apply what they learned from management development, the impact is affected by other people, resources available, timing, and other elements out of their control. So, again, you have to rely on participant reactions and self-reports of impact. However, the use of assessment center methodologies has advanced evaluation in this area of training.

Question: How does management development differ from organization development? Your previous job title indicates you were in charge of both.

Huegli: There are clear overlaps between the two. The key to both might be labeled "planned change." I see management development as a part of OD. In fact, part of the purpose of management development is to introduce organization development. We often use management development sessions to gather information from key parties, explore opportunities for change, and prepare the organization to use the results of training. No matter how good your training is, unless you prepare the organization to use it, most of the positive impact will be extinguished.

I believe a lot of trainers are thinking about their activities in a more "OD-like" fashion. In particular, training is not viewed as a one-shot affair by many people now. We use management development to work on individual behaviors within an OD effort aimed at the strategic planning of policies, structures, or procedures. To me, the key is to integrate OD and management development activities.

Question: What future directions would you like to see management development activities to take?

Huegli: I wish we could do something about the mentality that people learn best in groups. I don't mean they don't learn in those settings but I would like to see managers viewing learning as a daily, on-going activity. I think we may all be better off if we could offer more individualized management development. You don't need to form a class before launching a development activity. Interactive video equipment and one-on-one coaching from the boss should be utilized more fully within management development strategies. It must be viewed as part of the job, not some activity where you get away from your subordinates and phone calls.

One more little item. In the future I wish people in management development wouldn't label the completion of their programs as graduation. Graduation implies that you're done and that's inappropriate if you want the continuous nature of learning emphasized. Development means "under construction," with an emphasis on growing, nurturing, and the management of "health maintenance."

Chapter 10

THE ROLE OF
TRAINING IN OD _____

The previous two chapters focused on the content of training generally thought to be useful for several levels of employees: technical training and management development training. In this chapter we will attempt to identify the content of training efforts aimed at supplementing/enhancing organizational development (OD) applications. The domains of content of these three chapters are certainly not mutually exclusive. Technical training and management development activities are clearly part of many OD efforts. The purpose of this chapter is to examine the following questions:

1. What are the key defining characteristics of OD and what implications do these characteristics provide the field of training?
2. Why do trainers benefit from having the knowledge skills and perspectives of organizational development practitioners?
3. Why do OD practitioners need training knowledge and skills to enhance the likelihood of successful use of OD interventions?
4. What training needs should be assessed in order to capitalize on the unique features of the various OD interventions currently utilized in the field?

It is also our hope that this chapter will serve as an introduction for trainers to the many OD techniques. You may recall that we briefly described our perceptions of the field of OD and its utility to HRD work back in Chapter 1. Here, we will elaborate on our definition of OD and on our model for planned organizational change. We will also identify what we consider to be the most common training needs that emerge when organizations attempt to launch OD efforts. Appendix B at the end of this book provides the reader with a description of over 30 specific OD techniques. Key references have been provided for each technique in order to assist trainers who wish to learn more about a given technique.

SIMILARITIES BETWEEN ORGANIZATION DEVELOPMENT (OD) AND TRAINING

In Chapter 1, we described OD as having four key characteristics:

1. An open-systems theory perspective.
2. A long-term planned change perspective.
3. A behavioral science theory and technology base.
4. A process not a program orientation.

We, thus, define *OD* as a long-term planned change process that is based on behavioral science theories and open systems theory and aimed at simultaneously enhancing organizational effectiveness and individual employee perceptions of the quality of work life within that organization.

In Chapter 1, we spent considerable time explaining what we meant by an "open-systems theory perspective" and how it should provide valuable insights to HRD professionals. Let's now turn our attention to the other characteristics of OD.

OD Involves Long-term Planned Change Efforts

An effective OD intervention is characterized as a long-term planned change process. There appear to be clear parallels between the field of training and this OD characteristic. Our previous discussions of the definition of *training* emphasized that it is a "planned organizational activity" that attempts to "change human behavior and thought processes." Others (e.g., Amaya, 1980) have suggested that the impact of training can only be measured over the long run.

The need for change is bombarding organizations now more than ever before. Information travels faster, technology is being developed faster, market situations are changing faster, and educated employees are entering organizations faster than ever before. Trainers are often front-line soldiers in an organization's battle to keep up with change. Too often we have, as trainers, stressed short-term results in order to help keep production going or justify our budgets. Thus, proof of short-term results (at least until our check clears) has served us well. In fact, popular press articles (e.g., Seamonds, 1982) have suggested that the seductiveness of the short-term perspective is a major problem of which many American managers are also guilty. The field of OD stresses a long-term perspective. Instead of merely attempting to change individuals during a training session, we should, in addition, plan to address organizational elements that would support such changes (see Chapter 11) and have impact on the bottom-line results (see Chapter 5 on Evaluation).

As trainers, we can benefit from the OD perspective of *organizational change* in addition to our traditional focus on *individual change*. Let's review the similarities between the training process and the process of organizational change. Back in Chapter 1, we displayed a sequential model of how organizations change. It should be pointed out that organizations do not necessarily progress from step to step. In fact, resistance to change (a problem familiar to all trainers) is typically so strong that companies frequently fail to address systematically the change opportunities.

The stimulus for change may be a negative experience (e.g., new restricting government regulations; decreases in productivity) or a positive one (e.g., new market opportunities; newly hired, highly skilled personnel). It may come from forces external to the organization or from within. Many organizations attempt to cope with these stimuli by maintaining business as usual. Some ignore or discount the *stimulus* for change. Others see it as an opportunity rather than a nuisance and declare a need for change.

This recognition that a problem exists may stimulate some data-gathering and goal-setting activity. The organization must establish what its present state is and where it would like to be. Effective trainers also perform such activities and Chapter 2 of this book provided guidelines on how to perform needs assessments and how to set goals. It should be noted at this point that it is not sufficient merely to detail the *symptoms* of the problem recognized by the organization. The *causes* of the problem must also be identified. If the cause of the problem includes a lack of employee knowledge skills or abilities, then perhaps training programs should be developed to address the deficiency. However, other causes (such as poor equipment, lack of sufficiently motivating compensation, unhealthy working conditions, etc.) must also be considered as possible contributors to the problem.

Once the cause(s) has been clearly established, it is useful to identify *many possible interventions* that may resolve the problem. Unfortunately, trainers and managers frequently jump to the first solution offered rather than think through several alternatives. The research on OD activities indicates that it is useful to utilize the people closest to the causes of the problem in this brainstorming phase since this will reduce resistance to the change process (see, for example, Huse, 1980).

The pro's and con's of each intervention should be weighed. When selecting an intervention, one must consider factors such as (1) the likelihood of its acceptance by those who will have to implement it, (2) the amount of time available to implement the solution, and (3) the quality of the solution. Answers to these kinds of questions dictate whether the decision as to which intervention is to be attempted should be made by an individual or a group (see Vroom & Yetton, 1973).

Once an intervention is selected, care and attention must be given to planning and implementing the change idea. Who should do what to whom? When, why, where, and how must be carefully considered. Effective trainers answer these very issues when designing training programs. Our OD model of organizational change suggests that such issues should be considered from the broader perspective of not only the personnel system, but the entire organization.

The fields of OD and training both pay considerable lip service to the importance of evaluation. Have the goals/objectives of the intervention been met? Are the problems resolved? What spin-off effects has the intervention created? This evaluation step is, in essence, another source of stimuli for the organization and may launch the whole change process over again. This is the reason why OD is defined as a *process*. OD is not a program that has a beginning and end. Nevertheless, the changes launched within the organization will have a long-term impact only if these changes become part of the everyday reality of the organization. The internalization process refreezes elements of the change effort—it becomes institutionalized. This process of internalization can be aided by coordinating changes in job descriptions, pay systems, company policy, performance appraisal criteria, etc., that reinforce the changes created by a training effort in a topic area such as performance review skills. Lawler (1981) cited an example of this from the trainees' perspective when he discussed the benefits of a "pay for knowledge" compensation system that reinforces job content knowledge gained through training programs.

Trainers may benefit from the basic OD model of planned change in a number of ways. It provides trainers with a systematic approach by which they can *plan* their training interventions. It urges them to broaden their typical horizons from attempting to have impact on given individuals (trainees) in a short-term perspective to a focus on *changing* organizational effectiveness through the development of its human resources *over the long run*. It reminds trainers of the importance of issues such as resistance to change, the establishment of a compelling need for change, the diagnosis of causes not just symptoms, strategy planning, evaluation, and transfer of learning (internalization) that are crucial to trainers as well as OD practitioners. We feel that the more that trainers act like strategy planners, the more credibility they will have with top management.

OD is Firmly Rooted in Behavioral Science Theory and Technology

Behavioral scientists have been studying and assisting organizations since the early part of this century. The very foundation of the behavioral sciences is systematic data gathering. This activity separates the art from the science in the understanding of human behavior. The same can be said of our understanding of the way organizations change. Systematic data collection is a basic activity that we feel trainers should practice. It enhances the effectiveness of training by providing a sound basis for a needs assessment (see Chapter 2). The training program can then be tailored to the needs of the specific organization and individuals involved. Systematic data collection is also the basic activity needed to conduct evaluations of training efforts (see Chapter 5). The usual lack of attention to evaluation has diminished trainers' credibility with higher levels of management. Without more sophisticated data gathering skills, trainers must often resort to justifying their budgets on the basis of how many training programs they have delivered or how many trainees attended their sessions. Trainers could be justifying budgets on a cost-effectiveness basis or at least in ways that demonstrate increases in skill levels. Improved data gathering skills would also allow trainers to learn more effectively from their experiences. These skills should also aid in the determination of which features of a training program generalize across sites. OD practitioners and trainers alike would benefit from greater adherence to the disciplined approach to data collection urged by behavioral scientists.

The fields of organizational development and training have both been criticized for their lack of unique theory development. Both fields rely heavily on the conceptualizations and models of behavioral scientists. Understanding how humans change and cope with problems has aided our understanding of how organizations go through similar processes. The theories of interpersonal dynamics, learning, attitude formation, motivation, and leadership (just to name a few) provide guidelines for trainers and OD practitioners in their efforts to promote change. The behavioral science theories provide trainers with opportunities to plan their activities in a knowledge-based manner rather than on an intuitive basis. Throughout this book you have seen references to theories established in the behavioral science literature as rationale for our advice to trainers. In particular, Chapter 3 provided a thorough review of the theory and research that has been conducted by behavioral scientists on how people learn.

A virtual merging of the fields of training and OD in their use of the behavioral sciences was evidenced in the use of "sensitivity training" in organizations (see Chapter 7 and Appendix A). In fact, the field of OD was virtually defined as sensitivity training (T-groups, if you prefer) throughout the 1960s. The lack of transfer of learning from the T-group experiences to on-the-job situations was a force for the application of systems theory to understand OD interventions. Although the use of T-groups as an OD or training intervention is now infrequent, some important lessons have been gained from their application. As a result, trainers and OD practitioners are now more aware of the importance of interpersonal skills and dynamics, organizational climate effects on longevity of learning, the potency of small group dynamics as a stimulus for learning, and the importance of a climate of experimentation. Behavioral scientists proved useful throughout the T-group era and their own techniques uncovered the flaws in the application of sensitivity groups as a training procedure. The behavioral sciences should be of continued assistance in the evolution of the fields of training and OD.

OD is a Process Not a Program

Many authors stress that OD practitioners should help the organization help itself (see, for example, Schein, 1969). Development of a self-generated problem-solving process is usually stressed rather than a change accomplished by some expert consultant coming in and "saving the organization" by telling it what to do. When people in the field of OD say it's a long-term change strategy, they mean the process of change never ends. Systems theory promotes this notion through the concept of negative entropy as was described earlier in Chapter 1.

Trainers, on the other hand, have often thought of their activities as discrete programs that have beginnings and endings. However, as the rate of organizational change continues to accelerate, training processes are needed that update the skill and knowledge levels of all human resources on a continuing basis. Trainers provide organizations with this needed function of training while using many of the same techniques that OD process consultants use (e.g., Grid OD, Survey Feedback, MBO; Wexley & Latham, 1981).

A process view of training would suggest a need for a continuous cycle of training activities. It also infers a need for a participative problem-solving approach for the identification of training needs and the planning of training events. Such an approach should reduce resistance to training efforts since the trainee is no longer having a program imposed on him or her. The process approach would suggest that training should be an attempt to help trainees help themselves in ways that would improve the "health" of the organization. The "continuous cycle" perspective would be in line with the need to maintain a long-term perspective in training that we suggested in an earlier section of this chapter. Looking at training as a process should encourage trainers not only to assess whether the trainees feel positive as a result of their training activities but to continually assess the extent to which their training activities are helping the organization to accomplish its objectives. It is our hope that this book has provided some detailed insights on how this "process" perspective can greatly aid the effectiveness of trainers.

WHY TRAINERS SHOULD BE TRAINED IN OD

Throughout this book, we have emphasized the benefits to be accrued by viewing the training process from an organizational perspective. In every chapter, we have advocated the utility of the knowledge base and technologies of the field of organizational development (OD) for the training profession. Organizations should obtain a greater return on the investment of their training dollar as a result of including OD elements in planning and operationalizing their training functions. By including an analysis of organizational problems as an integral part of the training needs assessment activities, an organization should not only end up with training programs addressing broader organizational concerns, but will also raise the awareness of problems that should be addressed by means other than training (Chapter 2). The problem-solving orientation of the field of OD promotes training in the important long-term planning skills—skills American managers generally need (Chapter 9). The OD emphasis on participative approaches to designing interventions ties line management directly into the training process and is likely to result in greater transfer of learning from the training room to the job situation (Chapter 4). Inclusion of measures designed to assess the impact of any behavioral intervention on organizational effectiveness is another issue stressed in the field of OD that organizations would benefit from incorporating into their training function (Chapter 5).

We also believe that the trainees themselves may benefit from training developed and implemented with elements from the field of OD. Such an orientation would create an active role for trainees, placing them in a position to have more control over what kinds of training opportunities they will experience. If a trainer utilizes the knowledge and skills of potential trainees in the *planning* stages of a training program, trainees are less likely to demonstrate resistance to the process. This increased openness should result in more motivation to learn and, thus, a greater likelihood of development of the trainee.

When trainers use an open systems theory perspective (see Chapter 1) to design the training process, the resulting connections between the programs and other organizational subsystems (e.g., the performance appraisal subsystem) provides legitimization for the trainee to utilize what he or she learned in training. Since OD advocates a dual-goal orientation for any intervention (i.e., enhanced organizational effectiveness and individual job satisfaction), further legitimacy is established for trainees to spend "work time" developing themselves.

Trainees sometimes leave training sessions feeling, "Well, that was interesting, but what does all this have to do with my job and this company?" By following the suggestions provided in the previous chapters regarding implications of the field of OD for trainers, we believe that an organizational context would be built into the planning, implementation, and evaluation of training efforts. This context should serve as a useful framework to aid trainees in their attempts to understand the concepts, principles, and skills being presented.

Trainers themselves will benefit from utilizing the field of OD, not only because they can increase their impact on the organizations and trainees they are serving, but because it will enrich their jobs. We have heard from many trainers (especially external professional trainers) who have experienced the frustration of putting together training programs that got trainees excited but did not see the people or organizations actually change. Like an assembly line worker who puts only one piece of the product on a moving target, trainers often do not get to see or understand the relationship between their piece and the final product. Even if a training program is designed to address specific identified needs, unless we, as trainers, help facilitate the practice of the end products of our training, transfer of learning might not occur. Learning the skills of being a consultant/change agent is a growth experience for many trainers who entered the field mainly on the strength of their platform skills.

Beyond the satisfaction of enrichment, trainers may benefit from utilizing the field of OD because the planning procedures help to more fully clarify what is needed in a given organizational situation and the technologies (techniques) of OD add to the arsenal of trainers hoping to help organizations and individuals change. Conversely, OD practitioners will benefit from the literature and practices of the field of training. The remainder of the chapter will describe the ways the field of training enhances the effectiveness of OD practitioners. Appendix B at the end of this book is designed to provide trainers with a short introduction to a multitude of OD techniques. We are trying to provide a concrete realization of the frequently heard call for the integration of the fields of OD and training.

WHY OD PRACTITIONERS NEED TRAINING KNOWLEDGE, SKILLS, AND PROGRAMS ─────────────────────────

As the field of OD matured from infancy to a point "perhaps approaching adolescence" (Bennis, 1981, p. 19), it has become apparent that OD efforts have not been universally successful. While the track record of OD is impressive (see review articles by Golembiewski, Proehl, & Sink, 1982; and Nicholas, 1982), it has become clear that inclusion of training programs as an integral part of an OD effort is a key ingredient to its success. A review of the knowledge and skills requirements necessary to operationalize the characteristics of OD is provided in this section.

Earlier in this chapter we defined OD as a long-term, planned change process. The knowledge requirements of such a process would logically include understanding an organization's present economic and strategic situation, where it would like to be in the future, and the factors that are likely to promote or hinder movement toward that future. Furthermore, knowledge of effective planning processes and of how individuals, groups, and organizations change across time are also necessary (though not sufficient) conditions to effectively operationalize this characteristic of OD.

Use of such knowledge requires problem-solving and planning skills. Since the OD process is commonly conducted in a manner that utilizes groups of people (teams, work groups, task forces, steering committees, etc.), *group* problem-solving and planning skills are needed. Nadler and Lawler (1983) pointed out that, "To assume that people will be able to solve new problems, in new settings, in new relationships in a completely new and unstructured way, is simply naive" (p. 28). Therefore, training to increase knowledge and skills in group processes may be a necessary element. Of course, OD practitioners should conduct a needs assessment before assuming such training should be provided to the particular audience one is working with.

OD practitioners who are unskilled at designing and implementing such training programs are likely to fail unless they collaborate with others who can perform this function. This situation can (and has) provided an excellent opportunity to involve internal (to the organization) training resources in a crucial feature of the OD intervention. This can result in obtaining a sense of ownership for the intervention from the organization's human resource function. This can significantly reduce the conflict sometimes experienced between the external consultant and the human resources function by providing a shared sense of mission (see, for example, the interviews with Don Arnoudse at the end of Chapter 1).

In order for an OD effort to truly be a *"long term* planned change effort," it must be institutionalized into the fabric of the organization. Goodman and Dean (1983) found only one-third of the efforts they studied exhibited a reasonable level of persistence (four or five years). The very first process they discuss as a key to whether OD is successfully institutionalized is training. "There are three major situations in which training is important: training as a program is started, retraining after the program has been in place for a while, and training of new members of the organization" (p. 287). They found many organizations providing the initial training in group problem solving and the like, as we suggested in the previous paragraph. However, it was those organizations that provided reinforcing follow-up training and training of new members that experienced long-term success with OD. These latter forms of training are probably necessary because complex skills such as communications and conflict resolution are not likely to change through one-shot exposures to new ideas. Retraining, in particular, helped participants investigate what habits required changing and reinforced the messages delivered in the initial training effort.

We have also suggested that a defining characteristic of OD is its open systems theory perspective. We stressed such principles as all subsystems within an organization affect one another in some way; the whole system is greater than the sum of its parts; there is more than one way to get from one point to another within any system; and unless a system has permeable boundaries and converts output into re-energizing input, a system dies (entropy). Potential training needs exist in both the knowledge and skill categories for those attempting to apply this perspective. OD practitioners should conduct a training needs assessment that will help identify any knowledge and skill deficiencies that would interfere in the promotion of an open systems perspective. To what extent are managers and their department members aware of the degree to which decisions made within their subsystem impact on other subsystems? Do department managers understand how the output of their department is converted into subsequent resource allocations for their departments? Are the organizational members who have the responsibility to coordinate activity between departments skilled at resolving intergroup conflicts? Is there sufficient communication between subsystems? Do organizational members understand the information that must be shared and are they skilled at presenting this information? Are their listening skills such that they receive valuable input/feedback with the accuracy needed to facilitate the systems functioning and with the empathy needed to encourage further openness?

The answers to the above questions should help establish the types of training OD practitioners must conduct or arrange for in order to capitalize on the open systems theory perspective. This perspective is a set of complex conceptualizations that are difficult to put into practice. We have heard from many OD practitioners who have found it difficult to present and utilize systems theory when working with organizations. In fact, Miner (1984) found no successful, direct applications of systems theory in OD literature. We suggest that training programs designed to address deficiencies of knowledge and skills as unearthed by the previously stated questions will help in the application of these difficult principles. Nielson (1984) and others have suggested that OD practitioners clarify the frameworks they are using to assist clients. Effective training aimed at concrete knowledge and skill deficiencies will help clarify the open systems theory framework and provide a base for solving many organizational problems. Thus, for example, training, could be provided to managers in how to convert productivity figures or reject rates into economic terms that demonstrate the value added to a product from work conducted in their department. This could help those managers understand the systems theory principle of how the output of their departments is converted into subsequent resource allocations.

OD efforts are aimed at the dual goals of (1) improving organizational effectiveness and (2) improving the quality of the work life experiences of organization members. The training implication of this orientation includes the potential need for programs designed to help organization members understand, set, and measure progress toward mutually useful goals. Research (see, for example, Locke, et al., 1981) has consistently shown that the setting of difficult but clear, attainable goals enhances motivation. The talent and opportunities to work toward such goals must also be present; but, just having a target tends to focus behavior. It is easy to advocate the dual goals of OD but a deficiency in knowledge of how to develop, set, and measure organization effectiveness and quality of work life is a training need we have witnessed at the onset of many OD efforts.

Finally, another defining characteristic of OD is its behavioral science base. The theories, research, and techniques of the behavioral sciences form a base for the field of training as well. However, exposure to this base for organization members is often deficient. While managers seemingly utilize self-developed pet theories to guide their actions, they often deny the existence of such theories and rarely question the nonsystematically derived assumptions underlying their theories (Argyris, 1980). OD practitioners should consider utilizing training programs that address knowledge deficiencies of organization members in theories of motivation, leadership, and group development. The behavioral sciences have also advanced our understanding of how to improve a number of skills including communication skills (see, for example, Rogers & Roethlisberger, 1952), conflict resolution skills (Blake, Shepard, & Mouton, 1964; Walton, 1969) and leadership skills (Hershey & Blanchard, 1982; Blake & Mouton, 1969), just to name a few. OD practitioners would obviously benefit from including training programs on these skills within their organizational change strategy if organization members demonstrate inadequate development of these skills.

TECHNIQUES OF OD

Thus far, we have explored general ways in which training programs and trainers can enhance OD efforts. The OD literature describes many specific techniques for change. In fact, the field of OD has been driven more by practitioners developing techniques than by theory and research. Each set of techniques can be enhanced by inclusion of effective training components, but each set poses its own training needs. The reader is again reminded that Appendix B at the back of the book provides brief descriptions of a wide variety of OD techniques, references for further information regarding these techniques, and descriptions of the types of training programs organization members *may* need in order to fully utilize the OD techniques. Some examples from training programs that have actually been used by practitioners to enhance OD efforts will be provided in this chapter. We are not recommending automatic inclusion of any training programs in OD efforts. We firmly believe that a thorough needs analysis should be conducted before assuming that any of the suggested training programs should be delivered to a given group of organization members during an OD effort.

Several authors have attempted to classify the techniques of the OD field (e.g., Friedlander & Brown, 1974; Beer, 1980). We have chosen to use a simple scheme of dividing the OD interventions based on their orientation.

We see three levels of orientation: (1) *macro* interventions designed to address system-wide issues of diagnosis, planning, coordination, and reward; (2) *group* interventions designed to improve the effectiveness of and satisfaction with work groups, teams, committees, and task forces in a manner that is planned and coordinated by some steering committee; and (3) *individual* interventions designed to improve the effectiveness and satisfaction of organization members in a manner consistent with some overall organizational policy or philosophy. The first category best fits our definition of what constitutes an OD effort. The second and third categories include many of the most popular interventions used by OD practitioners today. These interventions fit our definition of an OD effort when they are implemented in a manner that ties the effort to broader system structures, policies, and procedures.

Macro OD Interventions

Diagnostic and planning approaches   OD practitioners have served many organizations by facilitating efforts to determine where an organization is now (in terms of effectiveness and quality of work life), where it would like to be, and how it should get there. Some of the most popular approaches include survey/feedback interventions, sensing meetings, organizational mirroring, the action research model, force field analysis, the confrontation meeting, open systems planning, grid OD, and futuring. Each of these approaches have unique features but all emphasize systematic approaches to proactively addressing organizational problems. Practitioners successfully using these techniques have a clear conceptual framework to guide the problem-solving process. Meeting facilitation skills and data collection and analysis skills are also required. In order to reduce dependency on the initiator of these interventions, practitioners will want to facilitate the ability of organization members to use these techniques themselves. Thus, a successful change agent will empower organizational members in a manner that they can address future problems as well as follow through on the ones addressed in the initial sessions. A clear understanding of the procedures of each technique is, of course, also needed.

Macro OD interventions require certain knowledge and skill bases in order to succeed. The data gathering function of these interventions requires knowledge of developing measures, instrument availability, interpretation of statistical analysis, and feedback strategies. While the change agent can supply this knowledge and skill, assuring that internal organizational members possess these is a key to their use within a long-term planned change effort. Training programs on these topics, uniquely designed for the particular company, may be appropriate. However, the skill and knowledge bases of data collection and analysis may be readily available through research and statistics courses offered at local universities.

The comprehensive planning strategies of this category of OD interventions also require knowledge of the company's history, capabilities, and competition. Knowledge of how to interpret forecasts regarding the economy, legal, and regulatory actions, technology, and the marketplace is needed to successfully use the interventions. This often results in an opportunity for the OD practitioner to work with organization members to develop the member's skills in presenting this complex information to peers, superiors, and subordinates involved in the planning intervention in a manner that is comprehensible. Thus, a training program on presentation skills is likely to prove to be a very useful supplementary activity for implementing these macro OD interventions.

Skills required to feed back data in an effective manner do not appear to be widespread throughout the population. It is important to feed back the data so that it is understood and yet does not threaten the receivers of the feedback to the point that they become overly defensive. Nadler (1977) described several formats and the skills needed to maximize the effectiveness of data feedback sessions. Managers may need some "coaching" in how to present information in a nonbiased manner and how to resolve the conflicts that frequently arise when members are asked to interpret the data.

Since feedback and planning activities are typically conducted in group settings, use of process consultation skills by a manager in the group can generate an understanding of how the group works together. Process and procedural problems are often ignored as groups concentrate on the content of the issues they are addressing. Schein (1969) provided detailed suggestions on how to utilize process consultation skills to maximize the utility of feedback and to improve subsequent meetings through better agenda-setting procedures. Training in how to conduct action planning and how to facilitate meetings (see, for example, Doyle & Strauss, 1976) may also be necessary. Again, the reader is reminded that an assessment of whether the knowledge and skill requirements mentioned here exist in the population of the participating organization members should be conducted first but it is our hope that it is now clear that these interventions have definite training implications.

Technostructural approaches "Technostructural approaches to OD refer to theories of and interventions into the technology (e.g., task methods and processes) and the structure (e.g., the relationships, roles, arrangements) of the organization" (Freidlander & Brown, 1974, p. 320). They, thus, are used to change organizations by changing how the actual work is performed, by changing the responsibilities assigned to a given worker or group of workers, and/or by changing the reporting relationships established to determine formal decision making power and communication channels. Some of the most popular approaches to this category of OD interventions include job enrichment, job redesign, sociotechnical systems, collateral organization, matrix organization, and responsibility charting.

OD practitioners attempting to use these approaches must have solid knowledge bases of the theories of organization design, motivation, and communications. They must be skilled in the use of procedures designed to diagnose the tasks assigned to the various job classifications. They must also be able to reduce the resistance generated by organization members who frequently perceive threats to their job security when these interventions are first introduced.

The macro OD interventions of the technostructural variety require considerable knowledge of the work that needs to be done in order for the organization to achieve its outputs (products and/or services). In large organizations, few individuals (if any) will have all this knowledge. The OD processes provide a common procedural approach to help coordinate efforts to change work responsibilities and reporting relationships. Practitioners attempting to use the techniques of this set should assess organization members regarding the extent of their knowledge of the work process. Knowledge/understanding of theories, principles, and research on motivation, ergonomics, and logistics would help guide the content decisions to be made by organization members when attempting to use the technostructural techniques. Thus, training programs in these areas may be necessary in order to raise awareness of what is known and prepare members to apply this material to their own work situations.

Whenever one actually changes an organization's structure (reporting relationships), conflict resolution skills are likely to be needed. Training in this and problem-solving skills, in general, may be required. Since much of the effort to implement these OD techniques is conducted in small planning group sessions, understanding and skills related to group dynamics would facilitate the process. Since the end product of the reassignment of work and positions may be the displacement of some job holders, out placement skills may be needed. Training programs addressing these matters should, thus, be available to insure the success of the interventions.

Incentive systems approaches   In the short run, many OD interventions provide organization members with "psychic rewards." They enhance feelings of trust, provide a sense of belonging through inclusion in more decisions, enable people to take on more responsibility, and provide greater understanding of the rationale behind how work is conducted at their place of business. If successful, financial benefits are a likely outcome for the organization. Some OD interventions also establish a process for organization members to share in the financial gains. The most popular incentive plan interventions that utilize an OD framework are Scanlon plans, Rucker plans, and Improshare plans. There are also a growing number of firms experimenting with various worker ownership plans as a means of organizational development. Practitioners implementing these techniques must have a thorough understanding of compensation systems and work measurement methods in addition to their OD knowledge. Thus, quantitative skills as well as diagnostic and planning skills must be available before going ahead with these endeavors.

The macro-level OD interventions that incorporate financial incentive systems require a sophisticated degree of knowledge regarding the company's present and historical financial and market situation throughout a broad segment of the organization's membership. Knowledge of how to set fair performance and compensation standards is also crucial. Training/ education on these matters is generally needed when OD practitioners attempt to implement these strategies.

Training in a broad set of skills (e.g., participative leadership, communications, work measurement skills, etc.) and for many groups and individuals is also generally needed (see, for example, Lawler, 1981). The ad hoc steering committee that is generally used to develop the plan will need presentation skills to explain the resulting proposal to the whole membership. Accountants and comptrollers will be frequently called on to explain the company books in terms that all the participants can understand. Engineers will be called on to explain why suggestions for changes in the physical facilities may or may not work to various employee committees. Management's ability to competently utilize a participative style of leadership will be tested. The number of meetings required by such plans creates the need for facilitation and time management skills. The processes require problem-solving skills throughout the organization, including conflict resolution skills. Obviously, this category of OD interventions is heavily dependent on skill building training programs to supplement the present skill levels of organizational members.

Group-Oriented OD Interventions

Certainly the most commonly used approaches to OD utilize a small group orientation. As Leavitt (1975) pointed out, "Small groups have become the major tool of the applied behavioral scientist. Organizational development methods are group methods" (p. 371). While most employees, including managers, realize that they work for the larger organization, their work group (consisting of peers, a supervisor above them, and the directly reporting subordinates below them) *is* the organization. Their work group is generally a strong influence on the perceptions they hold of the organization—their attitudes toward the company and job and even their work performance. Cohesive work groups demonstrate less variance in their level of productivity than noncohesive groups (Wallace & Szilagyi, 1982). Cohesion also holds a strong positive relationship with job satisfaction. However, unless a high performance norm for the work group is established, cohesion may bring only satisfaction and little variance in a generally low level of productivity.

OD interventions dedicated to the dual goals of improved organizational effectiveness and quality of work life attempt to develop cohesion and high performance goals. As was described in Chapter 7, T-groups represented the major (almost only) OD intervention throughout the 1960s and early 1970s. Originally, T-groups attempted to improve organizational effectiveness primarily by focusing on the interpersonal skills of diverse groups of strangers. The transfer of learning problem was enormous and more and more trainers/OD practitioners decided to use intact work groups and broaden the focus from interpersonal issues alone to work-related goals, roles, procedures, and processes. Practitioners must be knowledgeable about group dynamics and labor relations and skilled in facilitating meetings, processing dynamics, negotiating conflicts, and problem solving in order to make effective use of the techniques of this category. Today, a wide array of group-oriented OD interventions are practiced in all types of organizations under the titles of teambuilding, joint union-management quality of work life (QWL)/employee involvement (EI) approaches, quality control circles, collaborative management—by objectives (CMBO), job expectation technique (JET), role analysis technique (RAT), role negotiation method, the transition meeting, process consultation, nominal group technique, intergroup mirroring, image exchange, and third party peacemaking.

Obviously, the field of OD contains a plethora of interventions aimed at enhancing group (and ultimately organizational) effectiveness and the satisfaction of group members. Training programs to prepare the organization and the individuals to be involved in and use these OD techniques have been established as a key factor to their success (see, for example, Mohrman, 1983; Nadler & Lawler, 1983; Goodman & Dean, 1983).

The knowledge required of organization members to maximize the utility of these techniques depends on the focus of the efforts. If group goal setting is the focus, knowledge of the limitations imposed on the group and the organization's goal-setting procedures stand out as important. If role clarification is the focus, understanding of the work required or expected from the group must be available. In addition, knowledge of the resources available to the group is crucial. Understanding group dynamics, communication theory, and problem-solving models would assist a group's efforts to improve the procedures it uses to work as a team. Understanding the pro's and con's of various conflict resolution styles, the differences between mediation and arbitration, and the characteristics of effective feedback would help deal with interpersonal and intergroup problems that hinder satisfaction and effectiveness. In addition, quality of work life efforts and virtually any small group OD intervention conducted in unionized settings requires extensive knowledge of the collective bargaining agreement. Training programs addressing deficiencies in these knowledge areas should assist group oriented OD interventions.

There are, of course, many skill requirements to maximize the effective use of these techniques. Clarity of language skills is needed to establish goals in a manner that group members know what they are aiming for. Assertiveness, presentation, and task analysis skills are required in group efforts focused on role clarification.

FIELD EXAMPLES

Examples of agendas of training programs that have been used to support OD efforts are provided on the next few pages. We are not advocating or denouncing these programs, but merely providing the interested reader with samples of programs that have actually been conducted in the field. Only the names of the companies involved and the location of the training have been deleted.

Example 1   Labor relations workshop: A program for hospital personnel staff.

Length:	Two days
Location:	Training room located in hospital library
Number of Participants:	35
Objectives:	Identify the elements that promote a high quality union-management relationship.
	Identify the pro's and con's of five styles of resolving conflict.
	Promote a clearer understanding of the current labor contract and the role of hospital supervisors.
	Increase understanding of how each person's personality influences the conduct of labor relations activities.
	Promote improvement in communication skills, especially listening skills.
	Further develop the action-planning skills of hospital supervisors.
	Explore interest in the development of nontraditional labor-management relations.
	Promote the appreciation of differences between people.
	Identify and promote attitudes likely to lead to further improvements in labor relations at this facility.

AGENDA
Day 1

8:00–8:15 a.m.	Registration
8:15–8:30 a.m.	Welcome and introduction by the director
8:30–8:45 a.m.	Clarification of workshop objectives
	Promote the appreciation of differences between people

	Identify and promote attitudes likely to lead to further improvements in labor relations at facility
8:45–9:45 a.m.	Sharing and listening: Key component skills for change
9:45–10:30 a.m.	Administration of three inventories:
	A. Meyers-Briggs Personality Type Indicator
	B. Thomas Kilman Conflict-Resolution Styles
	C. CSC Key Elements in Union-Management Relationships Inventory
10:30–10:45 a.m.	Break
10:45–12:00 Noon	Elements of high quality union management relationships and the principles of positive employee relations in hospital settings
12:00–1:00 p.m.	Lunch
1:00–2:30 p.m.	A. Legal issues in labor relations
	B. Do's and don'ts during organizing drives
	C. Clarify the union contract language
2:30–2:45 p.m.	Break
2:45–4:30 p.m.	A. Improving grievance-handling skills
	B. Grievance documentation
	C. Conflict resolution skill building

Day 2

8:00–10:00 a.m.	Understanding your personality type
10:00–10:15 a.m.	Break
10:15–11:15 a.m.	Developing a problem-solving model
11:15–12:00 Noon	Introduction to force field analysis
12:00–1:00 p.m.	Lunch
1:00–3:00 p.m.	Application of force field analysis: Action planning
3:00–3:15 p.m.	Break
3:15–4:00 p.m.	Beyond traditional labor relations: The quality of work life
4:00–4:30 p.m.	Summary and evaluation

Example 2   Team building workshop for upper management.

Length:	Three days
Location:	Off-site hotel conference room
Number of Participants:	25
Objectives:	To explore the steps needed to develop an even more effective top management team.
	To clarify the goals of the organization.
	To assess the degree of commitment to the organization's goals.

To clarify the roles and expectations of the top management team members.

To promote improvement in communication skills, especially listening skills.

To identify the pro's and con's of the five styles of resolving conflict.

To assess the conflict resolution styles of top management team members.

To increase awareness of group dynamics affecting group problem-solving efforts.

To promote improvement in problem-solving and action-planning skills.

To identify the personality types and management styles of top management team members.

To promote the appreciation of differences between people.

To apply the knowledge and skills addressed in this workshop to the resolution of problems presently facing the organization.

AGENDA

Day 1

8:00–8:30 a.m.	Registration
8:30–8:45 a.m.	Introduction and clarification of objectives
8:45–9:15 a.m.	Team building and its four major purposes defined
9:15–10:15 a.m.	Development of key component skills for sharing/listening
10:15–10:30 a.m.	Break
10:30–12:00 Noon	Data gathering task forces and initial team building
12:00–1:00 p.m.	Lunch
1:00–2:30 p.m.	Where are we now? Reports from the data gathering task forces
2:30–3:15 p.m.	Administration of three inventories A. The Meyers-Briggs Personality Type Indicator B. The Thomas-Kilman Conflict Resolution Style Inventory C. The Organization Climate Questionnaire
3:15–3:30 p.m.	Break
3:30–4:30 p.m.	Styles for conflict resolution

Day 2

8:00–9:30 a.m.	Intergroup problem-solving skills
9:30–10:30 a.m.	Understanding how personalities influence team dynamics
10:30–10:45 a.m.	Break
10:45–12:00 Noon	More feedback from the Meyers-Briggs Personality Type Inventory

12:00–1:00 p.m.	Lunch
1:00–2:00 p.m.	Problem-solving and planning skills
2:00–3:00 p.m.	Group dynamics
3:00–3:15 p.m.	Break
3:15–4:30 p.m.	Problem-solving and planning skills to goal and role problems

Day 3

8:00–9:00 a.m.	Recap learning and progress
9:00–12:00 Noon	Application of force field analysis to team development issues
12:00–1:00 p.m.	Lunch
1:00–2:30 p.m.	Career style inventory
2:30–2:45 p.m.	Break
2:45–4:00 p.m.	Looking to the future: What is the path ahead?
4:00–4:30 p.m.	Evaluation

Example 3   Communication workshops for union staff involved in QWL/EI efforts.

Length:	Three separate two-hour sessions
Location:	Education Center of International Union
Number of Participants:	20
Session I:	Interpersonal communications (one-on-one)

A. When do a union leader's interpersonal communication skills affect his or her ability to serve the union?
B. What are the common problems people have in being effective communicators in one-to-one conversations?
C. What skills and knowledge should you have in order to be an effective communicator?
D. How does your personality influence your communication style?
E. What roles does listening play in the communications process?
F. How do your emotions and reactions under stress affect your ability to communicate?
G. How do organizational politics affect communications?
H. What are you willing to try this week to improve your ability to communicate?

Activities Planned:	Self-assessment of your personality and your communication style
	Listening exercise

Readings: Class discussion of topics
Session II: Communications in Small Groups
          A. What is different about communicating in small groups (committees, staff meetings, etc.)?
          B. Why is understanding small-group communications important to unionists?
          C. What should you look for in group discussions?
          D. How do groups arrive at consensus decisions?
          E. What skills are needed to effectively lead (facilitate) small-group discussions?
          F. How do you resolve conflicts between group members?
          G. What are you willing to do this week to improve your ability to communicate?

Activities
Planned: "Lost at sea" group decision-making exercise
          Feedback on how you operate in a group
          Feedback on your conflict resolution style
          Class discussion of topics

Readings:
Session III: Organizational Communication—Key to Organizational Effectiveness
          A. Types of information that are communicated
            1. Information sent downward
            2. Information sent upward
          B. Flow of communication
            1. Network analysis
              a. Wheel
              b. Line
              c. Star
              d. Com-Con
            2. Network roles
              a. Members
              b. Gatekeepers
              c. Bridges
              d. Liaisons
              e. Isolates
            3. Problems with communication flow
              a. Communication overload
              b. Communication underload
              c. Serial distortion
          C. Strategies for analyzing organizational communication
            1. Communication models
            2. Network analyses
            3. Communication audits

Activities
Planned: A. Exercise involving decision making in various networks (line, star, com-con) evaluation of strengths and weaknesses.
B. Case Analysis

Readings: "Steps in Performing a Communication Audit" by Sincoff, Williams.

Example 4   Managers and QWL.

Length: One eight hour day

Location: Company training room

Number of Participants: 70 (in two separate sessions)

Objectives: 1. To identify the knowledge level of DDA managers about QWL
2. To assist DDA managers to learn more about their personal styles (especially how their personalities may help or hinder adjustment to QWL)
3. To explore options needed to promote QWL for managers of DDA

AGENDA

7:30–7:45 a.m.	Introductions
7:45–7:55 a.m.	How will you maximize learning from this workshop?
7:55–9:00 a.m.	Sharing/listening triads exercise
9:00–9:30 a.m.	Administration of Meyers-Briggs Personality Type Indicator
9:30–9:45 a.m.	Break
9:45–10:05 a.m.	What do you know about QWL
	Facts
	Opinions
	Goals/motives
	QWL structures, procedures, interpersonal issues
11:00–12:00 Noon	Lunch
12:45–1:30 p.m.	Why should managers of your level resist QWL processes? Why should managers of your level support QWL processes?
1:30–2:45 p.m.	What does QWL for managers mean? Goals? Roles? Procedures? Interpersonal issues?
2:45–3:00 p.m.	Break
3:00–4:30 p.m.	Results from the Meyers-Briggs Personality Type Indicator Personality type Management style

	Adjustment to QWL
	Benefits of differences
4:30–4:45 p.m.	Summary
4:45–5:00 p.m.	Evaluation

Example 5   Agenda for QWL exploration workshop.

Preworkshop Diagnostic Interviews

One hour interviews would be conducted with four to eight key workshop participants who are in leadership positions or who are recognized as opinion leaders. Information received through these interviews would be kept confidential but would be used to modify the proposed workshop agenda. Themes that emerge across interviewees would be shared at the workshop but "who said what about what" would be kept strictly confidential. Questions used during the interview would include:

- Is there a need for change in the present situation?
- What is your opinion of the present union-management relationship?
- What do you already know/feel about QWL efforts?
- What would you hope a QWL effort to accomplish?
- What obstacles would have to be overcome in order to create positive changes in the present situation?
- What should the objectives of a QWL exploration workshop be?

On-Site Group Sessions (separate from union and for management)

Part I: Common Features of QWL Efforts

- Definition of a QWL Effort
- Three typical goals of a QWL Effort
- Six Phases of QWL Efforts:
  Exploration of commitment
  Structural formation
  Skill development
  Implementation
  Evaluation
  Dissemination
- Potential benefits (for rank and filers, for managers, for union leaders)
- Examples of QWL efforts (successes and failures)
- Potential pitfalls of QWL efforts (for rank and files, for managers for union leaders)

Part II: Analysis of the Potential for QWL at this Site

- Description of present situation
- Description of how you would like things to be here
- Identification of sources of support for change
- Identification of sources of resistance to change

Part III: Summary/Wrap-Up
- Questions and Answers
- What was learned here today?
- Where do you go from here?
- Evaluation

Follow-up Procedures
- Strategy meeting to be held within one month of the exploration workshop to develop action plans to capitalize on the identified sources of support for QWL and to reduce the forces of concern against QWL.
- Confidential interviews to determine degree of commitment of top local union leaders and managers for implementing a QWL effort.
- Identification of corporate and international union resources for a QWL effort.
- Survey of all employees and managers to determine depth of interest in QWL and to establish baseline data.

Example 6   Working together: increasing the effectiveness of teams, groups, and committees.

Objectives:

Team diagnosis:	To assess the current strengths and weaknesses of the groups to which the training participants belong to.
Action planning:	To develop realistic action plans that participants will attempt to implement back in their groups.
Goals and roles:	To develop participants' skills at getting groups to set goals and clarify roles.
Effective meetings:	To develop participants' skills in conducting, participating and/or facilitating effective and efficient meetings.
Leadership:	To identify and develop leadership skills of team/group leaders.
Group dynamics:	To develop participants' skills in processing group dynamics in a manner that stimulates group effectiveness.
Group problem solving:	To develop participants' skills in group problem-solving techniques.
Resolving conflict:	To develop participants' skills in resolving conflict between group members.
Listening skills:	To develop the listening skills of participants.
Monitoring progress:	To provide participants with a simple, yet useful, means of monitoring group effectiveness.

Participants:	No restrictions, but a "buddy system" has proven to be most effective in past offerings. In such a system, two or three people from each group sign up for the sessions together.
Length:	Three sessions, four hours each, once a week.

SUMMARY

This chapter attempted to review the reasons why trainers should be trained in OD and descriptions of the major categories of OD techniques. Appendix B gives trainers an introduction to the many specific interventions used by OD practitioners. With each set of techniques, we attempted to identify the knowledge and skill requirements for successful utilization. In particular, the training needs associated with OD interventions in terms of the knowledge and skill required of organization members were highlighted throughout the chapter.

Certain trends emerge across the sets of OD interventions that were examined. Knowledge of the organization's environment, resources, and processes is necessary to succeed with nearly any OD approach. Knowledge of the conceptual frameworks underlying the OD strategies is also required. Training programs can and have been designed by OD practitioners and/or by internal training staff personnel to address these needs (see Examples 1 and 5).

Skills, particularly interpersonal skills, emerged as necessary prerequisites to successful use of the OD interventions. Communications, problem-solving, conflict resolution, and planning skills were cited as key elements in every set of strategies described. The more experientially oriented training techniques described in Chapter 7 are likely to be quite useful in designing these skills-oriented training programs.

Boss and McConkie (1974) pointed out the potentially fatal error of making training programs mandatory for all organization members involved in an OD effort. Throughout this chapter, we stressed the necessity of conducting a thorough needs assessment to determine which training programs are needed by which participants in which situations. We, thus, heartily recommend a contingency view of training. This view serves as the underlying message of the next chapter.

DISCUSSION QUESTIONS

1. Why should trainers develop OD skill and knowledge bases?
2. How would you determine whether a "communications skills workshop" should be a mandatory component of a group-oriented OD intervention?

3. What elements of the field of human resources development are most likely to be of benefit to an OD consultant?
4. Critique the design of any of the examples of training programs provided at the end of this chapter.
5. After reading this chapter and Appendix B, what is your personal definition of OD?

THE ROLE OF TRAINING IN OD:
AN INTERVIEW WITH TOM HILL

Tom Hill is the manager of the Personnel Research Department of the American Hospital Supply Corporation. Tom consults and manages productivity enhancement activities in the many and varied subsidiaries of AHSC worldwide. His division is responsible for organization development and management development. Before going to AHSC, he was a member of the corporate personnel research staff of Sears. Tom received his doctorate in Industrial Organizational Psychology from Michigan State University where he received much exposure to companies utilizing Scanlon Plans. Dr. Hill has been a long-time advocate of integrating training and OD activities and, thus, seemed to be an excellent choice to be interviewed for this chapter.

Question: How would you distinguish OD from training activities?

Hill: Is there a need to distinguish them? If you look at the goals of both activities, you will find more similarities than differences. In training we try to change the behaviors, the skill levels if you prefer, of the participants. We seek the same thing in OD activities. We want the participants to change behaviors.

Training today is conducted very differently than the traditional approach. It seems to me that the old view of training was, "Let's bring some folks into our training room and educate them." Nowadays, at least within AHSC, we view training not so much as an event but rather a part of an on-going series of activities. For example, we build the survey feedback approach into many of our training efforts. In addition, we contact, prior to training, the supervisors of potential trainees and get them to help us develop the objectives and agenda. We make sure we follow up with these supervisors on what impact they perceive the training had on their people.

Today we are also more likely to send an intact work group to a training event. As a result, we essentially conduct some team building while working on some knowledge or skill need. At such training programs, participants work on real, back-on-the-job problems rather than artificial exercises. So you can see it's hard to say whether such a session should be labeled a training program or an off-site OD planning event.

Question: Do you see any differences between training and OD?

Hill: Oh yes, we can point to some differences. I would say that training is more likely to be thought of as more programmatic than OD. By that I mean, training activities will be scheduled and will provide a detailed agenda where an event labeled as OD might not. OD has a longer time frame across a wider audience of the organization.

Training provides more quantifiable results. It's more likely to provide managers with clearer clues of progress. Training and the evaluation data generated by the training function provides "ah-ha" experiences. OD provides ideas and direction and training acts as a booster shot that enables the organization to act on those ideas. Thus, training speeds up organizational change efforts and makes them all more real and concrete.

Question: What kind of training programs do you see as particularly useful in organizations attempting to integrate the OD and training functions?

Hill: I can think of several that stand out in my mind. Training programs in the methodologies of problem-solving skills for one. Especially when those programs schedule time within the session to apply the problem-solving techniques to back-home problems. Programs in "improving communication skills," especially interpersonal communications, have been important features of team building and leadership style change efforts. Training in conflict resolution techniques and in how to facilitate meetings in a more effective manner has aided all kinds of OD efforts.

An OD effort within a given function, say production, can benefit from training in planning skills—like a seminar on "how to do production planning" or "project management skills." Training programs offered to participants across functional areas not only produce a common data base but help build networks and bridges that are so valuable in promoting a systemwide change effort. Some training programs even support OD in a cross-organizational manner. For instance, in order to apply open systems theory within an organization, one needs to get the management team to fully realize the impact of the external environment on each function and the organization as a whole. Thus, a common training program, say on some government regulations, might bring together vendors, customers, sales, and distribution.

I still want to drive my main point home. Training and OD are becoming more and more similar every year. We rarely view training activities as one-shot events and have developed quite a data base through our evaluation procedures.

Question: Since the trend you refer to is likely to continue, how should people planning to go into training prepare themselves for the future.

Hill: I would expect trainers to have the whole range of OD skills and knowledge. Like I said, this is already happening. In fact, even some safety trainers I recently observed have incresed their effectiveness by using more of an OD approach. They are systematically gathering data on safety related matters, feeding that data back to groups and work teams, getting those people to process the data, and analyzing the social system to discover components that could serve as reinforcers of proposed changes.

Trainers will need the skills of the helping professions and they still must have almost "show biz" skills to capture people's interest while driving home their points. Trainers must provide the focal points for efforts to change organization, effectiveness, climate, and behavior.

Chapter 11

A STRATEGIC PLANNING APPROACH TO TRAINING _____

The first ten chapters of this book were designed to illustrate how training can be used to increase individual and organizational effectiveness. Throughout these chapters, we have emphasized that training is not a cure-all. It is a process for solving a certain type of problem and must be implemented correctly in order to succeed. Earlier portions of this book have suggested that the application of behavioral science concepts and techniques (e.g., OD) to the field of training will improve its effectiveness. There is probably no concept more central to OD than the notion of planned change. This chapter examines the types of issues that should be considered in the development of a strategic plan for training. Finally, this chapter will also summarize the types of skills and knowledge needed for an effective training department.

The specific questions that will be answered in this chapter are:

1. What is meant by a strategic training plan and what should it consist of?
2. What SKs are needed for an effective training department?

STRATEGIC PLANNING FOR TRAINING _____

One of the most popular issues in current management literature is the topic of *strategic planning*. Given its popularity, it is somewhat surprising that there is a lack of agreement as to the appropriate definition of the term (Jemison, 1981) as well as what the subject matter should be (Bower, 1982). The definition upon which the following discussion is based was developed by Chandler (1962) who defined *strategy* as "the determination of the basic long-term goals and objectives of the enterprise and the adoption of courses of action and the allocation of resources necessary for carrying out these goals" (p. 13). The advantages of a consciously formulated strategy are: (1) the guidance it provides employees, (2) its contribution to coordination among subunits, (3) a comprehensive logic for the allocation of resources, and (4) the development of a proactive rather than reactive approach to problems (Thompson & Strickland, 1980). Recently, the need to integrate human resource planning into the organization's strategic planning process has been advocated by several authors (e.g., Fossum & Parker, 1983). If advancements are to occur in this area, there is a need to recognize the strategic issues and alternatives in each area of human resource management. The following discussion is designed to focus on these issues in relationship to training.

Mission Statement

Most strategic planning approaches recognize the need for an *organizational mission statement.* Drucker (1974) noted:

> A business is not defined by the company's name, statutes, or articles of corporation. It is defined by the want the customer satisfies when he buys a product or service. To satisfy the customer is the mission and purpose of every business. The question, "What is our business?" can, therefore, be answered only by looking at the business from the outside, from the point of view of customer and market. What the customer sees, thinks, believes and wants, at any given time, must be accepted by management as an objective fact . . .
>
> . . . any serious attempt to state "what our business is" must start with the customer, his realities, his situation, his behavior, his expectations and his values. (pp. 77–79)

Drucker also noted the need to consider "what our business should be" (p. 82). It is our feeling that training departments should undergo a similar self-scrutiny. Efforts should be undertaken to determine how the department is viewed by other areas of the organization. Such efforts could range from formal attitude surveys and interviews to a few meetings with department heads. At first glance, it might seem easy to develop a mission statement for a training department. After all, the purpose of training is to train. Yet this statement is too broad to provide any direction. Will all types of training programs be offered to all employees? Will career development activities (see Chapter 8) be handled by training? The "fit" between training and other human resource management activities must also be considered in developing a mission statement. In Chapter 1 we noted that these activities impact each other. For example, more sophisticated selection systems may reduce the need for training. Similarly, an organization that has a compensation policy of paying employees for skill development rather than job change will not require the training department to devote as much time to developing employee motivation to attend training.

Tichy (1982, 1983) developed a model of managing strategic change which may be of some use in determining the mission of a training department. He suggested that there are three core dilemmas for organizations: technical design problems, political allocation problems, and cultural/ideological mix problems. *Technical design problems* arise in determining how the organization will deal with its concern for productivity. *Political problems* arise since an organization needs to allocate power and resources. Finally, *cultural/ideological concerns* deal with the shared values and beliefs that an organization wishes its members to hold. Training can obviously impact design problems through increasing skill and knowledge. However, training also influences the other two areas. Regarding the cultural/ideological issue, the manner by which individuals are sent to training, the process by which they are trained, the extent to which they are encouraged to apply their SKA back on the job and are given feedback on the effectiveness of this application are signals to employees about values and beliefs of the organization. (See Chapter 8 on socialization.)

Training is also a political process in that it is a way of allocating a very precious resource (i.e., increased knowledge and skill). In this book, we have advocated that this allocation be based on the needs of the organization through an organizational analysis (see Chapter 2). However, since many training departments do not conduct this type of analysis, the decision as to whether to provide training is often based on the political power of the person requesting the training. This is not the rational process of allocating resources that most organizations strive for.

Taking into consideration all of the previous comments, an example of a mission statement for a training department might look something like the following:

> The XYZ Company is in the business of producing high technology products of such quality that customers are willing to pay a premium price for them. Correspondingly, the mission of the training department of XYZ Company is to assist the organization in accomplishing its mission by developing the job related skills and knowledge of its employees. The training department will emphasize:
>
> - Training needs assessment to assure that organizationally relevant training is conducted.
> - Training evaluation to determine when desired objectives are obtained.

- Gathering internal and/or external training sources to assure training is conducted in the most cost beneficial manner.

All of the activities described above will be conducted in such a manner that trainee's job performance will improve as a result of training, trainees and department supervisors will feel that the XYZ training department provides organizationally relevant skill and/or knowledge enhancement and the XYZ Company is concerned for the quality of life of its human resources.

CORRESPONDENCE BETWEEN STRATEGY, ENVIRONMENT, AND TECHNOLOGY _____

Most theories of strategy (e.g., Jauch & Osborn, 1981) note the need for congruence between an organization's strategy, environment, and technology. Similarly, training should also carefully assess these factors when formulating strategy. The training function is influenced by both an internal and external environment. The former can be thought of as the environment for training within the organization, the latter as the environment the organization operates in. Technology refers to the process used in performing the work of the organization. As mentioned in Chapter 8, the nature of an organization's technology can impact the method and source of training. For example, an organization with a rapidly changing technology might not find the use of programmed instruction or computer-assisted instruction cost-beneficial due to the high developmental costs of these approaches. Similarly, such an organization may develop a strategy of having the majority of their training conducted through universities or subject matter experts since such experts should be current in their field. This section focuses on the factors to consider in assessing the internal environment for training. The next section, which examines strategic alternatives, evaluates alternatives based on technological and environmental constraints.

Internal Environment

The internal environment of an organization can facilitate or hinder a training program. Trainers should constantly monitor the internal environment and attempt to modify it so that an effectively designed training program has the possibility of being successful. The following discussion focuses on these types of issues and how they might be dealt with to provide an optimal internal environment for training.

Is the Training Content Part of the Formal Evaluation Criteria?

One of the basic principles of human behavior is that people do things they receive some sort of reinforcement for doing and/or some sort of punishment for not doing. Similarly, people do not continually do things if there are no *perceived* consequences for their actions. The term *perceived* cannot be overemphasized since rewards and punishments differ depending upon what a person values. For example, a trainer may assume that, since a particular skill or knowledge (SK) is an aspect of an individual's job, training in this SK will be perceived as relevant. This is not necessarily true, even if the trainee realizes that the SK is related to effective job performance. The lack of interest in acquiring the SK should be expected if it is viewed by the trainee as something he or she will not get rewarded for having nor punished for not having.

An example of how this may occur is in the area of affirmative action. Many organizations have affirmative action plans that state that it is every manager's responsibility to take affirmative action in selection decisions. However, there are often no direct consequences for a manager taking or failing to take such action. Ironically, the individual who does fulfill this "stated" job requirement is placing himself or herself in a dilemma since he or she will have less opportunity to devote time to activities for which consequences do occur. Thus, it is not surprising that a manager who attends a well-developed and relevant workshop on affirmative action may pay little attention and view the effort as a waste of his or her time.

The example above assumes that the lack of the desired behavior (i.e., increased affirmative action efforts) is, in fact, a problem for the organization. Given this assumption, what can a trainer do to rectify it? One obvious answer is to include the desired end products of training as part of the formal evaluation process. For example, a category of affirmative action could be included on the appraisal form. However, this alone will not rectify the problem. If all managers receive an acceptable affirmative action evaluation regardless of their progress, they will soon learn that this area does not really warrant much attention. Such a situation will produce little motivation for acquiring skill in this area. Thus, there is the need to assure that employees are accurately evaluated on areas in which training is provided. This will only occur if the immediate supervisor of the trainees is committed to the training effort. This can be accomplished by involving supervisors in program development and/or actions by top management that illustrate their commitment to the training material. For example, trainees can receive personalized letters from top management (through wordprocessing technology) that they are aware what types of training the employee will be receiving and that this type of material is in line with the direction and philosophy of the organization. A higher level of commitment would be illustrated by top management dropping in on a training session to indicate their support or (ideally) teach a small portion of the material. Obviously, with scheduling difficulties, this may not always be possible. However, the use of audiovisuals (e.g., films) can resolve some of these problems.

In addition to the above, top management can exemplify their commitment to training by evaluating the job performance of employees who report directly to them based on their subordinate's skill or knowledge development in areas in which they have received training. Similarly, they can also evaluate subordinate managers on their skills in developing their own employees. Finally, top management can set policies that require the completion of certain types of training courses before an individual is allowed to be promoted to a particular job. For example, no one could be allowed to be promoted to a first-level supervisory position without either completing a course in basic supervision or documenting (e.g., taking a test) that they have the skill or knowledge that the course provides. Such a policy would clearly indicate to employees that the organization supports the content of the training course. More importantly, the opposite is also true. We are aware of an organization that allowed employees to be promoted to first-level supervisory positions without ever taking such a course. Many of these employees proved ineffective on their jobs and were later given such training. However, because the course was not viewed as a requirement to obtain the first-level supervisory job, many participants questioned whether the organization truly supported the course content.

One additional point must be added. The use of success in training as a criteria for promotion means that the training is actually a selection test. According to federal guidelines (*Equal Employment Opportunity Commission*, 1978), any selection test that leads to what has been called *adverse impact* must be validated. Adverse impact occurs when the proportion of one category of people who apply and are accepted (e.g., females) is less than 80 percent of the proportion of the majority group selected. To illustrate this issue, let's assume 50 males and 30 females attend a training course required for promotion. If 30 males and 10 females pass the course, this course has adversely impacted the ability of females to move to the higher level position since 60% of the males passed (30/50), but only about 33% (10/30) of the females passed. If 48% of the females who took the exam passed (roughly 15 people), adverse impact would not have occurred since 60% × 4/5 = 48%. If adverse impact does not occur, an organization can use any selection process it wishes, as long as it is applied to all applicants. When adverse impact does occur, the organization must validate the selection instrument (i.e., demonstrate that training success is a measure of job-related skills). This suggested that there are desirable consequences for using training as a criteria for promotion, we also suggest that if this is done the possibility of adverse impact should be carefully monitored and the training program should be validated to assume that the organization is in compliance with federal guidelines.

Use of the techniques described above should provide an internal environment that creates motivation to acquire the skill and/or knowledge presented in training. However, the rewards that these approaches provide are typically not immediate. Yet, many times it is short-term rewards that have the greatest impact on behavior. Ways that training can provide immediate or short-term rewards are outlined below.

Are There Short-term Rewards for Effective Performance in Training

Everyone at one time or another has succumbed to short-term temptation. Whether it be the extra piece of chocolate cake, the cigarette, or watching a television show rather than working around the house, people sometimes do things based on short-term rewards. This is also true for training. Even if people are aware that a particular training course (in the long-term) is valuable, there are short-term considerations that reduce a trainee's motivation to acquire the SKA provided in training.

One short-term concern is the workload that the trainee leaves to attend the training session. A trainee who attends a one to two day workshop often returns to the office to find that his or her work has simply piled up. The trainee is faced with producing the same quantity and quality of work in less time due to the time spent receiving training. For this reason, training is often viewed by trainees as more of a punishment than a reward. Therefore, it is not surprising that trainees' thoughts will often be centered "back at the office," rather than on the information provided.

One solution to this dilemma is to simply schedule training sessions during the trainee's "slow season." For example, the months that close the financial records of an organization for the business quarter or financial year are hectic times for accounting and data processing personnel. Efforts should be taken to assure that training sessions are not scheduled during these periods. Similarly, the often-used vacation months of July and August may short-staff a department and, if possible, training should not be scheduled during these times. Trainers can use this slack time to undertake other activities. Time periods for which no training is scheduled can be used to conduct training needs assessments, evaluations, and to develop training manuals and materials.

In addition to the above, it is also wise to take steps to assure that the trainee's supervisor will consider that the trainee will be attending training when job assignments are allocated. This can often be handled through a short meeting where a representive from the training department meets with the supervisor to discuss any problems in scheduling training sessions at a particular time. Realistically, there will be some situations where there is no ideal time. Rather than creating a conflict about scheduling, it is often better to use innovation to solve this dilemma. Other solutions to scheduling problems include:

- Developing training material using programmed instruction or audio cassettes that trainees can use on the ride or drive to and from work.
- Presenting training during the lunch or breakfast hour.

In some situations, it is better not to train people who must squeeze training into their schedule. One factor that may open up some schedules is if training provides some extrinsic reinforcers. It was suggested above that training might be provided during the lunch or breakfast hour. When training is conducted during these times, the training department might consider providing lunch or breakfast. We are aware of one organization that provided grades to trainees based on their knowledge acquired in training. Trainees who received an A or B grade received a cash reward; those that received a C or below were required to pay a fee to the organization for having taken the course. These types of innovative efforts not only bring trainees into sessions but also help maintain their interest. However, care should be taken to assure that training is not viewed as merely the "orange juice and donut hour." Without quality training content, the issues described above are meaningless. Similarly, these efforts will not be of any value if the trainees' previous efforts have not been rewarded. We now examine this issue.

Is This Trainee Intrinsically Motivated to Change/Grow and Develop?

To this point, we have focused on generating an internal environment to assure trainee motivation and commitment to training. What we have not examined or dealt with is the track record of training. This "historical environment" may be very important since it may influence a trainee's responsiveness to the current situation. One factor that should be carefully assessed is the extent to which the previous environment has created feelings of *learned helplessness*. This is the notion that, after repeated punishment or failure, persons may become passive and remain so even after changes in the environment make success possible. The concept was developed by Overmier and Seligman (1967). They discovered that when dogs were repeatedly exposed to inescapable electric shocks, the dogs eventually discontinued their efforts to escape even after the situation was changed so that escape was possible. Research has also documented analogous behavior in humans in a variety of settings (Diener & Dweck, 1980; Dweck & Bush, 1976; Roth & Kubal, 1975).

Martinko and Gardner (1982) applied this concept to organizations. They have developed an extensive model indicating how organizational factors can teach individuals that they are helpless to control their destiny. For example, they note that one survey has shown that over 600 managers perceived no relationship between their merit pay and their performance evaluation (Lawler, 1966). Similarly, researchers have documented biases in performance evaluations (Mitchell & Wood, 1980; McFillen & New, 1979). They suggested that these types of factors teach employees that they are in a no-win situation and that it is impossible to improve. They also suggested that there are individual differences to this perception. They noted that people with an external locus of control (Rotter, 1966) are especially susceptible to this feeling (Pittman & Pittman, 1980), while people with a high need for achievement life style are more resistant to it than people with opposite life styles (Krantz, Glass, & Snyder, 1974).

To the extent that trainees perceive themselves as helpless to improve their performance, training cannot accomplish its objectives. The symptoms of learned helplessness are low productivity, passivity, withdrawal, and expressed dissatisfaction. To investigate whether these are a result of learned helplessness, trainers will need to go beyond the current reward system. The consequences of the trainees' previous attempts to improve their behavior will need to be carefully examined along with the trainees' feelings about their current situation.

If learned helplessness is perceived to exist, it is best to deal with this issue prior to training. A variety of training approaches exist specifically for this problem (Klein & Seligman, 1976; Abramson, Seligman, & Teasdale, 1978). Recent research has shown that this type of training can increase performance (Brockner & Guare, 1983).

Is the Job Conducive to Development?

The final factor to consider in assessing whether training has the potential to be effective is the nature of the trainee's job. There is now a wealth of evidence that suggests that task characteristics influence employee motivation and performance (Griffin, 1982; Thomas & Griffin, 1983). There are two major task characteristics that will influence training: autonomy and feedback.

To the extent that a trainee has *autonomy* on his or her job, the trainee by definition has the opportunity to apply new skill and knowledge acquired in training. If autonomy does not exist, previously stated concerns regarding supervisory support for training become more acute. *Feedback* has been noted as an important component of effective instruction (see Chapter 4). Probably the most important feedback occurs when an individual actually attempts to apply skill or knowledge learned from training on the job. Appropriate feedback may lead to an enhancement of what was acquired in training. Inappropriate, or a lack of, feedback may lead to stagnation or even deterioration. Jobs differ in terms of the amount of feedback they provide. For example, a computer programmer may receive much more immediate and clear feedback about the effectiveness of a new programming language than the research scientist working on a five-year project.

Trainers need to take steps to assure that trainees receive quality feedback upon returning to the job. This can be accomplished through one or more of the following activities:

1. Trainers can assess trainee job performance through observation and/or conversations with peers and supervision. This data can be used as the basis for a follow-up discussion/feedback session with the trainee regarding problems with applying SKA acquired in training.

2. Trainers can form an agreement with the trainee's supervisor that he or she will take the steps described in point 1 above. Typically, it is best to formalize this agreement (in writing) prior to training. Trainers must also "follow-up" to assure that trainees are actually receiving the feedback and may take part in the feedback session.
3. Training can be structured so that trainees have the opportunity to apply their skill and/or knowledge on the job before their training is completed. Subsequent sessions can then be used as group discussions where trainees note problems in application and work collectively on solutions. Such activity is often a part of the behavioral modeling approach to training (see Chapter 7).

Summary of the Internal Environment

The discussion above was not meant to be an exhaustive list but merely illustrative of factors to consider in the internal environment for training. The number of factors noted should not lead to pessimism about the possibility of effective training. All interventions have situational constraints that limit their effectiveness. When constraints are recognized and dealt with, the probability of a successful intervention increases. While we have been focusing on the issue of the environment for training, we have not yet examined the various strategies that a training department may adopt. We now turn toward that issue.

STRATEGIC APPROACHES

Proactive vs. Reactive

One strategic approach that a training department should consider is the extent to which it wishes to be proactive in its training efforts. Some readers may find this statement peculiar, since the majority of the training literature calls for training to take a proactive stance. Ideally, we agree with this notion. However, we think it is important to be aware of the fact that there are both benefits and costs in this approach. There are also certain situational factors that influence the need for a proactive stance. These factors (described below) should be assessed before making a commitment to a proactive strategy.

One problem associated with a proactive approach is that it is an attempt to forecast and deal with problems in the future. To the extent that the forecast is poor or inaccurate, training efforts directed toward this problem may be a waste of money. If we predict that Mary will have a problem and implement a training program to resolve this deficiency, training money has been spent wisely only if Mary would have actually had a difficult time on the job without this training. If our prediction was inaccurate, even though Mary may have acquired a new SK, training was not cost-beneficial and Mary may also develop a perception that the training department wastes her time.

Stated another way, a proactive strategy is an attempt to maximize gain to the organization by dealing with problems before they result in significant harm. However, this strategy is one of maximum risk since it may be directing valuable time and resources toward problems that, in fact, will never actually occur. Therefore, we urge that the following factors be considered in assessing to what extent training strategy should take a proactive stance.

1. Is there a history of successful training? If training has implemented a series of successful training programs in the past, this will result in the development of an environment of trust and credibility in training. In such a situation, training can take more speculative approaches without damaging its position within the organization. However, if training does not have such an environment and takes a proactive approach that fails, the viability of training within the organization may be seriously damaged. We do not mean to suggest that a new training department should only take a reactive approach to training. What we are suggesting is that a training department carefully consider whether it is viewed by significant organizational members as having a history of developing training programs that have helped the organization. If not, we suggest training departments work in the short term toward building a series of efforts that solve tangible problems, before moving heavily toward a proactive strategy.

2. Does the training department possess or can it acquire sophisticated skills for conducting training needs assessment? We have noted that a proactive approach to training is an attempt to forecast the future. If the forecast is inaccurate, the training will probably not be of much value. Therefore, if training will have a successful proactive strategy, it must have the ability to identify and forecast behavioral problems. Chapter 2 on training needs assessments examined the issues and skills involved in making such forecasts (i.e., knowledge of job analysis, skill assessment, etc.). Although a model was provided for making such assessments, it was also noted that conducting TNA is as much an art as a science. Therefore, we suggest that training carefully consider its capabilities in this area, as well as recognize the need to commit considerable time and effort to the TNA process, before moving toward a proactive approach.

3. Is the technology and environment of the organization changing rapidly? Few organizations exist in a stagnant environment. Nevertheless, some organizations have a greater rate of change than others. Probably the classic example is the computer industry which is changing at an extremely rapid pace. Due to this rapidly changing environment, there is the need to provide proactive training in this industry. However, there are other businesses in which this problem is not as acute. We suggest that

training carefully analyze the environment and technology of the organization in assessing the need for proactive training.

Location

A second strategic alternative that training should consider is where the training function should be located. The alternatives on this issue range from a *centralized* training staff that provides training to all units versus a *decentralized* training staff. The latter has trainers operating within functional units who may report either to the head of the functional unit and/or a centralized training director.

The relative advantages of these approaches are analogus to those of the internal versus external change agent. A decentralized training function has trainers who can be considered internal change agents since they are members of the functional unit. Internal change agents typically have acquired greater depth of knowledge regarding the environment for change as a result of being a member of the organization or subunit. This membership also often allows the internal agent to develop an atmosphere of trust and acceptance. An external change agent typically can be more objective, since he or she is not a member of the environment. However, he or she must be skilled in diagnosing this environment if effective change is to occur. In our view, the criteria for determining whether the training function should be centralized or decentralized is the rate of change of the organization's technology and environment. Lawrence and Lorsch (1967) showed that effective organizations in rapidly changing environments have subunits that are highly differentiated. *Differentiation* means that subunits do not operate in a standarized manner, but function in a way that allows them to deal most effectively with their environments. Since an advantage of a decentralized training department is the understanding that the change agent has of the environment, we feel this approach is best when the organization's environment is fluid. A more centralized approach is beneficial when the environment is more stable.

It is important to add that the research of Lawrence and Lorsch (1967) also suggests that organizations need *integration mechanisms*. These mechanisms tie the subunits of an organization together and help them move toward a common goal. If training is centralized, integration should occur for this function because it operates under one common structure. A decentralized training structure may lack this integration. Therefore, some mechanism should be developed to assure that integration occurs. Ways this can be accomplished include:

1. Establishing a training advisory council that might consist of training representatives from each subunit. This council might meet on a monthly or quarterly basis to discuss common problems and directions of their training efforts.

2. Requiring that all trainers report to one training manager. One function of this manager would be to assure that integration occurs across subunits.
3. The transmission of written progress reports on training between subunits.
4. Developing an organizational strategic plan for training that is based on input from all subunits and has sections dealing with their respective concerns.

Training the Trainer

Another strategic question training should consider is the extent to which the training function will provide training in job-related areas versus training others to provide this information. The latter approach is often referred to as *training the trainer*. Again, the major consideration is the nature of the organization's technology. If an organization has a complex and rapidly changing technology, the wisest strategy is to either train or hire someone to provide the training. If the technology is less complex and stable, the internal training function can develop the SK needed to train others on this issue. For example, it may be cost-beneficial to train an accountant on new tax legislation rather than having the training department attempt to digest this information and then provide the training. The ability of a technician to deal with questions as to how the current material may impact other areas is an additional benefit of a technical trainer. However, care should be taken to ensure that the technician possesses the SK required of an effective trainer (see Chapters 3 and 4).

The factors listed above are clearly not all of the issues that need to be considered in the development of a strategic plan for training. Other factors such as budget constraints and training capabilities must also be examined. A list such as this can never be exhaustive since certain considerations will always be a function of the particular environment and technology of the organization. However, hopefully this discussion has indicated some of the major considerations in strategic planning for training.

Example of a Strategic Training Effort

An example of a training effort based on a carefully thought out strategy is the United Auto Worker (UAW)/Ford Motor Company Employee Development and Training Program (EDTP). The objectives of this program are to:

1. Provide training, retraining, and developmental opportunities for both active and displaced employees.
2. Support local and national UAW-Ford Employee Involvement efforts.
3. Provide opportunities for the exchange of ideas and innovations with respect to employee training.

The program is a result of the 1982 UAW-Ford Collective Bargaining agreement. It is funded by a worker contribution of 5¢ per hour worked. A UAW-Ford National Development and Training Center is the core of this effort. The center is supervised by a governing body consisting of UAW and Ford representatives. The center does not actually provide training but helps plants set up training and retraining programs. This involves the development of a joint union/management training committee. The center helps the plant committee organize and identify existing community, educational, and counseling resources. It is through these resources that the actual training is conducted. The center also administers the paperwork for approving and providing tuition. Courses are approved based on their quality. Tuition is approved for payment as it becomes due. The latter point is a radical change from most such programs which typically reimburse tuition if a certain minimum grade is obtained in the course.

We believe this program illustrates many of the points discussed in this chapter. Specifically, from the objectives listed above, it is clear that the training effort has a clear mission. Second, the strategy is designed to match its internal environment. The Ford Motor Company has given considerable time and effort to its employee involvement program. Briefly, this is an OD effort designed to improve the quality of products as well as the quality of workers' lives by involving them in the decision-making process. Similarly, the training center and any training effort involves considerable employee input. Third, and perhaps most importantly, it is clear from the structure that the decision makers realized that the training center could not be all things to all people. Clearly the range of training and retraining projects would be too broad to be provided within one center. Thus, through assessing its limitations, the center has structured itself in a way so it can help resolve this problem.

French, Bell and Zawacki (1983) noted that an OD program must "unfold according to a strategy" (p. 9). We believe that training programs should follow a similar pattern. Unfortunately, the lack of solid research in training (Goldstein, 1980; Wexley, 1984) and the infancy of development of strategic planning research (Tichy, 1983) means that this process will currently have to be considerably more art than science.

SKILL AND KNOWLEDGE NEEDS
OF TRAINING

Once a strategy has been formulated, the focus shifts to a concern for implementation. Hopefully, the reader sees that the factors that will determine the effective implementation of a training strategy are those outlined in Chapters 1 through 10 of this text. In these chapters, we have attempted to review the technical components (i.e., the knowledge base required for effective training). Briefly, these involve such things as knowing how to diagnose the problem (see Chapter 2 on training needs assessment), understanding how people learn, and providing instruction in a manner to maximize effectiveness. (See Chapters 3 and 4 on learning and instruction.) Effective instruction involves not only understanding how to teach, but also includes knowledge of alternative techniques of training (see Chapters 6 and 7 on experiential and nonexperiential approaches), as well as the instructional needs of various content areas (see Chapters 8–10 on technical, managerial, and training in OD). We have also tried to stress the importance and knowledge requirements for effective evaluation (see Chapter 5).

It is our belief that the knowledge and skill issues noted throughout this text will help training maximize both individual and organizational effectiveness. We doubt whether any one individual will possess all of the knowledge and skills we have described. As long as these are covered somewhere within the training department, this is not a concern. We are often asked how one knows if one is capable of being an effective trainer. A point we have attempted to stress is that a trainer is really a consultant to the organization on change. Burke (1982) noted the following ability requirements for an effective consultant:

The ability to tolerate ambiguity: Every organization is different, and what worked before may not work now; every OD effort starts from scratch, and it is best to enter with few preconceived notions other than with the general characteristics that we know about social systems.

The ability to influence: Unless the OD consultant enjoys power and has some talent for persuasion, he or she is likely to succeed in only minor ways in OD.

The ability to confront difficult issues: Much of OD work consists of exposing issues that organization members are reluctant to face.

The ability to support and nurture others: This ability is particularly important in times of conflict and stress.

The ability to listen well and empathize: This is especially important during interviews, in conflict situations, and when client stress is high.

The ability to recognize one's own feelings and intuitions quickly: It is important to be able to distinguish one's own sensations from those of the client's and also be able to use these feelings and intuitions as interventions when appropriate and timely.

The ability to conceptualize: It is necessary to think and express in understandable words certain relationships, such as the cause-effect and if-then linkages that exist within the systemic context of the client organization.

The ability to discover and mobilize human energy, both within oneself and within the client organization: There is energy in resistance, for example, and the consultant's interventions are likely to be most effective when they tap existing energy within the organization and provide direction for the productive use of the energy.

The ability to teach or create learning opportunities: This ability should not be reserved for classroom activities but should be utilized on the job, during meetings, and within the mainstream of the overall change effort.

The ability to maintain a sense of humor, both on the client's behalf and to help sustain perspective: Humor can be useful for reducing tension. It is also useful for the consultant to be able to laugh at himself or herself; not taking oneself too seriously is critical for maintaining perspective about an OD effort, especially since nothing ever goes exactly according to plan, even though OD is supposed to be a *planned* change effort. (pp. 353–354)

In summary, it is our belief that the skill and knowledge requirements we have noted in this text will be those mandated of the training department of the future. As technology advances and organizations become more sophisticated, so too must the training function if it is to be a viable force for change.

DISCUSSION QUESTIONS _____

1. Describe two organizations that have different environments and technologies. Would the training strategies for these organizations be different or similar? Why?
2. Describe another internal environment characteristic that may inhibit the effectiveness of training.
3. What are some other considerations, beyond those listed in the text, in developing a training strategy?
4. What factors may have hindered trainers from viewing training in a strategic perspective? How could these problems be resolved?
5. What are the consequences of *not* taking a strategic approach to training?
6. What skills and knowledge are needed to be an effective trainer? Rank them in order or importance and compare your ranking to how you responded to question 5 in Chapter 1.

A STRATEGY PLANNING APPROACH
TO TRAINING:
AN INTERVIEW WITH DON MICHALAK ─────────────

Donald Michalak is President of Michalak Training Associates, Inc., a nationally known training/consulting firm headquartered in Tucson, Arizona. Don has developed and conducted a wide variety of training programs and authored a book entitled *Making the Training Process Work*. Don has consistently been noted as a competent and charismatic presenter throughout his careers as a high school teacher, a human resources specialist for Ford Motor Company, and an external consultant and trainer to companies and organizations throughout the U.S. He received his Ed.D. and MBA degrees from Wayne State University in Detroit where he studied the relationships between learning processes and training practices in industry. Don Michalak firmly believes in the importance of matching training styles to audience and situational needs. He and his associates have produced a series of behaviorally oriented instruments to provide trainees feedback about their styles and needs. They believe this feedback creates the awareness that is the first step of the change process to be promoted through their training programs. Since Don takes this contingency based approach to his training practices, we felt he would be an ideal interviewee for this chapter.

Question: What factors do you consider when attempting to match your training approach to the training situations you are involved with?

Michalak: There certainly are many factors that can be considered. I have found, however, that the size of the audience and the objectives of the training itself are the key factors to consider when choosing a style that will be appropriate for a given assignment. The number of trainees in the audience influences my style simply because there are some things you can do with four people that you cannot do with 300. A smaller audience allows for more individual practice time and individual coaching. Practice is still important in dealing with larger audiences when the training objective is to develop skills. However, the trainer needs to consider using more demonstration or design in time for the trainees to break from the larger group into smaller groups to practice the skills with each other and provide each other the feedback they will need in order to learn.

I would say that clearly understanding the training objectives is the main factor involved in using a contingency approach to training. I believe that the client must set the objectives and then the trainer chooses the methodologies best suited to meet those objectives. While I believe that, I must also admit that I have been burned by clients who set inappropriate objectives. I have found that many supervisors know how a job should be done, that is, the skill and knowledge requirements, but are unaware that the system they are a part of won't support real change on the part of their subordinates. Thus, I have been told by supervisors what they believe to be the reasons for some performance deficiency only to find out later that they only provided me with the symptoms not the causes of the problem. Using a training approach that deals with symptoms won't produce change. You must uncover the causes. I must admit that I have also run across another problem related to this matter. I call it the "Pontius Pilate" approach to training. The manager washes his or her hands of the matter, expecting me to determine the training objectives and/or claiming he or she can't do anything anything about a system that doesn't support real change on the part of trainees.

Question: What do you do to remedy these problems? How do you help your clients to set appropriate objectives?

Michalak: Well, for one thing, I no longer only talk to the supervisor of the trainees that I hope to help. I ask to talk to some of their people to get a feel for the organization and to help sort through what are the causes and what are the symptoms of the presenting problems. I make it clear that these will be confidential discussions and that I will not report back to the supervisor everything I hear. When management agrees that I should conduct these sessions, I essentially ask the people three questions: (1) What do you need to do in order to be more effective in your job? (2) What do you need to know in order to be more effective in your job? (3) What gets in your way or is likely to get in your way when you attempt to do things differently on your job? I probe in order to help classify what are the "don't do," "won't do," and can't do" problems. If differing perceptions of the presenting problems emerge, I try to feed back the information as data to the managers and get them to interpret the data. I want training to be treated as a line management responsibility so I will say things to supervisors like, "Sixty percent of the people think the problem is X, what does that mean to you?" Remember, I am committed to having the client set the objectives and my job is to provide the training approach best matched to accomplish the objectives. By the way, I never label these sessions as "diagnoses" or even "interviews." I do whatever I can to get the supervisors and their people to open up and talk. I try to instill in each training effort, the importance of setting "doing" objectives. I key in to what they say about the overt behaviors that they want to see come out of training.

Question: Do you have a system for matching training approaches with training objectives?

Michalak: Yes, I do. It's not a perfect system but I have found it enormously useful in helping me sort out the tremendous amount of information that typically results from the pretraining discussions I have been referring to. I evaluate the conclusions reached through these discussions along two dimensions: (1) How much concern is there for *what* is specifically going to be taught in the training session? (2) How much concern is there for *who* will be taught?

I then choose one of four approaches to training. If there appears to be high concern for *what* is to be taught, but little concern over *who* specifically will be taught, I use what I call the "traditional" approach to training. I emphasize the technical skills and knowledge that has been determined that the trainees must master. I act more like a drill instructor or subject matter expert in these situations. For example, in the drug industry, compliance to various laws and regulations is crucial. Trainees in classes on these laws and regulations are told they must cover X amount of material. I don't approach such an assignment with the notion that the trainees should discover what the laws and regulations should be. I let the content of the material and the inherent danger in not knowing the material be the guiding forces to approach such training assignments.

A second approach to training that I use, I call the "student-centered" approach. I use it when I have determined that there is much more concern over *who* is being taught than *what* is being taught. This is generally the case when the causes of the problems being experienced are related to deficiencies in interpersonal skills, when it's a matter of the relationship between supervisor and subordinates. It is also the style I believe to be most effective when the training objectives can be classified as "personal development" in nature. When using this approach, I make sure the agenda is very flexible. The discovery of the needs, wants, insights of the trainees provides the direction for these sessions. T-groups were a classic example of the use of this approach but most forms of participant-involvement activities can be thought of as characteristic of the "student-centered" approach. It is essentially a warm, friendly style where the trainer abdicates most of the decision-making authority within the sessions to the trainees themselves.

Sometimes the pretraining discussions indicate that there is not much concern over who or what is to be taught. If it becomes clear that it is a situation where a training program must merely be administered, I recommend an uninvolved style where the trainer merely acts as a funnel necessary to pass on information to the trainees who must themselves decide how to act on the information. I call this the "administrative style" and it's not as bad as it may sound. What I am getting at are the situations where the material and/or equipment carries the day . . . situations like the use of computer-assisted instruction, programmed learning, and self-study units. The trainer's job is essentially complete before the training session begins. He or she must develop or discover the material or program that will guide the learning sessions. During the sessions themselves, the trainer takes a low profile, merely making sure the equipment works and enough material has been provided. He or she should avoid jumping in too early or too often. It's important in these situations that the trainee develop a relationship with the material or the learning process, not the instructor.

The final style I might consider when taking on a training assignment I label as the "integrated style." It's to be used when there is a high concern for both *what* and *who* is to be taught. It is essentially an "involved" style with the instructor sharing the responsibility for the learning that is to take place. It can be used to promote improvement in technical or interpersonal skills through structured practice sessions. It is assumed that the trainee is motivated to learn but the trainer using this style will apply extrinsic forces to get a trainee moving if he or she does not appear to be intrinsically interested. These trainers see methods as a means to the end and will generally use a greater variety of techniques than the other three approaches.

I must warn you, however, that my actual choice of using one of these four styles of training is also strongly influenced by the comfort zone experienced by the client and myself. For example, there have been times when an "uninvolved style" like the "administrative" approach seemed appropriate upon my analysis of the information I received in the pretraining interviews but used a more involved style because I didn't feel comfortable when working with the group or the client group strongly encouraged a different approach.

Question: That brings up the issue of whether this contingency approach to training is more "art" than "science." What do you think, based on your experience?

Michalak: I believe it to be a mixture of both. In fact, I believe you must master the art and the science of training in order to successfully serve organizations today. If you know the "science," you can be adequate. If you only have the "art" of training, you will probably be all flash but rarely effective. Too many trainers, in years past, have been entertainers ... spending so much energy trying to keep their audience interested or amused and not enough energy planning a design that matches the problems that are to be addressed by training. The science part has become increasingly important. The disciplined application of principles, the systematic collection of information before training begins, the use of quantitative methodologies to evaluate the impact of training will be some of the necessary skills of the trainers in today's organizations. It will still take some intuition, some risk-taking, to know when to deviate from a formula approach to training. The excitement of getting people involved in learning and the utility of producing more satisfied and skilled employees requires a special blend of art and science. When a trainer demonstrates this blend, he or she feels the special rewards of our profession.

AN IN-DEPTH REVIEW OF T-GROUPS AS A TRAINING AND AN OD STRATEGY _____

HISTORY OF THE T-GROUP MOVEMENT _____

A look at the development of this famous training approach should provide the reader with a perspective on the evolutionary nature of experiential training techniques over the last three decades. The account of the events is taken from several sources: Bradford, Gibb, and Benne, 1964; Bradford, 1967; Marrow, 1976; Yalom, 1970; Rogers, 1970; French and Bell, 1972; and Shaffer and Galinsky, 1974.

In 1946, Kurt Lewin was asked to conduct a workshop that focused on helping community leaders in Connecticut implement the Fair Employment Practices Act. Lewin brought with him Ronald Lippitt, a social psychologist and two experts in adult education, Kenneth D. Benne and Leland P. Bradford. These men all shared an interest in understanding group dynamics and in encouraging organizations to adopt more humane and less autocratic work practices. It was their belief that this would lead to more productive organizations and more satisfied adult employees. Lewin, Lippitt, and White (1939) had provided reason to believe this could be true in a study of work habits of groups of adolescents.

The workshop was originally designed in a traditional format with some lectures about Civil Rights issues directed at the participants but with considerable time set aside for discussions of the issues. Participants shared their experiences of problems they had encountered in attempting to implement the provisions of the Fair Employment Practices Act. In the evening, the four staff members met together and discussed their observations of the participants' behaviors, how these behaviors were affecting the group's dynamics, and how the group dynamics could influence the outcome of the workshop. A couple of the participants heard about these evening sessions and asked Lewin if they could attend. Much to the surprise of his research colleagues, Lewin agreed. The following evening, the staff felt the discomfort of trying to describe and interpret participant behavior with some of these participants right there. A heated discussion ensued when a participant vehemently disagreed with an interpretation. Soon the format of the evening sessions was expanded. All of the participants voluntarily attended and responded to the observations made by the staff as well as analyzed and interpreted their own behaviors. Participants reported that these evening sessions provided them with a new kind of learning and a rich understanding of their own behavior. The staff realized that they had inadvertently discovered a powerful technique of human relations education.

Kurt Lewin died a few months later before the T-group format was fully developed but the rest of the staff conducted a follow-up effort with the original workshop participants at the Gould Academy in Bethel, Maine. They called this effort a "basic skills training group" and stated that its purposes were to serve as a medium for learning how to encourage planned change in social systems and to understand and facilitate individual and group development. With its success and funding from the Office of Naval Research and sponsorship of the National Education Association and the Research Center for Group Dynamics, a series of workshops using a T-group format evolved under what was called the National Training Laboratory for Group Development (NTL). NTL is still the center of most T-group activity in this country, although the methods and emphases have changed over the years.

In the early years, NTL used a two-group format: (1) T-groups, to focus on small group dynamics and interpersonal styles through studying the group's own behavior and (2) A-groups (action groups) that used a more traditional, didactic format to focus on strategies to change large social systems. However, the T-group had such a powerful allure for the participants that its format spilled over into the A-group and eventually the A-group was abandoned. Originally, most of the participants attending the T-group sessions were managers from industry. It was thought that, by improving a manager's understanding of his or her own behavior, of group dynamics, and of how to understand the needs of others, he or she would be more effective in relating to subordinates and ultimately improving their productivity. However, while participants nearly always felt that their T-group experience was tremendously insightful, they also found it very difficult and frustrating to transfer their new skills and knowledge back to their jobs in traditional, complex organizations. Furthermore, NTL hired more and more clinical rather than social or industrial psychologists throughout the 1950s. This resulted in a greater focus on intrapsychic processes and individual behavior change rather than the process of influencing organizational change. This was of concern to the founders of the T-group movement since participants had contracted for an educational experience in human relations and not a short dose of psychotherapy. In the 1960s, as public attitudes toward institutions declined, the trend of focusing on one's own interpersonal style independent from its role in the improvement of organizational functioning grew stronger at NTL. This was even more true of the groups conducted at Esalen in Big Sur, California, which became the other major center in the U.S. for the study and use of small group techniques.

For a while (late 1950s, early 1960s) some companies (e.g., ESSO, Standard Oil, and Union Carbide; see McGregor, 1967 and Shepard, 1965) initiated T-groups for managers at their own sites rather than sending them to NTL in order to facilitate the transfer of learning to their organizations. Today, in the 1980s, use of the pure, unstructured T-group technique is far less common. However, quite a few companies still send managers to NTL (Wexley & Latham, 1981) and, as we will see later, the T-group technique has served as a basis for the development of a variety of more structured team-building training techniques.

TYPES OF T-GROUPS _____

Carl Rogers (1970) described T-groups as the most potent social invention of the century. T-groups are inventions that go under many names, most commonly "T-group," "laboratory education," "sensitivity training," and "encounter group." Laboratory education may be distinguished from T-groups as it is a more complete program with the T-group as its main ingredient but supplemented by the use of lectures, cases, role playing, and discussions of theory (Campbell, et al., 1970). Encounter groups tend to be more intensive experiences designed to put the "normally alienated individual" into closer contact—or encounter—with himself or herself with others and with sensations. Thus, the emphasis is on personal growth and leaders tend to use more psychodrama and Gestalt therapy methods than the traditional human relations skills orientation of T-groups (Shaffer & Galinsky, 1974). Sensitivity training may resemble T-groups or encounter groups (Rogers, 1970). Training groups labeled as "human potential groups," "sensory awareness groups," "Synanon groups," or "human enrichment groups" share features in common with T-group methodology but typically have different emphases.

While these definitions should help the reader understand the range of phenomena under these rubrics, variation in groups using the same title may be greater than the actual variation between groups using different titles. Variations revolve around the role of the trainer (nondirective to directive), type of agenda (unstructured to structured), length of sessions (10 to 15 two-hour sessions, 24 to 72 hour marathons, numerous 15-minute compressed microlabs), and composition of the group (strangers, cousins, employees of the same company who don't ordinarily work together, family, employees from the same company who work together on a daily basis).

BASIC CHARACTERISTICS OF T-GROUPS

Many authors have described what they feel to be the key components of a T-group experience (see, for example, Bradford, Gibb, & Benne, 1964; Schein & Bennis 1965; Rogers, 1970; Yalom, 1970; Shaffer & Galinsky, 1974). Our summary, which follows, is based on the previous literature and on the experiences of one of the authors as a T-group participant and facilitator.

Here-and-Now Focus

The traditional T-group has no structured agenda. The content for group discussion is the present behavior of members and their feelings regarding efforts to relate to one another in the group. "There and then" discussions of past problems, especially those problems related to people not present in the group, are considered inappropriate. Since the typical business environment provides managers with guidelines, agendas, and expectations, it is thought that the removal of these structures will facilitate a reflection on how one actually behaves in the absence of established protocol. It will also generate anxiety but many feel that this will stimulate learning.

Self-Disclosure

Members learn about themselves by revealing to the group how they feel and what they perceive to be happening. The founders of the T-group movement felt that the competitive business environment encouraged managers to put on a facade in their relations with others. This lack of genuineness was thought to lead to relationship problems.

Feedback

Some of the self-disclosure that is expected to take place is feedback to other members about how they come across to the rest of the group.

Members thus learn quickly and directly what they are like to relate to. It is also hoped that members will learn how to give constructive, specific feedback through this process. It has long been recognized that life in business organizations often operates without much feedback to individual managers. This is an anxiety-provoking problem especially to younger managers (Schein, 1964). The founders of the movement felt T-groups could fill that gap and encourage managers to provide more feedback in back-home situations.

Climate of Experimenttaion

T-groups are to provide a "cultural island" where group members provide support and build the trust to open up and take some behavioral risks. By stretching beyond one's typical behavioral repertoire in a safe setting, an individual may discover new ways of relating to others and receive feedback on those attempts. It is especially hoped that participants will be able to let down their facades and experience and learn from their emotional reactions—something not typically encouraged in business set-tings. As Camus once wrote, "My greatest wish is to remain lucid in ecstasy." It was thought that the coupling of cognitive appraisal with emotional experimentation would provide trainees with the most effective experience.

This notion of a climate of experimentation is based on Lewin's belief in an action research model. He felt that the trainer and trainees should treat what is said and done as real data to be analyzed and acted upon. He felt that interpersonal styles are based on long held beliefs, and that they can only be changed and improved when individuals are able to examine them personally and discover whether their beliefs are satisfactory or not.

Trainer as Facilitator-Member

The founders of the T-group movement envisioned a very different role for the trainer than is typically prescribed for other forms of training sessions. The T-group trainer was not to be the focus or main provider of insight/information. He or she was to facilitate a climate of experimentation and occasionally intervene if a boisterous member was perceived as possibly doing harm to another member. However, the leader was primarily meant to be another member attempting to further his or her learning about self, others, group dynamics, and learning how to learn. It was hoped that he or she would model a number of key behaviors and values including openness, how to give and receive feedback, nondefensiveness, and listening skills. He or she would occasionally comment on group processes, although some (particularly Rogers, 1970) caution against this since the group may then depend on the leader to validate their experiences. Rogers also cautioned against the leader introducing structured exercises designed to explore interpersonal issues. However, many if not most T-group leaders do this, especially in more recent times. The founders of the T-group movement, reacting in part to the horrors of autocratic rule in Nazi Germany, were interested in developing a more democratic style of leadership for managers. They believed such a style would be more productive and had personal concerns about autocratic approaches. Lewin, for example, had escaped his native Germany before the war and had a deep interest in developing techniques to re-educate Hitler youth and change anti-Semitic attitudes. Thus, the fathers of the T-group movement were deeply committed to displaying a model of leadership that was far more participative than traditional models. The key to the T-group leader's role was, and still is, to facilitate, not control, the learning of the rest of the members.

Stages of the T-Group Process

Although each group is influenced by the style of the leader and the backgrounds of the participants, certain sequences of events very commonly occur. Many detailed descriptions of the events occurring in T-group experiences are available in the literature (see, for example, Klaw, 1961; Bradford, Gibb, & Benne, 1964; Schein & Bennis, 1965, Rogers, 1970). Typically, the leader begins the group by saying something about being here to learn about how people relate to one another and how they behave in groups. This learning is to take place by experiencing what it is like to be a group member. Carl Rogers reported using very simple opening statements such as "I suspect we will know each other a great deal better at the end of these group sessions than we do now," or "Here we are. We can make this group experience what we wish," or "I'm a little uneasy, but I feel somewhat reassured when I look around at you and realize we're all in the same boat. Where do we start?" (1970, p. 50). Other T-group leaders say nothing. When comments are directed to them, they merely reflect the message back to the sender.

The purpose of the vague, short opening of T-groups is to establish a leadership vacuum. Most trainees will look to the trainer for guidance to establish how they are supposed to act here. Since the purpose of a T-group is to learn about our actions from observing our actions, the leader purposely subverts the natural inclination to depend on the leader. He or she then occasionally comments on how he or she sees people dealing with this leadership vacuum.

Trainees typically display anxious behaviors. They are usually polite at first but after a few abortive attempts by members to get something started, frustration sets in. Frustration tends to lead to aggression which is verbally directed at the leader who suggests that the group explore these feelings of frustration. After some initial resistance, the behavioral styles of one or two members dealing with frustration is usually explored. The leader attempts to keep the discussion of these feelings in a here-and-now perspective.

As a couple of members start exploring their feelings and interpersonal styles, someone notices the support given to members willing to explore. This leads to more members opening up and a sense of group caring and cohesion begins to develop. As facades break down, feedback is provided and trainees attempt to verbalize what they are learning about themselves.

As the predetermined number of sessions begins to run out, the quiet members are encouraged to open up and if they don't open up they are often attacked then ignored by the rest of the group. During the last session, trainees express their sadness that the experience is ending and nearly all state that it has been a meaningful experience.

Upon returning home, they find it difficult to express just what it is they have learned. As they attempt to be more open, sensitive, and caring to others in their organization, they are often treated with suspicion. As their frustration grows from attempting to apply their new learning and skills in a "real world" setting, they frequently abandon their efforts or sign up for another T-group.

Clearly, not all the events and reactions described above occur as a result of every T-group, but the pattern is common enough that several authors and researchers have labeled specific stages of the T-group experience. These descriptions (see, for example, Bradford, Gibb, & Benne, 1964; Rogers, 1970; Shaffer & Galinsky, 1974) vary as to the number of stages, the specificity of stages, and the biases of the authors. Lundgren and Knight (1978) carefully studied transcripts of 20 two-week NTL Institute T-groups and could only identify three common stages: (1) the initial encounter, (2) interpersonal confrontation, and (3) mutual acceptance.

Problems with the Use of T-Groups

Not all T-groups end happily nor is everyone enamored with the approach. From the very beginnings of the T-group movement, participants have complained about the difficulties in applying what they learned to organizational settings. Risks taken in the safety of "the cultural island" of a T-group are often not well received in the competitive realities of the business world. Rogers (1970) reported some executives leaving the rat race of corporate life after their consciousnesses had been raised through T-groups. Others have reported being burned by superiors and subordinates alike when they approached their old jobs with a greater degrees of self-disclosure. Individual change may be difficult to achieve, but generalizing those changes to other settings appears to be very difficult.

As the T-group movement grew in the 1950s and 1960s, certain excesses became evident as well. Some trainers acted on the *reductio ad absurdum* that if something is good, then more must be better. Thus, if self-disclosure was good, then indiscriminate disclosure in the nude must be better. If expression of feeling is good, then screaming one's anger at others must be better. Admittedly, the number of nude encounter groups and other excessively oriented groups was probably small in relation to the number of traditional groups. However, they received publicity and were often offensive to public taste (Yalom, 1970). Congressman Rarick even read into the House Congressional Record a 30,000 word diatribe against sensitivity training referring to it as "brainwashing," a "Communist conspiracy," a "Nazi plot" and a form of "thought control" that would be forced on teachers during their college training (*Congressional Record*—House, June 10, 1969, pp. H4666–H4679.).

The excesses were, at least in part, due to a lack of control over who could lead T-groups and the general lack of information about what one was getting in to before starting T-group sessions. There were also very few trainers or companies who screened potential participants in T-group training. As a result of all this, some participants suffered psychological damage. Perhaps the most extensive study of psychological damage attributable to T-groups and their spin-offs was conducted in the late 1960s (reported in Yalom & Lieberman, 1971 and in Lieberman, Yalom, & Miles, 1973). They studied nine types of groups and found a casualty rate of 10 percent. This included any individual who felt the need to consult mental health professionals within six months of attending the group sessions or who merely reported feeling worse off as a result of the experience. They found the casualty rate to vary according to the type of group. In particular, they found certain leadership styles to be present in groups with higher casualty rates. Leaders who provided high amounts of stimulus, who played a central role in the group, were aggressive but charismatic and, who used an individual (as opposed to group) focus were more likely to be associated with groups having high casualty rates. Furthermore, participants who were described as having a low self-concept and unrealistically high expectations for change were more prone to become T-group casualties.

Wexley and Latham (1981) and Shaffer and Galinsky (1974) pointed out that T-groups were not based on any systematic theory of individual change. Their techniques were developed on the basis of experience and practice and their objectives were often stated in vague terms. It is thus difficult to explain why T-groups produced changes when they succeeded and difficult to prescribe what should be changed when problems occurred. Unstructured T-groups were a fad in the 1950s and early 1960s that were promoted by testimonials rather than sound training evaluations. Research studies with more rigorous designs appeared in the 1960s and 1970s but public reaction to excesses in the T-group movement reduced the likelihood that the popularity of this training technique would be revived even with improvements. The techniques and procedures described on the previous pages are still practiced today but rarely do trainers call such sessions "T-groups." Titles such as "human potential seminars," "interaction labs," and "teambuilding skill training" have been used to describe sessions that are strongly based on T-group methods. Today, such efforts are typically far more structured and far more likely to use in-tact work groups than was the practice in the heydays of T-groups.

RECOMMENDATIONS FOR IMPROVED USE OF T-GROUPS AND THEIR MODERN DAY COUNTERPARTS

A number of authors have suggested procedures to enhance the effectiveness of T-groups as a training technique. The most common suggestion is to develop and use a screening procedure to eliminate from consideration these participants who are likely to suffer psychological damage. Most suggest interviewing prospective trainees to determine if they match a certain psychological profile (like that described by Lieberman, Yalom, & Miles, 1973). Lakin (1972) identified three specific groups of people who may need to be excluded from T-group training:

1. People who become quite upset or mad under the stress of criticism.
2. People who are so intense that the others in the group are likely to feel victimized since they will have to spend so much time dealing with that person.
3. Person who have such low self-esteem that their needs for reassurance are not likely to be fulfilled by the group.

Wexley and Yukl (1977) suggested that voluntary participation and withdrawal is a helpful safeguard when using T-groups. They also felt that participants should be prescreened using psychometrically sound instruments that measure level of adjustment. Participants desiring therapy should be encouraged to utilize other resources, not T-groups, to obtain such help.

On the other hand, Gibb (1970) reviewed the research literature and concluded that there is no basis for making *a priori* restrictions as to group membership. Carl Rogers (1970) concurred, stating "One of the commonest myths regarding groups is that only certain people should be included, or that there should be a careful screening of participants. This does not fit my experience at all. In fact when asked such questions in public I have facetiously replied that I thought very careful screening should be done, and no one should be admitted unless he was a person!" (p. 130). His own systematic follow-up of 500 participants attending his groups indicated that only two people reported themselves as having been damaged (i.e., "It changed my behavior in ways I do not like.").

Rogers, unlike many others, blurred the distinction between the goals of therapy and the goals of T-groups. (See Yalom, 1970, for an in-depth discussion of the differences and similarities between group therapy and T-groups.) A suggestion made by Egan (1970) and others involves having the participants develop a contract specifying the goals and behavior guidelines for the leader and members in the conduct of the rest of their T-group experience. This sort of activity, which has been used extensively by the author of this chapter as well, provides an excellent starting point, helps some participants screen themselves out of a potentially harmful situation, develops more realistic expectations, and facilitates subsequent evaluation of the training sessions. While nearly every author writing about T-groups lists a set of goals for them (see, for example, Schein & Bennis, 1965; Campbell et al., 1970; Rogers, 1970), we would suggest that all these lists can be categorized into four sets of goals.

1. Increased awareness of self, especially in terms of how one relates to others.
2. Increased awareness of and sensitivity to others.
3. Increased understanding of how groups work.
4. Increased understanding of new ways to learn.

A group then might benefit by operationalizing in behavioral terms what they would like to accomplish within each of these categories. They should clarify whether their goals include changing their behaviors as well as their awareness and whether they want to change their behaviors within the group experience or change their behaviors in "real world" settings.

Other suggestions for improving T-groups involve changing the typical format. Campbell and Dunnette (1968) urged that greater, more direct efforts be made to insure that members are provided a sense of support in order to benefit from the opportunity to take behavioral risks within the group. Their review of the research casts some doubt over whether anxiety necessarily leads to learning. In order for learning to take place under anxiety-provoking situations, it is best to insure that reinforcement for risk-taking and for the positive features of the new behavior takes place. This may mean that the leader needs to take a more directive role by intervening more than has been traditionally recommended. It also suggests that, unless the organization's climate is supportive of change, any benefits acquired during the T-group sessions are not likely to be established back on the job.

Kelly (1973) claimed that his "structured sensitivity training" (SST) harnesses the benefits of T-groups without the disadvantages of slow pace, excessive introspection, and psychiatric casualties. SST is more task-oriented and far more structured than the traditional T-group. Kelly, however, failed to provide sound research evidence for his claims. Nonetheless, the trend toward introducing more structured exercises into T-group experiences is clearly evident especially in the 1970s and 1980s.

RESEARCH EVIDENCE ON THE EFFECTIVENESS OF T-GROUPS

As Gibb (1970) pointed out, statements regarding the paucity of research on T-groups are simply untrue. Literally hundreds of studies have been reported in the literature. Space does not even permit us to discuss all of the reviews of the research literature let alone the individual studies. Reviews of the research literature include Buchanan, 1965 and 1969; House, 1967; Campbell and Dunnette, 1968; Gibb, 1970; Smith, 1975; and Cooper, 1975. Many studies have failed to use sound research designs (control groups, long-term time series, self-report measures, etc.) but enough research has been conducted that certain highlights deserve special attention.

- Few studies provide evidence that back-home behaviors change in ways that enhance organizational effectiveness (see, for example, Campbell & Dunnette, 1968).
- Several studies provide strong evidence that knowledge of self, interpersonal relations, and group dynamics can occur and participants frequently *attempt to change* back-home behaviors (Wexley & Latham, 1981).
- Frequently reported changes include a more favorable self-concept, reduced prejudice, changed test scores of knowledge of interpersonal relations, and changed interpersonal behavior as perceived by others (Smith, 1975).
- Training directors believe that sensitivity training is the most effective means of changing attitudes and interpersonal skills (Carroll et al., 1972).
- T-groups had a long-term positive effect in 21 of the 31 studies reviewed by Smith (1975).
- Psychological dangers of T-groups are not unreasonable considering the potential for positive change (Cooper, 1975).
- Criteria for clear measurement of the outcome of T-groups are complex and elusive (Campbell & Dunnette, 1968).
- The T-group method is differentially effective in a wide variety of situations across a variety of individuals and is a potentially powerful tool for changing behavior (House, 1967).
- T-group methods can be successful in foreign settings as well as in the U.S. (Miller, 1980; Smith, 1980; Moscow, 1971).

A PERSONAL NOTE ABOUT T-GROUPS

In 1968, the author of this chapter was sent to a T-group as a participant. I will always remember one particular session when we were describing ways our values influenced the way we related to each other. I commented that I had been raised to believe that "It is better to give than receive." A group member commented that I should note that it is easier to give than receive and that I had frequently "used" the value of giving in a way that kept her and others in the group at arm's length and to control situations where I felt uncomfortable. That insightful comment strikes me even today. I believe I have improved some on that dimension but, unless a researcher had had a careful baseline of my giving and receiving behaviors prior to that T-group, he or she probably would not have discovered the extent to which that experience changed my approach to key relationships, my teaching style, and my approach to consulting.

In my second T-group experience, a group member attempted suicide between sessions and I felt, first-hand, why many have suggested the need to screen potential participants. In subsequent training sessions, I discovered the utility of "training the trainer sessions" to prepare T-group leaders. Later, as a T-group trainer, I found I preferred including structured exercises (as well as the development of a group contract) as useful devices for capitalizing on the power of the basic T-group format. I still receive letters from some participants that attended T-groups I led. I rarely receive letters from former trainees who participated in other forms of training sessions. I can attest from personal observation that T-groups seem to be better at providing insight/knowledge than at changing behaviors and that efforts to apply insights from T-groups to on-the-job situations often fail.

T-GROUPS AND OD

T-groups represent the first training methodology that bridged the fields of training and OD. In fact, as late as 1970, T-groups remained as virtually the only technique used by OD practitioners. The legacy of the popularity of the T-group remains as an influence today as is demonstrated by the preponderance of small group-oriented methods used as OD techniques. The power of the small group discussions has been tapped through "team building," "Q.C. circles," "employee participation groups," "group problem-solving sessions," "role clarification techniques," and "collaborative management-by-objectives," just to name a few. The emphasis has changed from understanding one's self or "understanding group dynamics" to "clarifying one's role in a department" or "understanding how one's work group operates." Such changes are expected to result in the use of small group training techniques in a manner that should result in organizational as well as individual impact.

Appendix B

A GUIDE FOR TRAINERS TO THE TECHNIQUES OF ORGANIZATION DEVELOPMENT (OD) _____

MACRO OD INTERVENTIONS _____

Diagnostic and Planning Approaches

Survey/feedback interventions Survey/feedback interventions consist of a process of collecting systematic perceptions of an organization by its members through written questionnaires or face-to-face interviews. The data thus gathered is summarized and fed back to organization members for their interpretation of the results. It is typically used to identify organizational strengths and problems, compare perceptions across groups and hierarchical levels within the organization, and to establish a baseline to be used to evaluate change following subsequent actions. Organization members themselves are expected to formulate action plans to address the issues identified through the survey. Nadler's 1977 book (*Feedback and Organizational Development: Using Data Based Methods*) provided a handy reference for using the survey/feedback approach as an OD intervention.

Sensing meetings Sensing meetings should be thought of as a diagnostic tool for an organized collection of information. As an OD intervention, it takes the format of a series of unstructured but tape recorded group interviews of employees of similar rank but differing units. The manager or change agent conducting the interviews asks general questions to gain information on the needs, concerns, issues, and resources as seen by a broad spectrum of organization members. Polling methods are used to assess the relative strength of feelings regarding issues and the tape recordings are reviewed to find quotes that epitomize the feelings of the members. Fordyce and Weil (1971) provided a description of how to utilize this approach.

Organizational mirroring Organizational mirroring utilizes the perspectives of individuals and/or organizations (e.g., clients, customers, vendors, divisional counterparts, etc.) who interface with the focal organization being examined. They are asked to spend some time directly observing a group or organization as it functions. Perceptions are then fed back to the focal organization. McGill (1977) described this technique in his book *Organization Development for Operating Managers.*

Action research Action research is an application of the scientific method of a data gathering, problem identification, solution exploration, experimentation, evaluation cycle. It provides a framework for the use of the survey/feedback approach but represents a framework for an OD intervention that includes any form of data collection and action planning. Frohman et al. (1976) provided a clear description of the cycles of the action research model.

The force field analysis This is a framework for the examination of perceptions, goals, problems, and causes of organizational behavior. It culminates in action plans aimed at reducing obstacles to change and capitalizing on forces that would support movement toward desired goals. The model, originally designed by Kurt Lewin (1951) to analyze group dynamics, recommends that members describe the organization's present and ideal state; estimate the strength of each of the forces; and develop action plans emphasizing the reduction of the restraining forces. Hall et al. (1982) described the application of these procedures for the interested reader.

The confrontation meeting This is a four to eight hour meeting of a total management group drawn from all levels of the organization to take a quick reading on the organization's health and set action plans for improving it. After top management has explained the goals for the meeting and set a tone of openness, managers are assigned to small groups representing a "diagonal slice" of the organization's hierarchy. The groups are to identify and discuss what they see as the major concerns facing organization members and what the causes of these concerns seem to be. Each group records the main points of their discussion on large newsprint sheets. After the sheets are posted and reviewed by the total group, managers are reassigned to functional/natural work units (e.g., all sales managers in one group, manufacturing to another, etc.) to discuss how the concerns as posted affect their area. The groups then prioritize the concerns according to the order they feel top management should address them. Action plans are developed. The total group is reconvened and each unit reports to a panel of top managers. This panel provides immediate reactions to the reports and makes commitments to action as they see fit. All managers are asked to make plans for reporting what went on at the meeting to their subordinates. Top managers are expected to follow through on their commitments immediately. Beckhard (1969) provided interested readers with a short but excellent reference.

Open systems planning Open systems planning is an approach that highlights the need to understand the external as well as the internal environment of an organization in order to assess and plan changes. Planning groups are formed and asked to create a description of the organization's present situation in terms of expectations for and interactions between its external and internal environments. The groups are then asked to focus on the future and predict changes in the external and internal environments if no deliberate intervention is instituted ("realistic future scenario") and again if changes are planned and executed ("idealistic future scenario"). The scenarios are shared and discussed and plans are developed across groups for action programs. Jayaram (1976) presented examples of how to use this model. Adams (1975) presented an alternative approach.

Grid OD As presented by Blake and Mouton (1969), Grid OD represents a comprehensive strategy that involves virtually the entire organization in a longitudinal effort. Leader's styles are assessed along two dimensions: concern for productivity and concern for people. Individual development plans are established to encourage leaders to improve on both dimensions. Each leader convenes his or her team to identify strengths and problems experienced by the team. Goals are established and a realistic schedule for achievement of these goals is developed. Representatives from all groups then meet to identify a model of desired relationships between groups and plans are drawn up to move the groups toward that model. A planning group is formed to utilize the information generated by the Grid process and develop a strategic plan to move the entire organization's procedures, objectives, structure, policy, etc., toward becoming an ideal model. The strategic plan is implemented, monitored, and critiqued. The process generally takes place across a three to six year span if all phases are attempted.

Futuring Futuring is a popular goal-setting and planning approach used to encourage members to influence the future direction their organization will take. Participants respond and share answers to a series of questions such as "Imagine it is 10 years from today. Will this organization still exist? How will it be different? Would you want to belong to it? Why?" (Lindaman & Lippitt, 1979, p. 9). Participants may also be asked to describe their observations of what their organization is like now and how they feel about that, to quickly share what they are proud and sorry about regarding current activities, nonactivities, and characteristics of their organization, as well as to fantasize what they would prefer their organization to be like at some point in the future. Lindaman and Lippitt (1979) provided the interested reader with a whole series of questions and exercises to facilitate this process. Once some future goals are agreed to, task forces are formed to plan what is needed to assist the organization's effort to achieve these goals. Public celebrations of progress toward goal attainment are recommended by most futurists.

Technostructural Approaches

Job enrichment/job redesign This includes any systematic effort to increase the motivating factors of a job in order to enhance the job holder's satisfaction and performance levels simultaneously. Herzberg's famous "Two Factor Theory of Job Satisfaction" (Herzberg, 1968) provided the basis for many of these efforts. According to the theory, "hygiene factors" (e.g., pay, job security, working conditions, safety) do not create satisfaction or motivation in workers, but merely prevent dissatisfaction if provided for. "Motivator factors" (e.g., responsibility, achievement, accomplishment, learning, growth opportunities) available to a worker on his or her job determine job satisfaction/motivation. So the jobs of targeted workers are changed so that more motivator factor opportunities are built into the performance of the job. If the job is changed such that only hygiene factors are improved and/or variety increased by including new, but routine, tasks in the person's assignments, it is referred to as *job enlargement.*

Hackman and Oldham (1980) suggested a strategy that involves assessing the characteristics of the job(s) targeted for change on five core dimensions (skill variety, task identity, task significance, autonomy, and feedback) using the Job Diagnostic Survey (Hackman & Oldham, 1975). The survey generates a measure of the motivation potential of a given job. The job holder's motivation, satisfaction, growth needs, and performance levels are also assessed to determine whether there is room and desire for improvement. The job holders participate in the planning of the redesign of their jobs. Principles such as forming jobs into natural work units to insure a sense of connection to the end product, removing controls while maintaining accountability, and opening up more direct feedback channels are used to guide the redesign process. A useful adaptation of this model is available (Hackman, 1977) to redesign jobs for entire work groups. The interested reader should also consult Herzberg's 1974 article in the *Harvard Business Review.*

Sociotechnical systems This is an approach to work redesign focusing on the interface between people and technology. The sociotechnical systems approach is more a set of principles than a specific technique. Some famous applications of these principles include their use in the design of work at the Volvo and Saab plants in Sweden, the hydroelectric plant in Norway, the General Foods plant in Topeka, Kansas, and a textile plant and coal mine in England (see Walton, 1975, for details). Most applications seem to result in the development of autonomous work groups that are collectively responsible for the outputs. The principles have been found to be particularly useful in the development of work systems for new facilities. The interested reader should refer to Trist (1969) or Walton (1977).

Collateral organization   This is a strategy to enhance the creative problem-solving capacity of an organization by developing a supplemental (subparallel) structure as a means of increasing flexibility. The collateral organization is thus a secondary mode of organization co-existing with the usual formal organization, but with the focus of resolving nonroutine, "ill-structured" problems that the hierarchical (formal) structure typically has difficulty dealing with. As problems are brought to the managers' attention, a decision is made to either attempt resolution within the "regular" hierarchy or assign the problem to a collateral organization. Within the later, status differentials are minimized; all channels of communications are open; norms of questioning and analysis of goals, assumptions, methods, and alternatives are encouraged; and members are allowed to approach and enlist others in the organization to help solve a problem without being restricted to formal sets of subordinates. Successful uses of this technique are described by Zand (1974).

Matrix organization   This is an alternative organization structure wherein a horizontal structure of a project coordinator is superimposed on the standard vertical hierarchical structure. This approach to change is used primarily in organizations whose business involves a number of projects (unit or small batch production systems) such as in the aerospace industry. Technical direction comes from the function managers while administrative control is exercised by various project leaders. Thus, most employees will have two "bosses" and coordination between the two sets of managers is the key for operating this approach. Davis and Lawrence (1977) provided an excellent reference for the interested readers.

Responsibility charting   Responsibility charting is a technique to manage a change effort in a large system and to focus on allocating work responsibilities. A grid is constructed such that one axis describes the types of decisions and classes of actions that need to be taken in the total area of work under discussion. The other axis is a list of the actors that might play some part in the decision making and/or execution of the issues identified. Four classes of behaviors are assigned to the actors: (1) responsibility (R) to initiate and carry out the decision, (2) review with the right of approval or veto (A-V) regarding the item, (3) providing logistical support (S) and resources for the particular item, and (4) reception of information (I) about the item without influence. Only one "R" can be assigned for any item listed.

This decision is made by consensus of the planning group. Completion of the chart clarifies who will do what to or with whom and clarifies the role description of each actor involved. The interested reader should consult Beckhard and Harris (1977) for more details.

Incentive Systems Approaches

Scanlon plans   Scanlon plans are really full systems designed to operationalize a philosophy of participative management. They combine a productivity gains/cost savings bonus formula, a representative committee structure to insure communication from and with managers and workers, and a suggestive system. Originally developed as an incentive plan by a union president of a steelworkers' union in the 1940s, consultants and scholars (most notably Lesieur, 1958, and Frost, 1978) have evolved the plan into an OD strategy. First, top management and union leaders are asked to assess to what extent do present employees identify with the company's situation and understand the current financial and market situation. An ad hoc steering committee is formed to analyze the compensation system, performance standards, managerial competency, feelings of equity, and opportunities to participate. The ad hoc committee generates a proposal that describes an education plan for the management and workforce, a bonus formula based on a historical ratio of labor cost to the sales volume of production, and a permanent, multitiered committee structure to insure representative input of suggestions for improvement. The entire workforce votes on whether to accept the proposal. If they do, suggestions for change are reviewed through the committee structure and gains reflected in the bonus formula ratio are shared between the company and every member of the organization on a percentage of salary basis each month. The most thorough reference on Scanlon plans as an OD intervention are books by Frost, Wakeley, and Ruh (1974) and Moore and Ross (1978).

Rucker plans   Rucker plans also combine a group incentive system and an employee participation plan to reduce costs and improve productivity. Opportunities for productivity gains are researched by plant productivity groups that are established on a rotating membership basis. Productivity gains are measured in money terms (value added) rather than physical units. A bonus formula is established to share the gains between the participants (added pay) and the company (added margin). Heyel (1973) provided a more detailed description for the interested reader.

Worker ownership plans   These are efforts whereby part or all of the company's assets are purchased or given to the employees of that company. Employee Stock Ownership Plans (ESOPs) and worker buyouts are two common examples. Sometimes these approaches are utilized as an OD effort to gain organizational performance benefits and increase commitment/ morale of the employees. More commonly, they are used to gain more favorable tax advantages or to avoid the closing of a business. Occasionally, employees are allowed to participate in the decision processes involved in establishing these plans. The interested reader should refer to O'Toole's (1979) article on the uneven track record of these efforts.

GROUP-ORIENTED OD INTERVENTIONS

Teambuilding

This is a set of team development activities aimed at accomplishing one or more of the following purposes:

1. To set goals and/or priorities.
2. To analyze or allocate the way work is performed.
3. To examine the way a group is working; its processes (such as norms, decision making, communications).
4. To examine relationships among the people doing the work (Beckhard, 1972, p. 23).

Teambuilding methodologies can be applied to any group of people with common organizational relationships (committees, departments, top management, etc.) and/or common purpose. Dyer's 1977 book served as a useful overview of the methodologies and procedures involved.

QWL/EI Processes

Joint Union-Management Quality of Work Life (QWL/Employee Involvement (EI) Approaches are actually almost any OD intervention in a unionized setting. However, most QWL/EI efforts rely heavily on small group interventions for structural and developmental reasons. Nadler and Lawler (1983) suggested that the distinctive elements of a QWL/EI effort are "(1) a concern for the impact of work on people as well as on organization effectiveness and (2) the idea of participation in organizational problem solving and decision making" (p. 26). After exploring whether to commit to experimenting with QWL/EI, a group (usually entitled a QWL/EI Steering Committee) is formed and a consultant attempts to help the group function. Its purpose is to determine the mission of the QWL/EI effort, the principles to govern the process, the pilot sites where experiments will be attempted, the progress of the effort, the support and resources needed to continue the effort, and the means to diffuse the QWL process throughout all organizational subsystems. This process is expected to avoid involvement in matters under the domain of the collective bargaining process. The process is usually coordinated on a day-to-day process by co-facilitators (one from management and one from the union) who report to the steering committee. Problem-solving groups are developed at departmental (often called employee participation groups, or employee involvement groups, or core groups) or hierarchical levels on a permanent basis or cross-functional, ad hoc task forces focused on a specific problem on a temporary basis. These groups generally meet once a week for one to one and one-half hours. The steering committee generally meets once a month, but more frequently prior to the launch of the other groups.

Quality Control Circles

QC circles are an intervention developed by Americans, such as Drs. Deming and Juran, to address the quality control problems in Japanese industries after World War II. Employees working together in small problem solving groups (circles) are trained primarily in statistical process control and problem-solving techniques. The groups apply the training to identify problems (especially quality control problems) occurring in their group's work performance. Solutions to the problems are developed by the groups and presented to management who retains the power to accept or reject the solutions. Most implementations of QCs are not truly OD efforts, but can assist job enrichment, QWL, and other OD approaches (Yager, 1981). Any of several recent books will provide the interested reader with comprehensive views on QC circles (e.g., Dewar, 1982; Ingle, 1982; Barra, 1983).

The increased popularity of teambuilding interventions has also resulted in the development of a number of other OD interventions aimed at enhancing teambuilding efforts. In particular, techniques to clarify team goals, roles, decision-making procedures, and group processes have been successfully advanced. In addition, methods to assist coordination and reduce conflict between groups have also been developed. These two sets of techniques belong here in our discussion of group-oriented OD techniques and include the following.

Collaborative Management-By-Objectives (CMBO)

This is a team-centered approach to goal setting. It is modeled after the management-by-objectives (MBO) approach (see section on Individual Oriented OD techniques) but emphasizes the development of mutual support systems within a group and attempts to utilize these informal networks in order to accomplish agreed upon team goals. A cross-section of organization members are asked to identify and analyze problems facing the organization as a whole. A series of workshops are then conducted through-out the organization to explain the CMBO process and share the group's analysis of the organization's problems. The readiness of the organization for CMBO is assessed and, if ready, the top management team is asked to decide by consensus what the organization's overall goals and objectives will be.

Each unit then meets and decides (by consensus again, if possible) what unit goals and objectives are essential to achieving the overall organization goals and objectives. Individual managers are then expected to develop specific, results—oriented objectives that also address career and development goals. If the roles and responsibilities of team members are unclear, time must first be taken to achieve clarity on these matters throughout the team. Progress toward objectives should be reviewed on a continuous basis, but superior and subordinate must schedule a formal performance review at the end of the agreed upon time period. The CMBO process should be rediagnosed, adjusted, and recycled on a yearly basis. The interested reader is referred to French and Hollman (1975).

JET and RAT

The job expectation technique (JET) and role analysis technique (RAT) are two very similar techniques used to enhance a teambuilding effort by clarifying the roles and expectations of every member of a group including its manager. They can be very useful when a new team is formed, a new member is added to an existing team, or as a means to resolve problems stemming from role ambiguity or role conflict. After verifying the need for RAT or JET, enough time must be found to address the issues (allowing approximately three hours per role) at an off-site session. A clear commitment to the process must be gained and confirmed by management. Each job incumbent, beginning with the manager, describes his or her own duties, responsibilities, and what expectations he or she has of other group members. Group members comment on the incumbent's perceptions and suggest additions and deletions. The incumbent then agrees to write up his or her new job description to incorporate any changes decided on and submit it to the group for approval. Each member in turn goes through the same process. Interested readers will find Dayal and Thomas (1968) a useful reference on the RAT and Huse and Barebo (1980) on the JET. Huse (1980) pointed out that "JET and RAT both appear in the literature, but are different terms for what is essentially an identical process" (p. 293).

Role Negotiation Method

The role negotiation method was depicted as a "tough minded approach" to role clarification by Harrison (1973). Individuals institute changes, through direct negotiation, in the roles performed by other individuals of the same group. Negotiations on elements listed on a person's formal job description, as well as informal understandings, arrangements, and expectations, are allowed as long as they are directly related to the work performance. This technique is not to be used to deal with interpersonal issues such as how group members feel about each other. Under a very structured procedure, individuals develop lists of what they want each other member to do less often, more often, or differently. Lists are exchanged and behavioral changes are agreed to on a one-to-one, *quid pro quo* basis. Sanctions for failing to live up to an agreement are identified and all negotiations are described in writing and signed by each party. The technique's procedures are clear cut and logical and based on the premise that most people prefer a fair, negotiated settlement to a state of unresolved conflict. Interested readers should refer to Harrison's 1973 article for more details.

The Transition Meeting

The transition meeting is a team goals and roles clarification technique utilized when there is a change in team leadership. Its purpose is to reduce misconceptions, alleviate subordinates' apprehension, and reduce the time needed for the new leader to effectively work with the group. Premeeting interviews are conducted by a consultant or staff person with the outgoing leader, the new leader, and possibly one or two group members. Issues identified through these interviews help establish the agenda for the meeting. The meeting itself should primarily clarify expectations. Follow-up discussions should be arranged to encourage support for actions and to identify new problem areas. Mitchell (1976) provides the interested reader with more information.

Process Consultation

Process consultation is a feedback and agenda-setting intervention whereby a consultant describes his or her observations of how the group works as a team and/or sets aside some time for the group to address process issues listed by the consultant. The purpose is to raise awareness of strengths as well as obstacles the group generatates in efforts to work together. The discussion is not to address the content of the work the group is attempting nor merely to evaluate the group's overall effectiveness. It is to help the group improve its own problem-solving capacity. The intervention can be used with individuals as well as groups. Once the group is aware of how it goes about functioning as a team, it should generate action plans for how to capitalize on its strengths and how to overcome its obstacles. Much has been written on this approach to OD work. The interested reader might best start with Schein's 1969 book on the topic.

The Nominal Group Technique

The nominal group technique is a carefully structured, problem-solving technique to gain ideas or make decisions in a time-efficient manner. An issue or problem is defined for a chosen group of people and each member is asked to silently write down his or her response to the matter. The instructions may be to identify causes of the problem or solutions to the problem. The facilitator asks each member to read aloud the most important response on his or her list and the facilitator posts the response on a flip chart. Several rounds of having each person read elements off his or her list are conducted and members are asked not to provide a response that someone in the group has already listed. Group members may question respondents in order to clarify the meaning of an item provided but they are asked not to discuss whether they agree or disagree. After all responses from the group are exhausted, each member is given a certain number of votes (usually 10) to cast for the items he or she feels are the most important responses to the issue. The votes are tabulated and used as a reflection of the group's decision on the matter. Interested readers are referred to Van de Ven and Delbecq (1971) for more information on this technique.

Intergroup Mirroring or Image Exchange

This is a technique used to uncover misperceptions and sources of conflict between two groups. Groups first work separately to complete three lists in response to these questions: (1) How do we perceive ourselves as a group? (2) How do we perceive the other group? and (3) What do we predict that the other group will say about our group? The two groups exchange lists and sufficient time is allocated to read each other's responses. A discussion is then facilitated by the OD practitioner (or staff person, manager, etc.) to identify what perceptions were held in common by both groups and what misperceptions and problems appear to exist. Subgroups are formed with equal representation from the original groups with the purpose of identifying solutions for the problems uncovered in the discussion. The solutions are later presented at a meeting with all parties to agree to a course of action. The interested reader should refer to Burke (1975) for more information.

Third-Party Peacemaking

This is an intergroup conflict resolution effort where the OD practitioner takes on the role of mediator. The consultant attempts to establish his or her neutrality and get the parties involved in the conflict to develop an objective statement defining the dispute. Attempting to use rational problem-solving methods and active listening skills, the consultant facilitates the parties coming to a solution themselves. The consultant should avoid attempting to solve the problem himself or herself, but rather comment throughout the process on how the parties are progressing (or failing to progress). Interested readers have a large variety of sources to turn to, but might best start with Walton's book (1969) on the matter.

INDIVIDUAL-ORIENTED OD INTERVENTIONS

Management-By-Objectives

This is a system of management driven by the setting of specific goals and objectives for individual employees in a manner that supports the overall organization's goals and objectives. After being familiarized with how the system works, the top management team defines measures of organizational performance and sets goals relevant to these measures. Each top manager then meets with his or her subordinate managers and establishes (by edict or via participatory means) goals appropriate for that level of the hierarchy, yet conducive toward the established organizational goals. The procedure cascades down the chain of command until all employees have goals to guide their actions. A bottom-up approach to MBO is theoretically possible whereby goals established by members of lower levels of the organization are collected and managers attempt to coordinate the resulting activities in a manner that insures a viable organization. Progress toward goal accomplishment in either the top-down or bottom-up approach is closely monitored and appropriate rewards should be granted to individuals achieving their goals. Odiorne wrote a classic text on MBO in 1965, if more information is desired.

Career Planning and Development

Career planning and development is a system to monitor, develop, and promote the talent of the individual human resources of an organization. After top management agrees to support such a system, awareness workshops are conducted to assist individuals to become more aware of their potential and of means the organization has of using that potential. A career path for each participating individual is developed that identifies which positions within the organization the employee should apply for at what stage of his or her career. The interested reader is referred to Hall's 1976 book on the topic.

Training and Development

Training and development can be an OD intervention in and of itself when it is designed and implemented as a long-term planned change process. Throughout much of the OD literature, training and development has been described as an OD strategy (see, for example, Chin & Benne, 1983; Miles & Schmuck, 1976; Porras & Berg, 1978), although some have contrasted the two as well (see Beckhard, 1969). Since training and development is expected to exhance the performance and satisfaction levels of trainees and efforts are expected to be made to sustain the impact of the learning and skill development acquired during the conduct of the training program itself, we consider training and development efforts to be OD interventions. The interested reader should refer to this book (again and again) for more details.

Meeting facilitation, communication (especially listening), problem-solving, and conflict-resolution skills will be called upon in the use of these methods. Data gathering and analysis skills are needed in the use of Quality Circles. Finally, most of the techniques listed in this category require participative management skills in order to gain the advantage produced by having groups, rather than individuals, solve problems facing an organization.

Trainers and OD practitioners should assess whether training programs to address all the above-mentioned areas are needed in a given situation. A needs assessment should always be conducted first. In this category in particular, we have observed consultants implementing OD interventions (e.g., QWL, QC efforts) by merely plugging in a package of training programs. This despite the fact that time and resources could have been better spent in other activities to enhance the change effort at the location.

Some OD interventions are designed to enhance the effectiveness and satisfaction of a variety of individuals with the idea that, if enough individuals are thus affected, the organization will also be improved. Interventions of this category include management-by-objectives, career planning and development, and even training and development. One might question whether these approaches are truly OD interventions. We believe the label fits only if they are implemented in a manner consistent with the four characteristics of OD that we discussed previously.

REFERENCES

CHAPTER 1

Amaya, T., Organization Development in Japan. *Journal of Enterprise Management,* 1980, *2,* 221–236.

American Society for Training and Development. *Models for Excellence: The Conclusions and Recommendations of the ASTD Training and Development Competency Study.* Washington, D.C.: ASTD, 1983.

Anonymous, Training Budgets '84: In the pink—and green. *Training,* 1984, *21,* 16–39.

Beer, M. *Organization Change and Development: A Systems View.* Santa Monica, CA: Goodyear, 1980.

Bennis, W. G., *Organization Development: Its Nature, Origins, and Prospects.* Reading, MA: Addison-Wesley Publishing, 1969, 2.

Brown, M. G. Evaluating Training via Multiple Baseline Designs. *Training and Development Journal,* October, 1980, *34,* 11–17.

Coch, L. and French, J. R., Overcoming Resistance to Change. *Human Relations,* 1948, *4,* 512–533.

Connellan, T. K., *How to Improve Human Performance.* New York: Harper & Row, 1978, 74–89.

Davis, R. W. Financial Aspects of HRD. In L. Nadler (ed.) *The Handbook of Human Resource Development,* New York, John Wiley & Sons, 1984, 3.1–3.34.

Dewar, D. L., *The Quality Circle Guide to Participation Management.* Englewood Cliffs, N.J.: Prentice-Hall, Inc., 1980.

Eckstrand, G. A., Current Status of the Technology of Training. *AMRL Document Technical Report 64–86,* September, 1964, 3.

French, W. L., Bell, C. H. & Zawacki, R. A. (Eds.) *Organization Development: Theory, Practice and Research.* Plano, TX: Business Publications, Inc., 1983.

Gagné, R. M., Military Training and Principles of Learning. *American Psychologist,* 1962, *17,* 83–91.

Goldstein, I. L., *Training: Program Development and Evaluation.* Monterey, CA: Wadsworth Publishing Co., 1974.

————, Training in Work Organizations. *Annual Review of Psychology*, 1980, *31*, 229–272.

Hinrichs, J. R., Personnel Training. In Dunnette, M.D. (Ed.), *Handbook of Industrial and Organizational Psychology*, Chicago: Rand McNally, 1976, 829–860.

House, R. J., T-Group Education and Leadership Effectiveness: A Review of the Empirical Literature and a Critical Evaluation. *Personnel Psychology*, 1967, *20*, 1–32.

Huse, E. F., *Organization Development and Change* (2nd Edition). New York: West Publishing Co., 1980.

Jamieson, D. W., Training and OD: Crossing Disciplines. *Training and Development Journal*, April, 1981, 12–17.

Jucius, M. J., *Personnel Management* (Seventh Edition). Homewood, IL: Richard D. Irwin, Inc., 1971, 243–263.

Katz, D. and Kahn, R. L., *The Social Psychology of Organizations*. New York: Wiley, 1978.

Lawler, E. E., *Pay and Organization Development*. Reading, MA: Addison-Wesley Publishing, 1981.

Leavitt, H. J. and Bass, B. M., Organizational Psychology. *Annual Review of Psychology*, 1964, *15*, 371–398.

Lippit, G. L. *Organizational Renewal*. Prentice-Hall, Inc., Englewood Cliffs, New Jersey, 1982.

Maier, N. R. F., *Problem Solving and Creativity in Individuals and Groups*. Belmont, CA: Brooks/Cole, 1970.

Mankin, D., Ames, R. E., Jr., and Grodsky, M. A. Training. In D. Mankin, R. E. Ames, Jr., and M. A. Grodsky (eds). *Classics of Industrial and Organizational Psychology*, Oak Park, Illinois: Moore Publishing Co., 1980, 171–173.

Nadler, L. *Designing Training Programs: The Critical Events Model*. Reading, MA: Addison-Wesley Publishing, 1982.

Nadler, L. Human Resource Development. In L. Nadler (ed.) *The Handbook of Human Resource Development*, New York, John Wiley & Sons, 1984, 1.1–1.47.

Olivas, L. Using Assessment Centers for Individual and Organization Development. *Personnel*, May/June, 1980, *57*, 63–67.

Plovnick, M. S., Fry, R. E. & Burke, W. W. *Organization Development: Exercises, Cases, and Readings*. Boston, MA: Little, Brown and Co., 1982.

Pondy, L. R. and Mitroff, I. I., Beyond Open System Models of Organization. In *Research in Organizational Behavior*, 1979, *1*, 3–39.

Putnam, T. Pragmatic Evaluation. *Training and Development Journal*, October, 1980, *34*, 36–44.

Quinn, R. P. and Kahn, R. L., Organizational Psychology. *Annual Review of Psychology*, 1967, *18*, 437–466.

Royland, C. Organization Development: Structures, Process or Systems. In Cummings, T. (Ed.), *Systems Theory and Organization Development*. London: John Wiley & Sons, Ltd., 1980.

Schein, E. H. *Organizational Psychology* (3rd Edition). Englewood Cliffs, N.J.: Prentice-Hall, 1980.

————, *Process Consultation: Its Role in Organization Development*. Reading, MA: Addison-Wesley, 1979.

Seamonds, J. A., Prof Hurls Stinging Indictment at Bosses. *Lansing State Journal*, December 19, 1982, 8E.

Strauss, G., Organizational Behavior and Personnel Relations. In *Review of Industrial Relations Research*, 1970, *1*, 145–205.

Tauber, M. S. New Employee Orientation: A Comprehensive Systems Approach. *Personnel Administrator*, January, 1981, *26*, 65–69.

Taylor, F. W. *Principles of Scientific Management.* New York: Harper & Row, 1911.

Thurow, L., Productivity: Japan Has a Better Way. *New York Times,* February 8, 1981, 2F.

Toffler, A., *The Third Wave.* New York: William Murrow and Co., 1980.

U.S. Training Census and Trends Report (Special Issue). *Training,* October, 1982.

Vroom, V. and Yetton, P., *Leadership and Decision Making.* Pittsburgh: University of Pittsburgh Press, 1973.

Warrick, D. (ed.), Definitions of OD by the Experts. *The Academy of Management OD Newsletter,* Winter, 1978.

Wexley, K. N. and Latham, G. P., *Developing and Training Human Resources in Organizations.* Glenview, IL: Scott, Foresman and Co., 1981.

Zemke, R., Does HRD need a PR consultant? *Training,* October, 1982, 8–9.

CHAPTER 2

Allen, R. F., Silverzwerg, S. Group norms: Their influence on training effectiveness. In R. Craig (Ed.) *Handbook of Training and Development,* 1976.

Arval, D. and Stumpf, S. A. Differentiating between perceived organization and work group climates. *Journal of Management,* 1981, *7,* 33–42.

Arvey, R. D., Davis, G. A., McGowen, S. L., and Dipboye, R. L. Potential sources of bias in job analytic processes. *Academy of Management Journal,* 1982, *25,* 618–629.

Arvey, R. D., and Mossholder, K. M. A proposed methodology for determining similarities and differences among jobs. *Personnel Psychology,* 1977, *30,* 363–374.

Arvey, R. D., Passino, E. M., and Lounsbury, J. W. Job analysis results as influenced by sex of incumbent and sex of analyst. *Journal of Applied Psychology,* 1977, *62,* 411–416.

Baumgartel, H., and Jeanpierre, F. Applying new knowledge in the back-home setting: A study of Indian managers' adoptive efforts. *Journal of Applied Behavioral Science,* 1972, *8,* 674–694.

Boehm, V. R., and Hoyle, D. F. Assessment and management development. In J. L. Moses and W. C. Byham (eds.), *Applying the assessment center method,* New York: Pergamon, 1977, 203–224.

Borman, W. C. Effects of instruction to avoid halo error on reliability and validity of performance evaluation ratings. *Journal of Applied Psychology,* 1975, *60,* 556–560.

Bradley, G. W. "Self-serving Biases in the Attribution Process: A Re-examination of the Fact or Fiction Question," *Journal of Personality and Social Psychology,* 1978, *36,* 56–71.

Burke, R. J., Weitzel, W., and Weir, T. Characteristics of effective employee performance review and development interviews: Replication and extension, *Personnel Psychology,* 1978, *31,* 903–919.

Cederblom, D. and Lounsbury, J. W. An investigation of user acceptance of peer evaluations. *Personnel Psychology,* 1980, *33,* 567–579.

Cohen, S. L., Groner, D. M., Muxworthy, D. G., and Glickman, E. I. Incorporating assessment center techniques into management training and development at Xerox. *Journal of Assessment Center Technology,* 1979, *2,* 1–5.

Cronbach, L. J., and Gleser, G. C. *Psychological tests and personnel decisions,* Urbana, Illinois, University of Illinois Press, 1965.

Dayal, I. and Thomas, J. Operation KPE: Developing a new organization. *Journal of Behavioral Science,* 1968, *4,* 473–506.

Deaux, K., and Emswiller, T. "Explanations of Successful Performance on Sex-linked Tasks: What is Skill for the Male is Luck for the Female," *Journal of Personality and Social Psychology*, 1974, *29*, 80–85.

Feather, N. T. "Attribution of Responsibility and Valance of Success and Failure in Relation to Initial Confidence and Task Performance," *Journal of Personality and Social Psychology*, 1969, *13*, 129–144.

Feather, N. T., and Simon, J. G. "Causal Attributions for Success and Failure in Relation to Expectations of Success Based Upon Selective or Manipulative Control," *Journal of Personality*, 1971, *39*, 527–541.

Feild, H. S., and Schoenfeldt, L. F. Ward and Hook revisited: A two-part procedure for overcoming a deficiency in the grouping of persons. *Educational and Psychological Measurement*, 1975, *35*, 171–173.

Fine, S. A. *Functional job analysis scales: A desk aid.* Kalamazoo, Mich.: Upjohn Institute for Employment Research, 1973.

Fleishman, E. A. Evaluating physical abilities required by jobs. *The Personnel Administrator*, 1979, *24*, 82–92.

Gallegos, R. C., and Phelan, J. G. Using behavioral objectives in industrial training. *Training and Development Journal*, 1974, *28*, 42–48.

Garland, A., and Price, K. H. Attitudes toward women in management and attributions for their success and failure in managerial positions. *Journal of Applied Psychology*, 1977, *62*, 29–33.

Goldstein, I. L. Training in work organizations. *Annual Review of Psychology*, 1980, *31*, 229–272.

Gordon, M. E., and Cohen, S. L. Training Behavior as a Predictor of Trainability, *Personnel Psychology*, 1973, *26*, 261–272.

Gorman, L., and Malloy, E. *People, Jobs and Organizations.* Dublin: Irish Management Institute, 1972.

Hansen, R. D., and Donoghue, J. M. "The Power of Consensus: Information Derived from One's Own and Other's Behavior," *Journal of Personality and Social Psychology*, 1977, *35*, 294–302.

Hansen, R. D., and Lowe, C. A. "Distinctiveness and Consensus: The Influence of Behavioral Information on Actors' and Observers' Attributions," *Journal of Personality and Social Psychology*, 1976, *34*, 425–433.

Helmreich, R., Boheman, R., and Radloff, R. The life history questionnaire as a predictor of performance in Navy diver training. *Journal of Applied Psychology*, 1973, *57*, 148–153.

Ilgen, D. R., Fisher, C. D., and Taylor, M. S. Consequences of individual feedback on behavior in organizations. *Journal of Applied Psychology*, 1979, *64*, 349–371.

Kane, J. S., and Lawler, E. E., III Methods of peer assessment. *Psychological Bulletin*, 1978, *85*, 555–586.

Kelley, H. H. "Attribution Theory in Social Psychology. In D. Levine (ed.), Nebraska Symposium on Motivation (Vol. 15), Lincoln: University of Nebraska Press, 1967.

————"Attribution in Social Interaction." In E. Jones, D. Kanouse, H. Kelley, R. Nisbett, S. Valins, and B. Weiner (eds.), *Attribution: Perceiving the Causes of Behavior*, Morristown, N.J.: General Learning Press. 1972A.

————"Causal Schemata and the Attribution Process." In E. Jones, D. Kanouse, H. Kelley, R. Nisbett, S. Valins, and B. Weiner (eds.) *Attribution: Perceiving the Causes of Behavior.* Morristown, N.J.: General Learning Press. 1972B.

————"The Processes of Causal Attribution," *American Psychologist*, 1973, *28*, 107–128.

Klimonski, R. J., and London, M. Role of the rater in performance appraisal. *Journal of Applied Psychology*, 1974, *59*, 445–451.

Kneller, G. A. Behavioral objectives? No! *Educational Leadership,* 1972, *29,* 397–400.

Knowles, M. S. *The Adult Learner: A Neglected Species,* Houston: Gulf Publishing Co., 1978.

Kolb, D. A. *Learning style inventory* Boston, Mass.: McBer, 1976.

Laird, D. *Approaches to Training and Development,* Reading, MA.: Addison-Wesley, 1978.

Lawler, E. E., III *Pay and Organizational Development.* Addison-Wesley, 1982.

Lewin, K. *Field theory in social science.* New York: Harper and Brothers, 1951.

Locke, E. A., and Schweiger, D. M. Participation in decision-making: One more look. In B. M. Staw (Ed.), *Research in organizational behaviorial,* Greenwich, Conn.: JAI Press, 1979.

Locke, E. A., Shaw, K. N., Saari, L. M., and Latham, G. P. Goal-setting and task performance: 1969-1980. *Psychological Bulletin* 1981, *90,* 125–152.

Love, K. G. Comparison of peer assessment methods: Reliability, validity, friendship bias and user reaction. *Journal of Applied Psychology,* 1981, *66,* 451–457.

Mager, R. F., & Pipe, P. *Analyzing Performance Problems or "You Really Oughta Wanna,"* 2nd Edition. Belmont, CA.: David Lake Publishing, 1984.

Martinko, M. J. and Gardner, W. L. Learned helplessness: An Alternative explanation for performance deficits. *Academy of Management Review,* 1982, *7,* 195–204.

McCormick, E. J. *Job Analysis.* New York: AMACOM, 1979.

McGehee, W., and Thayer, P. W. Training in Business and Industry. New York: Wiley, 1961.

Miller, D., and Ross, M. Self-serving biases in the attribution of casuality: Fact or fiction? *Psychological Bulletin,* 1975, *82,* 213–225.

Miller, R. W. and Zeller, F. A. Social psychological factors associated with responses to retraining. Morgantown, W. Va: *U. S. Department of Labor, Office of Research and Development,* Appalachian Center, West Virginia University, *Final Report,* 1967.

Mintzberg, H. *The nature of managerial work.* New York: Harper and Row, 1973.

Mitchell, T. R., Green, S. G., and Wood, R. E. An attributional model of leadership and the poor performing subordinate: development and validation. In L. L. Cummings and B. M. Staw (Eds.) *Research in Organizational Behavior; Volume 3,* Greenwich, Connecticut; JAI Press, 1981.

Moore, M. L., and Dutton, P. Training needs analysis: Review and critique. *Academy of Management Review.* 1978, *3,* 532–545.

Pace, C. R. The measurement of college environments. In R. Tagluri & G. A. Litwin (Eds.), *Organizational climate: Exploration of a concept.* Cambridge: Harvard University, 1968.

Payne, R. L. Organizational climate: The concept of some research findings. *Prakseologia.* NR 39/40/Rok,1971.

Payne, R., and Pugh, D. Organizational structure and climate. In M. D. Dunnette (ed). *Handbook of Industrial and Organizational Psychology,* Chicago, Illinois: Rand McNally, 1976, 1125–1173.

Perrow, C. *Organizational Analysis: A Sociological View,* Belmont, California: Wadsworth, 1970.

Regan, D. T., Strays, E., and Fazio R. Liking and the attribution process. *Journal of Experimental and Social Psychology,* 1974, *10,* 385–397.

Reilley, R. R., and Manese, W. R. The validation of a minicourse for telephone company switching technicians. *Personnel Psychology,* 1979, *32,* 83–90.

Roadman, H. E. An industrial use of peer ratings, *Journal of Applied Psychology,* 1964, *48,* 211–214.

Robertson, I., Downs, S. Learning and the prediction of performance: Development of trainability testing in the United Kingdom. *Journal of Applied Psychology,* 1979, *64,* 42–50.

Ryman, D. H., and Biersner, R. J. Attitudes predictive of diving training success. *Personnel Psychology*, 1975, *28*, 181–188.

Schein, E. H. Management development as a process of influence. *Industrial Management Review*, 1961, *2*, 59–77.

Schwab, D. P., Heneman, H. G., and De Cotiis, T. A. Behaviorally anchored rating scales: A review of the literature. *Personnel Psychology*, 1975, *28*, 549–562.

Sparks, C. P. Job Analysis. In K. Rowland and G. Ferris (eds.). *Personnel Management*, Boston, Mass.: Allyn and Bacon, 1982, 78–100.

Stern, G. G. *People in context: Measuring person-environment congruence in education and industry.* New York: Waley, 1970.

Trattner, M. A. Task analysis in the design of three concurrent validity studies of the Professional and Administrative Career Examination. *Personnel Psychology*, 1979, *32*, 109–119.

Weiner, B., Frieze, I., Kukla, A., Reed, L., Rest, S., and Rosenbaum, R. "Perceiving the Causes of Success and Failure." In E. Jones, D. Kanouse, H. Kelley, R. Nisbett, S. Valins, and B. Weiner (eds), *Attribution: Perceiving the Causes of Behavior.* Morristown, N. J.: General Learning Press, 1972.

Wexley, K. N. and Latham, G. P. *Developing and Training Human Resources in Organizations.* Glenview, Illinois: Scott Foresman, 1981.

Wittrock, M. C., and Lumsdaine, A. A. Instructional Psychology. In M. R. Rosenziwerg and L. W. Porter (eds). *Annual Review of Psychology*, 1977, *28*, 417–459.

Zedeck, S., Imparato, N., Krausz, M. and Oleno, T. Development of behaviorally anchored rating scales as a function of organizational level. *Journal of Applied Psychology*, 1974, *59*, 249–252.

Zeira, Y. Training the top-management team for planned change. *Training and Development Journal*, 1974, *28*, 30–36.

CHAPTER 3

Ausubel, D. P. *The Psychology of Meaningful Verbal Learning.* New York: Grune & Stratton, 1963.

Baltes, P. B., and Willis, S. L. Toward Psychological Theories of Aging. In J. E. Birren & K. W. Schaie (Eds.), *Handbook on Psychology of Aging.* New York: Reinhold-VanNostrand, 1976.

Bandura, A. Analysis of modeling processes. In Bandura, A. (Ed.), *Psychological Modeling: Conflicting Theories.* Chicago: Aldine-Atherton, 1971.

Bandura, A. *Social Learning Theory.* Englewood Cliffs, N.J.: Prentice-Hall, 1977.(a).

Bandura, A. Self Efficacy: Towards a unifying theory of behavioral change. *Psychological Review*, 1977, 84, 191–215.(b).

Ebbinghaus, H. As reported by G. Murphy and J. Kovach in *Historical Introduction to Modern Psychology.* New York: Harcourt Brace Jovanovich, Inc., 1972. The original works were: *Uber das Gedachtnis.* Leipzig: Duncker and Humbolt, 1885 and *Grundzuge des Psychologie.* 2 Vols., Leipzig: Veit, 1902–11.

Gagné, R.M. Military training and principles of learning, *American Psychologist*, 1962, *17*, 83–91.

Gagné, R.M. *The Conditions of Learning.* New York: Holt, Reinhart & Winston, 1965.

Gagné, R.M. *Essentials of Learning for Instruction.* Hinsdale, Ill: Dryden Press, 1974.

Gagné, R.M. Study of retention of some topics of elementary non-metric geometry. *Journal of Educational Psychology*, 1963, *54*, 123–131.

Gagné, R.M. and Bassler, O.C. Study of retention of some topics of elementary non-metric geometry. *Journal of Educational Psychology*, 1963, *54*, 123–131.

Griffith, G., Tough, A., Barnard, W. and Brundage, D. *The Design of Self-Directed Learning.* Toronto: Ontario Institute for Studies in Education, 1980.

Guthie, E.R. *The Psychology of Learning.* Rev. Ed. New York: Harper & Row, 1952.

Jarvick, L.F., and Cohen, A. A Biobehavioral Approach to Intellectual Changes With Aging. In Eisdorfer & Lawton (Eds.) *The Psychology of Adult Development and Aging.* Washington, D.C.: American Psychological Association, 1973.

Knowles, M.S. *The Adult Learner: A Neglected Species.* Houston: Gulf Publishing Co., 1978.

Knowles, M.S. Adult Learning: Theory and Practice. In L. Nadler (Ed.), *The Handbook of Human Resource Development,* New York: John Wiley & Sons, 1984.

Kraut, A.J. Behavior modeling symposium: Developing managerial skills via modeling techniques. *Personnel Psychology,* 1976, *29,* 325–328.

Labouvie Vief, G. Adult cognitive development: In search of alternative interpretations. *Merrill-Palmer Quarterly,* 1977, *23,* 227–263.

Latham, G.P. and Saari, L.M. Application of social learning theory to training supervisors through behavioral modeling. *Journal of Applied Psychology,* 1979, *64,* 239–246.

Manz, C.C. and Sims, H.P., Jr. Vicarious Learning: The influence of modeling on organizational behavior. *Academy of Management Review,* 1981, *6,* 105–113.

Pavlov, I.P. *Lectures on the Work of the Principle Digestive Glands,* St. Petersburg: Kushnereff, 1897.

Pavlov, I.P. Principle Laws of the Activity of the Central Nervous System as They Find Expression in Conditioned Reflexes. *Russhaii Vrack,* 11, 1912, 1502–11 (as reported by G. Murphy and J. Kovach in Historical Introduction to Modern Psychology, New York: Harcourt Brace Jovanovich, Inc., 1972).

Riegel, K.F. On the history of psychological genentology. In C. Eisdorfer & M. Lawton (Eds.) *The Psychology of Adult Development and Aging.* Washington, D.C. American Psychological Association, 1973.

Short, R.R. Managing unlearning. *Training and Development Journal,* July, 1981, 37–44.

Skinner, B.F. The steep and thorny way to a science of behavior. *American Psychologist,* 1975,30, 42–49.

Skinner, B.F. Beyond Freedom and Dignity. New York: Bantam/Vintage, 1971.

Skinner, B.F. *The Technology of Teaching.* New York: Appleton-Century-Crofts, 1968.

Skinner, B.F. *Science and Human Behavior.* New York: Macmillan, 1953.

Skinner, B.F. Are theories of learning necessary? *Psychological Review,* 1950,57, 193–216.

Skinner, B.F. *The Behavior of Organisms.* New York: Appleton-Century-Crofts, 1938.

Thorndike, E.L. *The Elements of Psychology.* New York: Seiler, 1905.

Thorndike, E.L. The Psychology of Learning. (*Educational Psychology, Vol. 2*) New York: Teachers College, Columbia University Press, 1913.

Thorndike, E.L. *The Fundamentals of Learning.* New York: Teachers College, Columbia University Press, 1932.

Tolman, E.L. *Purposive Behavior in Animals and Men.* New York, Appleton-Century, 1932.

Tough, A. New Conclusions on why and how adults learn. *Training,* Jan. 1979, 8–10.

Vroom, V.H. *Work and Motivation.* New York: Wiley, 1964.

CHAPTER 4

Anderson, J.R. and Bower, G.H. *Human associative memory.* Washington, D.C.: D.H. Winston, 1973.

Anderson, J.R. and Bower, G.H. Recognition and retrieval processes in free recall. *Psychological Review,* 1972, *79,* 97–123.

Anderson, R.; Kulhavey, R., and Andre, T. Feedback procedures in programmed instruction. *Journal of Educational Psychology*, 1971, *62*, 148–156.

Annette, J. *Feedback and Human Behavior*. Baltimore, MD: Penguin Books, 1969.

Bandura, A. *Social learning theory*. Englewood Cliffs, N.J.: Prentice-Hall, 1977.

Bass, B.M. and Vaughan, J.A. *Training in Industry: the management of learning*. Monterey, CA: Brooks/Cole, 1966.

Bilodeau, E.A. and Bilodeau, I.M. Motor skills learning. *Annual Review of Psychology*, 1961, *12*, 243–280.

Bloom, B. (ed.) *Taxonomy of Educational Objectives: The cognitive domain*. New York: Donald McKay, 1956.

Bloom, B. (ed.) *Taxonomy of Educational Objectives: The cognitive domain*. New York: Donald McKay, 1964.

Burke, R.J.; Weitzel, W. and Weir, T. Characteristics of effective employer performance review and development interviews: replication and extension. *Personnel Psychology*, 1978, *31*, 903–919.

Chapanis, A. Knowledge of performance as an incentive in repetitive monotonous tasks. *Journal of Applied Psychology*, 1964, *48*, 263–267.

Cook, D.M. The impact on managers of frequency of feedback. *Academy of Management Journal*, 1968, *11*, 263–277.

Cronbach, L.J. and Snow, R.E. *Aptitudes and instructional methods*. New York: Irvington, 1977.

Decker, P. J., The enhancement of behavior modeling training of supervisory skills by the inclusion of retention processes. *Personnel Psychology*, 1982, *35*, 323–332.

Fisher, C.D. The effects of personal control, competence and extrinsic reward systems on intrinsic motivation. *Organizational Behavior and Human Performance*, 1978, *21*, 273–288.

French, J.P., Jr.; Kay, E. and Meyer, H.H. Participation and the appraisal system. *Human Relations*, 1966, *19*, 3–19.

Gagné, R.M. *The Conditions of Learning*. New York: Holt, Rinehart and Winston, 1977.

Gagné, R.M. Learning outcomes and their effects. *American Psychologist*, 1984, *39*, 377–385.

Goldstein, I.L. Training in work organizations. *Annual Review of Psychology*, 1980, 229–272.

Hilley, J.M. and Wexley, K.N. Participation in appraisal interviews conducted in a training situation. *Journal of Applied Psychology*, 1974, *59*, 168–171.

Hundel, P.S. Knowledge of performance as an incentive in repetitive industrial work. *Journal of Applied Psychology*, 1969, *53*, 224–226.

Huysman, J. The effectiveness of the cognitive style constraint in implementing operations research proposals. *Management Science*, 1970, *17*, 92–104. (a)

Huysman, J. *The implementation of operations research*. New York: Wiley, 1970. (b)

Ilgen, D.R.; Fisher, C.D. and Taylor, M.S. Consequences of individual feedback on behavior in organizations. *Journal of Applied Psychology*, 1979, *64*, 349–371.

Ivancevich, J.M.; Donnelly, J.H. and Lyon, H.L. A study of the impact of management by objectives on perceived need satisfaction. *Personnel Psychology*, 1970, *23*, 139–151.

Kay, E.; Meyer, H.H. and French, J.R., Jr. Effects of threat in a performance appraisal interview. *Journal of Applied Psychology*, 1965, *49*, 311–317.

Kirby, P. *Cognitive style, learning style, and transfer skill acquisition*. Columbus, Ohio: National Center for Vocational Education, 1979.

Kirby, P.G. Performance improvement the adult way. *Personnel*, 1980, Nov.–Dec., 35–43.

Klatzky, R.L. *Human Memory: Structures and processes*. San Francisco: Freeman, 1975.

Kolb, D.A. Experiential learning theory and the learning style inventory: A reply to Friedman and Stumpf. *Academy of Management Review*, 1981, *6*, 289–296.

Kolb, D.A. *The Learning Style Inventory: Technical Manual.* Boston: McBer & Company, 1979.

Kolb, D.A. *The Learning Style Inventory: Self Scoring Test and Interpretation Booklet.* Boston: McBer & Company, 1976.

Kondrasuk, J. *Training and Development Journal.* 1979, Aug., 23–29.

Laird, D. *Approaches to Training and Development.* Reading, MA: Addison-Wesley, 1978.

Latham, G.P. and Locke, E.A. Goal setting: A motivational technique that works. *Organizational Dynamics*, 1979, Autumn, 69–80.

Latham, G.P.; Mitchel, T.R. and Dossett, D.L. Importance of participative goal setting and anticipated rewards on goal difficulty and job performance. *Journal of Applied Psychology*, 1978, *63*, 163–171.

Latham, G.P. and Yukl, G.A. Assigned versus participative goal setting with educated and uneducated woodworkers. *Journal of Applied Psychology*, 1975, *60*, 299–302.

Leifer, M.S. and Newstrom, J.W. Solving the transfer of training problems. *Training and Development Journal*, 1980, Aug., 42–51.

Lindsay, P.H. and Norman, D.A. *Human Information Processing: An introduction to psychology*. New York: Academic Press, 1972.

Lippitt, G. and Lippitt, R. The Consulting Function of the Human Resource Development Professional. In (L. Nadler, Ed.) *The Handbook of Human Resource Development*, John Wiley & Sons, New York, 1984.

Locke, E.A.; Shaw, K.N.; Saari, L.M. and Latham, G.P. Goal setting and task performance: 1969–1980. *Psychological Bulletin*, 1981, *90*, 125–152.

Mager, R.F. *Preparing Instructional Objectives*. Belmont, CA: Pitman Learning, Inc., 1975.

Mager, R.F. and Beach, K.M., Jr. *Developing Vocational Instruction*. Belmont, CA: Pitman Learning, Inc., 1967.

McVey, G.F. *Sensory Factors in the School Learning Environment*. Washington, D.C.: National Education Association, 1971.

Melton, A.W. and Martin, E. (Eds.) *Coding Processes in Human Memory*. Washington, D.C.: V.H. Winston, 1972.

Michalak, D.F. and Yager, E.G. *Making the Training Process Work*. New York: Harper & Row, 1979.

Myers, I.B. *The Myers-Briggs Type Indicator*. Palo Alto, CA: Consulting Psychologists Press, 1962.

Naylor, J.C. and Briggs, G.E. The effect of task complexity and task organization on the relative efficiency of part and whole training methods. *Journal of Experimental Psychology*, 1963, *65*, 217–224.

Nemerff, W.F. and Wexley, K.N. An exploration of the relationships between performance feedback interview characteristics and interview outcomes as perceived by managers and subordinates. *Journal of Occupational Psychology*, 1979, *52*, 25–34.

Popham, W.J. and Baker, E.L. *Establishing Instructional Goals*. Englewood Cliffs, N.J.: Prentice-Hall, 1970.

Rackham, N. The coaching controversy. *Training and Development Journal*, 1979, Nov., 12–17.

Reilly, R.R. and Manose, W.R. The validation of a minicourse for telephone company switching techniques. *Personnel Psychology*, 1979, *32*, 83–90.

Robey, D. and Taggart, W. Measuring managers' minds: The assessment of style in human information processing. *Academy of Management Review* 1981, *6*, 375–383.

Ross, P. C. A relationship between training efficiency and employee selection. *Improve Human Performance*, 1974, *3*, 108–117.

Saint, A.M. *Learning at Work: Human Resources and Organization Development*. Chicago: Nelson-Hall, 1978.

Vasarhelyi, M.A. Man-machine planning system: A cognitive style examination of interactive decision making. *Journal of Accounting Research*, 1977, *15*, 138–153.

Wade, T.C. Relative effect on performance and motivation for self-monitoring correct and incorrect responses. Journal of Experimental Psychology, 1974, 103, 245–248.

Wexley, K.N. and Latham, G.P. *Developing and Training Human Resources in Organizations*. Glenview, IL: Scott, Foresman & Co., 1981.

Wexley, K.N.; Singh, J.P. and Yukl, G.A. Subordinate personality as a moderator of the effects of participation in three types of appraisal interviews. *Journal of Applied Psychology*, 1973, *58*, 54–59.

Within, H.A.; Oltman, P.K.; Raskin, E. and Karp, S.A. *A Manual for the Embedded Figures Test*. Palo Alto, CA: Consulting Psychologists Press, 1971.

Xerox International Center for Training and Development—"A place to Learn." From *Training and Development Journal*, October, 1977.

CHAPTER 5

Aronson, E. and Carlsmith, J. M. Experimentation in social psychology. In: *The Handbook of Social Psychology*, Vol. II, G. Linsday and E. Aronson (Eds.), Reading, Mass.: Addison-Wesley, 1968.

Bass, B. M. and Vaughan, J. A. *Training in Industry: The Management of Learning*. Monterey, CA.: Brooks/Cole, 1966.

Campbell, D. J. and Stanley, J. C. *Experimental and Quasi-experimental Designs for Research*. Chicago: Rand McNally, 1963.

Campbell, D. T. and Fiske, D. W. Convergent and discriminant validation by the multitrait multimethod matrix *Psychological Bulletin*, 1959, *56*, 81–105.

Cascio, W. F. *Applied Psychology in Personnel Management*, Reston, Va.: Reston Publishing Co. 1982.

Chase, C. I. *Measurement for Eduational Evaluation*, 2nd. Ed. Reading, Mass.: Addison-Wesley, 1978.

Clement, R. W. Testing the hierarchy theory of training evaluation: An expanded role for trainee reactions. *Public Personnel Management Journal*, 1982, Summer, 176–184.

Cohen, M. and Nagel, E. *An Introduction to Logic and Scientific Method*. New York: Harcourt, Brace and Company, 1934.

Cook, T. D. and Campbell, D. T. The design and conduct of quasi-experiments and true experiments in field settings. *Handbook of Industrial and Organizational Psychology*, M.D. Dunnette (Ed.), Chicago: Rand McNally, 1976.

Cronbach, L. J. *Essentials of Psychological Testing* (2nd Ed.). New York: Harper and Row, 1960.

Goldstein, I. L. *Training: Program Development and Evaluation*. Monterey, Ca.: Brooks/Cole, 1974.

Hamblin, A. C. *Evaluation and Control of Training*. London: McGraw-Hill, 1974.

Hunter, J. E. and Schmidt, F. L. Quantifying the effects of psychological interventions on employee job performance and work productivity. *American Psychologist*, April, 1983, 473–478.

Johnson, S. L. A cost analysis method of establishing training criteria. *Ergonomics*, 1980, *23*, 12, 1137–1145.

Kirkpatrick, D. L. Techniques for evaluating training programs. *Journal of the American Society of Training Directors*, 1959, *13*, 3–9, 21–26.

Kirkpatrick, D. L. Evaluation of training. In R. L. Craig and L. R. Bittell (Eds.) *Training and Development Handbook.* New York: McGraw-Hill, 1967, 87–112.

Magnusson, D. *Test Theory.* Reading, Mass.: Addison-Wesley, 1967.

Mezoff, B. Six More Benefits of Pretesting Trainees. *Training*, 1983, 45–47.

Nunnally, J. C. *Psychometric Theory.* New York, McGraw-Hill, 1967.

Putnam, A. O. Pragmatic evaluation. *Training and Development Journal*, Oct., 1980.

Roche, W. J. The Cronbach-Gleser utility function in fixed treatment employee selection. As reported by W. F. Cascio in *Applied Psychology in Personnel Management*, Reston, Va.: Reston Pub. Co., 1982.

Ryan, P. The costs of job training for a transferable skill. *British Journal of Industrial Relations*, 1980, Nov., 334–352.

Scriven, M. The methodology of evaluation. In *Perspectives of Curricular Evaluation*. Chicago: Rand McNally, 1967.

Thorndike, R. L. *Personnel Selection: Test and Measurement Technique.* New York: Wiley, 1949.

Wexley, K. N. and Latham, G. P. *Developing and Training Human Resources in Organizations.* Glenview, Ill.: Scott Foresman, 1981.

CHAPTER 6

Anonymous. Cleveland Twist Drill's Best Sales Tool: CAI. *Training*, 1981, *18*, 51–53.

Anonymous. How USAIR made training take off with slides. *Training*, 1982, *19*, 26–33.

Bligh, D.A. *What's the use of lectures?* Middlesex, England: Penguin Education, 1974.

Bork, A. and Franklin, S.D. The role of computer systems in education. *Association for Educational Data Systems*, 13, 1979, 17–30.

Broadwell, M.M., *The lecture method of instruction*. Englewood Cliffs, New Jersey: Educational Technology Publications, 1980.

Brown, G. *Lecturing and explaining.* New Fetter Lane, London: Methuen & Co., 1978.

Carrol, S.J., Jr., Paine, F.T., and Ivancevich, J.J., The Relative effectiveness of training methods—Expert opinion and research. *Personnel Psychology*, 25, 1972, 495–510.

Casciero, A.J., and Roney, R.G. *Introduction to AV for technical assistants* Littleton, Colorado: Libraries Unlimited, Inc. 1981.

Chu, G. C., and Schramm, W. *Learning from Television: What the Research Says.* Washington, D.C.: National Association of Education Broadcasters, 1967.

Crowder, N.A. Automatic tutoring by means of intrinsic programming. In A.A. Lumsdaine & R. Glaser (Eds.) *Teaching machines and programmed learning*. Washington, D.C.: National Educational Association, 1960.

Dallman, B.E., and DeLeo, P.J. Evaluation of Plato IV in vehicle maintenance training. *AFHRL Technical Report 77-59.* Brooks Air Force Base, Texas 1977.

Dossett, D.L., and Hulvershorn, P. Increasing technical training efficiency: Peer training via computer assisted instruction. *Journal of Applied Psychology*. In Press.

Evans, J.L., Homme, L.E. and Glaser, R. The ruleg system for the construction of programmed verbal learning sequences. *Journal of Educational Research*, 55, 1962, 513–518.

Fleishman, E.A. Leadership climate, human relations training and supervisory behavior. *Personnel Psychology*, 6, 1953, 205–222.

French, J., Jr., and Raven, B. *Studies in Social Power*, Ann Arbor: Institute for Social Research, 1959.

Gagné, R.M., *The Conditions of learning*. New York: Holt Rinehart and Winston, 1977.

Goldstein, I.L. *Training, program development and evaluation*. Monterey, California: Brooks/Cole Publishing Company, 1974.

Goldstein, I.L. Training in work organizations. *Annual Review of Psychology*, 31, 1980, 229–273.

Hall, E.R., and Freda, J.S. A comparison of individualized and conventional instruction in navy technical training. *Train. Anal. Eval. Group Tech. Rep. 117*. Orlando, Fla., 1982.

Johnstone, A.H. and Percival, F. Attention breaks in lectures. *Education in Chemistry*, 13, 1976, 273–304.

Kulik, J.A., Julip C. and Cohen P.A. Effectiveness of computer-based college teaching: A meta-analysis of findings. *Review of Educational Research*, 50, 1980, 525–544.

Lerner, J. *Children with learning disabilities* (ed. 2) Boston: Houghton Mifflin Co., 1976.

Lloyd, D.H. A concept of improvement of learning response in the taught lesson. *Visual Education*, 1968, 23–25.

Luongo, R. Managers take a new look at mailroom training programs. *ZIP*, 1980, *3*, 35–38.

Maddox, H. and Hode E. Performance decrement in the lecture. *Educational Research*, 28, 1975, 17–30.

Mechner, F. *Programming for automated instruction*. New York, Basic Systems, Inc., 1961 (mimeo).

Merril, I.R. and Drob H.A. *Criteria for planning the college and university learning resources center*. Washington, D.C.: Association for Educational Communication and Technology, 1977.

Nash, A.N., Muczyk, J.P., and Vettare, F.L., The relative practical effectiveness of programmed instruction. *Personnel Psychology*, 24, 1971, 397–418.

Neider, L.L. Training effectiveness: Changing attitudes. *Training and Development Journal*. Dec., 1981, 24–28.

O'Sullivan, K. Audiovisuals and the training process. In R.L. Craig (Ed), *Training and Development Handbook*. (2nd Ed.) New York: McGraw-Hill, 1976.

Patten, T. H., Jr., and Stermer, E.P. Training foremen in work standards. *Training and Development Journal*, 1969, *23*, 25–37.

Reynolds, A. and Davis, R. The five most frequent questions (plus one) about computer based learning. *Training and Development Journal*, May 5, 1983, 42–48.

Romiszowski, A.J. *The Selection and Use of Instructional Media*. Wiley and Sons, New York. 1974.

Schein, E.H. *Process consultation: Its role in Organizational Development*. Reading, Massachusetts: Addison-Wesley Co. 1969.

Schramm, W., Mass Communication. *Annual Review of Psychology*, 1, 1962, 251–284.

Seltzer, R.A. Computer-assisted instruction—what it can and can't do. *American Psychologist*, 26, 1971, 373–377.

Silverman, R.E. *Automated teaching: A review of theory and research*. (NAVTRADEVCEN Technical Report 507-2) Port Washington, New York: U.S. Naval Training Device Center, 1960.

Solomon, G. *Interaction of Media, Cognition and Learning.* San Francisco, California: Jossey Bass Publishing, 1979.

Stovall, T.F., Lecture versus discussion *Phi Delta Kappan,* 39, 1958, 255–258.

Sullivan, E. GM looks to videodiscs for sales training. *Sales and Marketing Management,* 1982, *128,* 73–76.

Trist, E.L., & Bamforth, K. W. Some social and psychological consequences of the long-wall method of coal-getting. *Human Relations,* 4, 1951, 3–38.

Valett, R. *Developing cognitive abilities.* St. Louis: The C.V. Mashy Co., 1978.

Wexley, K.N. Personnel Training. *Annual Review of Psychology,* 35, 1984, 519–551.

Wexley, K.N. and Latham, G.P. *Developing and training human resources in organizations.* Glenview, Illinois: Scott, Foresman and Company, 1981.

CHAPTER 7

Adams, J. A. On the Evaluation of Training Devices. Presented at the 86th Annual Meeting of the American Psychological Association, Toronto, 1978.

Ancipink, P. Readin' and Writin' and the Multi-Media Conference Center. *Best's Review,* 1981, *81* (8), 70–72.

Argyris, C. Some Limitations of the Case Method: Experiences in a Management Development Program. *Academy of Management Review,* 1980, *5,* 291–298.

Bandura, A. *Social Learning Theory.* Englewood Cliffs, NJ: Prentice-Hall, 1977.

Baron, A.S. Communication Skills for the Woman Manager—A Practice Seminar. *Personnel Journal,* 1980, *59* (1), 55–63.

Barrett, G.F., Benko, T.W. and Riddle G. Programmable Simulator Speeds Operator Training. *Bell Laboratories Record,* 1981, *59* (7), 213–216.

Berger, M. A. In defense of the case method: A reply to Argyris. *Academy of Management Review,* 1983, *8,* 329–333.

Boocock, S.S. and Schild, E.O. *Simulation Games in Learning.* Beverly Hills, CA: Sage Publications, Inc., 1968.

Borinstein, D. A Systematic Approach To Increasing Supervisory Skills. *Supervisory Management,* 1982, *27* (6), 35–39.

Broom, G.M. and Ferguson-DeThorne, M.A. PR Students, Teachers Welcome Corporate Case Study Packages. *Journalism Educator,* July, 1978, 26–30.

Burnaska, R.F. The Effects of Behavior Modeling Training Upon Managers' Behaviors and Employees' Perceptions. *Personnel Psychology,* 1976, *29,* 329–335.

Butler, E. E., An experimental study of the case method in teaching the social foundations of education. *Dissertation Abstracts,* 1967, *27,* 2912.

Byham, W.C., Adams, D. and Kiggins, A. Transfer of Modeling Training to the Job. *Personnel Psychology,* 1976, *29,* 345–349.

Byham, W. and Robinson, J. Interaction Modeling: A new concept in supervisory training. *Training and Development Journal,* 1976, *30,* 20–33.

Campbell, J.P., Dunnette, M.D., Lawler, E.E. and Weick, K.R. *Managerial Behavior, Performance and Effectiveness.* New York: McGraw Hill, 1970.

Carkhuff, R. R. and Berensons, B. G. *Beyond Counseling and Therapy,* New York: Holt, Rinehart and Winston, 1967.

Carroll, S.J., Paine, F.T. and Ivancevich, J.J. The Relative Effectiveness of Training Methods—Expert Opinion and Research. *Personnel Psychology,* 1972, *25,* 495–509.

Castore, G. F. Attitudes of students toward the case method of instruction in a human relations course. *Journal of Educational Research,* 1951, *45,* 201–213.

Colgrove, M.A. Stimulating Creative Problem Solving: Innovative Set. *Psychological Reports,* 1968, *22,* 1205–1211.

Davis, L.E. Evolving Alternative Organizational Designs: Their Sociotechnical Bases. *Human Relations*, 1977, *30* (3), 261–271.

Decker, P. J., Effects of symbolic coding and rehearsal in behavior modeling training. *Journal of Applied Psychology*, 1980, *65*, 627–634.

Decker, P. J., The enhancement of behavior modeling training of supervisory skills by the inclusion of retention processes. *Personnel Psychology*, 1982, *35*, 323–332.

Deichman, D.C. and Jardine, A.F. Preventing Sexual Harassment. *Personnel Journal*, 1981, *60* (5), 343.

Delamontagne, R.P. Games that Stimulate: A Fun Way to Serious Learning. *Training*, 1982, *19* (2), 18–23.

Edwards, D. S., Hahn, C. P., & Fleishman, E. A. Evaluation of laboratory methods for the study of driver behavior: Relations between simulator and street performance. *Journal of Applied Psychology*, 1977, *62*, 559–566.

Erwin, D. E. (ed). *Psychological Fidelity in Simulated Work Environments*, presented at 86th Annual Meeting of the American Psychological Association, Toronto, 1978.

Fink, C. D., Shriver, E. L. Simulators for Maintenance Training: Some Issues, Problems, and Areas for Future Research. *AFHRL Tech. Rep.*, 78–27. Brooks Air Force Base, Texas, 1978.

Freedman, R.D. and Stumpf, S.A. Learning Style Theory: Less Than Meets the Eye. *Academy of Management Review*, 1980, *5*, 445–447.

Freedman, R.D. and Stumpf, S.A. The Learning Style Inventory: Still Less Than Meets The Eye. *Academy of Management Review*, April, 1981, *6* (2), 297–299.

Gardner, J.M. Teaching Behavior Modification to Non Professionals. *Journal of Applied Behavior Analysis*, 1972, *5*, 517–521.

Gentry, J.W., Buns, A.C. and Zinkhan G.M. Want to Use a Computer Simulations Game in a Marketing Course? *Marketing News*, 1982, *16* (2), 14–15.

Goldstein, A.P. and Sorcher, M. *Changing Supervisor Behavior*. New York: Pergamon, 1974.

Goldstein, I.L. Training in Work Organizations. *Annual Review of Psychology*, 1980, *31*, 229–272.

Goudy, R.J. Two Years of Management Experience in Two Challenging Weeks. *ABA Banking Journal*, 1981, *73* (6), 74–77.

Gray, J.L. The Myths of the Myths about Behavior Mod in Organizations: A Reply to Locke's Criticisms of Behavior Modification. *Academy of Management Review*, 1979, *4*, 121–129.

Gray, D.B. and Ashmore, R.D. Comparing the Effects of Informational Role-Playing and Value-Discrepancy Treatments on Racial Attitude. *Journal of Applied Social Psychology*, 1975, *5*, 526–580.

Green, S. G. and Taber, T. D. Structuring experiential learning through experimentation. *Academy of Management Review*, 1978, *4*, 889–895.

Groth, J.C. and Phillips, C.A. What Would You Do If a Crisis Hit Your Firm. *Management World*, 1978, *7* (3), 12–16.

Hall, D.T., Bowen, D.D., Lewicki, R.J. and Hall, F.S. *Experiences in Management and Organizational Behavior*. New York: John Wiley & Sons, 1982.

Hoffman, L.R., Harburg, E. and Maier, N.R.F. Differences and Disagreement as Factors in Creative Group Problem Solving. *Journal of Abnormal and Social Psychology*, 1962, *64*, 206–214.

Horn, D.B. A Program for Aggressive Trust Selling. *Bank Marketing*, 1980, *12* (4), 18–20.

"How Sperry Made People Listen." *International Management*, February, 1981, *36* (2), 20–23.

Huegli, J.M. nd Tschirgi, H.D. Preparing the Student for the Initial Job Interview: Skills and Methods. *ABCA Bulletin*, 1980, *42* (4), 10–13.

Ingersoll, V. Role Playing, Attitude Change and Behavior. *Organizational Behavior and Human Performance*, 1973, *10*, 157–175.

Janis, I.L. Attitude Change via Role Playing. In Abelson, R.P., Aronson, E., McGuire, W.J., Newcomb, T.M., Rosenberg, M.J. and Tannenbaum, P.N. (eds.), *Theories of Cognitive Consistency: A Sourcebook*. Chicago: Rand McNally, 1968.

Janis, I.L. and King, D. The Influence of Role Playing on Opinion Change. *Journal of Abnormal and Social Psychology*, 1954, *49*, 211–218.

Janis, I.L., and Mann, L. Effectiveness of Emotional Role Playing in Modifying Smoking Habits and Attitudes. *Journal of Experimental Research in Personality*, 1965, *1*, 84–90.

Kelly, H. Case Method Training: What It Is, How It Works. *Training*, February, 1983, 46–49.

Kepner, C.H. and Tregoe, B.B. *The Rational Manager*. Princeton, NJ: Kepner-Tregoe, Inc., 1965.

Kidron, A.G. The Effectiveness of Experiential Methods in Training and Education: The Case of Role Playing. *Academy of Management Review*, July, 1977, *2*, 490–495.

Killian, D.C. The Impact of Flight Simulators on U.S. Airlines. *American Airlines Flight Academy*, Fort Worth, Texas, 1976.

King, B. and Janis, I.L. Comparison of Effectiveness of Improvised Role Playing in Producing Opinion Changes. *Human Relations*, 1956, *9*, 177–186.

Kirkpatrick, D.L. Evaluating Training Programs: Evidence vs. Proof. *Training and Development Journal*, 1977, *31* (11), 9–12.

Kolb, D.A., Rubin, I.M. and McIntyre, J.M. *Organizational Psychology*, Englewood Cliffs, NJ: Prentice-Hall, Inc., 1971.

Kolb, D.A. Experiential Learning Theory and the Learning Style Inventory: A Reply to Freedman and Stumpf. *Academy of Management Review*. April, 1981, *6* (2), 289–296.

Latham, G.P. and Saari, L.M. The Application of Social Learning Theory to Training Supervisors Through Behavioral Modeling. *Journal of Applied Psychology*, 1979, *64*, 239–246.

Lawshe, C., Bolda, R. and Brune, R. Studies in Management Training Evaluation II. The Effects of Exposure to Role Playing. *Journal of Applied Psychology*, 1959, *43*, 287–292.

Leimberg, S.R. Consider the case study—An alternative educational tool for estate planners. *Trusts and Estates*, 1980, *119*, 24–28.

Lessem, R. Training Entrepreneurs. *Industrial and Commercial Training*, 1979, *11* (11), 464–466.

Lindenmeyer, C.R. and Chrisman, J.A. Work Sampling Training: A Simulation Gaming Approach. *Computers and Industrial Engineering*, 1980, *4* (1).

Locke, E.A. The Myths of Behavior Mod in Organizations. *Academy of Management Review*, 1977, *2*, 543–553.

Locke, E.A. Myths in "The Myths of the Myths about Behavior Mod in Organizations." *Academy of Management Review*, 1979, *4*, 131–136.

Maier, N.R.F. and Hoffman, L.R. Acceptance and Quality of Solutions as Related to Leaders' Attitudes toward Disagreement in Group Problem Solving. *Journal of Applied Behavioral Science*, 1965, *1*, 272–286.

Maier, N.R.F., Solem, A.R., and Maier, A.A. *Supervisors and Executive Development: A Manual for Role Playing*. New York: John Wiley & Sons, 1957.

McGhee, W. and Tullar, W.L. A Note on Evaluating Behavior Modification and Behavior Modeling as Industrial Training Techniques. *Personnel Psychology,* 1978, *31,* 477–484.

Miller, G. G. Some Considerations in the Design and Utilization of Simulators for Technical Training. *AFHRL Tech. Rep.,* 74–65. Brooks Air Force Base, Texas, 1974.

Moses, J.L. and Ritchie, R.J. Supervisory Relationships Training: A Behavioral Evaluation of a Behavior Modeling Program. *Personnel Psychology,* 1976, *29,* 337–343.

Onder, J.J. and Tuma, B. The Role Play Technique—Its Use in Real Estate Training. *Real Estate Today,* 1980, *13* (6), 30–36.

Otto, C.P. and Glaser, R.O. *The Management of Training.* Reading, MA: Addison-Wesley Publishing Co., 1972.

Paffet, J.A. Ships' Officers Use Simulators to Learn Vessel Operation. *Minicomputer News,* 1978, *4* (8), 11–13.

Parsons, H. M. *Man-Machine System Experiment,* Baltimore: Johns Hopkins Press, 1972.

Paul, N. Assertiveness Without Tears: A Training Programme for Executive Equality. *Personnel Management,* 1979, *11* (4), 37–40.

Pigors, P. and Pigors, F. *Case Method in Human Relations: The Incident Process.* New York: McGraw-Hill, 1961.

Raia, A. P. A study of the educational value of management games. *The Journal of Business,* 1966, *39,* 339–352.

Robinson, J.C. and Gaines, D.L. Seven Questions To Ask Yourself Before Using Behavior Modeling. *Training,* 1980, *17* (12), 60–69.

Rosenbaum, B.L. and Bakers, B. Do As I Do: The Trainer as a Behavior Model. *Training,* 1980, *16* (12), 90–93.

Rowland, K. M., Gardner, D. M., and Nealey, S. M. Business gaming in education and research in *Proceedings of the 13th Annual Midwest Academy of Management Conference,* East Lansing, Michigan, April, 1970.

Saint-Paul, F. Are We Implementing Our Excellent Training Programs? *Managers Magazine,* 1982, *57* (10), 28–31.

Schein, E.H. How to Break In the College Graduate. *Harvard Business Review,* 1964, *42,* 68–76.

Shaffer, J.B.P. and Galinsky, M.D. *Models of Group Therapy & Sensitivity Training.* Englewood Cliffs, NJ: Prentice-Hall, Inc., 1974.

Shaw, M.E. Role Playing. In Craig, R.L. and Bittel, L.R. (eds.) *Training and Development Handbook.* New York: McGraw Hill, 1967, 206–224.

Simmons, D.D. *The Case Method in Management Training.* In Taylors, B. and Lippitt, G.L. (eds.) *Management Development and Training Handbook,* London: McGraw Hill, 1975, 182–190.

Sims, H.P. and Manz, C.C. Modeling Influences on Employee Behavior. *Personnel Journal,* 1982, *61* (1), 58–65.

Skolnik, R. Sales Training. Coulter gets a second opinion. *Sales and Marketing Management.* 1981, *126,* 36–37.

Smith, P.E. Management Modeling Training to Improve Morale and Customer Satisfaction. *Personnel Psychology,* 1976, *29,* 251–259.

Solem, A.R. Human Relations Training: A Comparison of Case Studies. *Personnel Administration,* 1960, *23,* 29–37.

Sorcher, M., and Spence, R. The Interface project: Behavior modeling as social technology in South Africa. *Personnel Psychology,* 1982, *35,* 557–581.

Standke, L. Games Trainees Play Can Help Meet Your Training Objectives. *Training,* 1978, *15* (12), 42–46.

Thorpe, J. A., Varney, N. C., McFadden, R. W., LeMaster, W. D., and Short, L. H. Training effectiveness for three types of visual systems for KC-135 flight simulators. *AFHRL Tech. Rep.* 78–16. Williams Air Force Base, 1978.

Trist, E. L., Higgin, G. W., Murray, H. and Pollack, A. B. *Organizational Choice*, London: Tavistock Publications, 1963.

Utgaard, S. and Davis, R. The Most Frequently Used Training Techniques. *Training and Development Journal,* 1970, *24*, 40–43.

VanHemel, P.E., King, W.J. and Gambrell, C.B. Simulation Techniques in Operator and Maintenance Training, Performance Assessment, and Personnel Selection. *Computers & Industrial Engineering,* 1981, *5* (2), 105–112.

Veglan, P.A., Frazer, J.R. and Bommer, M.R. Computer Simulation—Training Tool for Collective Bargaining. *Personnel Journal,* 1978, *57* (11), 614–617.

VonNeumann, J. and Morgenstern, O. *The Theory of Games and Economic Behavior.* 1944.

Walton, R.E. From Hawthorne to Topeka and Kalmar. In Cass, E.L. and Zimmer, F.G. (eds.) *Man and Work in Society,* Van Nostrand Reinhold, Co., 1975.

Wexley, K.N. and Latham, G.P. *Developing and Training Human Resources in Organizations.* Glenview, IL: Scott, Foresman and Co., 1981.

Wohlking, W. Role Playing. In Craig, R.L. (ed.) *Training and Development Handbook.* New York: McGraw-Hill, 1976.

Zemke, R. Building Behavior Models That Work—The Way You Want Them To. *Training,* 1982, *19* (1), 22–27.

Zemke, R. Can Games and Simulations Improve Your Training Power? *Training,* 1982, *19* (2), 24–31.

Zoll, A.A. *Dynamic Management Education.* Reading, MA: Addison-Wesley Publishing Co., 1969.

CHAPTER 8

Anderson, J. C.; Milkovich, G. T.; and Tsui, A. A Model of Intra-Organizational Mobility. *Academy of Management Review,* 1981, *6*, 529–538.

Bandura, A. *Social Learning Theory,* Englewood Cliffs, New Jersey: Prentice-Hall, 1977.

Beach, D. S. *Personnel: The Management of People at Work* (fourth edition). New York: Macmillan, 1980.

Berlew, D. and Hall, D. The Socialization of Managers: Effects of expectations on Performance. *Administrative Science Quarterly,* September 1966, 207–223.

Breaugh, J. A. Realistic Job Previews: A Critical Appraisal and Future Research Directions. *Academy of Management Review,* 1983, *8* (4), 612–619.

Briggs, V. M. Jr., Conference Summary and Critique. In V. M. Briggs, Jr. and F. F. Foltman, (eds.). *Apprenticeship Research.* Ithaca, N.Y.: Cornell University, 1981, p. 218.

Bureau of Labor Statistics, *Major Characteristics of Collective Bargaining Agreements.* January 1, 1980. Washington, D.C.: U.S. Government Printing Office, 1981, p. 105.

Burke, R. J., Weitzel, W., and Weir, T. Characteristics of effective employee performance review and development interviews: Replication and extension. *Personnel Psychology,* 1978, *31*, 903–919.

Cascio, W. F. *Costing Human Resources: The Financial Impact of Behavior in Organizations.* Boston: Kent Publishing, 1982.

Dalton, G. W.; Thompson, P. H.; and Price, R. L. The Four Stages of Professional Careers: A New Look at Performance by Professionals. *Organizational Dynamics*, 1977, *6*, 19–42.

Dayal, I. and Thomas, J. Operations KPE: Developing a New Organization. *Journal of Applied Behavioral Science*, 4, 1968, 473–506.

Dugoni, B. L., and Ilgen, D. R. Realistic Job Previews and the Adjustment of New Employees. *Academy of Management Journal*, 1981, *24*, 579–591.

Dunnette, M. D. Critical Concepts in the Assessment of Human Capabilities. In M. D. Dunnette and E. A. Fleishman (Eds.), *Human Performance and Productivity.* (Volume 1), Hillsdale, N.J.: Lawrence Erlbaum Associates, 1982.

Dunnette, M. D., Arvey, R. D. and Banas, P. A. Why do they Leave? *Personnel*, 1973, *50*, 25–39.

Ekstrom, R. B., French, J. W., and Harman, H. H. *An Attempt to Confirm five Recently Identified Cognitive Factors.* (Technical Report No. 8, ONR Contract N000 14-71-C-0117, NR 150-329). Princeton, N.J.: Educational Testing Service, 1975.

Feldman, D. C. The Multiple Socialization of Organization Members. *Academy of Management Review*, 1981, *6* (2), 309–318.

Fine, S. A. *A Functional Approach to a Broad Scale Map of Work Behaviors*, HSR-RM-63/2. McLean, Va.: Human Sciences Research, September, 1963.

Finkleman, J. M. and Glass, D. C. Reappraisal of the Relationship between Noise and Human Performance by Means of a Subsidiary Task Measure. *Journal of Applied Psychology*, 1970, *54*, 211–213.

Franklin, W. A Comparison of Formally and Informally Trained Journeymen in Construction. *Industrial and Labor Relations Review*, July, 1973, 1086–1094.

Goldstein, I. L. and Buxton, V. M. Training and Human Performance. In M. D. Dunnette and E. A. Fleishman (Eds.) *Human Performance and Productivity.* (Volume 1) Hillsdale, N.J.: Lawrence Erlbaum Associates, 1982.

Hall, D. T. *Careers in Organizations.* Pacific Palisades, Calif.: Goodyear, 1976.

Holley, W. H. and Jennings, K. M. *The Labor Relations Process.* 2nd edition, New York, N.Y.: Dryden, 1984.

Hillery, J. M., and Wexley, K. N. Participation in appraisal interviews conducted in a training situation. *Journal of Applied Psychology*, 1974, *59*, 168–171.

Huse, E. F. *Organization Development and Change*, 2nd edition, St. Paul, Minn.: West, 1980.

Jones, D. The Employee Handbook. *Personnel Journal*, February 1973, 136–141.

Kantowitz, B. H. Interfacing Human Information Processing and Engineering Psychology. In W. C. Howell and E. A. Fleishman (Eds.), *Human Performance and Productivity* (Volume 2) Hillsdale, N.J.: Lawrence Erlbaum Associates, 1982.

Kondrasuk, J. Coaching vs. Classroom Training. *Training and Development Journal*, 1979, *8*, 12–16.

Latham, G. P. and Yukl, G. A. A review of research on the application of goal setting in organizations. *Academy of Management Journal*, 1975, *18*, 824–845.

Latham, G. P., Mitchell, T. R., and Dossett, D. L. Importance of participative goal setting and anticipated rewards on goal difficulty and job performance. *Journal of Applied Psychology*, 1978, *63*, 163–171.

Lee, C. HRD and the Computer Biz: Training Strategies in the 'Belly of the Beast.' *Training*, 1983, *20* (8), 35–41.

McCord, B. Job Instruction. In R. L. Craig (Ed.), *Training and Development Handbook: A Guide to Human Resources Development.* (2nd edition). New York: McGraw Hill, 1976.

McCormick, E. J. Job and Task Analysis. In M. D. Dunnette (Ed.), *Handbook of Industrial and Organizational Psychology.* Chicago, Ill.: Rand McNally, 1976.

Mecham, R. C. and McCormick, E.J. *The Rated Attribute Requirements of Job Element in the Position Analysis Questionnaire.* Lafayette, Ind.: Occupational Research Center, Purdue University, Report No. 1, 1969 (a).

Mecham, R. C. and McCormick, E. J. *The Use of Data Based on the Position Analysis Questionnaire in Developing Synthetically Derived Attribute Requirements of Jobs.* Lafayette, Ind.: Occupational Research Center, Purdue University, Report No. 4, 1969, (b).

Milkovich, G. T., and Anderson, J. C. Career Planning and Development Systems. In K. M. Rowland and G. R. Ferris (Eds.), *Personnel Management*, Boston, Mass.: Allyn and Bacon, 1982.

Mintzberg, A. *The Nature of Managerial Work.* New York, N.Y.: Harper and Row, 1973.

Nemeroff, W. F., and Wexley, K. N. An explanation of the relationships between performance feedback interview characteristics and interview outcomes as perceived by managers and subordinates. *Journal of Occupational Psychology,* 1979, *52,* 25–34.

Peterson, N. G. and Bownas, D. A. Skill, Task Structure and Performance Acquisition. In M.D. Dunnette and E. A. Fleishman (Eds.) *Human Performance and Productivity.* (Volume 1) Hillsdale, N.J.: Lawrence Erlbaum Associates, 1982.

Rackham, N. The Coaching Controversy. *Training and Development Journal,* 1979, *11,* 12–16.

Reilly, R. R., Brown, R., Blood, M., and Maletesta, C. The Effects of Realistic Job Previews: A Study and Discussion of the Literature. *Personnel Psychology,* 1981, *34,* 823–834.

Rush, J.; Peacock, A.; and Milkovich, G. Career Stages: A Partial Test of Levinson's Model of Life/Career Stages. *Journal of Vocational Behavior,* 1980, *16,* 347–359.

Schein, E. H. *Career Dynamics: Matching Individual and Organizational Needs.* Reading, Mass.: Addison-Wesley, 1978.

Schmidt, F. L., Hunter, J. E., and Pearlman, K. Assessing the Economic Impact of Personnel Programs on Workforce Productivity. *Personnel Psychology,* 1982, *35,* 333–347.

Schwab, D. P. Recruiting and Organizational Participation. In K. Rowland and G. Ferris (Eds.), *Personnel Management*, Boston, Mass.: Allyn and Bacon, 1982.

Shannon, M. J. Simulator Training for Corporate Pilots. *Wall Street Journal,* November 12, 1981, p. 1.

Strauss, G., *Union Policies toward the Admission of Apprentices.* Berkeley, California: University of California, 1971, Reprint No. 357.

Super, D., and Hall, D. T. Career Development: Exploration and Planning. In M. R. Rosenziwerg and L. W. Porter (Eds.), *Annual Review of Psychology* (Volume 29). Palo Alto, Calif.: Annual Reviews, 1978.

Theologus, G. C., Romashko, T., and Fleishman, E. A. Development of a Taxonomy of Human Performance: A feasibility Study of Ability Dimensions for Classifying Human tasks. *JSAS Catalog of Selected Documents in Psychology.*

U.S. Department of Labor, Bureau of Apprenticeship., *Apprenticeship Training.* Washington, D.C.: Government Printing Office, 1956.

Van Maanen, J. Breaking in: A Consideration of Organizational Socialization. In R. Duben (Ed.), *Handbook of Work Organization, on Society.* Chicago: Rand-McNally, 1975.

Van Maanen, J. People Processing: Strategies of Organizational Socialization. *Organizational Dynamics,* 1978, *7,* pp. 18–36.

Van Maanen, J. and Schein, E. H. Toward a Theory of Organizational Socialization. In B. M. Staw (ed.) *Research in Organizational Behavior, 1,* 1979, pp. 209–265.

Wanous, J. P. Effects of a Realistic Job Preview on Job Acceptance, Job Attitudes and Job Survival. *Journal of Applied Psychology*, 1973, *58*, 327–332.

Wanous, J. P. *Organizational Entry: Recruitment, Selection and Socialization of Newcomers.* Reading, Mass.: Addison-Wesley Publishing, 1980.

Webber, R. A. Career Problems of Young Managers. In M. Jelinek (Ed.), *Career Management: for the Individual and the Organization.* Chicago, Ill.: St. Clair Press, 1979.

Wexley, K. N. and Latham, G. P. *Developing and Training Human Resources in Organizations.* Glenview, Ill.: Scott, Foresman and Company, 1981.

Wexley, K. N., Singh, J. P., and Yukl, G. A. Subordinate personality as a moderator of the effects of participation in three types of appraisal interviews. *Journal of Applied Psychology*, 1973, *58*, 54–59.

Wickert, F. The Famous JIT Card: A Basic Way to Improve It. *Training and Development Journal*, February, 1974, 6–9.

Williams, T. A. Technological Innovation and Futures of Work Organization: A Choice of Social Design Principles. *Technological Forecasting and Social Change*, 1983, *24*, 79–90.

Williges, R. C. Applying the Human Information Process Approach to Human/Computer Interactions. In W. C. Howell and E. A. Fleishman (Eds.), *Human Performance and Productivity.* (Volume 2), Hillsdale, N.J.: Lawrence Erlbaum Associates, 1982.

CHAPTER 9

Bass, B.M. *Stogdill's Handbook of Leadership: A Survey of Theory and Research* (revised and expanded ed.). New York: Free Press, 1981.

Bentz, J. Research Findings from Personality Assessment of Executives. Paper Presented to the Michigan Association of Industrial and Organizational Psychologists, December, 1984, Novi, Michigan.

Berne, E. *Games People Play.* New York: Grove Press, 1964.

Blake, R.R. and Mouton, J.S. *The New Managerial Grid.* Houston, Texas: Gulf Publishing Co., 1978.

Bray, D.W. "New data from the management progress study," *Assessment and Development*, 1973, *1*, 3.

Bray, D.W. and Grant, D.L. "The assessment center in the measurement of potential for business management," *Psychological Monographs*, 1966, *80*, 1–27.

Bray, D.W.; Campbell, R.J. and Grant D.L. *Formative Years in Business: A Long-Term AT&T Study of Managerial Lives.* New York: John Wiley and Sons, 1974.

Bricker, G. *Bricker's International Directory.* Woodside, California: Woodside Press, 1981.

Byham, W.C. "Starting an assessment center," *Personnel Administrator*, Feb., 1980, *25*, 2, 27–32.

Campbell, J.P.; Dunnette, M.D., Lawler, E.E., III and Weick, K.R. *Managerial Behavior, Performance and Effectiveness.* New York: McGraw-Hill, 1970.

Coleman, E.C. and Campbell, M.E. *Supervisors: A corporate resource.* New York: AMACOM, 1975.

Couch, P.D. and Strother, G.S. "A critical incident evaluation of supervisory training," *Training and Development Journal*, 1971, *25*, 9, 6–11.

Dowell, B.E. and Wexley, K.N. "Development of a work behavior taxonomy for first line supervisors," *Journal of Applied Psychology*, 1978, *63*, 563–572.

Evans, M.G. "The effects of supervisory behavior on the path–goal relationship," *Organizational Behavior and Human Performance*, May, 1970, 277–298.

Fiedler, F.E. and Chemers, M.M. *Leadership and Effective Management*. New York: Scott Foresman, 1974.

Fiedler, F.E.; Chemers, M.M. and Mahar, L. *Improving Leadership Effectiveness: The Leader Match Concept*. New York: Wiley, 1976.

Griffin, R.W. *Management*. Boston, Massachusetts: Houghton Mifflin Co., 1984.

Harris, T.A. *I'm OK, You're OK*. New York: Harper and Row, 1969.

House, R.J. and Baetz, M.L. "Leadership: Some generalizations and new research directions," *Research in Organizational Behavior*. (B.M. Staw, Ed.), Greenwich, Connecticut: JAI Press, 1979.

House, R.J. and Mitchell, T.R. "Path-Goal theory of leadership," *Journal of Contemporary Business*, Autumn, 1974, 81–98.

Kepner, C.H. and Tregoe, B.B. *The Rational Manager: A Systematic Approach to Problem Solving and Decision Making*. New York: McGraw-Hill, 1965.

Kerr, S. and Jermeir, J.M. "Substitutes for leadership: Their meaning and measurement," *Organizational Behavior and Human Performance*, December, 1978, 375–403.

Koontz, H., O'Donnell, C. and Weihrich, H. *Management* (8th ed.). New York: McGraw-Hill, 1984.

Latham, G.P. and Wexley, K.W. *Developing and Training Human Resources in Organizations*. Glenview, Illinois: Scott Foresman & Co., 1981.

Lerda, L.W. "Conference Methods," in R.L. Craig and L.R. Bittel (Eds.) *Training and Development Handbook*. New York: McGraw-Hill, 1967, 154–173.

Maddi, S.R. *Personality Theories: A Comparative Analysis*. Homewood, Illinois: Dorsey Press, 1980.

Maier, N.R. *Problem Solving Discussions and Conferences*. New York: McGraw-Hill, 1963.

Maier, N.R. *Psychology in Industrial Organizations*, (5th ed.). Boston, Houghton Mifflin, 1982.

McClelland, D.C. *The Achieving Society*. New York: VanNostrand, 1961.

McClelland, D.C. "Toward a theory of motive acquisition," *American Psychologist*, 1965, *20*, 5, 321–333.

McClelland, D.C. and Winter, D.G. *Motivating Economic Achievement*. New York: The Free Press, 1969.

Miner, J.B. "Management Appraisal: A review of procedures and practices," *Business Horizons*, October, 1968.

Miner, J.B. *The Human Constraint: The Upcoming Shortage of Managerial Talent*. Washington, D.C.: BNA Books, 1974.

Miner, J.B. *The Challenge of Managing*. Philadelphia: W.B. Saunders Co., 1975.

Miner, J.B. *The Management Process: Theory, Research and Practice*. New York: Macmillan, 1978.

Mintzberg, H. *The Nature of Managerial Work*. New York: Harper and Row, 1973.

Mintzberg, H. "The manager's job: Folklore and fact," *Harvard Business Review*, 1975, *53*, 4, 49–61.

Miron, D. and McClelland, D.C. "The impact of achievement motivation training on small businesses," *California Management Review*, 1979, *21*, 13–28.

Nealey, S.M. and Fiedler, F.E. "Leadership functions of middle managers," *Psychological Bulletin*, 1968, *70*, 313–329.

Niehoff, M.D. and Romans, M.J. "Needs assessment as step one toward enhancing productivity," *Personnel Administrator*, May, 1982, 35–39.

Pavett, C.M. and Lau, A.W. "Managerial Work: The influence of hierarchical level and functional specialty," *Academy of Management Journal*, March, 1983, 170–177.

Peters, T. and Waterman, R. *In Search of Excellence*, N.Y.: Harper and Row, 1982.

Rackham, N. and Morgan, T. *Behavior Analysis in Training*. Maidenhead, Great Britain: McGraw-Hill, 1977.

Roberts, T. *Developing Effective Managers*. Stratford-upon-Avon, Great Britain: Edward Fox and Son, 1974.

Sayles, L.R. *Leadership: What Effective Managers Really Do and How They Really Do It*. New York: McGraw-Hill, 1979.

Scanlon, B. and Keys, B. *Management and Organizational Behavior* (2nd.) New York, N.Y.: John Wiley and Sons, 1983.

Starcevich, M.M. and Sykes, J.A. "Internal advanced management programs for executive development: The experience of Phillips Petroleum," *Personnel Administrator*, June, 1982, 27–33.

Steers, R. "Individual differences in participative decision making," *Human Relations*, September, 1977, 837–847.

Thornton, G.C. and Byham, W.C. *Assessment Centers and Managerial Performance*. New York: Academic Press, 1982.

Vroom, V.H. "Can leaders learn to lead," *Organizational Dynamics*, 1976, *4*, 3, 17–28.

Vroom, V.H. and Yetton, P.W. *Leadership and Decision Making*. Pittsburgh: University of Pittsburgh Press, 1973.

Waters, J.A. "Managerial skill development," *Academy of Management Review*, 1980, *5*, 3, 449–453.

Ways, M. "The hall of fame for business leadership," *Fortune*, January 30, 1978, 91–97.

Wexley, K. N. and Latham, G. P. *Developing and Training Human Resources in Organizations*. Glenview, Illinois: Scott Foresman, 1981.

CHAPTER 10

Amaya, T. Organization Development in Japan. *Journal of Enterprise Management*, 1980, 2, 221–236.

Argyris, C. Some Limitations of the Case Method: Experiences in a Management Development Program. *Academy of Management Review*, 1980, 5, 291–298.

Beer, M. *Organization Change and Development: A Systems View*. Santa Monica, CA: Goodyear Publishing Company, Inc., 1980.

Bennis, W. G. Organizational development at the crossroads: A dialogue with Warren Bennis (and David Jamieson). *Training and Development Journal*, 1981, *35*, 19–26.

Blake, R.R., Shepard, H.A. and Mouton, J.S. *Managing Intergroup Conflict in Industry*. Houston: Gulf Publishing, 1964.

Blake, R.R. and Mouton, J.S. *Building a Dynamic Corporation Through Grid Organizational Development*. Reading, MA: Addison-Wesley, 1969.

Boss, R.W. and McConkie, M.L. An Autopsy of an Intended OD Project. *Group and Organization Studies*, June, 1974, 183–200.

Doyle, M. and Strauss, D. *How To Make Meetings Work*. New York: The Berkley Publishing Group, 1976.

Friedlander, F. and Brown, L.D. Organization Development. In *Annual Review of Psychology*, 1974, 25, 313–316, 320–331, 336–341.

Golembiewski, R.T., Proehl, C.W. and Sink, D. Estimating the Success of OD Applications. *Training and Development Journal*, April, 1982, 86–95.

Goodman, P.S. and Dean, J.W. Why Productivity Efforts Fail. In French, W.L., Bell, C.H. and Aawacki, R.A. [Eds.]. *Organization Development: Theory, Practice, and Research*. Plano, TX: Business Publications, Inc., 1983.

Hershey, P. and Blanchard, K.H. *Management of Organizational Behavior: Utilizing Human Resources*. Englewood Cliffs, NJ: Prentice-Hall, Inc., 1982.

Huse, E. *Organization Development and Change*. New York: West Publishing, Co., 1980.

Ivancevich, J.M. Changes in Performance in a Management by Objectives Program. *Administrative Science Quarterly*, 1974, *19*, 563–574.

Lawler, E.E. *Pay and Organization Development*. Reading, MA: Addison-Wesley, 1981.

Leavitt, H.J. Suppose We Took Groups Seriously. In Cass, E.L. and Zimmer, F.G. [Eds.] *Man and Work in Society*. New York: Van Nostrand Reinhold Co., 1975.

Locke, E.A., Shaw, K.N., Saari, L.M. and Latham, G.P. Goal Setting and Task Performance: 1969–1980. *Psychological Bulletin*, 1981, *90*, 125–152.

Miner, J.B. Failures of Implementation. *The Industrial-Organizational Psychologies*, February, 1984, *21* (2), 9–20.

Mohrman, S.A. Employee Participation Programs: Implications for Productivity Improvement. *The Industrial-Organizational Psychologist*, February, 1983, *20*(2), 38–43.

Nadler, D.A. *Feedback and Organization Development: Using Data-Based Methods*. Reading, MA: Addison-Wesley, 1977.

Nadler, D.A. and Lawler, E.E. Quality of Work Life: Perspectives and Directions. *Organizational Dynamics*, Winter, 1983, 20–30.

Nielson, E.H. *Becoming an OD Practitioner*. Englewood Cliffs, NJ: Prentice-Hall, Inc., 1984.

Nicholas, J.M. The Comparative Impact of Organization Development Interventions on Hard Criteria Measures. *Academy of Management Review*, October, 1982, 7 (4), 531–542.

Rogers, C.R. and Roethlisberger, F.J. Barriers and Gateways to Communication. *Harvard Business Review*, July-August, 1952, 46–52.

Seamonds, J. A. Professor Hurls Stinging Indictment at Bosses. *Lansing State Journal*, December 19, 1982, 8E.

Schein, E.H. *Process Consultation: Its Role in Organization Development*. Reading, MA: Addison-Wesley Publishing Co., 1969.

Vroom, V.H., and Yetton, P.W. *Leadership and Decision-Making*. Pittsburgh: University of Pittsburgh Press, 1973.

Wallace, M.J. and Szilagyi, A.D. *Managing Behavior in Organizations*. Glenview, IL: Scott, Foresman, and Company, 1982.

Walton, R.E. *Interpersonal Peacemaking: Confrontations and Third Party Consultation*. Reading, MA: Addison-Wesley, 1969.

Wexley, K.N., and Latham, G.P. *Developing and Training Human Resources in Organizations*. Glenview, IL: Scott, Foresman and Co., 1981.

CHAPTER 11

Abramson, L. Y., Seligman, M. E. P., & Teasdale, J.D. Learned helplessness in humans: Critique and reformulation. *Journal of Abnormal Psychology*, 1978, *87*, 49–74.

Bower, J. L. Business policy in the 80's. *Academy of Management Review*, 1982, 7, 630–638.

Brockner, J., and Guare, J. Improving the performance of low self-esteem individuals: An attributional approach. *Academy of Management Journal*, 1983, *26*, 642–656.

Burke, W. W. *Organization Development: Principles and practices*. Boston, Mass.: Little Brown Publishing Co., 1982.

Chandler, A. *Strategy and structure*. Cambridge: MIT Press, 1962.

Diener, C. I., & Dweck, C. S. An analysis of learned helplessness: II. The processing of success. *Journal of Personality and Social Psychology*, 1980, *39*, 940–952.

Drucker, P. F. *Management: Tasks, responsibilities, practices.* New York: Harper and Row, 1974.

Dweck, C. S., & Bush, E. S. Sex differences in learned helplessness: I. Differential debilitation with peer and adult evaluators. *Developmental Psychology*, 1976, *12*, 147–156.

Equal Employment Opportunity Commission, U.S. Civil Service Commission, Department of Justice, Department of Labor, 1978. Uniform guidelines on employee selection procedures. *Federal Register*, 1978, *43*, 38290–39315.

Fiedler, F. E., and Leister, A. F. Leader intelligence and task performance: A test of a multiple screen model. *Organizational Behavior and Human Performance*. 1977, *1*, 1–14.

Fossum, J. R. and Parker, D. F. Building state of the art human resource strategies. *Human Resource Management*, 1983, *22*, 97–111.

French, W. L., Bell, C. H., Jr., and Zawacki, R. A. Part One: Mapping the territory. In W. Bell, C. H. Bell and A. R. Zawacki, (eds), *Organizational Development: Theory, practice and research.* Revised edition. Plano, Texas: Business Publications, Inc. 1983.

Goldstein, I. L. Training in work organizations. In M. R. Rosenzwerg and L. W. Porter, (eds), *Annual Review of Psychology*, 1980, *31*, 229–273.

Griffin, R. W. *Task design.* Glenview, Ill.: Scott-Foresman, 1982.

Hindricks, J. R. Personnel training. In M. D. Dunnette, (ed), *Handbook of Industrial and Organizational Psychology.* Chicago: Rand McNally, 1976, 829–860.

House, R. J. A path goal theory of leader effectiveness. *Administrative Science Quarterly*, 1971, *16*, 321–338.

Jauch, L. R. and Osborn, R. N. Toward an integrated theory of straegy. *Academy of Management Review*, 1981, *6*, 491–498.

Jemison, D. B. The importance of an integrative approach to strategic management research. *Academy of Management Review*, 1981, *6*, 601–608.

Klein, D. C., & Seligman, M. E. P. Reversal of performance deficits in learned helplessness and depression. *Journal of Abnormal Psychology*, 1976, *85*, 11–26.

Krantz, D. S., Glass, D. C., & Snyder, M. L. Helplessness, stress level, and the coronary-prone behavior pattern. *Journal of Experimental Social Psychology*, 1974, *10*, 284–300.

Lawler, E. E. The mythology of management compensation. *California Management Review*, 1966, *9*, 11–22.

Lawrence, P. R., and Lorsch, J. W. Differentiation and integration in complex organizations. *Administrative Science Quarterly*, 1967, *12*, 1–47.

Martinko, M. J., and Gardner, W. I. Learned helplessness: An alternative explanation for performance deficits. *Academy of Management Review*, 1982, *7*, 195–204.

McFillen, J. M., & New, J. R. Situational determinants of supervisor attributions and behavior. *Academy of Management Journal*, 1979, *22*, 793–809.

Mitchell, T. R., & Wood, R. E. Supervisor's responses to subordinate's poor performance: A test of an attribution model. *Organizational Behavior and Human Performance*, 1980, *25*, 123–138.

Overmier, J. B., & Seligman, M. E. P. Effects of inescapable shock upon subsequent escape and avoidance learning. *Journal of Comparative and Physiological Psychology*, 1967, *63*, 28–33.

Pittman, T. S., & Pittman, N. L. Deprivation of control and the attribution process. *Journal of Personality and Social Psychology*, 1980, *39*, 377–389.

Roth, S., & Kubal, L. Effects of noncontigent reinforcement on tasks of differing importance: Facilitation and learned helplessness. *Journal of Personality and Social Psychology*, 1975, *32*, 680–691.

Rotter, J. B. Generalized expectations for internal versus external control of reinforcement. *Psychological Monographs*, 1966, *80*, 1–28.

Tichy, N. M. *Managing strategic change: Technical, political and cultural dynamics.* New York: Wiley, 1983.

Tichy, N. M. Managing change strategically: The technical, political and cultural keys. *Organizational Dynamics*, 1982, *2*, 59–80.

Thomas, J and Griffin, R. The social information processing model of task design: A review of the literature. *Academy of Management Review*, 1983, *8*, 672–682.

Thompson, A. A., Jr. and Strickland, A. J. III. *Strategy formulation and implementation.* Dallas, Texas: Business Publications, Inc. 1980.

Wexley, K. N. Personnel Training. In M. R. Rosenzweig and L. W. Porter (eds). *Annual Review of Psychology*, 1984, *35*, 519–551.

APPENDIX A

Bradford, L.P. Biography of an Institution. *Journal of Applied Behavioral Science*, 1967, *3*, 127–144.

Bradford, L.P., Gibb, J.R. and Benne, K.D. (eds.) *T-Group Theory and Laboratory Method.* New York, John Wiley & Sons, 1964.

Buchanan, P.C. Evaluating the Effectiveness of Laboratory Training in Industry. *In Explorations in Human Relations Training and Research. No. 1.* Washington, D.C. National Training Laboratories, 1965.

Buchanan, P.C. Laboratory Training and Organization Development. *Administrative Science Quarterly*, 1969, *14*, 466–480.

Campbell, J.P., and Dunnette, M.D. Effectiveness of T-Group Experiences in Managerial Training and Development. *Psychological Bulletin*, 1968, *70*, 73–104.

Campbell, J.P., Dunnette, M.D., Lawler, E.E. and Weick, K.R. *Managerial Behavior, Performance and Effectiveness.* New York: McGraw Hill, 1970.

Carroll, S.J., Paine, F.T. and Ivancevich, J.J. The Relative Effectiveness of Training Methods—Expert Opinion and Research. *Personnel Psychology*, 1972, *25*, 495–509.

Cooper, C.L. How Psychologically Dangerous Are T-Groups and Encounter Groups? *Human Relations*, 1975, *28*, 249–260.

Egan, G. *Encounter: Group Processes for Interpersonal Growth.* Belmont, CA: Brooks/Cole Pub. Co., 1970.

French, W.L. and Bell, C.H. *Organization Development: Behavioral Science Interventions for Organization Improvement.* Englewood Cliffs, NJ: Prentice-Hall, 1972.

Gibb, J.R. The Effects of Human Relations Training. In Bergin, A.E. and Garfield, S.L. (eds.) *Handbook of Psychotherapy and Behavior Change.* New York: John Wiley & Sons, 1970, 2114–2176.

House, R.J. T-Group Education and Leadership Effectiveness: A Review of the Empiric Literature and a Critical Evaluation. *Personnel Psychology*, 1967, *20*, 1–30.

Kelly, J. Organizational Development Through Structured Sensitivity Training. *Management International Review*, 1973, 83–96.

Klaw, S. Two Weeks In a T-Group. *Fortune Magazine*, August, 1961.

Lakin, M. *Interpersonal Encounter: Theory and Practice in Sensitivity Training.* New York: McGraw-Hill, 1972.

Leiberman, M.A., Yalom, I.D. and Miles, M.B. *Encounter Groups: First Facts.* New York: Basic Books, 1973.

Lewin, K., Lippitt, R. and White, R.K. Patterns of Aggressive Behavior in Experimentally Created 'Social Climates.' *Journal of Social Psychology*, 1939, *10*, 271–299.

Lundgren, D.C. and Knight, D.J. Sequential Stages of Development in Sensitivity Training Groups. *Journal of Applied Behavioral Science*, 1978, *14* (2), 204–222.

Marrow, A. Events Leading to the Establishment of the National Training Laboratories. *Journal of Applied Behavioral Science*, 1967, *3*, 144–150.

McGregor, D. *The Professional Manager*. New York: McGraw-Hill, 1967.

Mezoff, B. Cognitive Style and Interpersonal Behavior: A Review With Implications for Human Relations Training. *Group and Organization Studies*, 1982, 7 (1), 13–34.

Miller, G.J. Overseas Applications of Behavioral Science Technology. *Southern Review of Public Administration*. 1980, *4* (2), 229–252.

Moscow, D. T-Group Training in the Netherlands—An Evaluation and Cross-Culture Comparison. *Journal of Applied Behavioral Science*, 1971, *7* (4), 427.

Rogers, C.R. *Carl Rogers on Encounter Groups*. New York: Harper & Row, 1970.

Schein, E.H. How to Break In the College Graduate. *Harvard Business Review*, 1964, *42*, 68–76.

Schein, E.H. and Bennis, W.G. (Eds.) *Personal and Organizational Change Through Group Methods: The Laboratory Approach*. New York: Wiley & Sons, 1965.

"Sensitivity Training" *Congressional Record-House*. June 10, 1969, H4666-H4679.

Shaffer, J.B.P. and Galinsky, M.D. *Models of Group Therapy & Sensitivity Training*. Englewood Cliffs, NJ: Prentice-Hall, Inc., 1974.

Shepard, H.A. Changing Relationships in Organizations. In March, J.G. (ed.) *Handbook of Organizations*. Chicago: Rand McNally, 1965, 1115–1143.

Smith, P.B. Controlled Studies of the Outcome of Sensitivity Training. *Psychological Bulletin*, 1975, *82* (4), 597–622.

Smith, P.B. The T-Group Trainer: Group Facilitator or Prisoner of Circumstance. *Journal of Applied Behavioral Science*, 1980, *16* (1), 63–77.

Wexley, K.N. and Latham, G.P. *Developing and Training Human Resources in Organizations*. Glenview, IL: Scott, Foresman and Co., 1981.

Wexley, K.N. and Yukl, G.A. *Organizational Behavior and Personnel Psychology*. Homewood, IL: Irwin, 1977.

Yalom, I.D. *The Theory and Practice of Group Psychotherapy*. New York: Basic Books, 1970.

Yalom, I.D. and Lieberman, M.A. A Study of Encounter Group Casualties. *Archives of General Psychiatry*, 1971, *25*, 16–30.

APPENDIX B

Adams, J.D. [Ed.] *New Technologies in Organization Development: 2*. San Diego: University Associates, Inc., 1975.

Barra, R. *Putting Quality Circles To Work*. New York: McGraw-Hill Book Company, 1983.

Beckhard, R. Optimizing Team-Building Efforts. *Journal of Contemporary Business*, Summer, 1972, *1* (3), 23–32.

Beckhard, R. *Organization Development: Strategies and Models*. Reading, MA: Addison-Wesley, 1969.

Beckhard, R. and Harris, R.T. Planning Procedures/Managing Interfaces/Charting Responsibility. In Beckhard, R. and Harris, R.T. (eds.) *Organization Transactions: Managing Complex Change*. Reading, MA: Addison-Wesley, 1977, 76–82.

Blake, R.R. and Mouton, J.S. *Building a Dynamic Corporation Through Grid Organizational Development*. Reading, MA: Addison-Wesley, 1969.

Burke, W.W. Managing Conflict Between Groups. In Adams, J.D. [Ed.] *New Technologies in Organization Development.* San Diego: University Associates, Inc., 1975, 255–268.

Chin, R. and Benne, K.D. General Strategies for Effecting Changes in Human Systems. In French, W.L., Bell, C.H. and Zawacki, R.A. [Eds.], *Organization Development: Theory, Practice and Research.* Plano, TX: Business Publications, Inc., 1983, 67–84.

Davis, S.M. and Lawrence, P.R. *Matrix.* Reading, MA: Addison-Wesley, 1977.

Dayal, I. and Thomas, J.M. Operation KPE: Developing a New Organization. *The Journal of Applied Behavioral Science,* 1968, *4* (4), 473–505.

Dewar, D.L. *The Quality Circle Guide to Participation Management.* Englewood Cliffs, NJ: Prentice-Hall, Inc., 1982.

Dyer, W.G. *Teambuilding: Issues and Alternatives.* Reading, MA: Addison-Wesley, 1977.

Fordyce, J.K. and Weil, R. *Managing With People: A Manager's Handbook of Organization Development Methods.* Reading, MA: Addison-Wesley, 1971.

Franch, W.L. and Hollman, R.W. Management by Objectives: The Team Approach. *California Management Review.* Spring, 1975, *17* (3), 13–22.

Frohman, M.A., Sashkin, M. and Kavanagh, M.J. Action Research as Applied to Organization Development. *Organization and Administrative Sciences,* Spring/Summer, 1976, 7, 129–142.

Frost, C.F. The Scanlon Plan: Anyone for Free Enterprise? *MSU Business Topics,* 1978 (Winter), 25–33.

Frost, C., Wakeley, J. and Ruh, R. *The Scanlon Plan for Organization Development: Identity, Participation, and Equity.* East Lansing, MI: Michigan State University Press, 1974.

Hackman, J.R. Work Design. In Hackman, J.R. and Suttle, J.L. [Eds.]. *Improving Life at Work: Behavioral Science Approaches to Organizational Change.* Santa Monica, CA: Goodyear, 1977, 96–162.

Hackman, J.R. and Oldham, G.R. *Work Redesign.* Reading, MA: Addison-Wesley Publishing Co., 1980.

Hackman, J.R. & Oldham, G.R. Motivation through the design of work: Test of a theory. *Organizational Behavior and Human Performance,* 1975, *16,* 250–279.

Hall, D.T. *Careers in Organizations.* Glenview, IL: Scott, Foresman and Co., 1976.

Hall, D.T., Bowen, D.D., Lewicki, R.J. and Hall, F.S. *Experiences in Management and Organizational Behavior.* New York: John Wiley & Sons, 1982.

Harrison, R. Role Negotiation: A Tough Minded Approach to Team Development. In Burke, W.W. and Hornstein, H.E. [Eds.] *The Social Technology of Organization Development.* Fairfax, VA: NTL Learning Resource Corporation, 1973, 84–96.

Herzberg, F. The wise old turk. *Harvard Business Review,* September-October, 1974, 70–80.

Herzberg, F. One More Time: How Do You Motivate Employees? *Harvard Business Review.* January-February, 1968, *46* (1), 53–62.

Heyel, C. Rucker Plan of Group Incentives. In *The Encyclopedia of Management.* New York: Van Nostrand Reinhold Co., 1973, 895–900.

Huse, E. and Barebo, C. Beyond the T-Group: Increasing Organizational Effectiveness. *California Management Review,* 1980.

Huse, E. *Organization Development and Change.* New York: West Publishing, Co., 1980.

Ingle, S. *Quality Circles Master Guide.* Englewood Cliffs, NJ: Prentice-Hall, Inc., 1982.

Jayaram, G.K. Open Systems Planning. In Bennis, W.G., Benne, K.D., Chin, R., and Corey, K. [Eds.] *The Planning of Change.* New York: Holt, Rinehart and Winston, 1976, 275–283.

Lesieur, F.G. *The Scanlon Plan: A Frontier in Labor-Management Cooperation.* Cambridge, MA: MIT Press, 1958.

Lewin, K. *Field Theory in Social Science.* New York: Harper and Row, 1951.

Lindaman, E.B. and Lippitt, R.O. *Choosing the Future You Prefer: A Goal Setting Guide.* Washington, D.C.: Development Publications, 1979.

McGill, M.E. *Organization Development for Operating Managers.* New York: AMACOM, 1977.

Miles, M.B. and Schmuck, R.A. The Nature of Organization Development. In Schmuck, R.A. and Miles, M.A. [Eds.] *Organization Development In Schools.* LaJolla, CA: University Associates, 1976, 2–3, 7–10.

Mitchell, M.D. Dealing with Personnel Changes in a Working Team. In Adams, J., Hayes, J. and Hopson, B. [Eds.] *Transition: Understanding and Managing Personal Change.* London, England: Martin Robertson and Co., 1976, 188–220.

Moore, B.E. and Ross, T.L. *Improving Productivity Using Scanlon Principles for Organization Development: A Practical Guide.* New York: Wiley-Interscience, 1978.

Nadler, D.A. *Feedback and Organization Development: Using Data-Based Methods.* Reading, MA: Addison-Wesley, 1977.

Nadler, D.A. and Lawler, E.E. Quality of Work Life: Perspectives and Directions. *Organizational Dynamics,* Winter, 1983, 20–30.

Odiorne, G.S. *MBO II: A System of Managerial Leadership for the 80's.* Belmont, CA: Pitman Learning, Inc., 1979 (Revised edition of *Management By Objectives,* 1965).

O'Toole, J. The Uneven Record of Employee Ownership. *Harvard Business Review,* November-December, 1979, 185–197.

Porras, J.I. and Berg, P.O. The Impact of Organization Development. *The Academy of Management Review,* April, 1978, 249–266.

Schein, E.H. *Process Consultation: Its Role in Organization Development.* Reading, MA: Addison-Wesley Publishing Co., 1969.

Trist, E.L. On Socio-Technical Systems. In Bennis, W.G., Benne, K.D. and Chin, R. [Eds.] *The Planning of Change.* New York: Holt, Rinehart, and Winston, Inc., 1969, 269–281.

Van de Ven, A. and Delbecq, A.L. Nominal vs. Interacting Group Processes for Committee Decision-Making Effectiveness. *Academy of Management Journal,* 1971, *14,* 201–212.

Walton, R.E. *Interpersonal Peacemaking: Confrontations and Third Party Consultation.* Reading, MA: Addison-Wesley, 1969.

Walton, R.E. From Hawthorne to Topeka to Kalmar. In Cass, E.L. and Zimmer, F.G. [Eds.]. *Man and Work in Society.* New York: Van Nostrand Reinhold, 1975, 116–129.

Walton, R.E. Work Innovation at Topeka: After Six Years. *Journal of Applied Behavioral Science,* 1977, *13,* 422–433.

Yager, E.G. The Quality Control Circle Explosion. *Training and Development Journal,* April, 1981, 98–105.

Zand, D.E. Collateral Organization: A New Change Strategy. *The Journal of Applied Behavioral Science,* 1974, *10* (1), 63–89.

INDEX

Abstract-reflective learner 108
Accommodation 82
Active practice 117
Adult learners 88–90
Adverse impact 329
American Society for Training and
    Development (ASTD) 6
Anticipatory learning 76
Apprenticeships 247–248
Aptitude-treatment interaction (ATI)
    106–107
Assessment, of training needs. *See*
    Training needs assessment
Assimilation 82
Attention 77, 112–114
Audience identification 147–150
Audio-visuals (AV) 188–198
    evaluation 197–198
    implementation 196–197
    planning 192–195
Authority reliance 132–133

Bandura, Albert 75
Behavior modeling 230–235
Behavior modeling approach 333
Behavioral reproduction 77
Behavioral science theory 298–299
Behaviorists 63
Branching program, in programmed
    instruction 201–202

Bureau of Apprenticeship Training
    (BAT) 247

Career 258–262
    from individual perspective 258
    from organization perspective 258
    stages 258–262, 263
Career planning and development 368
Case-study method 221–224
Chaining 71–72
Change
    climate for 244–245
    forces for 26–28
    in technology and training 249,
        264–265
    organizational 17, 98–99, 296–297
Classical conditioning 65
Coaching 243–245
Cognitive map 67, 90
Cognitive theorists 63
Collaborative management-by-objectives
    (CMBO) 310, 364–365
Computer-assisted instruction 198–205,
    249
Concept learning 85–86
Concrete-active learner 108
Control groups 146–147
Convergent validity 155
Criterion development 139–143
Criterion evaluation 151–156

Criterion relevancy, contamination, and deficiency 140–143
Cronbach's coefficient alpha 153

Decisional roles 273–274, 280
Diagnostic and planning approach, to OD 306–307, 357–360
Discriminant validity 156
Discrimination 81
Distributed practice 64
Domains of learning 102

Ebbinghaus, Hermann 64, 117
Encoding 115–116
Equafinality principle 13
Equal Employment Opportunity Commission 329
Evaluation 130–177, 327–329
    arguments for or against 131–135
    costs 167–172
    criterion development for 139–143
    criterion measurement 151–156
    design 156
        external validity 157–158
        types of 158–166
    internal validity of 143
    procedure for developing 147–151
    restrictions on 166–167
    types of 135–139
        outcome 136, 138–139
        process 135–136, 137
Evaluation design 156–166
    external validity 157–158
    types of 158–166
        multiple baseline design 159, 164–166
        post-test only control group 159, 161–162
        pretest, post-test control group 159, 162
        Soloman four-group 159, 162–163
        time series analysis 159, 163–164
Expectancy theory 72–74
Expectancy model of motivation 109
Experiential learning 211–215

Experiential training techniques. See Training techniques, experiential
Expert power 180
Extinction 65
Extrinsic reinforcement 331
Extrinsically oriented individuals 124

Face validity 264
Feedback 120–125, 255, 332
Feldman, D. C. 250–256
Fitzgerald Act 247
Follow-up 333
Formal authority 273
Formative evaluation 135
Functional job analysis 257

Gagné, Robert 78, 79, 101, 102, 115
Generalization 81
Goals, organizational 33–34
Guide practice 117
Guthrie, E. R. 66

Hemisphericity 107
Hierarchy model of evaluation 136–139
Human resource development training
    change in 16–17
    definition of 3–4
    designing, for effective learning 97–129
    evaluation 130–177
    field of 2–3
    learning and behavior in 62–96
    model of 4–6
    needs assessment 25–61
    of managers 271–294
    open systems theory of 10–16
    overview 1–24
    role in organizations 9–10
    role of trainers in 6–8
    role of, in organization development 17–18, 295–323
    strategic approach to 324–343
    technical 242–270
    techniques
        experiential 211–241
        nonexperiential 178–210

Identical-elements approach to transfer 119

Image exchange 310, 367

In-basket technique 221

Incentive system approaches, to OD 308–309, 362–363

Incident method 224

Informational roles 273–274, 280

Instructional objectives 100

Intergroup mirroring 310, 367

Internal environment 327

Internal validity
    methodological precautions 145
    threats to 143

Interpersonal roles 273–274, 280

Intrinsic motivation 331

Intrinsic program, in programmed instruction 202

Intrinsically oriented individuals 124

Instrumentality 72

Job analysis 38, 40–42, 43, 44

Job description 38

Job expectation technique (JET) 310, 365

Job instructive technique (JIT) 245–247

Joint union-management quality of worklife (QWL)/employee involvement (EI) approach 310, 363–364

Keystone image 196

Kirkpatrick, D. L. 136–139

Knowledge, skills, and abilities (KSA)
    and determining skill level 262
    and job analysis 38
    and person analysis 42–51
    and training programs 3
    as part of evaluation criteria 328
    matching with job requirements 254
    needed in training 337–339
    requirements for managers 276–285

Kolb, David 108, 212

Laboratory education 235

Latham, G. P. 75

Law of associative shifting 66

Law of effect 65–66

Learned helplessness 331–332

Learning and behavior
    adult learners 88–90
    expectancy model of 72–74
    historical background 63–67
        E. C. Tolman 66–67
        E. L. Thorndike 65–66
        E. R. Guthrie 66
        Hermann Ebbinghaus 64
        I. Pavlov 64–65
    learning hierarchy 78–88
        concept learning 85–87
        multiple discrimination learning 81–84
        principle learning 87
        problem solving 87–88
        verbal association 78–81
    learning vs. performance 74–75
    operant conditioning 67–68
        reinforcement and punishment 68–71
        shaping and chaining 71–72
    social learning theory 75–78
        attention 77
        behavioral reproduction 77–78
        symbolic rehearsal 77

Learning hierarchy 78–88
    concept learning 85–86
    multiple discrimination 81–85
    principle learning 87
    problem solving 87–88
    verbal association 78, 80–81

Learning objectives 100–109
    advantages of 101–102
    individual differences 105–109
    prior learning 105
    using domains of learning in 102–105

Learning style inventory 213–214

Learning vs. performance 74–75

Lecture 179–188
    evaluation 186–188
    implementation 185–186
    planning 183–185

Lesson plan 183–185
Linear programming, in programmed
    instruction 201

Management development. *See* Training
    and management development
Management development programs
    and techniques 286–289
Management-By-Objectives (MBO) 368
Managerial roles 273–276, 280–281
Managerial skills framework 283
Managers, knowledge and skill
    requirements of 276–281
        administrative 277
        integration of job and
            requirements 280–281
        interpersonal 278
        personal 278–279
            intellectual 279–280
            personality 279–280
        technical 277–278
Managers, sources of knowledge/skill
    acquisition for 282–285
Matching 161–162
Mintzberg, Henry 273–275, 280, 287
Mission statement 325–326
Motivation 109
Multi-trait, multi-method matrix 155
Multiple baseline design 159, 164–166
Multiple discrimination 81–85

Needs assessment 299
Negative reinforcement 68
Nominal group technique 310, 366–367
Nonexperiential training techniques. *See*
    Training techniques, nonexperiential
Nonprint media 188

Objectives. *See* Learning Objectives
Observational learning 76–77
Off-the-job training 249–250
On-the-job training. *See* Coaching
Open systems theory 10, 12

Operant conditioning 67–72, 211
    reinforcement and punishment
        68–71
            negative reinforcement 68
            positive reinforcement 68
            punishment 68
    shaping and chaining 71–72
Organization development
    and business games 220
    and coaching 244–245
    and role playing 229
    and T-groups 235, 345–356
    and technological change 264–265
    definition of 17–18
    interventions 357–369
    origin of 10
    role of training in 295–323
    sociotechnical approach to 205,
        217
Organizational development techniques
    305–311, 357–369
        group-oriented interventions
            309–310, 363–367
        individual-oriented interventions
            368–369
        macro interventions 306–309,
            357–363
Organizational analysis
    data sources for 35–36
    goals 33–34
    related to technical training 256
Organizational socialization 250
Outcome evaluation 136–139
Overlearning 116, 117
Overlearning process 64

Pavlov, I. 64–65
Perceived performance deficiency 26
Person analysis 42–51, 258–262
Physical fidelity, in simulation 249
Platform errors 186–187
Position analysis questionnaire (PAQ)
    257
Positive reinforcement 68
Practice effects 77
Pretesting and post-testing 145–146,
    158–162

Principle learning 87
Primary reinforcer 72
Print media 188
Proactive TNA 29
for developmental purposes 29
preventive approach to 29
Proactive vs. reactive 333–335
Problem solving 87–88
Process consultation 310, 366
Process evaluation 135–136
Programmed instruction (PI) 198–205, 249
Progressive-part training 116–117
Psychological fidelity, in simulation 249
Punishment 68
Pure part training 116–117
Pure whole training 116–117

Quality control circle 310, 364

Reactive TNA 29
Realistic job preview (RJP) 253
Reinforcement and punishment 68–71
Reliability 152–153
Reliability coefficient 152
Retention 77, 115–116
Robey, D. 107
Role analysis technique (RAT) 310, 365
Role negotiation method 310, 365–366
Role playing 224–229
Roles, managerial 273–276, 280–281

Saari, L. M. 75
Sayles, Leonard 275
Scientific method of evaluation 133–135
Secondary reinforcer 72
Sensitivity training 235, 299
Shaping 71–72
Simulation 215–220, 249
business games and functional simulation 217–220
equipment simulation 216
Skinner, B. F. 67–71, 74
Socialization, in training 250–256

Socialization process model 250–252
anticipatory socialization phase 251
change and acquisition phase 252
encounter phase 251–252
Social learning model 109
Social learning theory 75–78
attention 77
behavioral reproduction 77–78
symbolic rehearsal 77
Social system 11
Soloman four-group evaluation 159, 162–163
Spaced practice 64
State apprenticeship council (SAC) 247
Strategic planning. See Training, strategic planning for
Subsystem 11
Success spiral syndrome 250
Symbolic coding 77
Symbolic rehearsal 77
Synergy 14
System, larger 11
Systematic data collection 299
Systems errors 14

Taggart, W. 107
Task objectives 100
Task-oriented approach 38
Task structure 85–86
Team building 310, 363
Technical training. See Training, technical
Technostructural approaches, to OD 307–308, 360–362
Test-retest reliability 153
T-groups 235, 299–300, 310, 345–356
and OD 356
basic characteristics of 348–353
history of 345–347
recommendations for use of 353–354
research evidence on effectiveness of 354–355
types of 347–348
Third-party peacemaking 310, 367–368
Thorndike, E. R. 65, 139–140

Time series analysis 159, 163–164
Tolman, E. C. 66–67, 74
Trainer, role of 99–100, 262–264
Trainer, training of 336
Training. *See* Human resources
  development/training
Training and development 368–369
Training and Development Journal 194,
  286
Training and management development
  271–294
    knowledge and skill requirements
      of managers 276–281
    nature of managerial job 272–276
    programs and techniques 286–289
    sources of knowledge/skill
      acquisition 282–285
Training, costs and return on
  investment 168–172
Training, designing for effective learning
    arrangement of training activities
      116–125
        amount and type of practice
          117–119
        amount to be learned
          116–117
        behavioral reproduction and
          feedback 120
        motivation to use feedback
          123–125
        recipient's acceptance of
          feedback 122–123
        recipient's perception of
          feedback 121–122
        transfer of training 119–120
    developing learning objectives in
      100–109
        advantages of 101–102
        individual differences
          105–109
        prior learning 105
        using domains of learning in
          102–105
    facilitating the learning process
      109–116
        attention 112–114
        gaining support of supervisor
          110–111

gaining support of trainee
  111–112
motivation 109–110
retention 115–116
role of trainer in 99–100
Training/HRD 286
Training magazine 194
Training magazine survey 2
Training needs assessment (TNA)
    as system component 256–258
    conducting of 31–52
    contributions of research to 53–57
    definition of 25–28
    model of 32
    overview 53
    reactive and proactive 29–31
    types of 28–29
    value of 30–31
Training, role in organization
  development 295–323, 357–369
    field examples 311–319
    need for OD practitioners to have
      training knowledge 302–305
    need for trainers to know OD
      300–302
    OD techniques 305–311, 357–369
    similarities between OD and
      training 296–300
Training, strategic planning for 324–343
    correspondence between strategy,
      environment, and technology
      327–333
    mission statement 325–327
    skill and knowledge needs 337–339
    strategic approaches 333–337
Training, system components of 256–265
    evaluation 264
    implementation 262–264
    person analysis 258–262
    skill level 262
    technological change and OD
      264–265
    training needs assessment 256–258
Training, technical 242–270
    approaches to 243–249
        apprenticeships 247–248
        coaching 243–245
        job instruction technique

(JIT) 245–247
off-the-job training 249–250
definition of 242
innovative approaches:
    socialization 250–256
system components 256–265
    evaluation 264
    implementation 262–264
    person analysis 258–262
    skill level 262
    technological change and OD
        264–265
    training needs assessment
        256–262
Training techniques, experiential
    211–241
    behavior modeling 230–235
    case-study method 221–224
    in-basket technique 221
    incident method 224
    philosophy of 211–215
    role playing 224–229
    simulation 215–220
    T-groups, sensitivity training and
        laboratory education 235
Training techniques, nonexperiential
    audio-visual 188–198
        evaluation 197–198

implementation 196–197
    planning 192–195
lecture 179–188
    evaluation 186–188
    implementation 185–186
    planning 183–185
programmed and computer-
    assisted instruction 198–205
    evaluation 204–205
    implementation 204
    planning 203–204
Transfer of training 119–120, 248
Transfer-through-principles approach to
    transfer 119–120
Transition meeting 310, 366

Valence 72
Validity 151, 154–156, 264
Verbal association 78
Vestibule training 249
Vicarious learning 76
Vroom, Victor 72

Waters, J. 283–285
Williams, T. A. 265
Work environment analysis 51–52
Worker-oriented approach 38–39